DAY HIKING
SNOQUALMIE PASS

DAY HIKING
SNOQUALMIE PASS

Tami Asars

1001 SW Klickitat Way, Suite 201, Seattle, WA 98134
800-553-4453, www.mountaineersbooks.org

Printed in China
First edition, 2026
Design and layout: Jen Grable
Cartographer: Bart Wright, Lohnes+Wright
All photographs by the author unless credited otherwise
Cover photograph: *Mountains stand watch as Tuck Lake (Hike 93) sleeps in forested silence.*

Frontispiece: *On a sunny fall day, the areas near Snoqualmie Pass are often alive with color.*
Photo page 384: *The deep, cold water of Snow Lake (Hike 79) is guarded by rugged Chair Peak and serrated mountain ridgelines.*

The background maps for this book were produced using CalTopo. For more information, visit caltopo.com.
Leave No Trace Seven Principles © Leave No Trace, www.LNT.org

Library of Congress Cataloging-in-Publication Data is on file for this title.

Mountaineers Books titles may be purchased for corporate, educational, or other promotional sales, and our authors are available for a wide range of events. For information on special discounts or booking an author, contact our customer service at 800-553-4453 or mbooks@mountaineersbooks.org.

Printed on FSC®-certifiedmaterials

FSC
www.fsc.org
MIX
Paper | Supporting responsible forestry
FSC® C188448

ISBN (paperback): 978-1-68051-703-3
ISBN (ebook): 978-1-68051-704-0

An independent nonprofit publisher since 1960

Contents

MIDDLE FORK SNOQUALMIE NATURAL AREA

SNOQUALMIE PASS

Snoqualmie Pass West

Snoqualmie Pass Summit

Snoqualmie Pass East

CLE ELUM AND SALMON LA SAC

TEANAWAY AREA AND BLEWETT PASS

ELLENSBURG AREA

HIKE LOCATOR

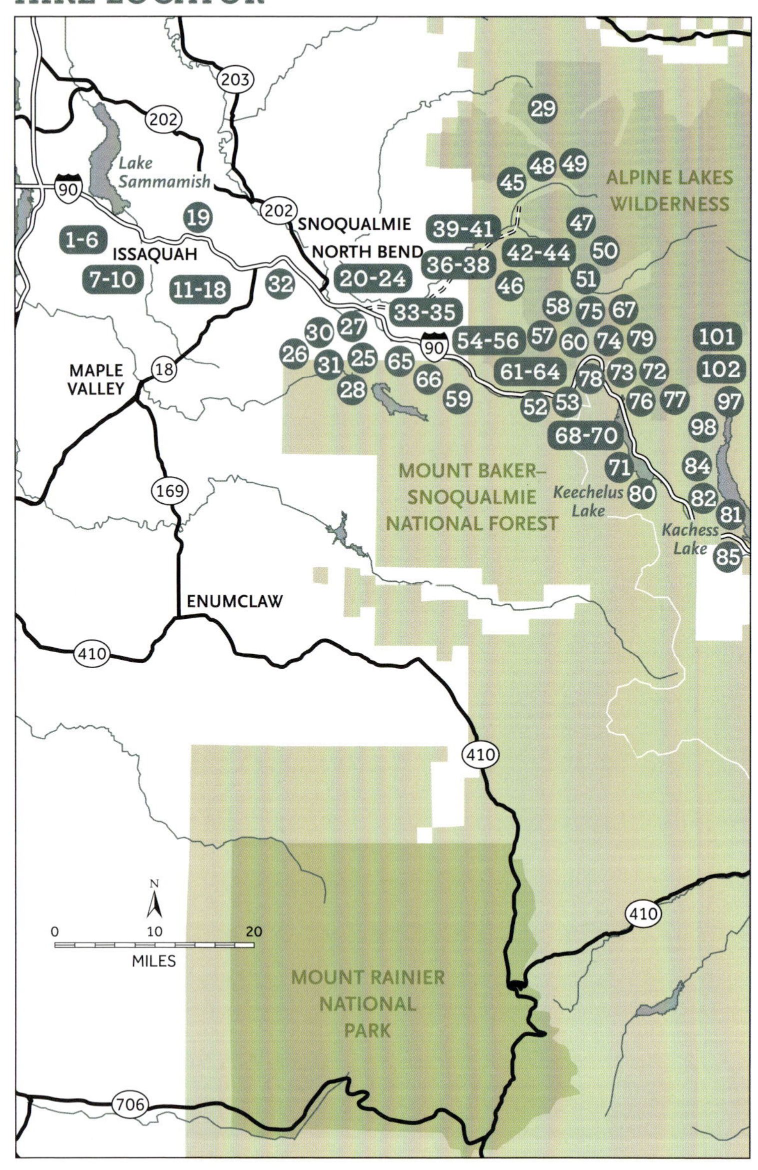

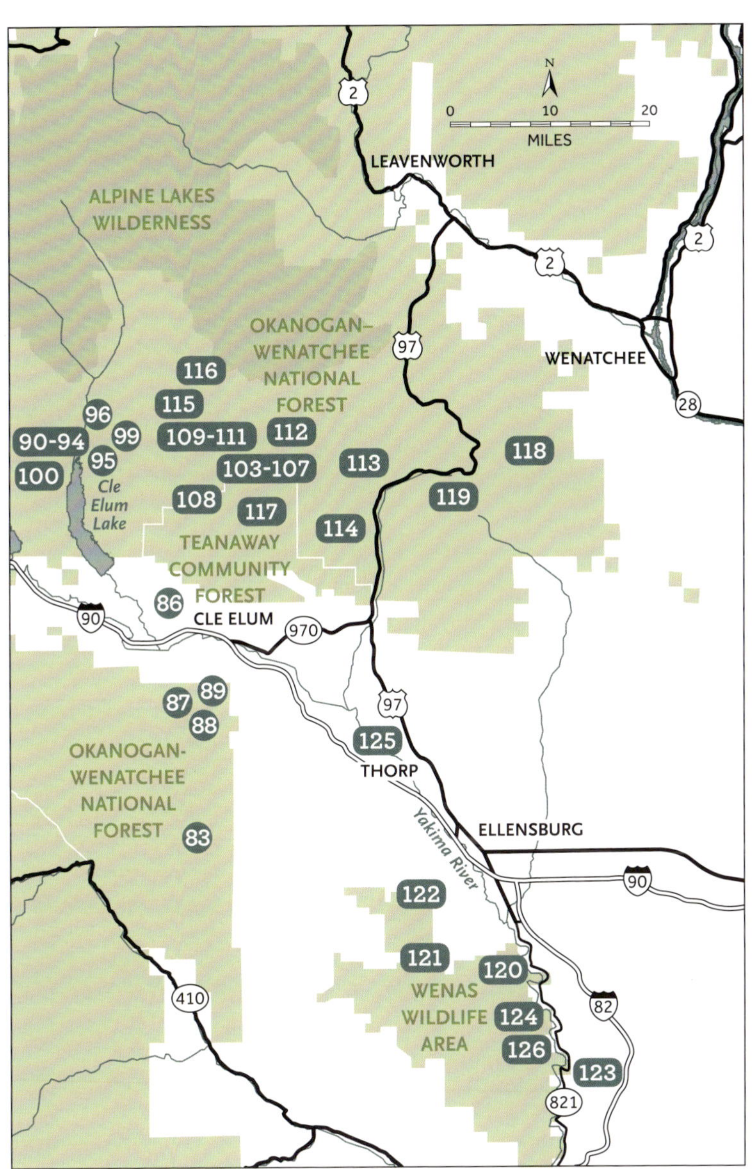
N
0
10
20
MILES
2
LEAVENWORTH
ALPINE LAKES
WILDERNESS
2
2
OKANOGAN–
WENATCHEE
NATIONAL
FOREST
97
WENATCHEE
116
115
28
96
99
109-111
112
90-94
95
118
103-107
113
100
Cle
Elum
Lake
108
119
117
114
TEANAWAY
COMMUNITY
FOREST
86
90
CLE ELUM
970
89
87
88
97
125
OKANOGAN-
WENATCHEE
NATIONAL
FOREST
THORP
Yakima River
83
ELLENSBURG
90
122
121
120
WENAS
WILDLIFE
AREA
410
82
124
126
123
821

Hikes at a Glance

HIKE	ROUNDTRIP DISTANCE (IN MILES)	RATING	DIFFICULTY
ISSAQUAH ALPS			
Cougar Mountain Regional Wildland Park			
1. Anti-Aircraft Ramble	4.5	***	2
2. Wilderness Peak Loop	6.5	***	3
3. Coal Creek Falls	3.1	**	2
4. Doughty Falls Ramble	6.4	**	3
5. Red Town Meadow Loop	2	**	1
6. Wildside Trail and De Leo Wall	4.7	**	2
Squak Mountain			
7. Bullitt Fireplace Trail	3.8	****	3
8. East Side Squak Loop	9.8	**	4
9. Margaret's Way to Debbie's View	7.5	***	3
10. May Valley Loop	7.8	**	3
Tiger Mountain			
11. Bus Trail and Around the Lake Trail	1.7	***	1
12. Tradition Lake and Round Lake	2.6	***	2
13 Ruth Kees Big Tree Trail	2.5	**	1
14. Nook Trail and Talus Rock Loop	2.5	**	2
15. Tiger Mountain Trail to West Tiger No. 2	7.4 one way	**	4
16. West Tiger No. 3	5.8	***	3
17. Poo Poo Point: High School Trail	7.2	**	3
18. Poo Poo Point: Chirico Trail	4	****	3
19. Grand Ridge Loop	4.3	**	2
NORTH BEND			
20. Mount Si	8	****	5
21. Talus Loop Trail	5.4	**	3
22. Little Si	4.1	***	3

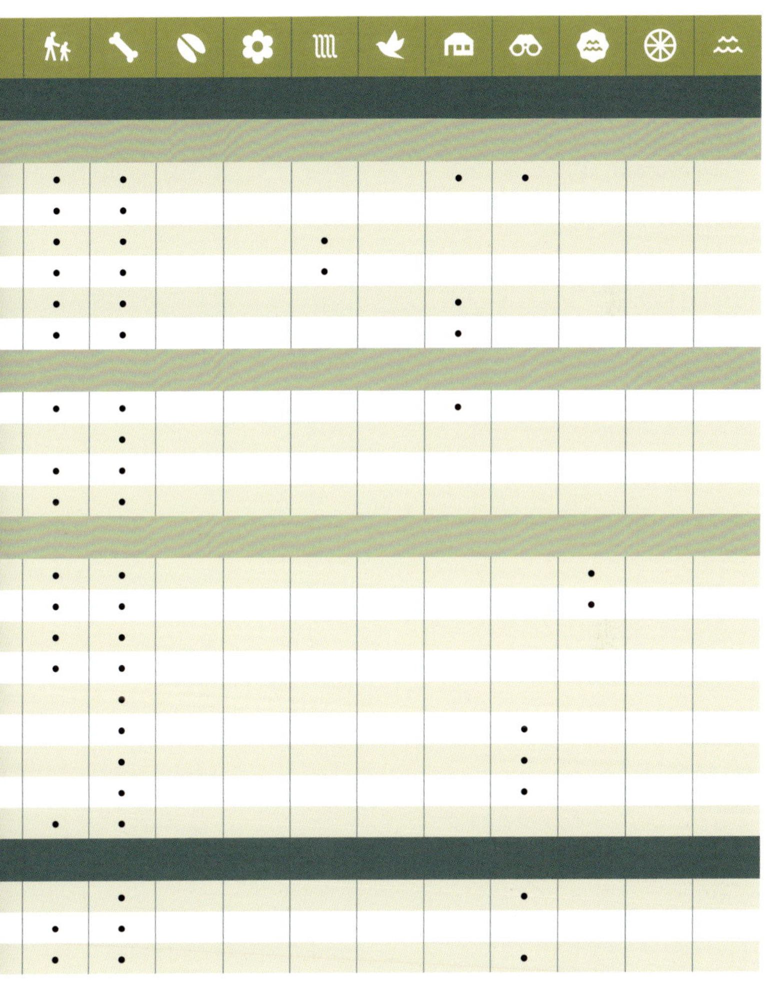

Kid Friendly	Dog Friendly	Wildlife	Wildflowers	Waterfalls	Bird Watching	Historical	Views	Lakes	Multiuse	Rivers & Streams
•	•					•	•			
•	•									
•	•			•						
•	•			•						
•	•					•				
•	•					•				
•	•					•				
	•									
•	•									
•	•									
•	•							•		
•	•							•		
•	•									
•	•									
	•									
	•						•			
	•						•			
	•						•			
•	•									
	•						•			
•	•									
•	•						•			

KID FRIENDLY · DOG FRIENDLY · WILDLIFE · WILDFLOWERS · WATERFALLS · BIRD WATCHING · HISTORICAL · VIEWS · LAKES · MULTIUSE · RIVERS & STREAMS

HIKE	ROUNDTRIP DISTANCE (IN MILES)	RATING	DIFFICULTY
23. Mount Teneriffe	13	****	5
24. Teneriffe Falls	6.2	****	3
25. Palouse to Cascades: Homestead Valley to Mine Creek Trestle	5.4	**	2
26. Palouse to Cascades: Cedar Falls to Iron Horse Falls	6.2	**	1
27. Cedar Butte	4.4	***	3
28. Twin Falls	2.5	*****	2
29. Bare Mountain	8.3	***	4
30. Rattlesnake Ledge	4.6	*****	3
31. Rattlesnake Lake Pathway	1.5	***	1
32. Rattlesnake Mountain	10.7 one way	****	4
MIDDLE FORK SNOQUALMIE NATURAL AREA			
33. Mailbox Peak	10.2	****	5
34. Mailbox Peak: Old Trail	6.6	****	5
35. Granite Lakes	8.4	****	3
36. South Bessemer Mountain	13.4	***	4
37. Lower CCC Trail	6.9	**	2
38. Last Chance Promontory on Green Mountain	12.5	**	4
39. Middle CCC Trail	6.2	**	2
40. Pratt Balcony	2.4	****	2
41. Upper CCC Trail	6.8	***	2
42. Garfield Ledges	2.1	****	2
43. Stegosaurus Butte	2.4	**	4
44. Pratt River Trail and Big Tree	8.8	***	3
45. Camp Brown	0.5	**	1
46. Oxbow Loop	1.4	***	1
47. Middle Fork Trail	12.5	***	3
48. Marten Lake	9	****	5
49. Otter Falls and Lipsy Lake	10.1	****	3
50. Hester Lake	11.4	****	4
51. Dutch Miller Gap Trail	10.2	***	3
SNOQUALMIE PASS			
Snoqualmie Pass West			
52. Annette Lake	7.2	****	3
53. Asahel Curtis Nature Trail	0.8	***	1

							•			
•	•			•						
•	•					•				
•	•			•						
•	•					•				
•	•			•						
							•			
•	•						•			
•	•				•			•		
•	•						•			
							•			
							•			
•	•							•		
							•			
•	•									
	•						•			
•	•									
•	•						•			•
•	•									
•	•						•			
							•			
•	•									•
•	•									•
•	•				•					
•	•									•
								•		•
•	•							•		•
								•		
•	•			•						•
•	•							•		
•	•									•

HIKE	ROUNDTRIP DISTANCE (IN MILES)	RATING	DIFFICULTY
54. Bandera Mountain	7	***	4
55. Mason Lake	6.8	****	3
56. Mount Defiance	10	****	4
57. Denny Creek to Keekwulee Falls	4	****	3
58. Melakwa Lake	8.8	*****	4
59. Dirty Harrys Balcony	4.5	***	3
60. Franklin Falls and Wagon Road Trail Loop	2.3	****	2
61. Granite Mountain	8.5	****	5
62. Pratt Lake	13	****	4
63. Talapus and Olallie Lakes	6.8	***	3
64. Island and Rainbow Lakes	11.8	***	4
65. Mount Washington	8.6	***	4
66. McClellan Butte	11.6	****	5
Snoqualmie Pass Summit			
67. Commonwealth Basin to Lundin Peak	9.8	****	4
68. Silver Peak	5.6	****	4
69. Cold Creek Loop	6.6	****	3
70. Mount Catherine	2.8	***	3
71. Cottonwood and Mirror Lakes	3	*****	2
72. Gold Creek Pond Loop	1.3	*****	1
73. Palouse to Cascades: Snoqualmie Tunnel	5.4	****	1
74. Kendall Katwalk	12.5	****	4
75. Kendall Peak Lakes	8.4	***	3
76. Lake Lillian and Twin Lakes	9.2	***	4
77. Margaret Lake and Mount Margaret	7	***	3
78. Lodge Lake	3.8	****	2
79. Snow Lake	6.8	****	3
80. Stirrup Lake	2.3	***	2
Snoqualmie Pass East			
81. Kachess Ridge to Kachess Beacon	6.4	***	3
82. Easton Ridge	6.9	***	4
83. Lost and Manastash Lakes	8	****	4
84. Rachel Lake and Rampart Ridge	10.6	****	4
85. Lake Easton Loop	5.8	**	2

	•			•			•			
	•							•		
							•	•		
•	•			•						•
	•			•				•		
•	•						•			
•	•			•						•
		•					•			
							•	•		
•	•							•		
							•	•		
							•			
		•				•	•			
							•			•
							•			
•	•							•		
•	•						•			
•	•							•		
•	•				•	•		•		
•						•				
						•	•			
•	•							•		
	•							•		
•	•							•		
•	•							•		
•	•							•		
								•		
	•		•		•	•				
	•		•		•					
•	•							•	•	
	•						•	•		
•	•							•		

HIKE	ROUNDTRIP DISTANCE (IN MILES)	RATING	DIFFICULTY
CLE ELUM/SALMON LA SAC			
86. Coal Mines Trail	6.2	**	1
87. North Fork Taneum Creek	10	**	2
88. Taneum Ridge	9.4	**	4
89. Palouse to Cascades: South Cle Elum	4.9	****	2
90. Cathedral Rock	9.2	*****	3
91. Hyas Lake	5.4	***	2
92. Peggys Pond	11	*****	5
93. Tuck and Robin Lakes	15	*****	5
94. Cooper River	6.6	**	2
95. Polallie Ridge to Diamond Lake	8.5	***	4
96. Davis Peak	10.4	*****	5
97. French Cabin Creek	4.6	**	3
98. French Cabin Mountain	11.4	**	4
99. Jolly Mountain	14	****	5
100. Paddy-Go-Easy Pass to Sprite Lake	7.7	*****	4
101. Pete Lake	9.1	*****	3
102. Thorp Lake and Thorp Mountain Lookout	8	****	4
TEANAWAY AREA/BLEWETT PASS			
103. Standup Creek Trail	9.3	***	3
104. Navaho Pass via Stafford Creek	10.8	****	4
105. Bean Basin	8.2	***	4
106. Beverly Turnpike and Iron Peak	10.2	****	4
107. Earl Peak via Bean Creek Trail	8	*****	5
108. Elbow Peak via Yellow Hill	11.5	**	4
109. Esmerelda Basin and Fortune Creek Pass	7	****	3
110. Lake Ingalls	9	*****	3
111. Longs Pass	5.8	****	4
112. Miller Peak	8.9	****	5
113. Iron Bear and Teanaway Ridge	6.5	****	3
114. Red Top Lookout	1.3	****	2
115. Boulder–De Roux Trail	9	**	3
116. Koppen Mountain	7.7	***	4
117. Johnson Creek to Medra Pass	8.2	***	4

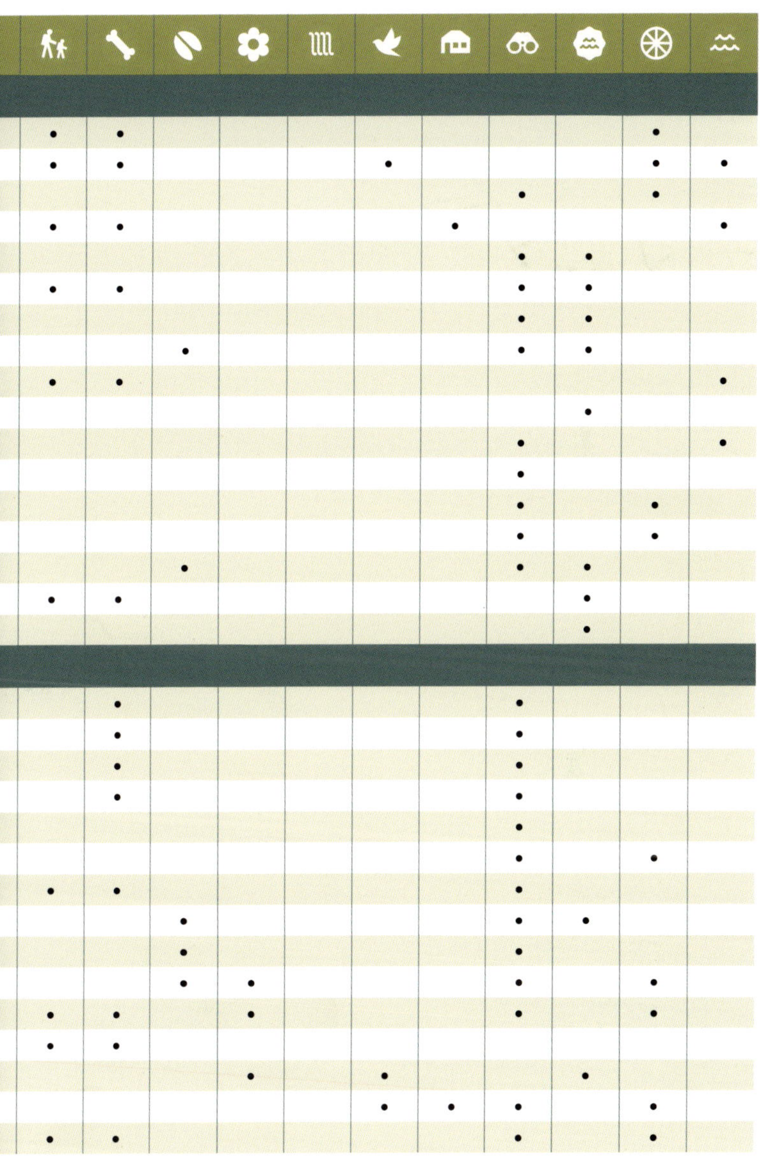

•	•								•	
•	•				•				•	•
							•		•	
•	•					•				•
							•	•		
•	•						•	•		
							•	•		
		•					•	•		
•	•									•
								•		
							•			•
							•			
							•		•	
							•		•	
		•					•	•		
•	•							•		
								•		
	•						•			
	•						•			
	•						•			
	•						•			
							•			
							•		•	
•	•						•			
		•					•	•		
		•					•			
		•	•				•		•	
•	•		•				•		•	
•	•									
			•		•			•		
					•	•	•		•	
•	•						•		•	

HIKE	ROUNDTRIP DISTANCE (IN MILES)	RATING	DIFFICULTY
118. Tronson Ridge	9.4	***	3
119. Swauk Forest Discovery Trail	2.9	****	2
ELLENSBURG AREA			
120. Rattlesnake Dance Ridge	2	****	3
121. Umtanum Creek Falls	2	****	1
122. Westberg and Boy Scout Trail Loop	4.3	***	3
123. Baldy Mountain	4.3	****	4
124. Umtanum Creek Canyon	5.5	**	1
125. Palouse to Cascades: Thorp Tunnels	11.8	***	1
126. Vista Trail to Umtanum Ridge	5.3	***	3

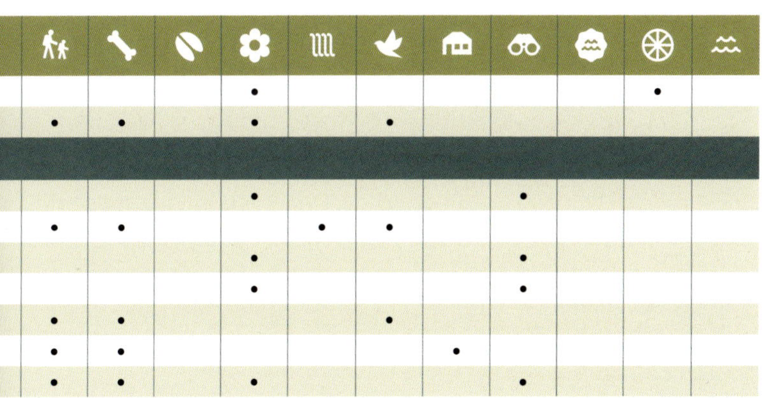

Introduction

The Snoqualmie region is made up of a plethora of landscapes, and this book covers them all. From the bumps and humps of the Issaquah Alps to the rugged, rocky shoulders of the Stuart Range, there is something for everyone.

The region holds large stands of ancient Sitka spruce trees, happily growing in poorly drained soil, as well as groves of sweeping western red cedars, important in historical uses to Indigenous peoples. There are barren mountaintops and summits laden with brush. Each path has a unique ambiance that encapsulates its spirit as you follow where it leads.

There are sweeping panoramas that you have to work hard to achieve and some that come much easier within a short distance. I've included trails for all, including ADA paths and those suitable for small kids or elderly folks. Some of these hikes will be all-day, heart-pumping affairs, while others will be wonderful leisurely strolls. Wherever possible, I noted extended hiking opportunities that would be suitable for trail runners or those who are interested in logging more miles.

Mountain goats frequent the peaks and pathways of many of the trails in the book, as do Columbian black-tailed deer, Rocky Mountain elk, and even the occasional coyote or black bear. You may see hoary marmots, pikas, golden-mantled ground squirrels, and a variety of birds, such as the sooty grouse, an upland ground bird. Keep your eyes open as you wander, and enjoy the magic of the surrounding wildlife.

I have been enjoying the pathways between these pages for decades and am blessed to call the Snoqualmie region home. I know these trails like good friends, as they are my treadmills and playgrounds as well as my sanctuaries from a crazy world, and I'm honored to share them with you! Perhaps you are a seasoned hiker who has already hiked many of these, or maybe you are new to hiking or to the Pacific Northwest; either way, I hope you find some new trails within these pages to fill your soul's cookie jar. Happy trails!

Before you head out into the hinterland, here are a few important details that are key to planning. Some of this stuff is straightforward, while some might feel foreign, especially if you're from out of town.

PERMITS, REGULATIONS, AND FEES

These days there are so many permits, passes, and regulations, it's often hard to know which one is which and what you need for where. Wouldn't it be great if there was one big pass that worked for all locations? Until that happens, we will unravel the mystery together. Every so often, you'll stumble upon a hike that doesn't have a note about a parking pass. This means one is not required for you to park at that spot. They are rare gems, but they do exist!

OPPOSITE: *The serene waters of Humpback Creek dance through boulders along Asahel Curtis Nature Trail (Hike 53).*

Discover Pass: If you plan to play or park on land that belongs to the State of Washington, you'll need to get a Discover Pass. It comes in two versions, the annual pass and the day-use pass. The Discover Pass can be purchased at various vendors and retail locations as well as online (see Resources). Every year there are a handful of free entry days as well, so be sure to check the website for those dates.

Peggys Pond (Hike 92) may be small and still, but with Mount Daniel looming above, the view is anything but ordinary.

Interagency Pass: As far as a comprehensive pass goes, this one is about as good as it gets. Although it doesn't cover Washington State recreational lands, which still require the Discover Pass, you can use it in lieu of the Northwest Forest Pass (see below) for federally operated recreation lands as well as national parks. The pass is actually a card, the same size as a credit card, which you show the gate attendees at national parks or put on your dashboard when you park in pass-required areas. America the Beautiful is the name of the primary interagency pass, which is available to everyone for purchase. However, other versions, with different designs, are available at a discount or even free to various groups of people such as senior citizens and those with permanent disabilities. Other qualifying groups include volunteers who offer 250 hours of service in one year on federally managed recreation sites, US military personnel and their dependents, and US fourth-grade students through Every Kid Outdoors. See Resources to learn how to order the Interagency Pass.

Northwest Forest Pass: For developed Forest Service trailheads in Washington, such as those with designated parking areas, toilets, or picnic areas, you'll either need an Interagency Pass or the Northwest Forest Pass. The latter is available both online (see Resources) and at select retailers and can be purchased as either an annual pass, good for one year from date of purchase, or a one-day pass.

Wilderness-Use Permits: This one is less of a permit or pass and more of a free, informational form that the Forest Service requests you fill out if you are visiting a wilderness area. The information on it helps the Forest Service gauge the number of visitors using the area, which in turn helps them get

SACRED TRAILS, STORIED LANDS

Indigenous communities have walked these trails and lands for generations, long before they became a recreational playground. The Snoqualmie, Muckleshoot, and Puyallup Tribes, among others, were deeply connected through shared traditions, ceremonies, and cultural practices. Their languages, largely dialects of Lushootseed, carried the stories and wisdom of their ancestors.

The Muckleshoot Tribe descends from the Duwamish and Upper Puyallup peoples, who lived throughout the Puget Sound region for thousands of years. Their ancestors relied on salmon fishing, hunting, and gathering, forming strong kinship networks that extended across the Cascade Mountains. The Snoqualmie people, known as the "People of Moon the Transformer," have a rich mythological and cultural history tied to the land.

In recent years, efforts to reclaim and protect sacred lands have gained momentum. The Snoqualmie Tribe, in partnership with the Muckleshoot Tribe, successfully secured the return of the land surrounding Snoqualmie Falls, a site of immense spiritual significance. This historic agreement underscores the ongoing commitment of Indigenous communities to preserve their heritage and steward their lands.

Today, we honor their enduring legacy and recognize the privilege of experiencing these native lands. As we hike, camp, and explore, we do so with respect—acknowledging the deep history beneath our feet and committing to responsible recreation. The echoes of their ancestors linger in these valleys and pathways and is woven into the land itself, a quiet reminder of those who walked before us.

grants and funding. It also gives them an idea of how many people are in the backcountry if something unfortunate happens, such as a wildfire. On most trails that cross into wilderness areas, you'll find a wooden box at the trailhead with the forms and a stubby golf pencil, if you are lucky. Frequently, the Forest Service can't keep up with the number of hikers using the forms and the box is empty or the writing utensil is AWOL. I generally keep pens in my car just in case and leave one for the next person, which I like to think brings me good pay-it-forward points as I head into the hinterlands.

WEATHER

It doesn't take a meteorologist to know that the Cascade Range can really throw some sky tantrums. When storms from the ocean force moist air inland, the high, rugged Cascades push the wet air up, creating clouds and rainy squalls. And we all know that in the mountains, things can change quickly. A beautiful, sunny day can turn into a rainy, cold mess over the course of several hours, so be sure to check the weather before you go and be prepared with the right gear. Reading the Doppler radar is a good idea to at least give you a general idea of where the rain showers might be and where they're headed. Knowing when the sun sets is also important to give you a guideline for darkness.

Another important skill is knowing how to respond if you get caught in a lightning storm. In a nutshell, descend from open terrain such as fields and mountaintops and off bodies of water to low-lying areas, and become the smallest possible object by crouching down into a ball with your heels touching the ground; maximize contact with the ground, but don't lie flat. If you are in the forest, head to a smaller group of trees tucked into the taller ones, and avoid single trees or stony outcroppings.

ROAD AND TRAIL CONDITIONS

Ask any trail crew leader about how fast trails can transform from year to year and you might get an earful. Blowdowns, fires, landslides, avalanches, and floods are just a few of the challenges that trails face as Mother Nature uses her tools to rearrange. With the help of volunteers, land managers do their best to keep the trails in tip-top shape, but change is inevitable and it's often one step forward, one step back; just when the blowdowns are cleared, another comes down with a windstorm.

Forest roads with potholes, water berms, blowdowns, and erosion can also change quickly and, at times, can make roads impassable.

Before you set out, contact land managers or read current online trip reports to see if your selected hike is affected by any challenging changes that might make the day an ordeal. And, if you find yourself with a little time on your hands, nonprofits like Washington Trails Association, Mountains to Sound Greenway Trust, and others always appreciate sweat equity (or wallet gifts) on volunteer trail projects. To learn more, visit the Trail and Conservation Club links in Resources.

The views from Rattlesnake Ledge (Hike 30) are lovely any time, but at sunset they turn magical.

IMPACT OF THE LABOR MOUNTAIN FIRE

The Teanaway/Blewett Pass Region, cherished for its alpine lakes, rugged ridgelines, and wildflower-filled basins, has been deeply affected by the Labor Mountain Fire, which burned in late summer and early fall of 2025.

Numerous trails featured in this book have been impacted, though with current closures the full extent of the damage remains undetermined. Affected areas include Standup Creek (Hike 103), Stafford Creek and County Line Trail (Hike 104), Beverly Turnpike and Iron Peak (Hike 106), Bean Creek (Hike 107), Esmerelda Basin (Hike 109), Ingalls Lake and Ingalls Creek (Hike 110), Miller Peak (Hike 112), Boulder-DeRoux Trail (Hike 115), Koppen Mountain (Hike 116), Iron Bear and Teanaway Ridge Trails (Hike 113), Johnson Creek and Medra Pass (Hike 117), and Tronson Ridge and Mount Lillian (Hike 118). Fire damage, falling debris, and unstable terrain may persist long after containment, so hikers should check with local land agencies for the latest conditions before heading out. Please respect all closures and reroutes and consider alternate destinations while the region recovers. The Cascades are resilient, but healing takes time. Please let the land rest and the wild regrow.

COMBAT PARKING

We can't blame folks for wanting to see the backcountry, and I believe if everyone had a little more of that peace tattooed on their souls, the world would be a better place. That said, the parking areas at trailheads are only so big, and on weekends and holidays, me, you, and half the zoo come out to frolic in the play areas.

If the parking area gets too crowded, you probably don't want to throw trail elbows anyway, so be flexible and have a plan B, such as an alternative hike or a timing change. Of course, obey all no-parking signs (even if the others don't), and don't block roadways or parking areas. No kidding, right? But you won't believe how much this happens.

Avoid weekends if you can, or pick up the second shift by starting your hike midmorning or even early afternoon. Carpool whenever possible. Some hikes in this book are more remote and less hiked than others, and I've indicated those in the trail descriptions. These are great hikes for weekends when other destinations are likely to be crowded. Also, be a weather warrior, and don't let the rain or clouds stop you! There are no bad days, only bad gear, and if people in the Pacific Northwest didn't hike in wet weather, we might not hike much at all. Perhaps you can relish in the coziness of a warm drink at a café après hike.

This is also a good place to note that in recent years, King County Metro teamed up with King County Parks to provide a **Trailhead Direct** bus, which goes from the Seattle area to a few select trailheads in North Bend during the busy summer months on weekends and holidays. If you are interested in learning more, please see the website (in Resources).

LEAVE NO TRACE AND WILDERNESS ETHICS

Since so many of us are sharing trails these days, a few guidelines from the Leave No

Patches of phlox grow happily in the rocky, well-drained soil near Silver Peak (Hike 68).

Trace Center for Outdoor Ethics can help everyone be safe and happy.

Plan ahead and be prepared. Aside from being prepared for weather and parking challenges, it's also good to have emergency supplies if something like a twisted ankle has you spending more time in the elements than you expected. Have a good idea of current road and trail conditions before you set out. Also, assess the fitness prowess and limitations of the group and pick something within everyone's capabilities.

Be considerate of other visitors. While I also love living in a world with great tunes, rocking out to jams on your Bluetooth speaker while pumping up the hills is frowned upon by those who came out to enjoy the sounds of nature. If you want to enjoy some music, consider using earbuds with transparency mode or bone-conduction technology so you can still hear sounds around you and stay alert.

Respect wildlife. We've all seen someone making bad choices in the name of a photo. One time at Lake Ingalls I saw a guy get charged by a grumpy mountain goat with a kid because he pushed his luck with a photo. Thankfully it ended well for both parties, but he may have soiled his drawers and probably learned his lesson. Carry a long lens for a classic camera or zoom in from a safe distance with your camera phone for that memorable wildlife moment. And for the love of all things wild, don't feed the fauna, Donna.

Dispose of waste properly. When you've gotta go, you've gotta go. Ladies—the new pee rags on the market work great for tinkles and eliminate the need for toilet paper, at least for number one. If you get a code brown on your hike, bury that sucker at least six to eight inches deep and at least 200 feet away from water. I recommend bringing some compostable doggie waste bags for picking up your toilet paper and/or sanitary products and packing them out. Don't bury it, as animals such as squirrels will often dig it up to use for nesting materials. And of course, please haul out the dog waste bags when the pup has to go too. Bring all wrappers and disposable water bottles down the mountains to toss 'em in the trash and recycle bins when you get to civilization.

Travel and camp on durable surfaces. Look for rocky outcroppings for sit breaks, and avoid fragile meadows or areas where foliage is present for sitting, walking, or standing.

Leave what you find. Mother Nature doesn't have a checkout area at her gift shop, so best not to steal any souvenirs. And while you and your sweetheart might want to remember the moment forever, consider a photo instead of carving or tagging your names or other notes in trees, signs, or natural features. Also, avoid cutting switchbacks, as it creates social trails and scars on the land that may cause erosion.

Minimize wildfire impacts. Should you feel the need for a warm fire glow, read up on the area's fire restrictions and be sure you are in a zone and time frame that they are permitted. Use designated fire rings if possible and be sure to extinguish your flame completely, breaking apart the fire ring if you created one. Or just enjoy the warm glow of accomplishment and save the fire time for a

A pika pops out to say hello—a tiny burst of life among the alpine stillness.

glass of something special by the fireplace when you get home.

Give uphill hikers the right of way. The easiest way to remember this one is to yield to whoever is pumping their heart the hardest. We've all been there—honor their efforts and maybe even lend a few encouraging words.

Step aside for stock and saddle animals. Move to the safest side of the trail to allow stock to pass without stepping off the trail and damaging vegetation. Also, keep in mind some horses get spooked when it comes to things like trekking poles in your hand, so be sure to ask the rider about what will make them most comfortable.

Treat your water. Parasites, such as giardia, may be present in PNW water sources, so always treat water by either filtering or using purification tablets before drinking.

THE 10+ ESSENTIALS

I have a little stuff sack or kit containing the 10+ essentials that lives in my pack. It doesn't get used unless necessary, and I check it periodically to replace expired food, meds, or batteries. This is a good idea if you plan to hike a lot, because it saves time and possible forgetfulness of rounding up all the supplies when you are hustling to meet a friend. Making a little 10+ essentials kit is also a great gift for your hiking partners.

1. Navigation (map and compass)
2. Headlamp (or flashlight)
3. Sun protection (sunglasses, hat, and/or sunscreen)
4. First-aid supplies
5. Knife (repair kit and tools)
6. Fire (firestarter, matches)
7. Emergency shelter (emergency blanket, bivy sack, tarp, etc.)

A nose-twitching but pretty patch of skunk cabbage blooms on the muddy shoreline of Lodge Lake (Hike 78).

A trailside western toad looks smug in the sweetest way.

8. Extra food
9. Extra water (for this one I also carry a small water filter in my 10+ essentials kit)
10. Extra clothing

STAYING SAFE

Having a safe and happy trip is always the goal. A few tips might help the odds of that happening.

Dress in layers and avoid cotton. Anyone who recreates in the shoulder seasons (not peak, or optimal, season) can tell you that regulating your body temp is tough. You need protection from the elements, but when you are working hard, you are often sweating up a storm. Layers help you stay protected but also allow you to take pieces off when you are overheated. I pack for hikes by starting at my head and going down to my toes so I don't forget anything: hat, neck gaiter, torso base layer, insulation layer, outer layer, gloves, etc. Even in summer months, it's not a bad idea to have more clothing than what you think you need, in case of an emergency or changing weather. Stay away from cotton and instead choose natural or synthetic fabrics that breathe and retain their warming properties even when wet.

Wear shoes with sufficient traction. Most of the hikes in this book have optimal timeframes listed when they are mostly snow-free. But some of the year-round destinations can have compacted snow or ice on the route during shoulder seasons or winter months. Invest in some shoe traction devices that are like tire chain or metal spikes that slide over your boots. These are a lifesaver—sometimes in the literal sense, on dangerously icy surfaces near cliffs or on steep inclines.

Let 'em know where you are going. Most folks know to let someone know where they are going and when they expect to return, but

Dwarf dogwood and mountain heather flourish along the damp edges of Pacific Northwest trails.

why not take it one step further and email them a map or trail description? That way they will know your plans to a T.

Consider carrying a messaging device. I don't mean your phone, though if you have cell service, this is the obvious choice. But in many places in this book, such as hikes in Salmon La Sac or the Teanaway region, service is nonexistent (at this book's publication date). Satellite communication devices such as SPOT messengers or Garmin inReach have recently flooded the market, making it easy and somewhat affordable for two-way satellite communication with others. Sure, it's one more electronic to keep charged and another subscription fee, but if you ever need it, it will be worth every effort and penny.

Know what to do if you or someone else in your group gets hurt. Take a basic first-aid class or, at the very least, watch a video online if you aren't sure how to treat common backcountry injuries or issues. Things like carrying a whistle, staying calm, agreeing on emergency plans, and having the right first-aid supplies can be a game changer if things go sideways.

Prevent bug hitchhikers. Wear insect repellent if the swarms are hatching and hunting your hemoglobin. And at the end of the hike, do a quick sweep to check for ticks; sadly, we've had more than ever before showing up in the PNW lately.

Strip your car of valuables. Car prowls are extremely common at trailheads—many trailheads still have glass on the ground from previous break-ins. Avoid tempting a thief by removing valuables from your car before you leave home, or carry all valuables with you. I deliberately spread trash around my car to make it look unappealing, and I also made a laminated sign for my driver's seat that reads, "No valuables in vehicle. No money, medication, jewelry, purses, paperwork, or even a candy bar." I haven't interviewed any would-be thieves lately, but knock on wood, so far, it's worked. According to the King County Sheriff's Office, it's perfectly legal to have a clear photo of your car's registration on your phone instead of in your glove box. Just be sure to save it to a specific album so you can find it quickly if need be. In fact, it's a good idea to remove any personal paperwork including car repair records or receipts. And if you have a physical garage-door opener, you may want to also take that with you.

Trust that red-flag feeling. You have enough years on this planet to know what is normal, so when something, or someone, feels off, trust that feeling. Avoid confrontation or conflict, and leave the area immediately.

WILDLIFE

We are fortunate to live in an area where wildlife is abundant and healthy. The odds of seeing them and having a great experience can be increased when you follow a few simple guidelines.

Bears

The Snoqualmie region has a healthy population of black bears. They come in other colors besides black, including tones of brown and auburn or cinnamon. To avoid confrontation:

- **Clap, sing, or shout.** Make noise on blind corners or in high brush to help bears know humans are nearby. Forget bear bells—they aren't a natural human sound. In fact, in one study done in Alaska, bears walked right by the testing blind without even acknowledging the ringing. You voice is a much better human-alert tool, and free too!
- **Walk in pairs or groups.** Hike together! It's more fun anyway, right?
- **Don't let kids wander off or run ahead.** Kids tend to get the wiggles out by running, so emphasize the importance of sticking close in areas with wildlife.
- **Keep the pup on a leash.** Most areas in this book require dogs to be on a leash, but if you are in an area where off-leash dogs are permitted, remember that roaming dogs can create quite a safety issue for you and them if a bear is encountered.
- **Avoid darkness if possible.** Hike during daylight hours when bears are less active.
- **Tone down scents.** Avoid fragrances that might make a bear stick his nose in the air with curiosity about you.
- **Be smart with headphones.** If using headphones, choose those with transparent mode or bone-induction technology so you can still hear the outside world and stay alert. Or just use one ear bud to still allow some sensory perception.

Bear Encounters

The odds of having a scary bear encounter are slim, but if you get approached by a bear, remain calm and appear as nonthreatening as possible. Don't run. Avoid sudden movement, avoid looking them in the eye, and identify yourself as human by speaking clearly and calmly. Don't try to climb a tree; black bears are much better climbers than humans. If the bear bluff-charges, stand your ground and deploy bear deterrent pepper spray if you brought some.

Bear Spray

Bear deterrent pepper spray is sold at a handful of sporting goods retailers throughout

"Who's that?" Three furry locals take a break from brunch to inspect the visitor.

the state, but for the most part, it's overkill for the hikes in this book. Some people feel better carrying it, and that's ok too. Usually, unless provoked, bears are well-behaved and want nothing to do with you. Rest assured that most bear-viewing opportunities result in lovely pictures of the bear's hind end, not fear-based interactions. Enjoy the backcountry and be prepared instead of worried.

Mountain Goats

Mountain goats are frequently seen in our PNW backcountry, especially just on the eastern side of the Cascade Crest. In some areas, the goats have been habituated and don't seem to be afraid of humans. While they are generally docile, they can be downright dangerous—after all, they are powerful and large and have knives growing out of their heads. To avoid confrontation:

- **Piddle on pumice.** Urinate off-trail on stones or rocky slabs, as goats will tear up vegetation to get at urine. They (disgustingly) seek the salt that you are expelling, and to some goats, you are a human vending machine for the mineral. I have even had them move in before I was finished!
- **Stay back.** As with all wildlife, keep your distance from these big, gorgeous creatures. They are agile and quick, and have been known to climb 1500 vertical feet in a matter of only 20 minutes. While they seem mellow, they can be easily agitated, especially if they are with their young. Give them plenty of space, and use your camera zoom or a longer lens when enjoying their company.

Deer and Elk

The biggest concern with deer and elk comes in rutting season, in the fall. When they seek mates, they tend to get a bit grumpy and can charge if you get too close. For the most part, common sense applies. To avoid a confrontation:

A NOTE ABOUT SAFETY

Safety is an important concern in all outdoor activities. No guidebook can alert you to every hazard or anticipate the limitations of every reader. Therefore, the descriptions of roads, trails, routes, and natural features in this book are not representations that a particular place or excursion will be safe for your party. When you follow any of the routes described in this book, you assume responsibility for your own safety. Under normal conditions, such excursions require the usual attention to traffic, road and trail conditions, weather, terrain, the capabilities of your party, and other factors. Keeping informed on current conditions and exercising common sense are the keys to a safe, enjoyable outing.

—Mountaineers Books

- **Stay back.** Resist the temptation of close-up pictures and give them plenty of space.
- **Keep dogs on a leash.** This is especially critical if you hear elk bugling or you are hiking in fall in general.

Mountain Lions

The most elusive beast in the Cascades doesn't come out from hiding very often. But if you do see a mountain lion, a few tips might help:

- **Get big.** Look them in the eye, make noise, wave your hands or poles above your head, and do everything possible to look large. Pick up small children and, if possible, put them up high on a stump or log to make them appear as big as possible.
- **Don't run!** They have an instinct to chase.

If necessary, fight back. Attacks are rare, but if one occurs, fight hard, fight dirty; use jabs, kicks, and punches to the most vulnerable spots, like the eyes.

How to Use This Guide

This book is laid out in a straightforward manner to get you hiking with clear-cut information and detailed guidance. Knowing a few tidbits about what the features mean might help if you have questions. The information block located prior to each hike helps you quickly decide if this is the right hike for you based on all the factors that define it.

Overall Rating: This rating is quite subjective, and some of you will no doubt feel differently than I do. But, since we can all only see through our own lens, I've done my best to qualify each hike with my best 1- to 5-star rating, which accounts for scenery, trail tread, and overall must-do quality of each hike. I don't give 5s out easily, so if you see one—be sure to put it on your list!

- ★★★★★ Bucket list or better; must do
- ★★★★ Get there! Scenic and impressive landscape features
- ★★★ Enjoyable hike with some noteworthy features and/or views
- ★★ Worthy of exploration but not a sock-knocker-off-er
- ★ Great leg stretcher or alternative place to check out if you are nearby

Difficulty Rating: This one is also super personal, but I've tried to rate these for the average hiker, with 5 being the hardest. If you are a trail runner, fitness guru, or thru hiker, these numbers probably won't help you much because nearly everything in your repertoire is probably easy to moderate. But I wanted to give a guideline for the majority of folks, so I did my best to take into account the steepness of the terrain, elevation gain, trail tread, and obstacles such as creek crossings or talus fields that might make it more challenging.

- 5 You might scream, "Uncle"—this one's as tough as it gets (extremely difficult, rough trail tread)
- 4 Have the pain relievers handy post-hike (steep sections or primitive stretches)
- 3 Not a gimme; you'll still work, but it's moderate grade and tread
- 2 You got this—some challenging elements but not too hard
- 1 Piece of cake—gentle terrain and trail tread, possibly ADA accessible

Roundtrip Mileage: I've hiked all of the hikes in this book with three GPS calculating devices: a fitness watch, a Garmin GPS with a quad helix antenna, and an app on my phone. Nearly every single hike read something slightly different for distance on each device. I then compared the mileage to that of Green Trails Maps to get their reading. The bottom line is that it's almost impossible to find a resolute number to the tenth of a mile, and I've beat my head on my desk a few times in the quest for perfection. Go a few steps off the trail to check out a viewpoint, squat

OPPOSITE: *As fleeting as spring mist, the calypso orchid appears only where the forest remains undisturbed near Easton Ridge (Hike 82). Step lightly, and admire from afar.*

behind a tree, or explore a connecting path, and the number changes again. But I've done my best to get in the ballpark of accuracy using my most scientific methods, so you know what you are up against when you set out. Your distance might vary slightly, but we will be close.

Elevation Gain/High Point: The elevation gain represents the total cumulative elevation you can expect on the hike, while the high point is the elevation of highest point you'll reach. Keep in mind that the high point of the hike isn't necessarily at the end. For example, you could climb to a high pass, then drop down to a lake basin. In that example, you would be climbing back out of the lake basin to return to the trailhead, so the trail would have ups and down, all of which would be accounted for in the total elevation gain number as listed.

Season: Many of these trails get used year-round for snowy pursuits, but since this book focuses on hiking, I've listed the optimal time to enjoy them when the trail is mostly snow-free and the roads to the trailheads are passable. Of course, Mother

MAP LEGEND

Symbol	Meaning	Symbol	Meaning
90	US Interstate		Caution
97	US highway	▲	Mountain/peak
821	State highway	■	Point of interest
9703	Forest Service road		Picnic area
	Other road		Gate/turnstyle
	Dirt road		Campground/campsite
45	Trail	)(	Bridge
→	Direction of travel		Wetland
	Other trail	)(	Pass
T	Trailhead		Waterfall
P	Parking		Waterbody
T	Alternate trailhead		River/stream
P	Alternate parking		Forest boundary
V	Viewpoint		Wilderness boundary

A couple of peaceful nooks like this one offer fine snack break spots on Stegosaurus Butte (Hike 43).

Nature has her own plans and might vary from the dates listed. Big snow years can leave lingering piles well into summer, and late or early snowstorms can change things up too. If you decide you want to check the trails out in winter, you may want to enroll in an avalanche awareness class and educate yourself on snowslides, hazards, and gear for traveling in the snowy backcountry.

Maps: Most maps in this book use Green Trails Maps—a boots-on-the-ground map-maker using physical 7.5-minute maps that are quite accurate and available at many retail locations around the area or online at Mountaineers Books (see Resources). Some hikes located on county or state land have their own online maps, which are listed in the maps section too. Digital mapping is also popular, but a backup printed version is a good idea since phone batteries get sucked down quickly when tracking.

Contact: The name of the government agency that manages the land for the hike is listed here, with its nitty-gritty contact details in Resources. These agencies are the best contact for up-to-date conditions and road issues.

Notes: Pay particularly close attention to the notes section, where important information about rough roads, facilities at trailheads, or specific hike details (water crossings, gun range proximity, etc.) is listed for your awareness. I list parking situation issues in here too, so read this carefully if you plan to hike on the weekends. The Open To subsection lists permitted users on that trail, which may

With tiny paws and big attitude, a Douglas squirrel greets a hiker from his perch.

include dogs, equestrians, mountain bikes, or motorcycles.

GPS: The coordinates get you to the trailhead, if you choose to go digital and follow them, and are listed in degrees and decimal minutes style according to WGS84 datum. But when trail excitement sets in, you could just use the directions; both will help you arrive.

Trail Introduction and Icons: The **trail overview** offers a high-level synopsis of the route, often with some tantalizing details about landscapes you might see on your way. Along with the quick-reference **icons**, you'll get a sense of the trail's best features or opportunities:

 Kid-friendly

 Dog-friendly

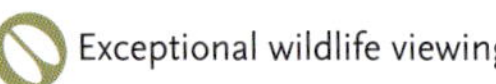 Exceptional wildlife viewing

 Exceptional wildflowers in season

 Waterfall

 Bird-watching

 Historical relevance

 Views

 Lakes

 Multiuse

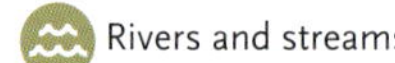 Rivers and streams

While most of the listed icons are self-evident, **Kid-friendly** can be more subjective. For me it means that the trail is either short enough, smooth enough, or level enough that bringing your children won't result in a miserable march. Keep in mind, though, kids come in a variety of ages and abilities. Some active kids might be able to do all the hikes in this book, while others are too young or too inexperienced to enjoy them. I did my best to label each appropriately, but you know your kids best.

Dog-friendly is also one of those labels that's hard to dial in. Do you hike with an active, young cattle dog or an old Lab? That makes a difference, and again, you know your dog and their abilities best. The dog-friendly label isn't just for hikes that are open to dogs but also hikes with dog-friendly trail tread, appropriate distances, or in some cases, water or swimming holes en route.

Getting There: Provided here are step-by-step directions to take you to the trailhead. In most cases, I list the directions from the largest town or obvious geographical point of reference to make the drive easier for you. I've made notes with my car's mileage on each of these hikes, but keep in mind, where I set my car's tripometer might have been a tiny bit different than from where you pressed yours, but it will be close enough to get you there.

The author admires Gem Lake (Hike 79) from a perfect shoreline perch.

Alligator lizards love the heat and the rocks. You might catch one lounging on Little Si's sunlit slopes (Hike 22).

On the Trail: The trail description is the main course. When I hiked these trails, I documented them using detailed notes and photos to describe them to a T. I like to provide heavy data with a lighthearted twist, so the trail descriptions are helpful as well as fun to read. Feel free to roll your eyes at my dumb dad jokes. On some hikes, I listed hike extension options for hikers or trail runners who are looking for longer, more challenging days.

OPPOSITE: *A creek winds through a vibrant, mossy woodland on the Tiger Mountain Trail (Hike 15).*

ISSAQUAH ALPS

THE ISSAQUAH ALPS—A TERM COINED by the late, great author Harvey Manning—are the result of years of private land acquisitions and advocacy to protect hidden, winding pathways through sword ferns, mossy bogs, and tall evergreens on peaks high above city development. After historical uses spanning from logging to mining and sometimes use as a dumping ground, the area was cleaned, protected, and preserved and now holds some of the best maintained and most used trails around the greater Seattle Eastside. Consisting primarily of Cougar, Squak, and Tiger Mountains and, to a lesser degree, Grand Ridge and Taylor Mountain, there are so many trails that even on a busy summer Saturday, you can find some solitude along the many pathways. I've outlined several good loops and out-and-back options, but with the crisscrossing trails and different approaches, this area is made for exploration, and I encourage you to spend the day discovering the many trails.

COUGAR MOUNTAIN REGIONAL WILDLAND PARK

1 Anti-Aircraft Ramble

RATING/DIFFICULTY: ***/2
ROUNDTRIP: 4.5 miles
ELEV GAIN/HIGH POINT: 480 feet/1440 feet
SEASON: Year-round

Maps: Green Trails Maps Cougar Mountain/Squak Mountain No. 203S, King County Parks Cougar Mountain map; **Contact:** King County Parks; **Notes:** As with all Cougar Mountain trails, there are plenty of options for variety in distances and elevations. Open to leashed dogs, stock (on some trails); **GPS:** N 47 53.347, W 122 11.335

While this northern section of Cougar Mountain was once a military defense area against potential attacks on Puget Sound, Mother Nature is a lover, not a fighter, so she has turned the area back into a peaceful habitat for birds, plants, and people alike. It's a great place for a walk in the woods, complete with a picturesque viewpoint and points of interest.

GETTING THERE

From I-90 near Issaquah: Take exit 13 and head south on Lakemont Boulevard. Follow Lakemont Boulevard for 2.3 miles, then head left (southeast) on SE Cougar Mountain Way. At 2.9 miles, turn right (south) on 166th Way SE. At 3.3 miles, enter a large signed area for Cougar Mountain Regional Wildlife Park. In 0.5 mile beyond the signed entrance (3.7 miles from I-90), locate a large parking area for Sky Country trailhead to the right, complete with pit toilets and a picnic area.

ON THE TRAIL

From the parking area, walk northeast and locate a small wooden footbridge connecting the trailhead with a service road. Follow the road, known as Clay Pit Road, for 0.5 mile, passing intersecting trails, until you reach an informational sign kiosk and the Klondike Swamp Trail on the road's left. Turn left onto the Klondike Swamp Trail and follow it for 1 mile, passing the Cougar Pass Trail and the Lost Beagle Trail, until you arrive at a T with the Coyote Creek Trail.

Turn right on the Coyote Creek Trail and at 1.8 miles, turn right onto the Shangri-La Trail. A short, steep climb takes you up into the hinterlands, but it's there you will find the view,

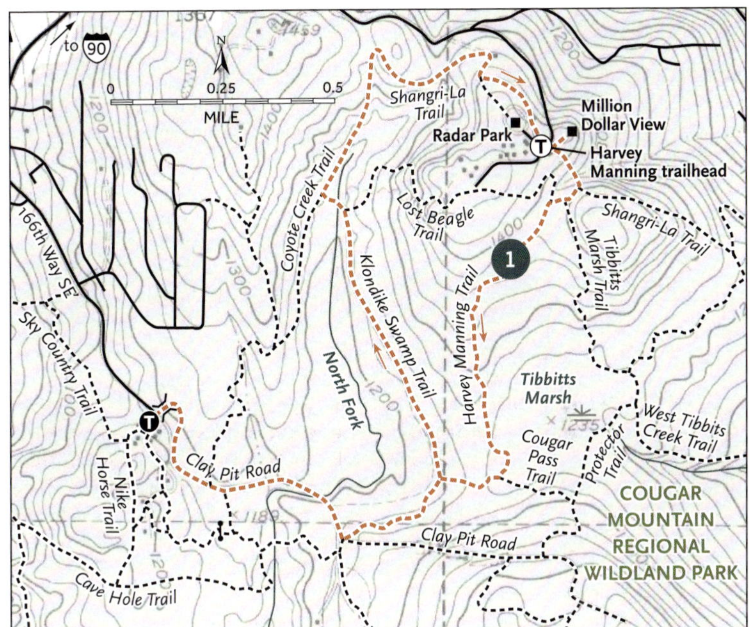

so onward! At 2.2 miles, arrive at a signed junction. The trail straight goes to Radar Park Field, but so does the unsigned trail to the left, which also winds around the outskirts through welcoming evergreens, so head left.

At 2.6 miles, arrive at the Harvey Manning trailhead as well as Radar Park to the right. The park, complete with informational signage, covered picnic areas, green grassy lawns, and outhouse toilets, is well worth a stop. From 1957 to 1964, this was the site of Nike anti-aircraft missiles and radar technology, designed for defenses against potential enemy bombing attacks on military and industrial facilities in the greater Puget Sound area during the Cold War.

After you've explored the park, wander over to the Harvey Manning trailhead, and locate the pathway between wooden fences that promises to lead to a Million Dollar View. Walk up this short spur trail and find . . . you guessed it . . . a serene view showcasing Mount Baker, Vesper Peak, Big Four Mountain, and other peaks, as well as the sparkling waters of Lake Sammamish in the valley below. A couple of picnic tables beg you to bust out a snack while you take a load off. A kiosk here tells of the famed guidebook author and hiking advocate Harvey Manning, whose vision created this very park. Tip your hat to him as you enjoy the sprawling view and nibble your PB&J.

Walk the spur back to Harvey's trailhead. Between the park and viewpoint exploration, we've likely burned 0.2 mile, so we will add this to our total, just in case you are keeping

Even on winter days, Cougar Mountain trails are ready for hikers.

track. At the trailhead, avail yourself of the map kiosk and trash can as needed. Next to the trash can, a sign points the way toward the Harvey Manning Trail. Follow the arrow and the trail southeast, for less than 0.1 mile, then turn right, staying on the Harvey Manning Trail at a junction with the Shangri-La Trail. Bear right again, staying on Harvey's Trail at another junction with the Tibbetts Marsh Trail in 0.1 mile.

At 3 miles, turn left at a signed junction with the Lost Beagle Trail to stay on the Harvey Manning Trail. At 3.7 miles, go right at a signed junction with the Cougar Pass Trail and soon reach the Klondike Swamp Trail. Look familiar? You've been here—you just made a full loop.

Turn left on the Klondike Swamp Trail and retrace your steps for another 0.2 mile until you arrive once again at the Clay Pit Road. Go right and follow the road 0.5 mile back to your waiting vehicle. Mission accomplished!

2 Wilderness Peak Loop

RATING/DIFFICULTY: ***/3
ROUNDTRIP: 6.5 miles
ELEV GAIN/HIGH POINT: 1040 feet/1598 feet
SEASON: Year-round

Maps: Green Trails Maps Cougar Mountain/Squak Mountain No. 203S, King County Parks Cougar Mountain map; **Contact:** King County Parks; **Notes:** You can also reach Wilderness Peak and the Wilderness Peak Loop from the Jim Whittaker Wilderness Peak trailhead, but this way provides a gentler trail grade to start and a longer adventure. What's more, it has more parking opportunities. Should you choose the Jim Whittaker Wilderness Peak trailhead, a roundtrip loop to Wilderness Peak and back is 3.9 miles with 1200 feet of elevation gain. As with all Cougar Mountain trails, multiple loops are possible depending on how much time and gumption you have for your adventure. Port-a-potties and picnic areas available at trailhead. Open to leashed dogs, stock (on some trails); **GPS:** N 47 53.347, W 122 11.335

Wilderness Peak is a peaceful nook on the top of a forested summit. A log bench offers a reflection stop, and a small trail register awaits your signature. There aren't stunning views, but the peak's tranquility makes you appreciate the Issaquah Alps for their soul food in the midst of development. This is only one of the many trails to explore in this maze of beautiful forested pathways.

GETTING THERE

Sky Country trailhead: From I-90, take exit 13 and head south on Lakemont Boulevard for 2.3 miles, then head left (southeast) on SE Cougar Mountain Way. At 2.9 miles, turn right (south) on 166th Way SE. At 3.3 miles, enter a large signed area for Cougar Mountain Regional Wildlife Park. In 0.5 mile beyond the signed entrance (3.7 miles from I-90), locate a large parking area to the right, complete with pit toilets and a picnic area.

Jim Whittaker Wilderness Peak trailhead: From I-90, take exit 15 and drive south on Renton/Issaquah Road (State Route 900) for 3.4 miles. Look closely for a small trailhead sign and a driveway heading uphill to the right to the parking area. It's easy to miss! Port-a-potty available here most years.

ON THE TRAIL

From the parking area, locate the trail behind a large blue sign for the Sky Country trailhead. An information kiosk sits to the right with maps and area information. In 0.1 mile, arrive at a T that was part of an old paved roadway and make a right (the left dead-ends in a log, but you can see Clay Pit Road beyond it). Follow the paved road for another 0.1 mile as it opens up into a rather large paved open space. Straight ahead of you is the signed C11 Old Man's Trail, a gravel forested single track.

Follow the Old Man's Trail as it bobs and weaves through deciduous trees and lowland forest shrubs before it exits through a wooden turnstile (designed to keep out horses) and arrives at a wide former road, now called the Cave Hole Trail, 0.4 mile from the trailhead. Turn right and follow the Cave Hole Trail for another 0.1 mile until you reach a forested Y intersection. The sign here is a bit confusing, as it seems to be pointing off in the brush. Bear left, signed for C9 By Pass Trail.

At 0.7 mile , arrive at Fred's Railroad Trail and go right. By now, your head is probably swimming—good thing you have a fantastic guidebook with step-by-step details to get you to these trails. It's so easy to get turned around in this maze!

Follow Fred's Railroad Trail for 0.6 mile, passing East Fork Trail and Quarry Trail and turning left onto Shy Bear Trail as you make your way toward Shy Bear Pass at 1.3 miles. If you think of a pass as a high mountain intersection, you might be surprised when you arrive here and find that it's simply a forested junction. Also, I've never seen any bashful bears in these parts, so it might be false advertising. Regardless, it's a good spot to look around and get your bearings. We will come back to this spot and retrace our steps to the parking lot after doing a loop.

If you are ready to see more of the area, follow along as I walk you through the other turns. However, if time is limited, or if you want to skip the main course and eat dessert first, you can get to Wilderness Peak by going left at this point and following the Whittaker Wilderness Peak Trail all the way to the top. If this is the route you take, your total mileage will be 1.6 miles out and back from this spot.

Otherwise, earn your steps! Turn right at Shy Bear Pass and in about 30 feet, bear left at the signed intersection with the Whittaker Wilderness Peak Trail. From here, prepare to descend! Down you go through lovely Douglas-firs and the occasional western red cedar to reach a narrow log boardwalk over a swampy area at 1.9 miles.

This trail was named for Jim Whittaker, a legendary local mountaineer who became the first American to reach the summit of Mount Everest. Later, you'll pass by a trail named after his climbing partner Sherpa Nawang

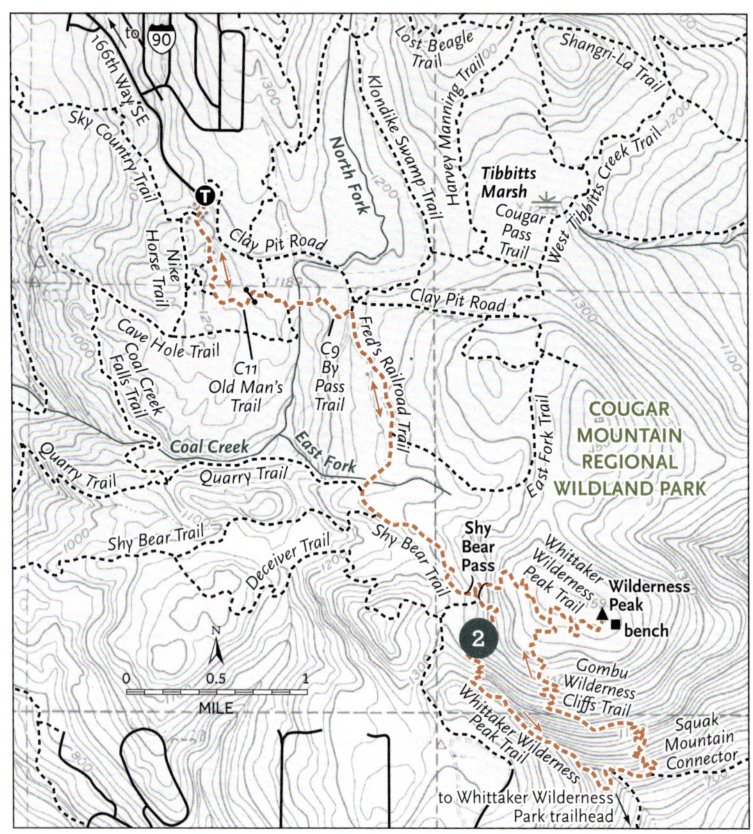

Clear signage at every junction reflects the thoughtful stewardship at Cougar Mountain.

Gombu. Jim Whittaker was also the CEO of REI in the 1960s, and you are probably wearing or carrying something you bought there, so you are within six degrees of separation from climbing Everest, naturally.

After a rather steep descent, reach a small wooden bridge over a seasonal creek at 2.8 miles. Roughly 50 feet after the bridge, arrive at a three-way signed trail junction. To the right, the Whittaker Wilderness Peak Trail descends toward the Jim Whittaker Wilderness Peak trailhead. Straight ahead is the Squak Mountain Connector Trail, and to the left is the trail we are taking: Gombu Wilderness Cliffs Trail. And, yes, you'll wish you had a Sherpa for this climb.

Up you go, burning calories and busting beads of sweat as you traverse through evergreen roots and forest canopies. This might be a good time to remind yourself that you came for a little exercise, right? The trail ebbs and flows with steepness, until at 4.1 miles, it rejoins the Whittaker Wilderness Peak Trail at a signed T intersection.

Wilderness Peak is an out-and-back spur trail from this point, so make a right and proceed for 0.3 mile on a gentle grade until the trail dead-ends at a bench and a wooden cubby for the trail register book. Though there aren't views, this is the high point of the Cougar Mountain area with an elevation of 1598 feet. Not quite Everest, but we'll take it.

The forest is peaceful and pleasant. The gorgeous split-log bench has a plaque dedicated to a Japanese American pair who suffered in the internment camps of World War II. Along with the message of inner peace and tranquility, the plaque says, "Follow the Path to Bushido." The word *Bushido* comes from Samurai warriors and literally translates to the "way of the warrior." Bushido is a system of ethics such as honor, loyalty, righteousness, respect, and self-control, and the pathway is assumedly within one's self. Sounds like a lovely place—onward to Bushido! But at some point, you'll want to head back physically too.

To do so, retrace your steps back 0.3 mile until you arrive at the Whittaker Wilderness Peak Trail–Gombu Wilderness Cliffs Trail intersection. Go straight here, following the Whittaker Wilderness Peak Trail back to Shy Bear Pass at 5.2 miles. From Shy Bear Pass, retrace your path back to your vehicle. If you make a mistake and end up at a forest road, that's Clay Pit Road. Go left and follow it downhill until you see the parking lot to the left. These twists and turns can really be befuddling.

3 Coal Creek Falls

RATING/DIFFICULTY: **/2

ROUNDTRIP: 3.1 miles

ELEV GAIN/HIGH POINT: 510 feet/1270 feet

SEASON: Year-round

Maps: Green Trails Maps Cougar Mountain/Squak Mountain No. 203S, King County Parks Cougar Mountain map; **Contact:** King County Parks; **Notes:** Port-a-potties and picnic areas available at trailhead. As with all Cougar Mountain trails, there are various approaches to Coal Creek Falls and plenty of options for variety in distances and elevations. The one listed here is a pleasant walk with just enough elevation gain to get the heart pumping. Open to leashed dogs, stock (on some trails); **GPS:** N 47 53.347, W 122 11.335

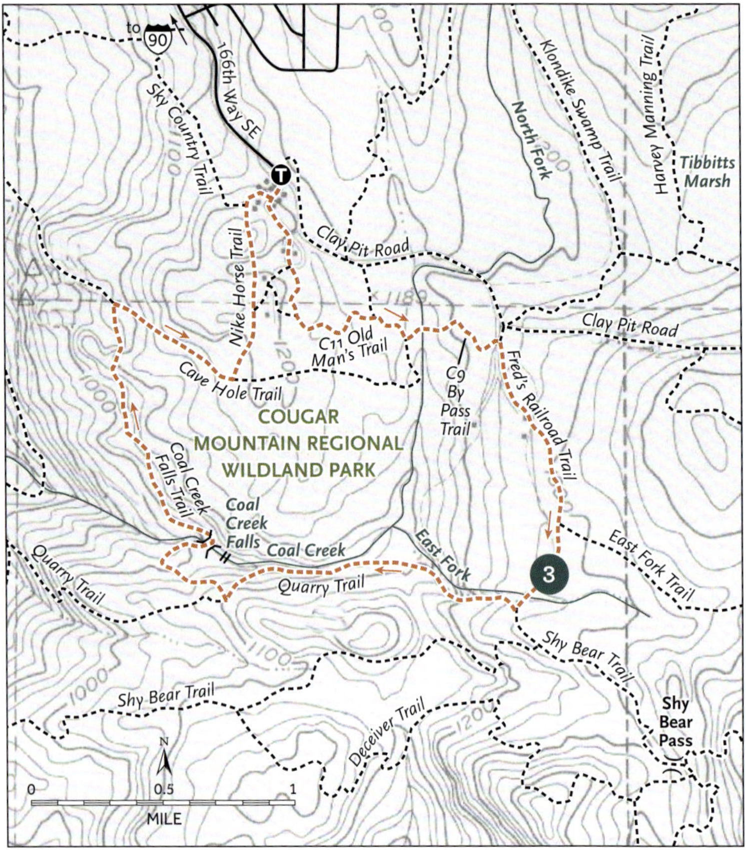

Coal Creek Falls flows over mossy rocks with a peaceful rhythm.

Coal Creek Falls, with a 28-foot drop and an average width of 5 feet, isn't huge, but it dances with light and shadows as it bounces over a mossy face. In the midst of Cougar Mountain's forests and mazes of trails, it's fun to locate this little gem.

GETTING THERE

Sky Country trailhead: From I-90, take exit 13 and head south on Lakemont Boulevard. Follow Lakemont Boulevard for 2.3 miles, then head left (southeast) on SE Cougar Mountain Way. In 0.6 mile more (2.9 miles from I-90), turn right (south) on 166th Way SE. At 0.4 mile, enter a large signed area for Cougar Mountain Regional Wildlife Park. In 0.5 mile beyond the signed entrance (3.7 miles from I-90), locate a large parking area to the right, complete with pit toilets and a picnic area.

ON THE TRAIL

From the parking area, locate the trail behind a large blue sign for the Sky Country trailhead. An information kiosk behind the sign contain maps and information on the area. In 0.1 mile, arrive at a T that was part of an old, paved roadway and make a right (the left dead-ends in a log, but you can see the Clay Pit Road beyond it). Follow the paved road for another 0.1 mile as it opens up into a rather large paved open space. Straight ahead of you is the signed C11 Old Man's Trail, a gravel forested single track.

Follow the Old Man's Trail as it winds around tranquil riparian areas and ferns, until it exits a wooden turnstile and arrives at a large former road, now called the Cave Hole Trail (0.4 mile from the parking area).

Turn right and follow the Cave Hole Trail for 0.1 mile (0.5 mile from where you parked), until you arrive at a Y intersection. Veer left at this spot onto the C9 By Pass Trail, and, in 0.2 mile beyond the Y (0.7 from the parking area), arrive at Fred's Railroad Trail and turn right. This place is a maze, right?

Follow Fred's Railroad Trail for 0.5 mile, (1.2 from the parking area) passing the East

Fork Trail, until you arrive at a sign to the right, for the Quarry Trail. Turn right and start descending through mixed deciduous and conifer trees on a well-tread pathway.

In 0.6 mile (1.8 from the parking area), turn right at a signed junction pointing toward Coal Creek Falls, and continue descending, listening as you walk for the running water.

In 0.2 mile more (2.0 from the parking area), arrive at a wooden bridge over Coal Creek Stream, with a good view of Coal Creek Falls to the right. The horsetail falls drops over a large mossy rock, providing a peaceful soundtrack to the area. A rough boot path just after the bridge heads up toward the waterfall's base for those who want a closer look.

Carry on with the hiking, climbing slightly now for 0.5 mile (2.5 miles from the parking area), to reach a T junction with the signed Cave Hole Trail. You were on a different part of this trail earlier, should it sound familiar. Turn right here, and walk for another 0.2 mile until you arrive at the signed Nike Horse Trail, where you'll go left.

The Nike Horse Trail wanders next to a large meadow bordered by a weathered split rail fence, until it connects with the Sky Country Trail in 0.4 mile. At this junction, the parking area, just several feet away to your right, is clearly visible. This is the southwest end of the parking area where you parked. Congratulations on your loop, and welcome back!

4 Doughty Falls Ramble

RATING/DIFFICULTY: **/3

ROUNDTRIP: 6.4 miles

ELEV GAIN/HIGH POINT: 1190 feet/1330 feet

SEASON: Year-round

Maps: Green Trails Maps Cougar Mountain/Squak Mountain No. 203S, King County Parks Cougar Mountain map; **Contact:** King County Parks; **Notes:** Port-a-potty and picnic areas available at trailhead. As with all Cougar Mountain trails, there are various options for variety in distances and elevations. Waterfalls in this area are best in the springtime. In summertime, they may be dry. Open to leashed dogs, stock (on some trails); **GPS:** N 47 53.462, W 122 12.880

Loop trails are great because you get to vary your view of the area without having to cover too much ground twice. This one makes a big loop on the slightly quieter western side of Cougar Mountain and is a great hike to catch up with friends or simply do some thinking on a solo trip. Long View Peak doesn't have much of a view anymore, thanks to overgrown trees, and the other trail features—such as Doughty Falls and Far Country Lookout—are quiet forest nooks rather than inspiring landscape spectacles. But the workout is energizing and the network of trails mesmerizing, so it's worth the time.

GETTING THERE

From I-90 near Issaquah: Take exit 13 and head south on Lakemont Boulevard for 3.1 miles to find the Red Town trailhead on your left.

From I-405 near Factoria: Take exit 10, Coal Creek Parkway/Factoria Boulevard, and proceed east for 2.6 miles, then turn left on Newcastle Way (near the shopping center). In 0.2 mile farther, at the stop sign, turn left onto Newcastle Golf Club Road. In 1.9 miles farther, locate the Red Town trailhead on the right (southeast) side of the road.

Surrounded by green that never fades, trails around Cougar Mountain lead deeper into nature's calm.

ON THE TRAIL

From the parking lot, walk toward the signed kiosk and arrive at a Y with two gravel roads. These roads are part of the trail system of the park and used only lightly by park personnel. A wooden sign points left to the Red Town Trail and right to the Wildside Trail. Turn left and begin a short, steep uphill warm-up on the gravel Red Town Trail.

Stay on the Red Town Trail, passing the Cave Hole Trail, Bagley Seam Trail, and Rainbow Town Trail. At 0.7 mile, the trail crosses the culverted Coal Creek and makes a sharp bend. At 0.8 mile, pass a junction with a

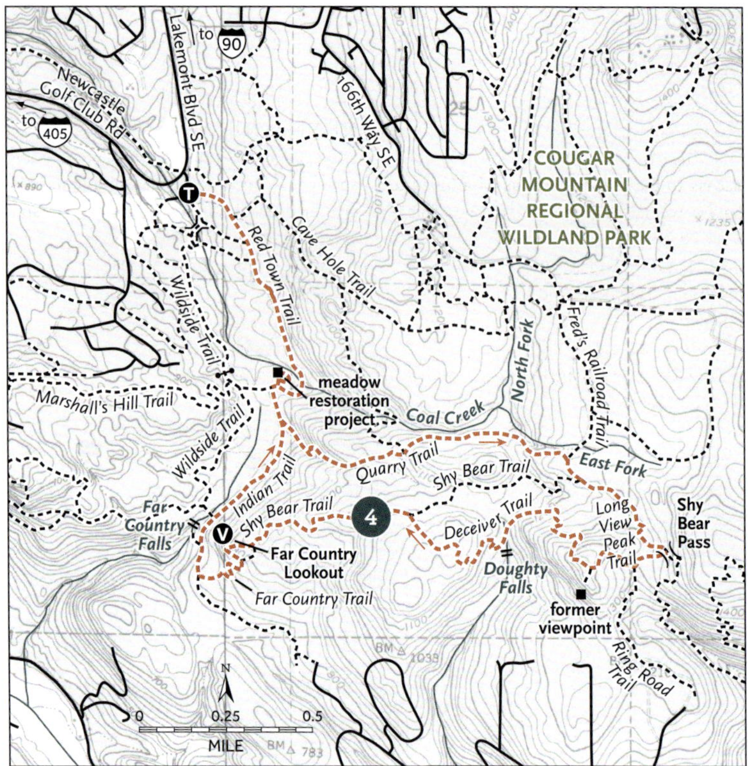

small wooden bridge to the right, leading to the meadow restoration project. A former baseball field for the coal-mining town near here, the meadow was restored to its native state thanks to volunteer efforts (see Hike 5).

Immediately after the meadow restoration junction, stay left at a signed intersection with the Indian Trail. Follow the Indian Trail for a short distance, and at 0.9 mile, begin the loop by turning left onto the Quarry Trail. A climb awaits, though it's not terrible compared to some.

At 1.4 miles, arrive at a junction with the Coal Creek Falls Trail (see Hike 2). If you have time and want to check it out, it's 0.4 mile from this spot to go out and back. If not, see it another day. Continue on the Quarry Trail until you reach Fred's Railroad Trail at 2 miles from the trailhead. Turn right here, passing the Shy Bear Trail coming in from the right.

Arrive at the signed junction with Shy Bear Pass at 2.5 miles. Turn right here and stay straight, avoiding the turn for the Whittaker Wilderness Peak Trail on the left. You are now on the Long View Peak Trail, and it's getting deeper into evergreens and quite peaceful, right?

Pass the Ring Road Trail and, at 2.9 miles, reach a signed junction with the Deceiver Trail, bearing right. Straight ahead is horse access to the area, as well as what used to be a viewpoint but is now overgrown. This is quite deceptive—no viewpoint on Long View Peak? Hmmm. Ponder that as you bear right on the Deceiver Trail and follow it, winding downhill to Doughty Falls at 3.3 miles. The signed spur trail takes you downhill to a small wooden viewpoint where the 10-foot split falls drop over moss-covered stone. It's not likely to leave you in awe, but everyone loves to watch water do its thing, so it's a cool place to hang out for a few minutes. Down and back is less than 0.1 mile.

In 0.6 mile from the Doughty Falls spur (3.6 miles from the trailhead), the Deceiver Trail ends in a T with the signed Shy Bear Trail. To complete our loop, go left and follow the Shy Bear Trail until you arrive at a Y at 4.2 miles. This is now the Far Country Trail, and you can go either way. The left branch of the Y descends along the loop and skips the viewpoint, while the right detours to it. You don't lose much elevation to get to the viewpoint, and it only adds about 800 feet to your hike, so why not? You came this far. Turn right and walk 0.1 mile to a wooden bench and a pleasant vista through the trees. It's a serene place to relax in a calmness you can almost feel through your skin.

After the viewpoint, the spur trail loops back around and reconnects with the Far Country Trail in another 0.1 mile. Turn right on the Far Country Trail and follow it to reach a T with the Indian Trail at 4.6 miles. Turn right, following the Indian Trail northbound past a small kiosk with some information on birds and wildlife. A map is also displayed if you want to see how many trails connect on Cougar Mountain.

At 4.8 miles, arrive at a signed spur trail for Far Country Falls, a 20-foot drop with steep cascades. It flows mostly during winter and spring months and can be quite unimpressive or even dry during summer. The spur takes you 0.2 mile down and back to see the playful water, so if it's flowing, stop and check it out. You've come 5 miles from the parking lot at this point, assuming you visited Doughty Falls, Far Country Lookout, and Far Country Falls. You rock!

After checking out Far Country Falls, continue northbound on the Indian Trail, and at 5.1 miles, pass the De Leo Wall Trail. At 5.4 miles, hit the Quarry Trail junction again, officially completing our loop. Now we turn left to retrace our path the way we arrived. In 0.1 mile farther, arrive back at the junction with the Marshall's Hill Trail, and make a right. You are now on the Red Town Trail, which will lead you back to your vehicle and hopefully to a milkshake at a nearby restaurant.

5 Red Town Meadow Loop

RATING/DIFFICULTY: **/1
ROUNDTRIP: 2 miles
ELEV GAIN/HIGH POINT: 120 feet/750 feet
SEASON: Year-round

Maps: Green Trails Maps Cougar Mountain/Squak Mountain No. 203S, King County Parks Cougar Mountain map; **Contact:** King County Parks; **Notes:** As with all Cougar Mountain trails, there are various options for variety in distances and elevations. Open to leashed dogs, stock (on some trails); **GPS:** N 47 53.462, W 122 12.880

Cougar Mountain is full of scenic pathways where you can crank out a short workout, soak in nature, and still have time for errands.

This is the perfect loop for hikers with small kids or couples looking for a romantic stroll. Conversations will flow easily, since you won't be breathless, and the forest teems with vibrant green foliage. What's more, you get a taste of the area's mining history.

GETTING THERE

From I-90 near Issaquah: Take exit 13 and head south on Lakemont Boulevard for 3.1 miles to find the Red Town trailhead on your left.

From I-405 near Factoria: Take exit 10, Coal Creek Parkway/Factoria Boulevard, and proceed east for 2.6 miles, then turn left on Newcastle Way (near the shopping center). At 2.8 miles, at the stop sign, turn left onto Newcastle Golf Club Road. At 4.7 miles, locate the Red Town trailhead on the right (southeast) side of the road.

ON THE TRAIL

From the parking lot, walk toward the picnic area and signed kiosk and arrive at a Y with two gravel roads. These roads are part of the trail system of the park and used only lightly by park personnel. A wooden sign points left toward the Red Town Trail and right to the Wildside Trail. Turn left and begin a short, steep uphill warm-up on the gravel Red Town Trail.

Stay on the Red Town Trail, passing the Cave Hole Trail, Bagley Seam Trail, and Rainbow Town Trail. At 0.7 mile, the trail crosses the culverted Coal Creek and makes a sharp bend. At 0.8 mile, pass a junction with a small wooden bridge to the right, leading to the meadow restoration project. Turn right and check out this pleasant spot, complete with a couple of benches and an informational kiosk. At the kiosk, you are standing on home plate of a former baseball field for the coal-mining community of Red Town. In the early 1900s, baseball was a popular pastime, with teams coming from other mining communities to play here. Coal Creek flowed elsewhere back then, and the meadow was bigger and more level than today's view, but you can almost imagine the field when you look at the displayed pictures.

Eventually, the meadow was restored to its native state thanks to volunteer efforts. Hike the 0.1-mile loop around the meadow, pausing for a moment to eat some peanuts and Cracker Jacks if it strikes you. Cross back over the bridge and turn right on Red Town Trail.

Immediately after the meadow restoration junction, bear right to stay on the Red Town Trail as two other trails (Indian Trail and Wildside Trail) come in from the left. At 1 mile, the trail you are following becomes the Wildside Trail and you pass the Marshall's Hill Trail on the left. Just after that, skirt around a wooden barrier designed to keep horses out, and continue for 0.5 mile to a small signed spur that goes right to the Steam Hoist exhibit. Take the side trip if you wish. The foundations are all that's left from the hoist engines that lifted coal carts from the mine, and an interpretive sign kiosk along with a bench is located at the spur's end (0.1-mile roundtrip).

From here, walk a couple hundred feet more on the Wildside Trail and arrive at a junction with the Rainbow Town Trail. You'll return to this spot after you check out the mining exhibit, so keep that in mind. For now,

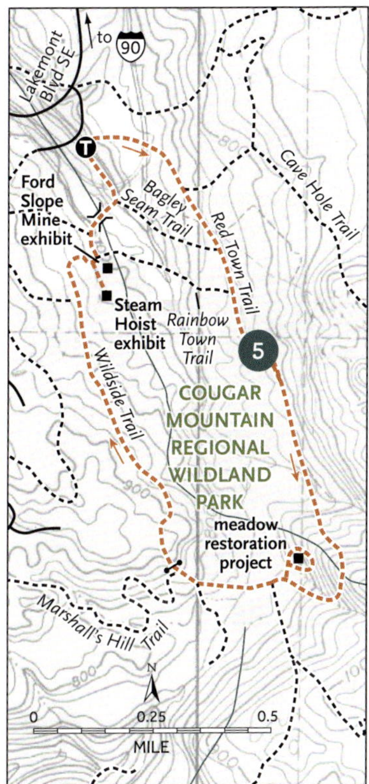

go right and in 0.1 mile, arrive at the Ford Slope Mine exhibit, where the mine entrance, a coal cart, and an interpretive kiosk give you a peek into coal mining that was productive in this area from 1906 to 1926. When you've enjoyed the exhibit, walk back on the Rainbow Town Trail and turn right on the Wildside Trail again. Stay on the Wildside Trail for less than 0.1 mile as it crosses a narrow pedestrian bridge over Coal Creek before it reaches a junction with the Bagley Seam Trail. Head left here and follow the Wildside Trail back to the trailhead.

6 Wildside Trail and De Leo Wall

RATING/DIFFICULTY: **/2
ROUNDTRIP: 4.7 miles
ELEV GAIN/HIGH POINT: 490 feet/1120 feet
SEASON: Year-round

Maps: Green Trails Maps Cougar Mountain/Squak Mountain No. 203S, King County Parks Cougar Mountain map; **Contact:** King County Parks; **Notes:** With side trails and exhibits, this hike becomes 5.1 miles and gains an additional 200 feet. As with all Cougar Mountain trails, many different loops and other trails can be taken to make your trip shorter or longer. Open to leashed dogs, stock (on some trails); **GPS:** N 47 32.077, W 122 07.728

Crossing Coal Creek at the forest's edge

You know those weekends where you want to get out, forget about the hustle and bustle, get some fresh air in your lungs, but still have time to run a couple of errands? This is a good place to do that. It's close to the metropolitan areas but feels like a world away as you wander through the trees, rocks, and ferns. This trail borders the far western side of Cougar Mountain Regional Wildland Park and has the solitude to soothe your soul, with time left over for the necessary chores of the weekend.

GETTING THERE

From I-90 near Issaquah: Take exit 13 and head south on Lakemont Boulevard for 3.1 miles to find the Red Town trailhead on your left.

From I-405 near Factoria: Take exit 10, Coal Creek Parkway/Factoria Boulevard, and proceed east for 2.6 miles, then turn left on Newcastle Way (near the shopping center). At 2.8 miles, at the stop sign, turn left onto Newcastle Golf Club Road. At 4.7 miles, locate the Red Town trailhead on the right (southeast) side of the road.

ON THE TRAIL

From the Red Town trailhead, pass the picnic area and make a right at the Y signed for the Wildside Trail.

At 0.1 mile arrive at a junction for the Bagley Seam Trail, and turn right, staying on the Wildside Trail. Cross a wooden pedestrian bridge over Coal Creek, and immediately afterward, bear left. At 0.3 mile, the trail makes a T with the Rainbow Town Trail. Go left here, and then in about 50 feet, the

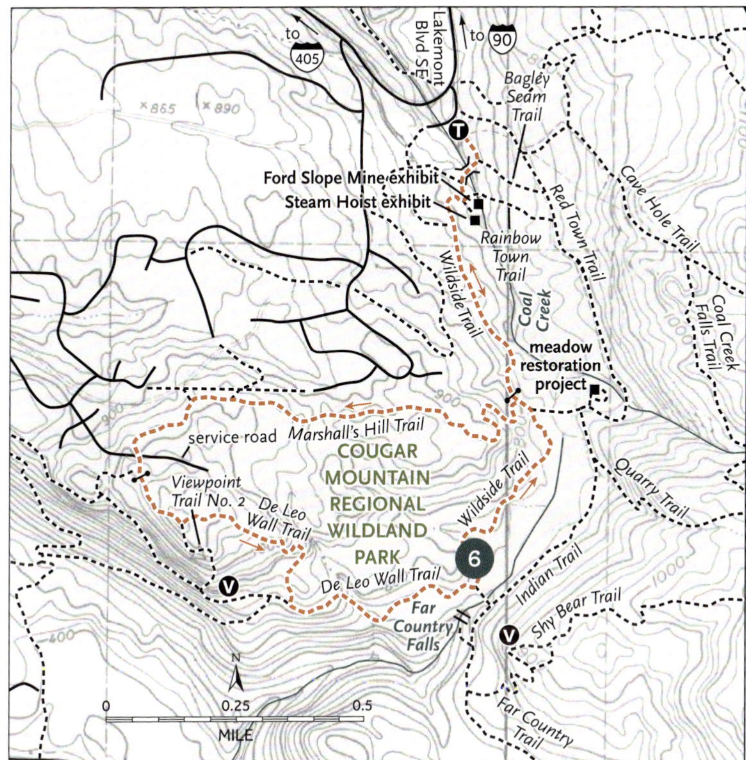

Wildside Trail shows up to the right again. A small detour—should you want to see a glimpse of history—takes you to the Ford Slope Mine exhibit, located straight ahead on the Rainbow Town Trail in 0.1 mile (0.2 roundtrip), where the mine entrance and a coal cart offer insight into coal mining in this area from 1906 to 1926. You are going to want to return to this spot if you visit the exhibit.

When done, or if you skip it, turn right (south) here on the Wildside Trail and in a couple hundred feet, arrive at another mining exhibit, the Steam Hoist. A spur trail takes you down and back in 0.1 mile to visit the foundations of steam-powered hoist engines that lifted coal carts from the mines. Visit if you wish; if not, bear right and continue on the Wildside Trail.

At 0.7 mile (not including detours), walk around the side of a wooden pedestrian gate and arrive at a junction with the Marshalls Hill Trail coming in from the right. Turn right here and start a gentle climb up switchbacks. Up you go, with peek-a-boo views of houses and several unsigned boot paths from them coming in from the right.

At 1.8 miles, the trail bears left at a park boundary sign, then in 0.2 mile beyond that, crosses a paved service road. On the other side of the road, the trail becomes the De Leo Wall Trail and is signed as such. In 185 feet, the trail reaches a Y with a wooden pedestrian gate. The De Leo Wall Trail goes around the pedestrian gate and keeps climbing, while the trails to the right carry on to other parts of Cougar Mountain. The *wall* refers to a unique geological feature that makes up the treed ridgeline and layers of minerals near where you walk.

The trail climbs steeply, then descends, and then at 2.6 miles arrives at a signed junction for the Viewpoint Trail No. 2 to the right. If time permits and the weather is clear, check out the viewpoint, a rocky perch with views of Mount Rainier and the vast valley below you, and return to this spot in 0.4 mile. It's roughly 200 feet down to the viewpoint, so just remember that what goes down must come back up. The viewpoint is on private property and is subject to closures, should the landowner decide to block it, but for now, we are able to enjoy it.

Shortly after the Viewpoint Trail No. 2 junction, the De Leo Wall Trail changes to a gentler grade, strolling through a variety of evergreens and healthy understory plants, until you reconnect with the Wildside Trail, 3.4 miles from where you started. Bear left on the Wildside until you reach a T intersection at 3.9 miles. Turn left here and stay on the Wildside Trail for another 0.1 mile until things look familiar! Not long ago, you were at this wooden pedestrian gate and turnoff for the Marshalls Hill Trail—you've completed the loop. From here, retrace your footsteps by walking around the horse barrier and following the Wildside Trail, reversing your twists and turns until you arrive back at the parking lot.

SQUAK MOUNTAIN

7 Bullitt Fireplace Trail

RATING/DIFFICULTY: ****/3
ROUNDTRIP: 3.8 miles
ELEV GAIN/HIGH POINT: 1220 feet/2024 feet
SEASON: Year-round

Maps: Green Trails Maps Cougar Mountain/Squak Mountain No. 203S, Squak Mountain State Park map; **Contact:** Washington State Parks; **Notes:** No toilets at trailhead; picnic table available at fireplace site. You can visit the fireplace and make several loops in the area if you wish. Open to leashed dogs, stock (on some trails). In January 2025, some park trails were closed due to storm damage. Please consult the state park website for updates.; **GPS:** N 47 31.707, W 122 02.075

In the 1940s, Charles Stimson "Stim" Bullitt purchased 590 acres of land on Squak Mountain as an intended private outdoor playground and quiet retreat. In 1952, he had a two-room cabin built on the land with the intention of giving his family a rustic shelter for a weekend away from the hustle and bustle of the city. However, they only ended up using the cabin minimally, and as it sat unoccupied and unkempt, it began to fall into a state of disrepair. The parcel and structure were given to his children, who by 1972 had decided to donate it as a public park. Eventually, the cabin burned down, but its fireplace remains and now serves as a pseudo mascot for Squak Mountain. This hike takes you to the seventy-plus-year-old fireplace, which also has a picnic

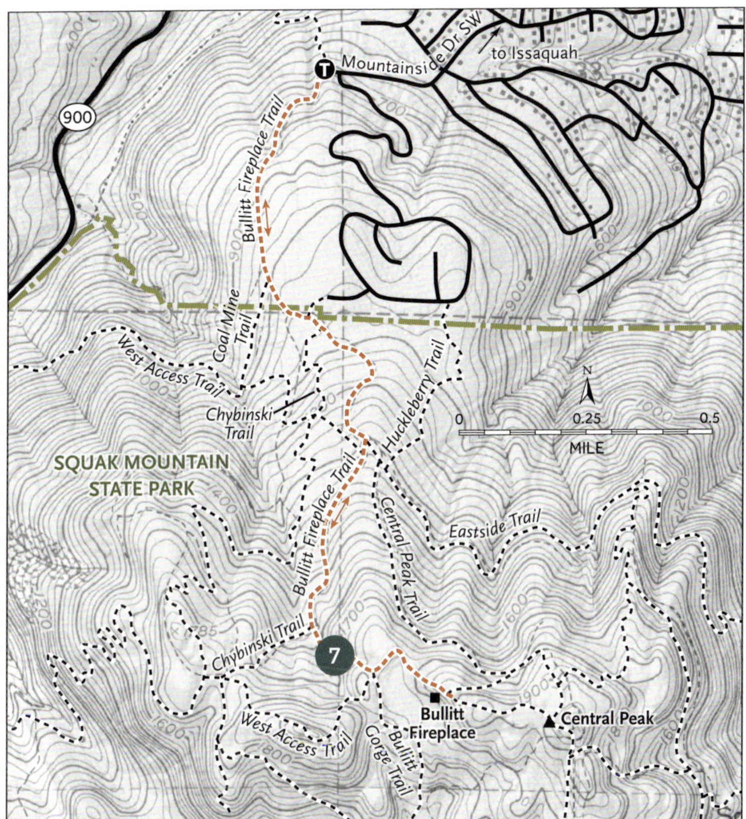

table waiting for you to spread out your feast.

GETTING THERE

From I-90 near Issaquah: Take exit 15 (State Route 900) and at the exit light, take SR 900 (17th Avenue NW) south. In 0.5 mile, take a left onto Newport Way NW. At 0.7 mile, turn right onto 12th Avenue NW and continue as the road bears left and becomes Mount Olympus Drive NW. At 1.5 miles, turn right at the stop sign to continue on Mount Olympus Drive NW. Stay on Mount Olympus Drive NW (which becomes Mountain Park Boulevard SW) to a junction at 2 miles. Here, Mount Olympus Drive goes right, but the road we want, Mountain Park Boulevard SW, goes left. Stay left and follow Mountain Park Boulevard SW to 2.2 total miles, then turn right on Mountainside Drive SW. At 2.5 miles, on a hairpin turn, find roadside parking for the Bullitt Fireplace Trail.

The Bullitt Fireplace is Squak Mountain's mascot, serving cozy wilderness vibes from its spot at the forest's edge.

ON THE TRAIL

The trail kicks off with a map kiosk and an interpretive sign about the area's natural and logging history. If you are like me, you'll be itching to get going, so take a picture to read later, or stop on your way back to read the nitty-gritty. Off you go, up a defunct forest road, climbing steadily and getting into your calorie-burning zone.

At 0.5 mile, reach a signed junction with the Coal Mine Trail heading off to the right. This is the first of several junctions in Squak Mountain State Park. If you have a good map and want to make loops, there are boundless opportunities to do so up here. For now, remain on the Bullitt Fireplace Trail as boot trails—from the private homes to the left—meet up with our trail.

The trail climbs through sword fern, Oregon grape, and second-growth forest until it reaches a signed junction with Chybinski Trail, which leads to Debbie's View (see Hike 9). Stay on the Bullitt Fireplace Trail and continue your uphill pursuit. A beautiful nurse log that is home to several teenage evergreens pops up just after the junction. Nurse logs are ecological mothers, offering nutrients, water, immune support, and decaying, rich humus to seeds that fall from above. This magical world of trees is so in sync that a nurse log's decaying schedule is often perfectly aligned with the lifespan of its host trees. Then the cycle repeats. Nature is in perfect harmony and timing: pure zen.

At 1 mile, reach a signed junction with the East Side Trail coming in from the left. The Bullitt Fireplace Trail curves right and continues through western red cedar, Douglas-fir, and western hemlock, as well as a sprinkling of deciduous trees. More trails, some signed, some not, hook into ours, but ours is obvious, so stay on the main path and keep traveling uphill.

At 1.4 miles, reach a signed junction where the Bullitt Fireplace Trail bears left, gets narrower, and ditches the old road for a steep single track climbing up, up, up. Grunt and groan your way up for just shy of 0.3 mile, until the grade eases a bit and reaches the signed Bullitt Gorge Trail coming in from the right.

Back on a wider old roadbed, continue climbing until the you reach the fireplace off to the right, 1.9 miles from the trailhead. The concrete foundation is also still here, along with several post footings and a picnic table on which to flop your pack. Walk around and imagine where the rooms were, and what it must have felt like to visit here in the mid-1950s.

The Bullitt family left quite a legacy in the Northwest. Not only were they responsible for saving this land from development, but Stim also founded *Seattle* magazine, served as president of King broadcasting (founded by his mother, Dorothy Bullitt), and was a visionary for environmental protection and minority rights. He founded Seattle's Harbor Properties, constructing over 1300 downtown residences and the landmark Harbor Steps Community just off First Avenue. He also was an accomplished outdoorsman and a fit athlete all the way into his eighties. His sister, Harriett, also left her imprint by donating more than $200 million to environmental causes, founding the Sleeping Lady Resort in Leavenworth and assisting in kicking off the careers of writers Ken Kesey and Ivan Doig, cartoonist Gary Larson, and photographer Art Wolfe. The family fell into fortune thanks to their grandfather, C. D. Stimson, who owned the largest sawmill in Seattle and was also a real-estate baron. His real-estate holdings helped rebuild the city of Seattle after the great fire of 1889. The list of accomplishments and accolades for the whole family is impressive and outstanding. Stim passed away in 2009, at age eighty-nine, while Harriet departed at age ninety-seven in 2022.

After visiting the fireplace, you have plenty of options. You could head back the way you came or add on more loops, including visiting Central Peak, Squak's highest point. Despite it being tower-filled and viewless, it's a good workout goal.

8 East Side Squak Loop

RATING/DIFFICULTY: **/4
ROUNDTRIP: 9.8 miles
ELEV GAIN/HIGH POINT: 2310 feet/2024 feet
SEASON: Year-round

Maps: Green Trails Maps Cougar Mountain/Squak Mountain No. 203S, Squak Mountain State Park map; **Contact:** Washington State Parks; **Notes:** There are two trailheads and parking options for this mountain. This trail description starts from the Issaquah Alps Trail Center, where parking options are plentiful. If you want a slightly shorter hike, use the Sunrise trailhead, which cuts off 2.2 miles. As with all trails on Squak Mountain, shorter or longer loops can be made. Consult your map

A green corridor along East Side Squak Loop wrapped in ferns and evergreens awaits footsteps.

for options. Open to leashed dogs, stock (on some trails); **GPS:** N 47 31.707, W 122 02.075

If you are interested in a less crowded hike than some of the others in the Issaquah Alps, and you don't mind hardy exercise, you'll probably enjoy the lesser-known east side of Squak. The trail crosses several crystal-clear seasonal streams as it works its way to Central Peak, the viewless apex of Squak Mountain. From the top, it descends through mature evergreens, giving you the occasional glimpse of Lake Sammamish and the surrounding Issaquah environs.

GETTING THERE

Trail Center trailhead (main): From I-90 in Issaquah, take exit 17 (Front Street/E. Lake Sammamish Parkway SE) and head south. Follow Front Street past old Issaquah for 0.8 mile, then turn left onto Bush Street. Follow Bush Street for 0.1 mile, past the Issaquah Trail Center (in the little yellow house), then turn left onto Rainier Boulevard S. Park here or in the vicinity, then wander back to the little yellow house for the hike's start.

Sunrise trailhead: If you want to shave 2.2 miles off the roundtrip distance, start your hike at the Sunrise trailhead. From I-90 in Issaquah, take exit 17 (Front Street/E. Lake Sammamish Parkway SE) and head south. Follow Front Street past old Issaquah for 1 mile, and turn right onto Newport Way SW. Follow Newport Way SW for 0.1 mile and turn left onto Wildwood Boulevard SW, then left again after 0.4 mile onto Sunrise Place SW. In 0.3 mile, find the trailhead on the road's right. Parking is available along the street. Note: Please respect nearby homes and park at the Trail Center trailhead if parking is crowded.

ON THE TRAIL

From the Trail Center trailhead, start off by paying your respects at the statue of Harvey Manning to the east of the trail center (the little yellow house, Issaquah Alps Trails Club headquarters). Not only was he the founder of the Issaquah Alps Trails Club, but he was also a fierce advocate for trails and an outdoors-focused author who was partially responsible for the creation of Mountaineers Books. In fact, the reason I write, and hence the reason you are holding this book, is primarily because of my collection of his books that I pored over and dreamed about throughout my youth. His grit made him a bold, robust protector of trails—sort of the Lorax for the Issaquah Alps. It's been said if you rub his hiking boots at the statue, you will have a safe and happy hike; true story.

From the trail center, head west down Bush Street. If you aren't known for your precise navigation skills, don't worry—I've got you covered. Point your right shoulder at the little yellow house and begin walking forward. Follow Bush to Front Street and turn left (south). From there, walk to Newport Way SW and turn right (west). At 0.3 mile, turn left on Wildwood Boulevard SW.

Follow a paved pathway, called Squak Mountain Access Trail, as it guides you through an open service gate and along Issaquah Creek. The path turns gravel and becomes narrower, and at 0.6 mile, it passes a pump house building, followed by a couple of parking areas for apartments. At 0.8 mile, the trail breaks into a Y. The left branch continues along the creek, but you knew we'd be climbing soon, right? Follow the right branch as it climbs past some more apartments and crosses a road (Sunrise Place SW). Across the road, at 1.1 miles, the path arrives at the Sunrise trailhead, complete with a sign and informational kiosk.

The climb after the Sunrise trailhead begins in a forest, made up of primarily deciduous trees, such as vine maple, black cottonwood, red alder, bigleaf maple, and Indian plum. A smattering of evergreens, such as western red cedar come to the party offering pops of deep green.

The trail reaches the Sycamore Access Trail coming in from the left at 2.1 miles. Bear right, and almost immediately, cross a creek on a footbridge. We are now officially on the East Ridge Trail.

Tall conifers guide you up, up, and away as you soon forget you are close to a city. At your feet is a sea of sword ferns, salal, and Oregon grape. At 3.3 miles from where you started, arrive at a signed junction with the East Side Trail, which scoots off to the right. Why so many "East" named trails? It's a bit confusing, but you got this. You'll be coming back to this intersection when you return on the East *Side* Trail, but for now, hang a left to keep rocking up the East *Ridge* Trail.

Two unsigned junctions appear to make you scratch your head. The first comes at 3.7 miles, where a boot path heads up to Squak Mountain's Southeast Peak. Our trail continues to the right.

The second unsigned junction arrives almost 0.2 mile after the last, where a boot path goes right. Our trail stays straight ahead. When in doubt, follow the path most traveled.

At 3.9 miles, arrive at the signed Phils Creek Trail and take a right, then roughly 300 feet later, arrive at what is known as Thrush

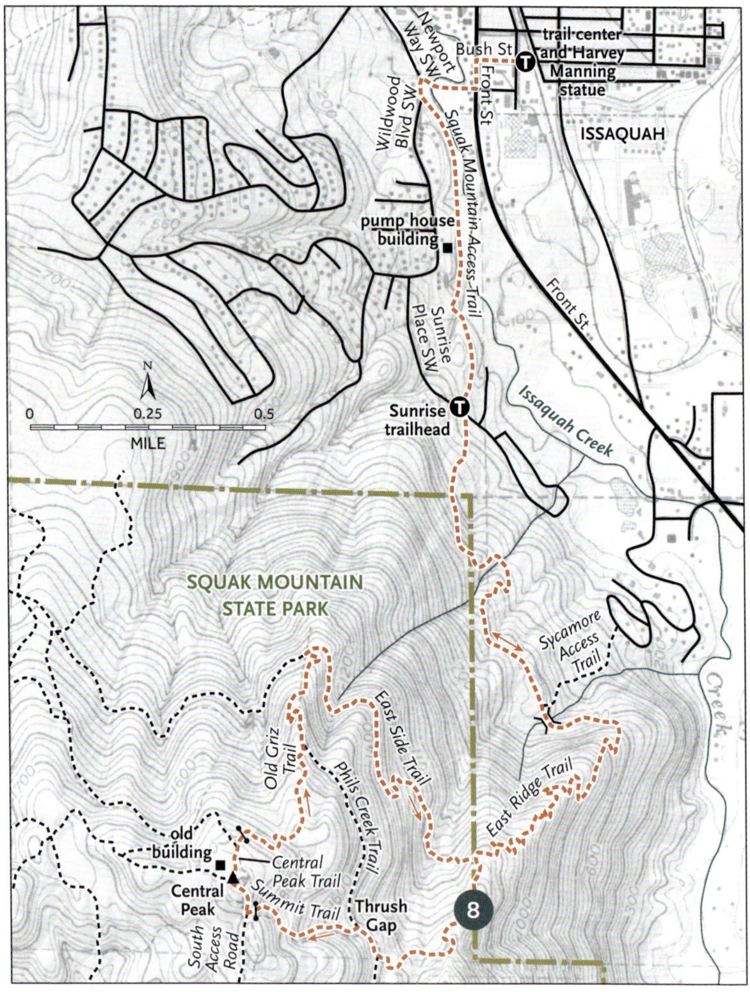

Gap, where we meet up with a few trails including the Summit Trail, our next huff and puff.

Follow the Summit Trail as it steeply climbs then arrives at a metal pedestrian turnstile followed by the South Access Road at 4.2 miles. Your quads will be glad that's over! Thankfully, it's only 0.1 mile to the right along the service road to reach Central Peak, our next destination.

The virtual sad trombone plays its depressing cry, as there is nowhere to sit on the summit. A guardrail or the ground might have to do. Radio towers and a lack of views make this place underwhelming, but hey, you are on the top of Squak and by golly, you worked hard to get here, so celebrate with a couple of dance moves. Maybe just move your arms a little if you are too tired to bust out the Running Man.

When your rear is dented from the guardrail and you are ready to continue, head about 200 feet down the road and look to your right for a trail that starts off wide. If you see the old building with a chain-link fence around the perimeter, you are on the right path!

Signs greet you just beyond the building—one saying Squak Mountain State Park Natural Area, and the now familiar trail signs pointing you along what is now the Central Peak Trail. An unsigned path heads off to the left down to Bullitt Fireplace (see Hike 7), but we stay straight and descend, crossing through another metal pedestrian gate.

At 4.6 miles, turn right at the signed junction for the Old Griz Trail and follow it downhill through mature evergreens. Pass the Phils Creek Trail to the right, at 5.1 miles, and continue on Old Griz. The way continues descending until it reaches the East Side Trail, where we turn right, continuing our loop. Note: The East Side Trail is spelled on maps and in literature both ways, East Side and Eastside. Do we need the space? Ponder this as you continue your walk.

The trail traverses across the slopes with a mellow grade until it climbs to cross a ravine at 5.8 miles. A giant boulder left over from the last ice age sits to the right, followed by a small wooden bridge over a seasonal dribble. The fern and moss-laden forest floor are a testament to the amount of rain this area sees.

Reach the East Ridge Trail again at 6.5 miles. Look familiar? You were just here not long ago! Loop complete. Now, retrace your steps by going left and following the East Ridge Trail back to the Squak Mountain Access Trail and maybe to infinity and beyond. Or . . . at least to the trail center, where you can thank Harvey for your safekeeping on your adventure.

9 Margaret's Way to Debbie's View

RATING/DIFFICULTY: ***/3

ROUNDTRIP: 7.5 miles

ELEV GAIN/HIGH POINT: 1670 feet/1780 feet

SEASON: Year-round

Maps: Green Trails Maps Cougar Mountain/Squak Mountain No. 203S, Squak Mountain State Park map; **Contact:** Washington State Parks; **Notes:** Port-a-potty and picnic area available at trailhead. Open to leashed dogs; **GPS:** N 47 30.469, W 122 05.246

This rather-steep-at-times hike leads to a few sweeping viewpoints and ample reward for your effort. What's more, it's close to town, so it's a good one to hit if you want to get a workout and still have time for other tasks.

GETTING THERE

From I-90 near Issaquah: Take exit 15 (17th Avenue NW/State Route 900). Head south on SR 900 for 3.2 miles to reach an easy-to-miss blue Cougar Mountain Regional Wildland Park sign on the road's left (east). Proceed 0.1 mile to find the parking area.

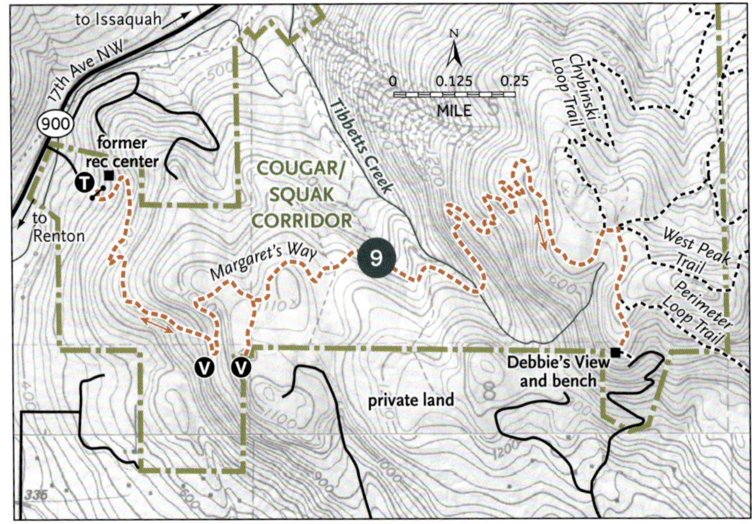

ON THE TRAIL

Years ago, part of this trail was home to the Issaquah Highlands Recreational Club, which contained an RV park and car-camping area on a meandering gravel road. In 2014, King County purchased the parcel and was able to link together trails in this area, creating even more public land and hiking opportunities for the Cougar/Squak Corridor.

Start by walking toward the hill to the parking area's right (southeast). Locate the former road with a metal service gate and walk around it. Just beyond the gate, a kiosk, dog waste bags, trash cans, and a picnic table are available for visitors. Head up the road and follow the signage, which is well-placed along this route.

To the left is the former recreation center for the campground, still in use for county business. In 0.1 mile, leave the roadway and find a beautifully constructed set of trail stairs followed by two bridges over a bubbling waterway. This gorgeous single-track trail connects you again to the road at 0.2 mile. Turn left on the road as instructed by the Margaret's Way sign, and continue your uphill push, switching back as you go.

The property has not been a campground for over twelve years, and it's fun to see how Mother Nature has come in and taken over the sites that once likely contained picnic tables, fire rings, and happy campers with marshmallow sticks. Sword ferns, devil's club, salmonberries, and other foliage popped up with reckless abandon when tires and commotion were no longer stifling their growth. With more years of progress, we might be hard-pressed to even see where these former campsites were located. The mossy, old road signage is also interesting, with names of trees such as Hemlock and Cedar indicating the loops where campers likely were directed.

Back and forth on the road you go until 0.6 mile, when the trail leaves the road for a bit on another single track, eventually reconnecting with the roadway. At some point, the single track wins out over the road, and you find yourself on what feels more like a more conventional trail grinding up, up, and up.

At 1 mile, arrive at the first viewpoint, to the right. What a gorgeous sight on a sunny day! The Olympic Mountains pop up, along with views of May Valley and environs beyond. You could always turn back here if you brought the wee ones, content with getting this view . . . or keep on trucking because more viewpoints await!

At 1.4 miles, arrive at a signed junction for another viewpoint, located 0.1 mile down a spur trail to the right. You'll want to check it out because it's simply stunning. A log bench in a grassy clearing awaits your hindquarters as you stare out to the Puget Sound and the Olympics. The Brothers, Mount Ellinor, Mount Washington, and others pop out on the far horizon, and a keen eye will even see planes taking off in the pattern at SeaTac. Some lucky soul has a house that's close to this vista, a private property of dreams. In my humble opinion, this panorama is better than Debbie's View, but then again, it's a good workout and you came to see them all, so back down the spur and to the main trail you go.

Turn right at the main trail and continue onward, now through mature evergreens, such as western hemlock, western red cedar, and Douglas-fir. Margaret's Way continues to be extremely well marked, so you can just follow the arrows.

The trail is named for Margaret Macleod, an environmental leader and City of Issaquah park planner for twenty years. She was instrumental in coordinating with various nonprofit

A log bench at the second viewpoint can make a fine turnaround spot.

and government agencies throughout the years, with the goal of protecting hundreds of acres of land. I had the pleasure of working with Margaret on stewardship projects prior to her untimely passing of lung cancer in late 2013, and I can attest to her outstanding ability to secure grants for the acquisition of many key land parcels. She dug in to her goals with a pleasant countenance and a megawatt smile—more reasons she was successful. Each time I visit this trail, I'm reminded of her beautiful soul and how she used her time on earth for the betterment of us all.

The trail grade after the second viewpoint is gentler, climbing and dropping intermittently until it crosses the headwaters of Tibbetts Creek at 2.3 miles. The crossing simply requires a step across the ripples.

Now the climbing really kicks into gear, and a series of switchbacks grinds you up the steep hill through the evergreens. Sucking wind is not shameful, so wear your huff and puff proudly!

At 3.4 miles, arrive at a junction where Margaret's Way ends at the signed Chybinski Loop Trail heading off to the right. Follow it for about 150 feet to find a signed junction for Debbie's View. Turn right and then immediately pass the West Peak Trail coming in from the left. Continue straight for Debbie's View. At 3.6 miles, the trail splits. The unsigned left branch is more of a boot path going uphill, but the sign to Debbie's View points right, so follow the arrow.

At 3.7 miles, arrive at Debbie's View—a wooden bench looks out toward Mount Rainier high on the horizon. The Cedar Hills landfill is below you, but it's neither an eyesore nor a nose-twist. Several rocky areas near the bench give you another place to perch if the trail is busy. Debbie's View is named after Debbie Anschell, a longstanding steward of the Issaquah Alps Trails Club.

When you are done visiting this spot, you can either head back the way you came or extend your hike by connecting with other local trails.

10 May Valley Loop

RATING/DIFFICULTY: **/3
ROUNDTRIP: 7.8 miles
ELEV GAIN/HIGH POINT: 1900 feet/2024 feet
SEASON: Year-round

Maps: Green Trails Maps Cougar Mountain/Squak Mountain No. 203S, Squak Mountain State Park map; **Contact:** Washington State Parks; **Notes:** Discover Pass required. Pit toilets and picnic area available at trailhead. Park gates open 6:30 AM to dusk in summer/8 AM to dusk in winter. Open to leashed dogs, stock (on some trails). In January 2025, some park trails were closed due to storm damage. Please check the state parks website for updates; **GPS:** N 47 28.915, W 122 03.219

This hike is a wonky figure-eight loop. The lower half is bigger and available to equestrians, while only a portion of the upper half is. You'll get some hardy exercise as you climb to the top of Squak Mountain where towers, instead of views, await. So, what's to love? There is peacefulness to be found, even this close to town. What's more, some of this forest is as green, mossy, and vibrant as I've ever seen in the Northwest. Get your workout, enjoy some forest ambles, then pat yourself on your sweaty back for standing on the top.

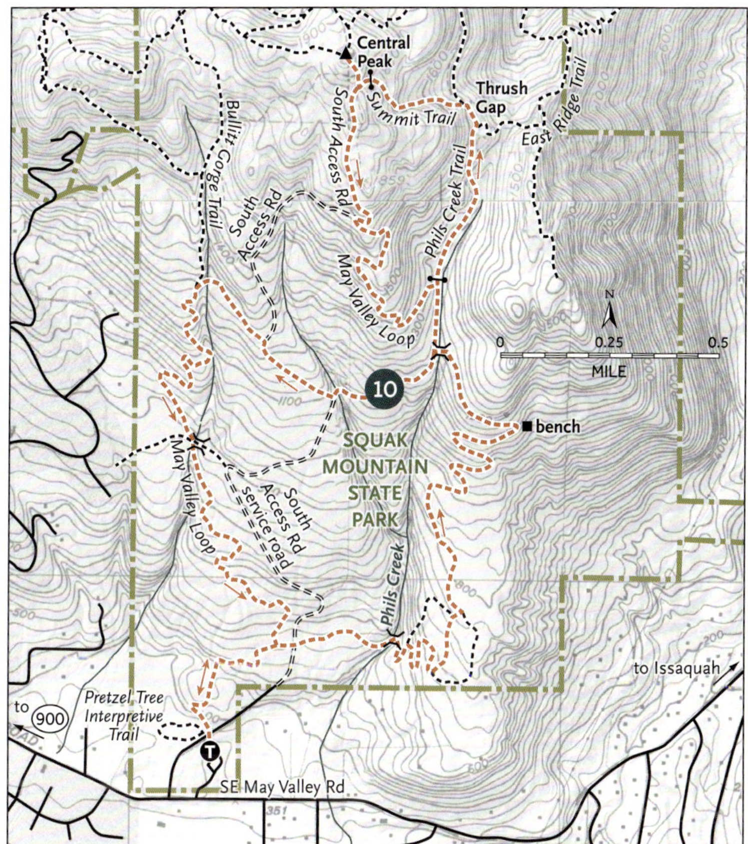

GETTING THERE

From I-90 near Issaquah: Take exit 15 (17th Avenue NW/State Route 900) and at the exit light, head south on SR 900 for 4.1 miles until SE May Valley Road. Turn left on SE May Valley Road and follow it until the signed Squak Mountain State Park to the road's left at 6.5 miles. Turn into the park and find the parking lot, toilets, and picnic area in 0.1 mile.

From Renton: Take exit 5 off I-405. Head east on SR 900 (NE Park Drive/Sunset Boulevard NE) for 5.3 miles. Turn right onto SE May Valley Road until you reach the signed Squak Mountain State Park to the road's left at 7.8 miles. Turn into the park and find the parking lot, toilets, and picnic area in 0.1 mile.

Sunlight peeks through mossy evergreens, bringing a soft, golden glow to the forest.

ON THE TRAIL

From the parking area, follow the well-signed trailhead path roughly 450 feet until you reach the South Access Road (service road). Straight ahead of you on the other side of the road is the Pretzel Tree Interpretive Trail, a 0.3-mile loop with a darling story located on signs along the route. If you have kids, or just want a short warm-up, this is a great place to wander. It isn't part of our trail, though, so skip it if you are short on time.

For our loop, walk about ten steps to the right on the access road to find the signed May Valley Loop Trail to the road's left. Swooping limbs of the drapey western red cedar above you, and thickets of sword ferns near your feet, guide you upward until the way levels out and crosses a puncheon bridge over a seasonal stream. At 0.4 mile, the signed May Valley Loop junction comes in from the left, our return trail. For now, stay right and begin the askew figure eight. In a few hundred feet beyond the junction, cross a service road and jog right a few steps until you see the continuation of the trail to the road's left.

At just shy of 0.8 mile, arrive at a large wooden bridge that crosses Phils Creek. It's in need of some repairs, as the wet weather has taken its toll on log spindles, but it's not a safety hazard, so onward! Just beyond the bridge, turn left and ascend through mixed forest, ignoring all the unofficial boot paths and game trails coming in from the main trail's right. Thankfully, the May Valley Loop is well marked, and signs with arrows guide you along the route.

The trail traverses a few switchbacks before delivering a peace offering with an easier grade, and then, without much warning, it kicks up the switchbacks again. At 2.3 miles, a trailside log bench appears on the final switchback, a welcome sight for tired legs or for anyone needing to catch their breath.

At 2.6 miles, the trail crosses a large wooden bridge over Phils Creek again. This bridge is newer and in much better shape than the last.

Immediately after the bridge, arrive at an unsigned T junction. We will come back to this spot after we work through the top loop of our figure eight, but if you want to skip the upper part, you can make this trip shorter by going left here.

For those ready for more sightseeing, turn right and follow the Phils Creek Trail as it wanders next to the playful Phils Creek. At just shy of 2.8 miles, the May Valley Loop comes in from the left—this will be our return trail. Almost immediately after that, enter a pedestrian-only metal turnstile, telling the horses that no hooves are allowed beyond this point.

At 3.3 miles, the East Ridge Trail comes in from the right. In roughly 300 feet beyond that junction, arrive at what is called Thrush Gap, where the Summit Trail—the trail we want—heads left toward Central Peak. Have a pep talk with your lungs because they are going to need all the help they can get as you suck wind up this steep incline. Thankfully its only 0.3 mile of climbing before it reaches another metal pedestrian-only gate, followed by the South Access Road.

To get to the highest point on Squak Mountain, Central Peak, turn right and walk 0.1 mile to the towers. There's really nothing more to see up here—no rewarding views or cool historic sights . . . but hey, you get the feather in your cap of accomplishment, so take a victory lap around the towers and then head back down the road the same way you arrived. This time, walk past the Summit Trail you came from and continue following the road until it turns hard to the right, just shy of 4.2 miles. Look to the left, find a sign pointing to the May Valley Loop, and hop on.

This trail doesn't get as much traffic, so it's a little narrower than the others, but it's quiet and peaceful all the same. I spotted mourning cloak butterflies, Douglas squirrels, and Pacific wrens on my last visit, a flutter of fun forest friends to keep me company.

At 5 miles, arrive back at the Phils Creek Trail. You've just completed the top portion of our wonky figure eight, and now you will walk south toward the bottom portion, retracing your steps to the T junction, where the newer bridge over Phils Creek is now on your left. We will be continuing on straight ahead.

Descend now through mixed conifers and deciduous forest, following the May Valley Loop signs and avoiding boot paths, until arriving at the South Access Road again at 5.5 miles. Climbing up to the right here feels really counterintuitive after descending for so long, but it's a beautiful forest and well worth a little extra effort once you get back on the trail. However, if you are tired of climbing, you can turn left instead and take the service road back down to the trailhead.

Pump up the rather steep roadway, questioning your decision to climb, until you find yourself back on the signed trail to the road's left at 5.7 miles.

At 5.9 miles, arrive at a signed junction with the Bullitt Gorge Trail to the right. Our trail, the May Valley Loop, goes left on a gorgeous descent through pristine, mature evergreens and an understory teeming with moss, ferns, salal, Oregon grape, and other PNW characters. At 6.6 miles, an unsigned T arrives. Our path goes left over a wooden bridge, while the well-worn boot path heads off to the right to connect with private homes.

Just after the wooden bridge, a signed junction pointing you along the May Valley Loop Trail goes right, and at 7.4 miles, arrive back at the beginning of the May Valley Loop and the official end of our figure eight. Go right and retrace your steps, back to the parking area, in 0.4 mile. What a playground!

TIGER MOUNTAIN

11 Bus Trail and Around the Lake Trail

RATING/DIFFICULTY: ***/1
ROUNDTRIP: 1.7 miles
ELEV GAIN/HIGH POINT: 90 feet/540 feet
SEASON: Year-round

Map: Green Trails Maps Tiger Mountain/Taylor Mountain No. 204S; **Contact:** Department of Natural Resources, South Puget Sound Region; **Notes:** Discover Pass required. Pit toilets and picnic areas available near the trailhead. Parking on weekends is difficult, so arrive early or have a plan B hike. Open to leashed dogs; see map, page 76; **GPS:** N 47 31.775, W 121 59.733

This loop showcases some of the easier trails on Tiger Mountain, perfect for taking kids, strolling as a couple, catching up with friends, or getting the dog out. Those who just want to roam can extend this hike by following the many trails on Tradition Plateau as they twist in all directions through large conifers hosting knocking woodpeckers and small songbirds.

GETTING THERE

From I-90 near Issaquah: Take exit 20, for High Point Way, and head south. In a couple hundred feet, turn right onto SE 79th Street, which parallels the freeway heading westbound. Stay on this road as it passes through an open gate and continues to the High Point trailhead, 0.8 mile from the exit. Note: The gate is usually slated to be open from dawn to dusk; however, staffing issues in the last several years have kept the gate open all the time. This could change without notice, so you may want to park on the road's edge on the east side of the gate and take the obvious connecting spur trail 0.5 mile (one-way) toward the trailhead if you have concerns about timing.

ON THE TRAIL

There are a couple of ways to pop into the hiking trails from the parking area, but the easiest way to start is to follow the trails (and your nose) to the outhouses. From there, walk west (put the outhouses on your left and walk forward, if you are directionally challenged). In about 350 feet, arrive at a junction with a sign for the Bus Trail and many other hiking trails. Turn left and follow the Bus Trail and, in 0.2 mile, arrive at a junction with West Tiger No. 3. Bear right here. At 0.2 mile, find the signed Nook Trail coming in from the left, just after crossing a seasonal creek on a wood-and-metal bridge, but continue straight.

The main dirt-and-gravel pathway continues wandering through cottonwoods, western red cedars, and sword ferns for 0.5 mile, where it arrives at the hike's namesake, an old bus frame resting on its side.

The mystery of the rusty, sideways bus is anyone's best guess. The area is fairly flat, and what is now a system of trails was once forest and logging roads that networked through the various commercial camps and operations. Odds are, it was abandoned here by one of the many companies that mined, logged, or supplied power during the mid-twentieth century. But why it tipped over is perplexing. Be careful in your exploration and watch dog paws, little fingers, and soft-soled shoes, as bits of glass and rusty metal have detached and come to rest on the ground.

Once you've traveled back in time on the mystery bus, continue on the Bus Trail for just shy of 200 feet until you reach a signed junction with the continuation of the Bus Trail going straight ahead and the Connector Trail going to the right. There are a lot of loops you can explore on the plateau, so pull out your map if you want to continue on the Bus Trail and loop back around. Otherwise, continue onward with the trail description I've outlined.

Follow the Connector Trail about 370 feet until you reach another signed junction with the Around the Lake Trail. Bear left here and

An old bus, the star of the obviously named Bus Trail, is a surprise dose of civilization in the middle of the woods.

follow the Around the Lake Trail as it wanders . . . well, you guessed it, around Tradition Lake.

The trail tread is more primitive at this point, with roots, rocks, and the occasional patch of mud in the rainy season instead of gravel. The quiet lake hides well through the evergreens, though you know it's there from small glimpses and the occasional honk or quack of waterfowl. At 0.7 mile, a hollow tree appears to the right, just big enough for kids and dogs to explore and have their pictures taken.

At 0.8 mile, arrive at a sitting area with four benches and a peek-a-boo, overgrown view of the lake. Meander more underneath the healthy Douglas-firs, western red cedars, and western hemlocks until you arrive at the Puget Power Road, at 1.1 miles. You have options. If you still have pep in your step and want to hike/run/walk more, turn left on the road and explore more loops on the plateau. If the kids are tired or you are short on time, turn right and head back toward the parking lot, reaching it in 0.6 mile.

12 Tradition Lake and Round Lake

RATING/DIFFICULTY: ***/2

ROUNDTRIP: 2.6 miles

ELEV GAIN/HIGH POINT: 220 feet/540 feet

SEASON: Year-round

Map: Green Trails Maps Tiger Mountain/Taylor Mountain No. 204S; **Contact:** Department of Natural Resources, South Puget Sound Region; **Notes:** Discover Pass required. Pit toilets and picnic areas available near the trailhead. Parking on weekends is difficult, so arrive early or have a plan B hike. Open to leashed dogs; **GPS:** N 47 31.775, W 121 59.733

Like all the Issaquah Alps, Tiger Mountain is packed with networks of trails that make loops. This is a fun ramble if you want to explore the two lakes on Tradition Plateau or if you want to just take a pleasant walk with minimal elevation gain.

GETTING THERE

From I-90 near Issaquah: Take exit 20 for High Point Way and head south. In a couple hundred feet, turn right onto SE 79th Street, which parallels the freeway heading westbound. Stay on this road as it passes through an open gate and continues to the High Point trailhead, 0.8 mile from the exit. Note: The gate is usually slated to be open from dawn to dusk; however, staffing issues in the last several years have kept the gate open all the time. This could change without notice, so you may want to park on the road's edge on the east side of the gate and take the obvious connecting spur trail 0.5 mile (one-way) toward the trailhead if you have concerns about timing.

ON THE TRAIL

Wander south from the parking lot and locate the pit toilets. Walk west (signed "Main Hiking Trails") until you arrive at a signed junction with the Bus Trail and the Swamp Trail and others in roughly 350 feet. Turn left and follow the Bus Trail for about 50 feet, where you arrive at a sign for Tradition Lake and the Around the Lake Trail. Go right here and wander through the sword ferns, mossy downed logs, western red cedar, and salmonberries. A few interpretive signs tell about the natural world, and benches provide opportunities to sit and enjoy the peacefulness. At 0.5 mile, arrive at a viewing platform for Tradition Lake to the right. The evergreens are blocking a crystal-clear view, but you'll at least get a

Round Lake reflects tall trees along its peaceful shoreline.

sneak peek of the lake's edges and be able to scan for buffleheads and mallards.

Just after the platform, the trail arrives at a signed junction where the Around the Lake Trail goes right and the Connector Trail (headed toward the Bus Trail) goes left. We will come back to this spot after we complete the loop, so for now, go left and follow the Connector Trail. At 0.6 mile, reach a junction with the Bus Trail going off to the right. Follow it into the forest and enjoy a woodsy walk. The trail you are following eventually spits you out at a wooden pedestrian turnstile. It then crosses a grassy strip of land that contains the unsigned Gas Line Trail before it finally delivers you to the Bonneville Trail at 1 mile. Turn right here and walk just shy of 100 feet to reach the Wetlands Trail to the road's left. A signed kiosk with a map and a you-are-here arrow helps you navigate if you are feeling a bit directionally befuddled.

The tranquil and scenic Round Lake appears next at 1.1 miles. Benches for picnicking or relaxing are positioned nicely by the water's edge, and your camera is begging to come out of your pocket to photograph this picturesque spot. Waterfowl such as Canada geese and mergansers cruise these shorelines too and, in the springtime, are often seen with chicks.

After enjoying Round Lake, continue your forest ramble until you reach a signed junction with the Wetlands Connector Trail at 1.3 miles. The main Wetlands Trail goes to the left at this spot, but we will take the connector and continue north until we reach the Puget

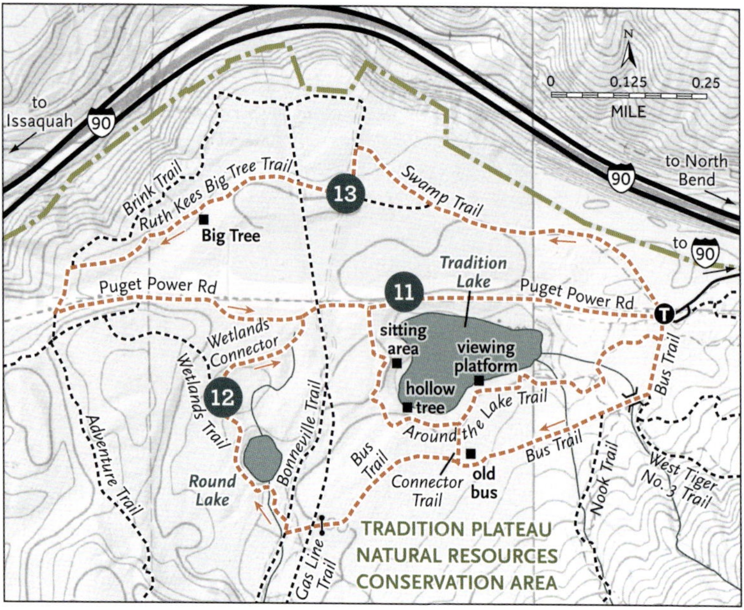

Power Road at 1.5 miles. Turn right on the road and walk the roadway until you arrive at the Around the Lake Trail to the right at 1.7 miles. Turn right here and duck back into the evergreens.

At 1.8 miles, a sitting area complete with four benches and an overgrown viewpoint of Tradition Lake appears to the left. If time permits, stop and enjoy the forested nook.

The pleasing grade and woodsy shrubs capture your attention until you arrive back at the junction with the Connector Trail at 2.1 miles. This spot might look familiar, but if not, it will likely do so soon as you retrace your steps. Turn left on the Around the Lake Trail and keep walking, passing the viewing platform and interpretive signage until completing your adventure the same way you arrived.

13 Ruth Kees Big Tree Trail

RATING/DIFFICULTY: **/1
ROUNDTRIP: 2.5 miles
ELEV GAIN/HIGH POINT: 190 feet/530 feet
SEASON: Year-round

Map: Green Trails Maps Tiger Mountain/Taylor Mountain No. 204S; **Contact:** Department of Natural Resources, South Puget Sound Region; **Notes:** Discover Pass required. Pit toilets and picnic areas available near the trailhead. Parking on weekends is difficult, so arrive early or have a plan B.

Open to leashed dogs; **GPS:** N 47 31.775, W 121 59.733

There might be no better trail on the Tiger Plateau to take kids than the Swamp Trail, which tells a cute tale via story signs of woodland creatures and their night in the swamp. The story boards have collected moss since they were installed, but it's all still readable and enjoyable, especially in the eyes of the little ones. Trail runners or anyone looking for a less strenuous walk will appreciate the gentle grade and maze of trail options.

GETTING THERE

From I-90 near Issaquah: Take exit 20 for High Point Way and head south. In a couple hundred feet, turn right onto SE 79th Street, which parallels the freeway heading westbound. Stay on this road as it passes through an open gate and continues to the High Point trailhead, 0.8 mile from the exit. Note: The gate is usually slated to be open from dawn to dusk; however, staffing issues in the last several years have kept the gate open all the time. This could change without notice, so you may want to park on the road's edge on the east side of the gate and take the obvious connecting spur trail 0.5 mile (one-way) toward the trailhead if you have concerns about timing.

ON THE TRAIL

To start this trail, wander south from the parking lot and locate the pit toilets. Walk west (signed "Main Hiking Trails") until you arrive at a junction with the Bus Trail and the Swamp Trail and others in roughly 350 feet. Turn right and follow the connector toward the Swamp Trail. In roughly 200 feet beyond the sign, cross the Puget Power Road and locate the Swamp Trail, signed "Zoe and the Swamp Monster: A Self-Guided Adventure."

The first sign comes up quickly and kicks off the story of Zoe the raccoon who, on a dare, must spend a night in the middle of the swamp. More signs come up as the terrain matches the story and gets a swampier feeling. In 0.5 mile, reach a signed Y junction. If you are following the story, you'll want to take the unsigned trail to the right at this intersection.

Heading toward the Ruth Kees Big Tree, a sentinel on the Tiger Mountain Plateau.

Zoe's adventure continues as a long boardwalk over a wetland, or swamp, guides you through the final story sign and pops you out at a powerline at 0.7 mile. Turn left here, knowing you and Zoe made it safely through the swamp, and follow the powerline trail until reaching another junction at 0.8 mile, this one for the Ruth Kees Big Tree Trail to the right.

Go right and follow the Ruth Kees Big Tree Trail through Douglas-firs and western red cedars until arriving at the signed Big Tree at 1 mile. A wooden fence protects one of the largest and oldest trees on Tiger Mountain, estimated to be between 200 and 400 years old. A sign tells us that no one knows why this tree was spared from logging operations and gives us other details at this spot. Ruth Kees, the trail's namesake, was an environmental advocate who was strong in her convictions to help Issaquah protect natural resources. She received a Lifetime Achievement Award from the Issaquah Environmental Council in 2003 before she passed away at age eighty-five in May of 2009.

At 1.3 miles, arrive at the end of the Ruth Kees Big Tree Trail. Here, a T junction connects you to the Brink Trail. Turn left and pop out at the Puget Power Road at 1.4 miles. As with nearly every turn on Tiger Mountain, you have options at this point. If the kiddos are tired, turn left on the road for 1.1 miles and follow it all the way back to the trailhead where you started, making a complete loop.

EXTENDING YOUR HIKE

If your group still has lots of energy, you might pull out your map and follow the Wetlands and Adventure Trails across the road as they twist and turn to your feet's content. Make your way back to the parking area when you've explored many great paths on the Tradition Plateau.

14 Nook Trail and Talus Rock Loop

RATING/DIFFICULTY: **/2
ROUNDTRIP: 2.5 miles
ELEV GAIN/HIGH POINT: 710 feet/1220 feet
SEASON: Year-round

Map: Green Trails Maps Tiger Mountain/Taylor Mountain No. 204S; **Contact:** Department of Natural Resources, South Puget Sound Region; **Notes:** Discover Pass required. Pit toilets and picnic areas available near the trailhead. Parking on weekends is difficult, so arrive early or have a plan B hike. Open to leashed dogs; **GPS:** N 47 31.775, W 121 59.733

This hike is perfect for those who want to have a short, steep workout and still have time for other connecting trails or running errands in town. Leftover from the Pleistocene ice age, the giant erratic boulders have been shaped by ancient history—worth checking out!

GETTING THERE

From I-90 near Issaquah: Take exit 20 for High Point Way and head south. In a couple hundred feet, turn right onto SE 79th Street, which parallels the freeway heading westbound. Stay on this road as it passes through an open gate and continues to the High Point trailhead, 0.8 mile from the exit. Note: The gate is usually slated to be open from dawn to dusk; however, staffing issues in the last several years have kept the gate open all the time. This could change without notice, so you may want to park on the road's edge on the east side of the gate and take the obvious connecting spur trail 0.5 mile (one-way) toward the trailhead if you have concerns about timing.

ON THE TRAIL

There are a couple of ways to pop into the hiking trails from the parking area, but the easiest way to start is to follow the trails (and your nose) to the south, toward the pit toilets. Once there, walk west (put the outhouses on your left and follow the trail forward, if you are directionally challenged). In about 350 feet, arrive at a junction with a sign for the Bus Trail and many other hiking trails. Turn left and follow the Bus Trail to arrive at a junction with West Tiger No. 3 Trail at 0.3 mile. Bear right here to stay on the Bus Trail and proceed to 0.4 mile where, just after crossing a seasonal creek on a wood-and-metal bridge, you'll find the signed Nook Trail coming in from the left.

Turn left and follow the Nook Trail as it ascends through abundant western red

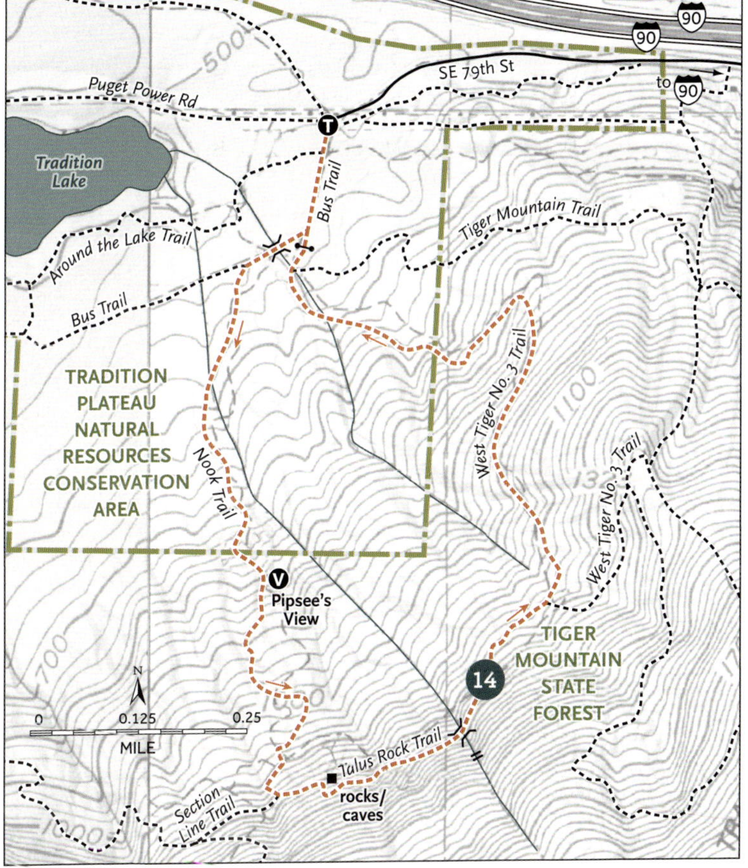

Well-built trails and sturdy bridges, like this one on the Nook Trail, are gifts from hardworking trail crews and volunteers.

cedars and seasonal creeklets. At 0.7 mile, a bench with a sign for Pipsee's View begs you to take a rest. Those in the know tell me that Pipsee, who is in her twilight years, hikes here frequently, so her family donated the bench in her honor. The viewpoint isn't overwhelmingly impressive as it peeks over a dribbling creek, but the bench makes a good perch if your legs are getting a little tired from walking uphill. Thank you, Pipsee and family, for the gift!

After the viewpoint, the trail kicks your heinie into high gear with some steep spots that will have you huffing and puffing until you reach a junction with the Section Line Trail on the right at 1.1 miles. Turn left here onto the Talus Rock Trail toward the ice-age era boulders. A few wooden fences discourage hikers from going into the shallow caves that are located underneath the behemoth rocks. Stay safe and enjoy from a distance. From here, the trail climbs up a series of well-constructed trail stairs and crosses the rocky area at the base of a seasonal trickling waterfall at 1.2 miles. If flowing, the waterfall is lovely as it careens over moss-covered stone slabs.

In another 0.1 mile, cross another seasonal creek, this time on a weathered bridge missing some of its boards. Teeter across, watching your feet so you don't slip and slide.

At 1.5 miles, arrive at a T with West Tiger No. 3 Trail. If you feel energized, you could turn right here (see Hike 16) and go to the top, but if you are ready to head back, turn left and start the descent on the final portion of our loop.

The Tiger Mountain Trail (see Hike 15) comes in from the right at 2.3 miles, and just beyond it, a wooden pedestrian turnstile leads you back to the Bus Trail. Retrace your steps back to the outhouse and to your car, or follow any of the other trails in the area to get a few more steps in.

15 Tiger Mountain Trail to West Tiger No. 2

RATING/DIFFICULTY: **/4
ONE-WAY: 7.4 miles
ELEV GAIN/HIGH POINT: 2450 feet/2740 feet
SEASON: Year-round

Map: Green Trails Maps Tiger Mountain/Taylor Mountain No. 204S; **Contact:** Department of Natural Resources (DNR), South Puget Sound Region; **Notes:** Discover Pass required. Pit toilets and picnic areas available near the trailhead. Parking on weekends is difficult, so arrive early or have a plan B hike. Many of the Tiger Mountain summits have been recently logged. Check DNR website for logging and trail rebuilding status. Open to leashed dogs, stock (southern 3 miles); **GPS:** N 47 31.775, W 121 59.733

The Tiger Mountain Trail (TMT) is a deep forest connector route that winds through lush coniferous woods and riparian zones, where the understory is richly carpeted with ferns. It offers a solid workout along its length and rewards hikers with panoramic views from a short side trip to Middle Tiger No. 2.

GETTING THERE

From I-90 near Issaquah: Take exit 20 for High Point Way and head south. In a couple hundred feet, turn right onto SE 79th Street, which parallels the freeway heading westbound. Stay on this road as it passes through

Fellow Mountaineers Books guidebook author Craig Romano enjoys a sunny walk through massive sword ferns along the Tiger Mountain Trail.

an open gate and continues to the High Point trailhead, 0.8 mile from the exit.

Note: The gate is usually slated to be open from dawn to dusk; however, staffing issues in the last several years have kept the gate open all the time. This could change without notice, so you may want to park on the road's edge on the east side of the gate and take the obvious connecting spur trail 0.5 mile (one-way) toward the trailhead if you have concerns about timing.

ON THE TRAIL

Wander to the pit toilets from the parking lot and once there, follow the sign for Main Hiking Trails west a short distance until you arrive at a signed junction. Turn left on the Bus Trail, toward the West Tiger No. 3 Trail, and at 0.3 mile, arrive at a sign for the West Tiger No. 3. The Bus Trail makes a right here, but our trail goes straight ahead and crosses through a wooden pedestrian turnstile. Find the signed Tiger Mountain Trail on the left in roughly 235 feet and take it.

The trail starts off on a gentle grade through spectacular moss-covered forest—a testament to the amount of rain this area gets. The trail wastes no time with its uphill trajectory, passing by the occasional dripping creeklet and damp drainage but mostly staying in thick forest. At 0.9 mile, cross the unsigned Cable Line Trail. This trail is a wicked-steep, primitive approach to the summit of West Tiger No. 3—an option if you want a grueling climb, hence killer workout, of 1.5 miles to the viewpoint.

If not, continue onward, and reach the first of two wooden bridges at 2.1 miles. The next one you'll come to is more impressive, so keep rolling and reach it 0.1 mile after the last. This wooden bridge, spanning the width of a babbling creek, is tucked into the drapey boughs of western red cedars and the emerald limbs of Douglas-firs. Devil's club and lush sword ferns cover the ground, and the whole sight feels like a gnome might just pop out of this storybook setting at any time. If you aren't intent on a long day, you could make this your goal and turn back here. Getting to this point is still good conditioning for the heart, lungs, and legs and fills you with pride for carrying your carcass up this far.

The junction with the K-3 Trail appears at 2.3 miles. You have options here too. The K-3 Trail is a steep shortcut that reconnects with the TMT in 0.8 mile. If you're sticking to the recommended route, stay on the TMT; you'll hit the reconnection spot in 3.2 miles.

Either way, keep powering up to reach the signed junction to scoot up to the top of Middle Tiger No. 2 at 3.7 miles, where a bench and a summit sign await. It has been logged recently—however, the logging opened up swoon-worthy views. If you can overlook the glum landscape of the downed logs in this working forest, the sweeping panorama on a clear day will treat you to vistas of downtown Seattle, the Puget Sound, and even the Olympic Mountains.

EXTENDING YOUR HIKE

The full Tiger Mountain Trail is 15.7 miles one way with an elevation gain of roughly 2580 feet. It winds through a healthy dense forest before it hits recent logging efforts and crosses several old roadways. If you are in the mood for a long hike or a big trail run, you could follow the TMT from the start (as described here) to its end where it reaches an unsigned trailhead off Tiger Mountain Road SE (Issaquah), or just go as far as you wish.

To continue on, rejoin the TMT from the summit spur and turn left. Shortly, the TMT will pop you out just downhill from the summit (still with ample views) in the logging area. The trail becomes part of the logging road, where the trail has been reconstructed through the downed debris. Stay on the trail and look to the left for a new signed continuation of the TMT, now a single track, at 6.2 miles.

From here, continue following the TMT all the way to its southern terminus (another 6.5 miles ahead) if you wish, or consult your map for any number of other loops you can take back to the High Point trailhead.

16 West Tiger No. 3

RATING/DIFFICULTY: ***/3
ROUNDTRIP: 5.8 miles
ELEV GAIN/HIGH POINT: 2010 feet/2522 feet
SEASON: Year-round

Map: Green Trails Maps Tiger Mountain/Taylor Mountain No. 204S; **Contact:** Department of Natural Resources, South Puget Sound Region; **Notes:** Discover Pass required. Pit toilets and picnic areas available near the

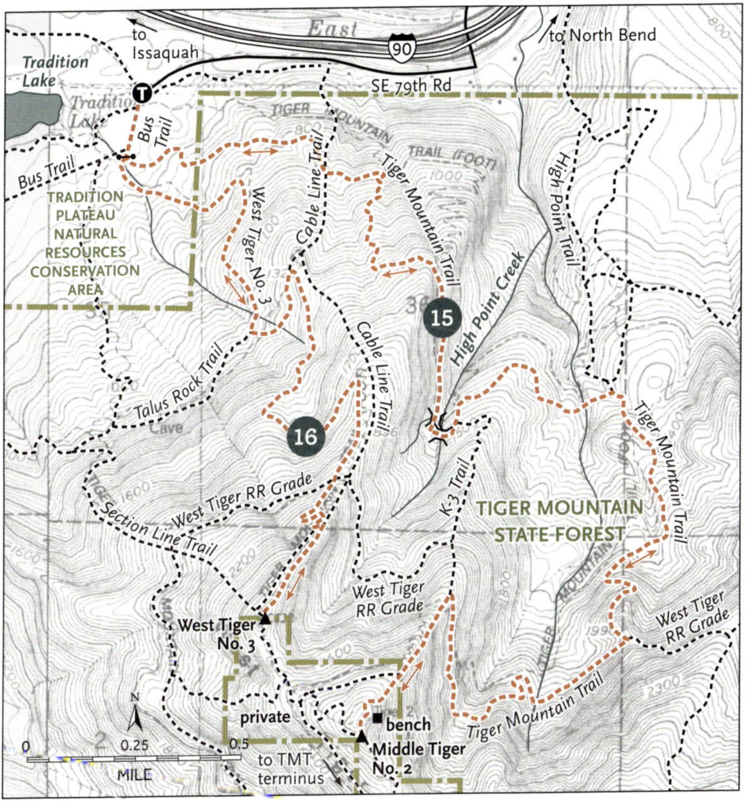

Where trees once stood on West Tiger No. 3, the land now offers broader views while reckoning with change.

trailhead. Parking on weekends is difficult, so arrive early or have a plan B hike. Many of the Tiger Mountain summits have been recently logged. Check DNR website for logging and trail rebuilding status. Open to leashed dogs; **GPS:** N 47 31.775, W 121 59.733

In the last several years, the summit of West Tiger No. 3 has turned from a treed forest with moderate views to a deforested landscape with boundless, sweeping views, thanks to the logging of the working forest on the top. Despite the decimated peak there's still a summit sign, a beautiful bench, and spectacular views waiting for those willing to put forth the effort to reach the often-windy summit.

GETTING THERE

From I-90 near Issaquah: Take exit 20 for High Point Way and head south. In a couple hundred feet, turn right onto SE 79th Street, which parallels the freeway heading westbound. Stay on this road as it passes through an open gate and continues to the High Point trailhead, 0.8 mile from the exit. Note: The gate is usually slated to be open from dawn to dusk; however, staffing issues in the last several years have kept the gate open all the time. This could change without notice, so you may want to park on the road's edge on the east side of the gate and take the obvious connecting spur trail 0.5 mile (one-way) toward the trailhead if you have concerns about timing.

ON THE TRAIL

From the parking lot, locate the pit toilets and once there, walk west a short distance on the Bus Trail (signed "Main Hiking Trails") until you arrive at a signed junction for West Tiger No. 3 and other trails. Follow the sign left and, at 0.2 mile, arrive at a signed junction for West Tiger No. 3. The Bus Trail makes a right here, but our trail goes straight ahead and crosses through a wooden pedestrian turnstile and passes the Tiger Mountain Trail (TMT) coming in from the left.

The climbing officially commences, and boy howdy, does it get going! The river rocks that are firmly held in place by the soil and foot-pounding over the years can have a slippery surface to them, so you'll want to watch your foot placement. Up you go, breathing heavily, yet smiling for the gift of good health. At 1 mile, cross a trickling creek, then reach a junction with the Talus Rock Trail, which goes in the same direction we have been traveling; however, our trail makes a hairpin turn to the left and continues climbing.

At 1.2 miles, the trail passes an unsigned junction to the left. This is an unmaintained short cutover to the Cable Line Trail, which also climbs to the top of West Tiger No. 3. The Cable Line Trail, however, is a primitive trail that is steep and merciless, making short work out of what the official West Tiger No. 3 Trail more gently accomplishes. The Cable Line Trail cuts off roughly a half mile but takes most folks about the same amount of time with rest breaks. Get ready for the cardio burn if you decide to cut over.

The West Tiger No. 3 Trail makes a hairpin turn to the right at this point and continues working hard to get you to the summit on sweeping switchbacks. The fern groves here are some of the best on Tiger Mountain, and Douglas squirrels like to play in their leaves, occasionally scolding you for having the nerve to walk through their neighborhoods.

The trail crosses over the unsigned West Tiger Railroad Grade at 2.2 miles and makes a left on a switchback. Continue following a short series of switchbacks until the trail crosses over the unsigned Cable Line Trail again at 2.5 miles. Gaining elevation somewhat steeply now, the path continues toward the West Tiger No. 3 summit, giving the occasional peekaboo view until it reaches the logged top at 2.9 miles.

Views of Squak and Cougar Mountains are outstanding, as are glimpses of various peaks to the west and to the east, such as Fuller Mountain. Look for paragliders high up in the puffy clouds, launched from Poo Poo Point (Hikes 17 and 18), and peer down into the Issaquah Hobart Valley.

EXTENDING YOUR HIKE

If time and gumption permit, continue following the new trails over to West Tiger No. 2, where the views get even better! Getting lost is nearly impossible, since the previous forest is no longer present. Perhaps this is a silver lining? From West Tiger No. 2, you can either go back the way you arrived or consult your map and take the TMT (or the K-3 Trail) back to the High Point trailhead for a complete loop of 8.4 miles.

17 Poo Poo Point: High School Trail

RATING/DIFFICULTY: **/3
ROUNDTRIP: 7.2 miles
ELEV GAIN/HIGH POINT: 1810 feet/1850 feet
SEASON: Year-round

Map: Green Trails Maps Tiger Mountain/Taylor Mountain No. 204S; **Contact:** Department of Natural Resources, South Puget Sound Region; **Notes:** No facilities at either trailhead. The main trailhead is located next to a shooting range—so loud gunfire is common. Use caution with gun-shy dogs or sensitive humans. There are a couple of ways to

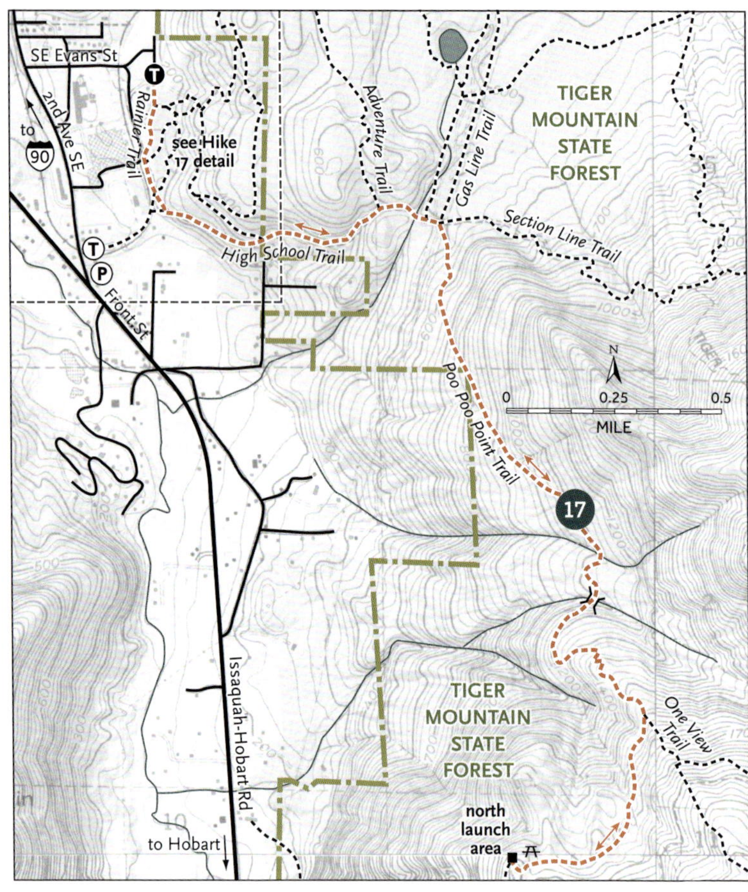

get to Poo Poo Point. This one is longer than the Chirico Trail (Hike 18), but it's usually less crowded and parking isn't as cutthroat. This trail also leads to the Tradition Plateau and connects with many trails, allowing for different loops and options. Open to leashed dogs, stock, mountain bikes (the High School Trail); **GPS:** N 47 31.474, W 122 01.569

The name invokes giggles. There are restrooms on the summit, but that's not what it's named after. Back in the day, loggers used whistles to communicate from towers to workers, and two blasts (POO POO) were frequently heard when the logging operation needed to convey information. Poo Poo Point has fantastic views of Lake Sammamish, Bellevue, and even the Olympic Mountains

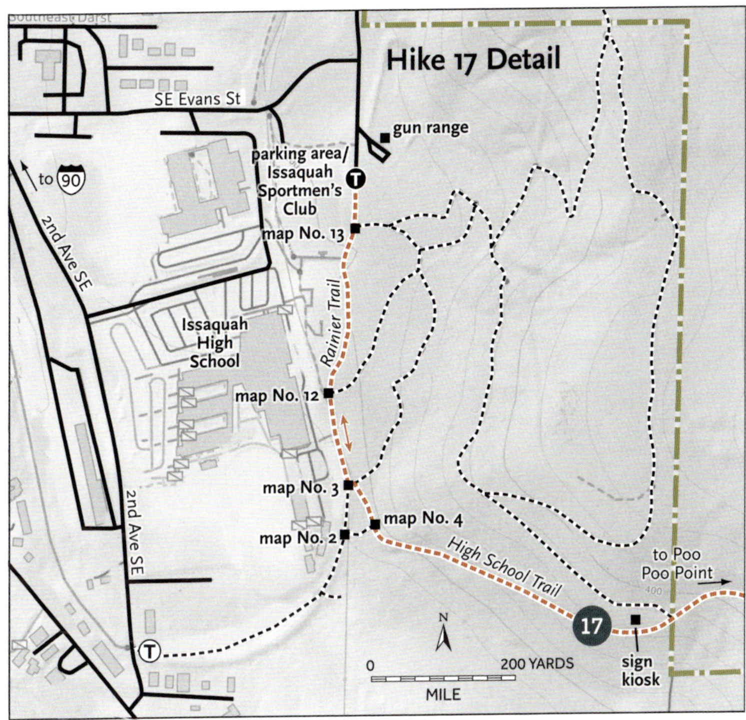

far to the west. It is the main launch point for local paragliders who wish to set sail on clear days, and it's entertaining to watch them take off.

GETTING THERE

Main parking area: From I-90 in Issaquah, take exit 18 for E. Sunset Way. Head south on E. Sunset Way and in 0.5 mile, turn left onto 2nd Avenue SE. At 0.8 mile, turn left onto SE Evans Street. Stay on SE Evans Street until it arrives at the parking area at 1 mile. The closest parking spots—and the trailhead—are located where the road winds to the right past the Issaquah Sportsmen's Club.

Alternate parking and trailhead: From I-90 in Issaquah, take exit 18 for E. Sunset Way. Head south on E. Sunset Way and in 0.5 mile, turn left onto 2nd Avenue SE. At 1.3 miles, look for a small parking lot with room for eight or nine cars on the left side of the road. Park here and walk east, then northeast as the trail curves, 0.2 mile. At map No. 2, go right. Then in just over 100 feet, go right at the sign marked for map No. 4. Follow directions in the trail description from this spot.

ON THE TRAIL

From the main trailhead, follow the wide path, known as the Rainier Trail, as it follows

The forest's longest song belongs to the tiniest singer; listen for the crisp, perfect warble of the Pacific wren.

the outer edges of Issaquah High School. In recent years, the Issaquah Alps Trails Club in conjunction with the City of Issaquah have marked this web of trails with numbered signs. There are so many that the numbers are often out of order, but each sign contains a map to help you find your way if you get turned around. In roughly 150 feet, arrive at map No. 13, noted by a giant number thirteen surrounded by a blue circle, and bear right, continuing your journey close to the high school's edge. Map No. 12 arrives at 0.2 mile and again, bear right, keeping close to the school. At almost 0.3 mile, arrive at map No. 3, and this time, go left, heading south. The trail almost immediately connects with another unsigned trail—go right. In 185 feet, arrive at map No. 4 and continue as the trail turns eastward, now climbing on a wide former road. If you came in from the secondary trail, this is the spot to start following along.

At 0.7 mile, a kiosk with wildlife information and a Green Trails topographical map shows up to the left. Don't let the bear and cougar information worry your sweet head—they hang out in this forest occasionally but mostly keep to themselves.

Continue climbing until at 0.9 mile the grade eases up at a swampy area and the Adventure Trail arrives to the left. The Adventure Trail is one of the many great lowland hikes you can take if the higher hills are snowy or muddy—just consult your map, as the trails are all a big maze in this area. Just beyond the swamp is a gorgeous stream where water abounds even well into hot summers.

At 1.1 miles, the trail nears some powerlines and arrives at a signed junction pointing you toward the Poo Poo Point Trail. Go right here and immediately pass the unsigned Gas Line Trail. In roughly 100 feet, the Poo Poo

Point Trail is signed again, where it meets a Y with the Section Line Trail. As a side note, you can make a big loop if you choose and come down the Section Line Trail, although it's steep and unmaintained and adds more distance to your day. You'll need to connect to other trails to get over to the Section Line Trail, so consult your map for more details if you want a bit more adventure.

For now, head south on the Poo Poo Point Trail, climbing on the fairly steep pitch. Grunt and snort your way up through the ferns, western red cedar, thimbleberry, and—in springtime—occasional trillium flowers, until the trail eases its grade at 2 miles. A large wooden bridge over a heavily vegetated waterway provides a good place to catch your breath and admire the woody shrubs and brushy landscape before continuing onward.

At nearly 3 miles, the trail arrives at a junction with the One View Trail to the left. If you want to do a return loop with the Section Line Trail, this is the connection you'll want upon your return from Poo Poo Point. I like to hike up the One View Trail, then turn left on the West Tiger Railroad Grade, which eventually joins to the Section Line Trail to the left. The Section Line Trail then takes you steeply back to the High School Trail. It's 4.5 miles from Poo Poo Point back to the High School Trail going this way. Longer and tougher, but fun to see different scenery.

For now, continue straight, following signs for the Poo Poo Point Trail, until you arrive at a parking area with pit toilets at 3.6 miles. In the offseason, these restrooms might be closed, so don't psych up your bladder. Bear right at the parking area and follow it up a small rise to the north launch area, where benches and picnic tables await. There might be more folks up here than you'd expected, since the Chirico Trail (Hike 18) leads up here from Issaquah-Hobart Road. In summer months, the parking area up here is used privately to shuttle paragliders and their gear to the top.

The artificial green swath and windsocks you see are the launch point for the paraglider pilots. If you feel the need to just run as fast as possible off the side of a mountain (with proper equipment) and let the wind carry you, you might want to try it sometime. Marc Chirico—of the Chirico Trail and the founder of Seattle Paragliding—and his team offer tandem jumps for newbies (see Resources). After coming up here for years and watching, I finally bit the bullet, did it, and had the time of my life.

If you prefer your feet on terra firma, enjoy the area as long as you wish before heading back the way you came or exploring other options for getting back down.

18 Poo Poo Point: Chirico Trail

RATING/DIFFICULTY: ****/3
ROUNDTRIP: 4 miles
ELEV GAIN/HIGH POINT: 1770 feet/1850 feet
SEASON: Year-round

Map: Green Trails Maps Tiger Mountain/Taylor Mountain No. 204S; **Contact:** Department of Natural Resources (DNR), South Puget Sound Region; **Notes:** No parking pass is required, as the parking area is located on King County property. Portable toilets are often found in the parking area, permanent restrooms on the summit. Parking is extremely tough at this location—hike weekdays early or late in the day, and be prepared to pay for private parking options on neighboring properties. Obey all no-parking signs. This trail also leads to Tradition Plateau and connects with many trails, allowing for different loop options. Open to

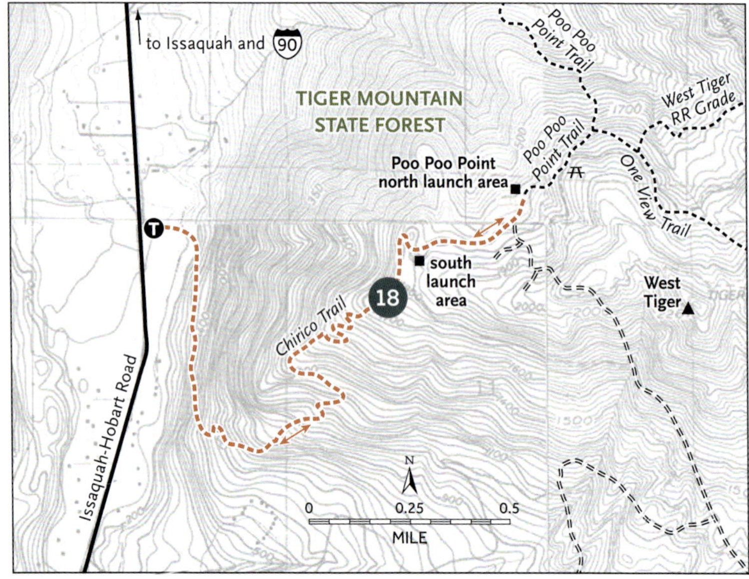

leashed dogs, stock; **GPS:** N 47 30.084, W 122 01.343

You have Marc Chirico (owner of Seattle Paragliding) and friends (a group he calls Team Chirico) to thank for constructing this steep, wonderful trail to the summit of Poo Poo Point. He lives and works next door, and he and Team Chirico created the trail from 1997 to 2000 to help paragliders access the summit. Since the trail's initial construction, DNR, trail clubs, and other volunteers have helped support the well-traveled pathway.

While the name Poo Poo is snicker-worthy, it's not named for the restrooms on the summit. Rather, the moniker comes from the whistles that once communicated from the towers to workers during logging operations. The views from the top are outstanding, and on clear days, even the Olympic Mountains are visible. This is the primary launch point for local paragliders, so enjoy a picnic on the top and watch the shenanigans if the wind and conditions are right.

GETTING THERE

From I-90 near Issaquah: Take exit 17 and turn south onto Front Street. Stay on Front Street, passing old-town Issaquah and farm communities, for 3.1 miles (the road changes names to Issaquah-Hobart Road) until you reach a large parking area to the left next to a large field. If the parking area is full, private property owners nearby often offer spots for a fee.

ON THE TRAIL

The trail is easy to find as it crosses the field to the east. Keep your eyes out for landing paragliders if you happen to be here when they are buzzing overhead, and avoid crossing until it's safe for all. At the far side of the field, the unofficial entrance to the forest is often highlighted with novelties such as a sturdy archway, statues, and flags. The personal touch is welcoming, and you begin your huff and puff up the slopes.

The steepness is not lost on anyone as you grunt, groan, and growl up the scenic pathway. A series of purposefully placed rocks makes a cobblestone pathway in places and shows the work this trail has received over the years. Ferns, Oregon grape, and mosses are your companions, along with second-growth forest—welcome shade on a hot day.

At 1 mile, the steepness lets up briefly and the trail reaches a road-turned-trail area, which it follows for a short 0.1 mile. A more open area follows, along with hopes that you are getting near the top. Not too long now! A few peekaboo views to the south pop up as a sneak peek of what's ahead.

At 1.7 miles, the trail busts out at the south launch area for paragliders to use if the wind is coming from this direction. The steep, hillside meadow opens views to the south of Mount Rainier and the valleys of Hobart, Ravensdale, and beyond. You can also see the Hobart landfill from this spot, so be sure to point that out to all your friends; nothing says vantage point like a bird's-eye view of the garbage dump. Thankfully, if you didn't know what it was, you might think it was an odd grassy knoll.

Stay on the main trail here and avoid the social trails, which have become increasingly well-used shortcuts. A couple more switchbacks through the forest deliver you to a grassy, wide-open meadow known as the north launch or the primary launch point. Picnic tables and wooden benches are out your nibbles. Restrooms are located to the south of the launch area, as is parking for the cheaters who get rides via the private access road for their jumps. From here, on a clear day, there is magic afoot. Lake Sammamish as well as the cities of Issaquah and Bellevue are twinkling below you, while Squak Mountain stares back from the west. It's a gorgeous place to sit and soak it all in before heading back the way you arrived. Oh, and

High above the trees, the launch site at Poo Poo Point offers a stunning overlook of Lake Sammamish far below.

by the way . . . if you get inspired to jump, newbies are welcome at Seattle Paragliding (see Resources).

19 Grand Ridge Loop

RATING/DIFFICULTY: **/2
ROUNDTRIP: 4.3 miles
ELEV GAIN/HIGH POINT: 600 feet/910 feet
SEASON: Year-round

Maps: Green Trails Maps Tiger Mountain/Taylor Mountain No. 204S, King County Parks Grand Ridge Park map; **Contact:** King County Parks; **Notes:** Parking lot is a high car prowl area; do not leave any valuables in vehicle (see Staying Safe in the Introduction). Several trailheads connect these trails, such as Central Park trailhead and South Pond trailhead—see map for various approaches. No toilet or picnic areas at trailhead, though Tiger Mountain (see Hike 15), a short distance away, offers them. Open to leashed dogs, mountain bikes; **GPS:** N 47 31.920, W 121 58.845

This trail is shared with mountain bikers, and on weekends they can be plentiful. But on weekdays, especially when snow still lingers in the high country, this is a pleasant place to walk under a healthy forest canopy of second-growth Douglas firs and western red cedars. The elevation gain isn't as grueling as other local hikes, so it makes this one more attainable for kids or hikers who aren't used to consistent climbs.

GETTING THERE

From I-90 near Issaquah: Take exit 20 for High Point Way. If going eastbound, turn left, cross back under the freeway, and find the trailhead in 0.1 mile to the left. If going westbound, turn right and almost immediately find the trailhead to the road's left. Grand Ridge Park is served by the Issaquah Highlands Park and Ride, Issaquah Transit Center, and Metro bus route 208 at High Point on I-90.

ON THE TRAIL

From the parking lot, begin walking westbound and immediately cross a large bridge over the East Fork Issaquah Creek. During spring, the creek flows heavily and attempts to cover the consistent freeway noise. You are now on a former railroad grade, which was part of the Seattle, Lake Shore and Eastern Railway that routed passengers and supplies from Seattle out to Snoqualmie Valley. In 1971 the lines were abandoned, and eventually, the tracks were removed and it was converted to a rails-to-trails path now called the Issaquah–Preston Trail. The grade slopes ever so slightly downhill, but you probably won't notice the incline until you come back this way.

The freeway buzzes loudly nearby, as East Fork Issaquah Creek babbles down a forested incline on the old railroad's left. Several unofficial boot paths wander down for a closer look, as a couple of trickling streams come in from the old road's right. Snap a few pics if the mood and light are in your favor.

At 0.6 mile, reach the signed East Fork Trail on the road's right. A trail map is available on the sign so you can get your bearings without having to fish your map out of your pack. Turn right and begin the majority of the hike's climbing.

With the classic Northwest suspects such as salal, sword fern, and moss at your feet, the trail guides you upward through switchbacks until the grade eases at 1.3 miles.

At 1.5 miles, continue straight at a junction with the Coal Mine Loop Trail, heading

The trails near Grand Ridge are welcoming spaces where you can get a good workout and breathe some fresh air.

off to the left. A map mounted on a post shows a big red dot as a you-are-here marker, making it pretty hard to get lost. If the kids are tired or you are ready for a downhill, you can take this trail back toward the railroad grade, but otherwise there is more to see!

At 1.8 miles, arrive at a signed T junction where the East Fork Trail heads right and the northern Coal Mine Loop Trail goes left. If you have a lot of time to burn and the map is at your fingertips, you could take a right turn and follow the East Fork Trail past Grand Ridge Drive, where more loops are available. For now, head left and follow the Coal Mine Loop as it begins descending. At 2.1 miles, cross the small South Pond Bridge over a meandering seasonal creek.

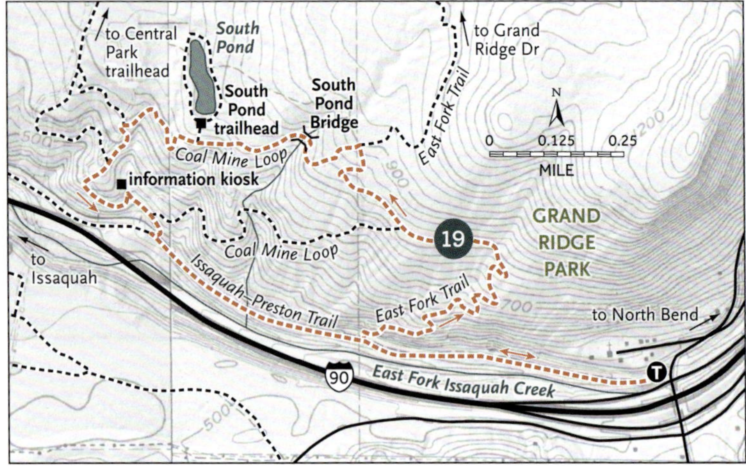

The forest is magical up here as western red cedars drape their long, graceful limbs around the trail's edges, somewhat obscuring the views of Tiger Mountain to the south. In the springtime, look for yellow violets in the mossy areas, with their delicate sunshine-colored petals lined with dark streaks. Oregon grape hides in the shade, producing gorgeous sprays of yellow flower clumps in the spring, followed by periwinkle berries in the months of August and September. Unlike a grape, the edible berries are very tart and are generally mixed with sugar or sweeter berries for jams and jellies. Civilization feels miles away, as the freeway noise is barely audible.

At 2.3 miles, arrive at a signed junction where a trail from the South Pond trailhead comes in from the right. Stay straight and continue going downhill. At 2.6 miles, rock-hop your way across a stream, and then in less than 500 feet, arrive at an unsigned junction. Stay straight, or slightly left, and continue your descent.

Another unsigned junction arrives at 2.8 miles, so stay straight—bearing left—here also. From here the trail winds downhill until it arrives at a kiosk at 3 miles. To the left are some mossy concrete pillars, which are footings from the Grand Ridge coal mine that was in operation from 1909 to 1934, then periodically until the 1950s. Imagine, what was once a bustling operation is now a nature walk.

At 2.9 miles, our trail connects with a signed junction to the left, but we stay straight—somewhat right—and reconnect to the railroad grade at 3.1 miles.

Turn left and follow the railroad grade back toward the trailhead, passing the East Fork Trail again and making a full loop back to your car at 4.3 miles.

OPPOSITE: *Little Si rewards your sweat equity with views of the Snoqualmie Valley and North Bend.*

NORTH BEND

THE ONCE SLEEPY COMMUNITY OF North Bend is now a bustling mountain town with plenty of fantastic trails and rural pathways to enjoy. Whether you admire the scenic panoramic from Mount Si—the most popular hike in Washington State—or discover a quiet pathway that's slightly less visited, you're sure to find somewhere fulfilling to get your workout while enjoying Mother Nature.

20 Mount Si

RATING/DIFFICULTY: ****/5
ROUNDTRIP: 8 miles
ELEV GAIN/HIGH POINT: 3150 feet/3900 feet
SEASON: May–Nov

Maps: Green Trails Maps Mount Si NRCA No. 206S, Department of Natural Resources Mount Si NRCA Trail Map; **Contact:** Department of Natural Resources (DNR); **Notes:** Discover Pass required. Pit toilets at trailhead. Parking can get full on sunny summer weekends; arrive early, avoid weekends, and if necessary, park at Mount Teneriffe trailhead and use connecting trails. Trailhead Direct bus (see Resources) is available most summers. Open to leashed dogs; **GPS:** N 47 29.210, W 121 45.206

Because it is a familiar landmark and boasts such amazing views, hiking to the top of Mount Si should be a requirement for every able-bodied person in the Pacific Northwest. With upward of 100,000 visitors a year, you'll have plenty of company, but perhaps the camaraderie of like-minded, tough hikers is all part of its charm. The consistent pitch makes it a true fitness challenge that is amply rewarded with big payoff views of the Snoqualmie Valley and distant peaks all the way to the Olympic Mountains.

GETTING THERE

From I-90 near North Bend: Take exit 32 (436th Avenue SE) and head north. In 0.3 mile, take the second exit (to stay straight) at the roundabout. At 0.5 mile, take the second exit (going left/northwest) on SE North Bend Way. At 0.9 mile, turn right onto SE Mount Si Road. Proceed to the signed trailhead and parking area to the road's left at 3.3 miles.

ON THE TRAIL

From the broad, well-traveled pathway at the trailhead, pass the pit toilets, picnic areas, and large interpretive sign. A side trail, called the Creekside Loop, shoots off to the left in roughly 50 feet. This short loop rejoins the main trail in 0.1 mile and is an option if you want to take it.

Cross a bridge over a tributary creek and reach the unofficial start to your climb. The Creekside Loop rejoins the trail here, and a bench provides a place to sit if you need to regroup before you start up.

The switchbacks start off slowly, then pick up as you get higher, so hang on for the ride. Salmonberries, drippy creeks, and a smattering of alders are present as you make your way into a thick evergreen forest. At 0.8 mile, the Mount Si Trail intersects a signed connector with the Talus Loop Trail and the Roaring Creek Trail going off to the right, then continues climbing before it reaches the Douglas Fir Trail, which goes straight ahead at 1.3 miles. Our trail switches back at the trail junction and continues the uphill grind.

At 1.5 miles, a couple of benches are strategically placed on a level spot en route and provide a perfect opportunity to take a load off. A sit break or a stop to shed some layers might be in order because the uphill grind is relentless.

Hiking to the rocky viewpoints near the top of Mount Si is a PNW must-do for all who are able.

At 1.8 miles, the trail reaches another signed junction with the Talus Loop Trail to the right just prior to delivering you to some welcome level ground, called Snag Flats. This interpretive area, complete with aging signs, a boardwalk exhibit, and a lovely bench is a good milestone—it means you are nearly halfway to the top. This area has some gorgeous old trees, including a large 350-year-old Douglas-fir that withstood the heat and vigor of the 1910 Mount Si Fire as well as logging efforts prior to 1977. After that timeframe, this landscape was turned into a state conservation area.

You have the 2005–6 restoration efforts of DNR and Mountains to Sound Greenway to thank for the improvements to the trail tread. Prior to this time, roots, rocks, and tripping hazards made this an obstacle course not only at the top but also all the way up the mountain.

The next couple of miles consist of tighter switchbacks and even more grueling uphill grades underneath the shade of thick conifers. A large Mount Si trail map is displayed by the side of the trail at 3.8 miles, with a you-are-here arrow showing that you are officially at the junction of the Mount Si Old Trail and the newer one (now the main one). Take notes! This could be a climbing option for a future trip (see Extending Your Hike) or

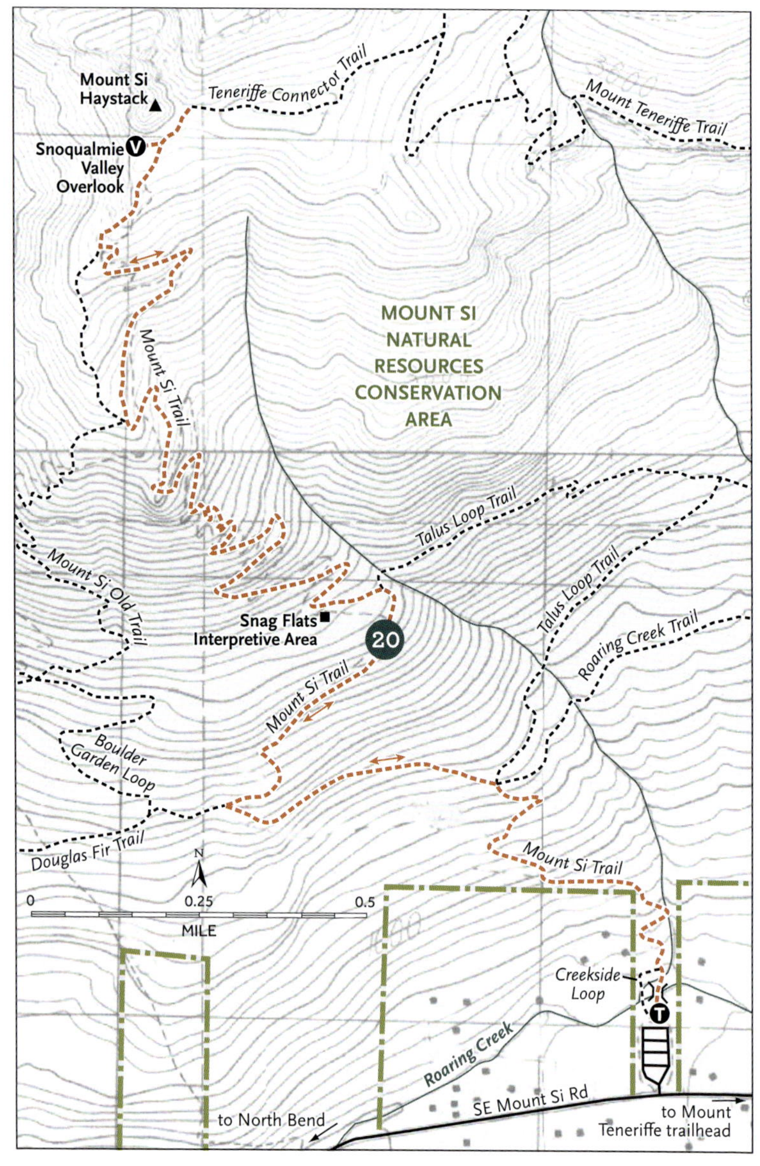

Mount Si Haystack
Snoqualmie Valley Overlook
Teneriffe Connector Trail
Mount Teneriffe Trail
MOUNT SI NATURAL RESOURCES CONSERVATION AREA
Mount Si Trail
Talus Loop Trail
Mount Si Old Trail
Snag Flats Interpretive Area
20
Talus Loop Trail
Roaring Creek Trail
Mount Si Trail
Boulder Garden Loop
Douglas Fir Trail
Mount Si Trail
N
0
0.25
0.5
MILE
Creekside Loop
Roaring Creek
SE Mount Si Rd
to North Bend
to Mount Teneriffe trailhead

maybe an alternative way down. There are so many choices!

Mount Si was named for an early pioneer of the area, Josiah Merritt, known as Uncle Si. He was a gruff, unusual man and was known for playing the fiddle, growing orchards and vegetable gardens, and raising pigs. He occupied a cabin, which he built in 1862 at Mount Si's base, near a creek that emptied into the Middle Fork Snoqualmie River. He passed away in 1882, but his legacy lives on.

Long before Uncle Si came on the scene, the Snoqualmie Tribe referred to the mountain as *qʷalbc* from the Lushootseed language. The mountain has enormous cultural significance in the Snoqualmie people's ancestry and history, and is considered a sacred site to them. Practicing good stewardship on Native soils is a way to honor their history and people.

The mountaintop is beckoning, so keep rolling up the steeps until you reach a rocky boulder field where there are usually plenty of rock lizards of the human variety, sunning themselves and feeding their hungry bellies. The views are outstanding here, but there's more to see!

The trail is a bit more obscure in this spot, but you'll know you are on it when you see the attempts at concrete fillers in between boulders, creating more official looking steps. Pick your way up, following the trail, until you reach the signed junction for the Snoqualmie Valley Overlook pointing you to the left at just shy of 4 miles. A few more steps on a spur trail, and there you are! The benches at the viewpoint are a great place to sit and take in the panorama, but if they are occupied, there are plenty of other rocky perches to sprawl out. Enjoy every sweet drop.

To the right of the Snoqualmie Valley Overlook, you will see a large rocky protrusion—the official summit known as the Haystack. While people do climb it, please think twice before attempting it yourself, especially if you have a fear of heights or limited rock climbing or scrambling experience, or if there is bad weather. The exposed, loose, and slippery rock has resulted in numerous accidents, so make an informed decision about your own capabilities! To climb it, follow the spur trail from the overlook back out to the main trail; turn left, walking a bit farther until you reach the obvious spot to start the scramble. Up and back down adds approximately another 0.5 mile to your day.

EXTENDING YOUR HIKE

UPPER SI–TENERIFFE CONNECTOR TRAIL: Keep going past the base of the Haystack and you'll find yourself on the Teneriffe Connector Trail that leads to the Mount Teneriffe Trail in 0.8 mile. From there, you could hit the summit of Mount Teneriffe (4.6 miles out and back from this junction), or simply head down the trail. You can make a loop with the Roaring Creek Trail, which leads back to the Mount Si Trail for an alternative descent. Doing this loop on your return adds 1 mile to your descent, but it's fun to not see the same thing twice.

THE OLD SI TRAIL: The steepness of this knee cruncher is tough on the body. However, if you are hoping for a new way to descend (or possibly ascend in the future), this is it. From the signed junction listed in the trail description above, head down 1.8 miles of tight switchbacks on jelly legs, until you reach the Boulder Garden Loop Trail. From there, turn left and in 0.1 mile, reach the signed Douglas Fir Trail. Turn left and climb (yes, you read that right) nearly 270 feet before dropping some to meet up with the Mount Si Trail again. It's approximately 0.1 mile shorter to come down this way verses the main trail, though you'll have some additional climbing on the last stretch, which makes it feel longer.

21 Talus Loop Trail

RATING/DIFFICULTY: **/3
ROUNDTRIP: 5.4 miles
ELEV GAIN/HIGH POINT: 1310 feet/2120 feet
SEASON: Year-round

Maps: Green Trails Maps Mount Si NRCA No. 206S, Department of Natural Resources Mount Si NRCA Trail Map; **Contact:** Department of Natural Resources; **Notes:** Discover Pass required. Pit toilets at trailhead. Trailhead Direct bus (see Resources) is available most summers. The former trailhead was farther east on SE Mount Si Road but no longer serves as a parking area. You could park at the Mount Si trailhead and also access this loop. Open to leashed dogs; **GPS:** N 47 29.207, W 121 45.599

While this loop keeps you in the woods, it's possible to branch out for longer hikes and go to Teneriffe Falls or even Mount Si. But you can also just enjoy the bounty of a classic PNW forested walk that affords some fresh air and a decent workout by simply following the trail description.

GETTING THERE

From I-90 near North Bend: Take exit 32 (436th Avenue SE) and head north. In 0.3 mile, take the second exit (to stay straight) at the roundabout. At 0.5 mile, take the second exit (going left/northwest) on SE North Bend Way. At 0.9 mile, turn right onto SE Mount Si Road. Continue on Mount Si Road to 3.9 miles, passing the trailheads for Little Si (1.5 miles) and Mount Si (3.3 miles), until arriving at the large signed Mount Teneriffe trailhead to the road's left.

ON THE TRAIL

Display your Discover Pass proudly at the parking area, then walk toward the pit toilets and the large map kiosk: the official trailhead. Just behind the kiosk, the trail begins its upward trajectory, guiding you gently through the evergreens, then throwing in a couple of switchbacks for good measure.

At 0.5 mile, reach a defunct logging road-turned-trail, and turn left to stay on the main trail. At a junction signed for Mount Teneriffe and Teneriffe Falls at 0.9 mile, continue left on the mellow grade.

Make a mental note to come back and see the gorgeous falls (Hike 24) if time and energy allow today, or put it on the calendar for another day. For now, continue onward, crossing a couple of wooden pedestrian bridges over playful brooks, including a beautiful one over Roaring Creek. The creek isn't roaring, as the name might imply, but rather dances over mossy rocks, through salmonberry and woody debris. It's tranquil in this spot and might even have you reaching for a picture or two.

At 1.4 miles, pass the Roaring Creek Trail on the left and make another mental note. This is where you'll come out after you complete the loop, so get your bearings and then continue uphill on the Mount Teneriffe Trail, steeper now. At 1.7 miles, arrive at a signed junction.

Take the left toward the Talus Loop Trail and arrive at a Y signed trail junction in 0.1 mile. You have options at this point, as you do at so many intersections in life. If you are feeling like you've had enough climbing or have the wee ones with you, you could take a left and drop down the Talus Loop Trail for 0.5 mile to reach the Roaring Creek Trail. Once there, turn left and go another 0.5 mile to complete the loop. This would give you less

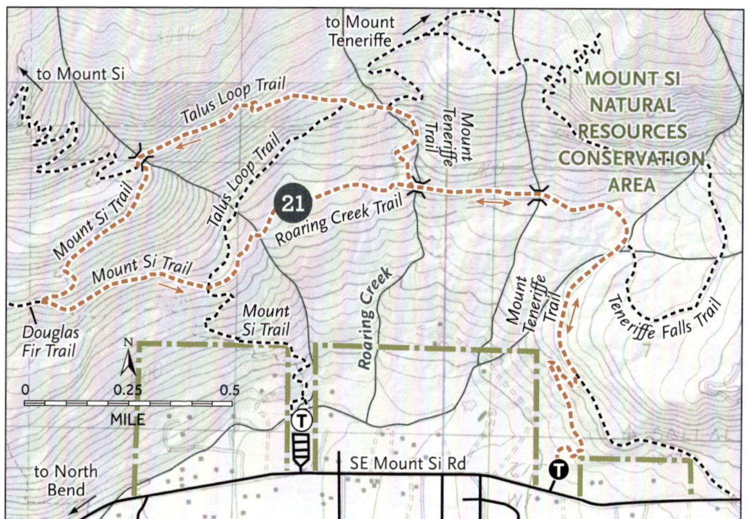

distance (0.5 mile shorter) and less elevation gain (just shy of 400 feet less) than the trail description here.

For the main hike, stay right at the Y at the start of the Talus Loop Trail and climb up through western hemlock, Douglas-fir, and western red cedar. Give yourself some good rah-rah to push harder and stronger; this is your last official climb on our trek (unless you visit the top of Mount Si). At 2.1 miles, you get rewarded with an open scree field, which allow for views to the southeast. Mount Washington shows up, as does Truck Town in North Bend, and even the ribbons of I-90. It's not a good place for a break, as the rocks are too small, but it's worth grabbing a pic or two.

At 2.5, cross a log footbridge over a dribbling brook, then almost immediately afterward, arrive at the Mount Si Trail. It's not signed as the Mount Si Trail at this point, but rather, the sign points back toward the Talus Loop Trail where we just came from. Still, you'll know you are on the Mount Si Trail because it's likely to have way more people than where we just were, and the trail is well used. Turn left on the Mount Si Trail (right if you want to visit the top) and follow it downhill. It's pretty much all gravy from here—woot!

The Douglas Fir Trail comes in from the right at 3 miles, but we stay on the Mount Si Trail as it makes a hard left. At 3.4 miles, a junction points to the Talus Loop Trail, which feels like it's straight ahead, since the Mount Si Trail turns slightly right at this point. Follow the sign toward Talus Loop, and then in about 20 feet, arrive at the Talus Loop Trail to the left and the Roaring Creek Trail straight ahead.

Follow the signs for the Roaring Creek Trail as it climbs slightly, then levels off and arrives back at Roaring Creek. You are only about 100 feet from reconnecting with the Mount Teneriffe Trail, so when you've finished taking

A wooden bridge along the Roaring Creek Trail offers a scenic and sturdy crossing.

pictures, carry on and arrive back at the end of the loop.

From this point, turn right and retrace your steps 1.4 miles back to the trailhead and then grab a nibble in town. You've earned it.

22 Little Si

RATING/DIFFICULTY: ***/3
ROUNDTRIP: 4.1 miles
ELEV GAIN/HIGH POINT: 1210 feet/1570 feet
SEASON: Year-round

Maps: Green Trails Maps Mount Si NRCA No. 206S, Department of Natural Resources Mount Si NRCA Trail Map; **Contact:** Department of Natural Resources; **Notes:** Discover Pass required. Pit toilets at trailhead. Limited parking options—arrive early and avoid weekends if possible. If overflow parking is full, please find a plan B trail. Trailhead Direct bus (see Resources) is available most summers. Open to leashed dogs; **GPS:** N 47 29.210, W 121 45.206

This is one of the most popular hikes along the I-90 corridor for good reason; it leads to fantastic views of the Snoqualmie Valley without the same grueling effort as its tougher brother, Mount Si. Though it's not a gimme in terms of being easy, it's moderate enough as it ebbs and flows in elevation to be enjoyed by kids and inexperienced hikers. Little Si is also a haven for rock climbers, who have designated routes along the walls near the trail.

GETTING THERE

From I-90 near North Bend: Take exit 32 (436th Avenue SE) and head north. In 0.3 mile, take the second exit (to stay straight) at the roundabout. At 0.5 mile, take the second exit (going left/northwest) on SE North Bend Way. At 0.9 mile, turn right onto

SE Mount Si Road. At 1 mile, pass Tanner Landing Park, then cross a large bridge over the Middle Fork Snoqualmie River. Just after the bridge, find the overflow parking lot to the road's left, followed by the main parking area at 1.7 miles.

ON THE TRAIL

From the trailhead, pass the pit toilets and informational kiosk and start up. The trail wastes no time climbing you into the hinterlands. In 0.1 mile, a rocky viewpoint to the left mysteriously pulls you over to enjoy a quick breather and a sneak peek of coming attractions at the top.

A steep ascent of a few rocky and rooty sections follows until the trail eases its grade and passes the Boulder Garden Loop at 0.3 mile (see Extending Your Hike). A gentle grade follows and at 0.6 mile, the trail catches up with the other side of the Boulder Garden Loop. The trail cruises over a trickling creek before entering an area with dense evergreens such as western red cedar and Douglas-fir. At 1 mile, the main trail makes a hard right at a signed

The rugged edge of Little Si, which gazes across the valley, eye to eye with its mighty sibling, Mount Si.

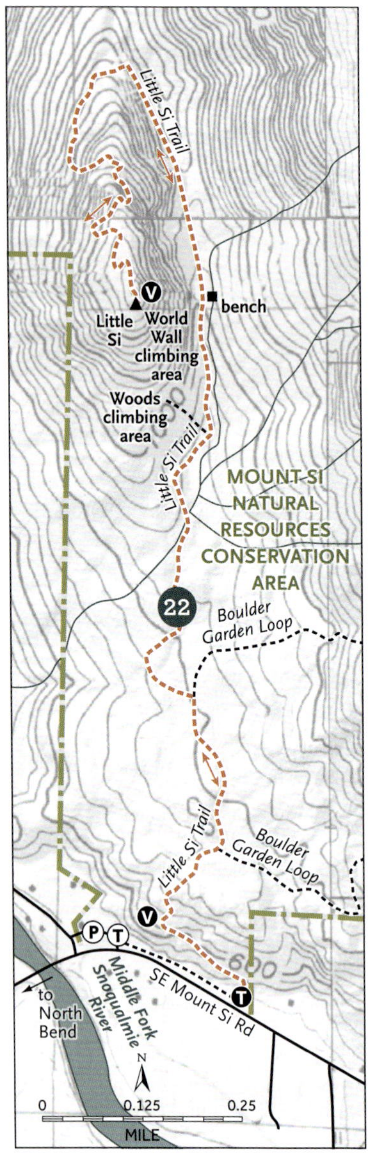

junction with a primitive trail for the Woods climbing area, which goes off to the left.

Up you go through evergreens, sword ferns, and thick mossy forest duff, until you arrive at a bench to the right at 1.1 miles. This bench is a tribute to the late Doug Hansen, a forty-six-year-old PNW local and postal worker who perished in the May 1996 Mount Everest disaster. The book *Into Thin Air* by Jon Krakauer, and the subsequent movie under the same title, outlines the catastrophe that killed eight people, including Doug. Their misfortune centered on a blizzard that overtook them as they descended from the summit.

Stop to catch your breath and pay your respects, or keep on trucking and pass the signed World Wall climbing area to your left just after the bench.

The trail winds around the rocky walls and begins a ramble up through the evergreens toward the summit. Some of the rocky areas are steep, requiring big step-ups and fancy footwork, so your trekking poles—if you brought them—come in handy.

At just beyond 2 miles, arrive at a viewpoint to the left, where some of your hard work starts to pay off. Mount Si is glorious as it watches over the smaller mountain and the lush green network of evergreens. The top is a hop, skip, and a jump beyond the viewpoint, and a metal benchmark affixed to the rock lists it as Small Si. The valley stretches out below you, along with views of Rattlesnake Mountain to the south; it's a breathtaking sight.

EXTENDING YOUR HIKE

Boulder Garden Loop is a side trail that ascends through a lovely forest and a series of gigantic stones to reconnect on both ends with the Little Si Trail. A couple of rock climbs are located off this trail, noted by bolts and chains near the clean routes traveling up the rock faces. This trail also serves as the approach to the Mount Si Old Trail, which leads to the top of Mount Si. It also connects to the Douglas Fir Trail, which traverses over to the newer and official Mount Si Trail (see Hike 20).

23 Mount Teneriffe

RATING/DIFFICULTY: ****/5
ROUNDTRIP: 13 miles
ELEV GAIN/HIGH POINT: 4240 feet/4788 feet
SEASON: Year-round

Maps: Green Trails Maps Mount Si NRCA No. 206S, Department of Natural Resources Mount Si NRCA Trail Map; **Contact:** Department of Natural Resources; **Notes:** Discover Pass required. Pit toilets at trailhead. Trailhead Direct bus (see Resources) is available most summers. The name of the waterfall near here was changed in recent years from Kamikaze Falls but may still appear this way on some maps/websites. The former trailhead was farther east on SE Mount Si Road and no longer serves as a parking area. Open to leashed dogs; **GPS:** N 47 29.207, W 121 45.599

Unlike Mount Si, Mount Teneriffe's neighbor, the trail to get to the top is not woodsy and pristine. In fact, you'll be following an old forest road nearly the whole time, with a few exceptions. But it's a popular trail all the same because the workout is stellar and the views from the top are some of the best in the area. What's more, you can make the day longer or varied with connections from this trail pop over to Teneriffe Falls (Hike 24) or loops with Mount Si. Whatever you choose, you are sure to feel your efforts in your quads!

GETTING THERE

From I-90 near North Bend: Take exit 32 (436th Avenue SE) and head north. In 0.3 mile, take the second exit (to stay straight) at the roundabout. At 0.5 mile, take the second exit (going left) on SE North Bend Way. At 0.9 mile, turn right onto SE Mount Si Road. Continue, passing the trailheads for Little Si and Mount Si, until 3.9 miles, when you arrive at the large signed Mount Teneriffe trailhead to the road's left.

ON THE TRAIL

From the trailhead, near the signed kiosk, walk through a gorgeous northwest forest of western hemlock, western red cedar, and Douglas-fir. Sword ferns and Oregon grape gather near the trail's edges for even more ambiance as you make your way up for 0.5 mile to reach the first intersection. A sign for Mount Teneriffe points you to the left, so turn and follow the gentle grade as it cruises along to reach a signed junction at 0.9 mile for Teneriffe Falls to the right.

If you want to visit the falls, you could do so via this junction, then rejoin the Mount Teneriffe Trail farther along via the brand-new Teneriffe Connector Trail. If you take this route, you add nearly 2 miles onto your day, with approximately 650 additional feet of elevation gain, but you get to see the waterfall! This might be a good time to add that some mapping apps show the former trail that leads to the top of Mount Teneriffe from Teneriffe Falls. This trail is still there; however, land managers request you refrain from using it. It's steep and loose in places near the top of the falls and quite risky with rock scrambles and natural hazards. A much safer

The author sits, slightly uncomfortably, for the classic summit shot atop Mount Teneriffe, embracing the soggy charm of a typical Northwest day.

bet is to visit the falls, retrace your steps 0.4 mile, then use the aforementioned Teneriffe Connector Trail.

If you're headed straight to the summit today, go left at the intersection with the Teneriffe Falls Trail, and at 1.4 miles from the trailhead, after crossing a couple of creeks by rock-hopping or on bridges, arrive at the signed junction with the Roaring Creek Trail to the left. This trail connects to Mount Si, and you can make several loops using it. For now, turn right and continue climbing until at 1.7 miles, you reach a signed junction pointing you toward the Talus Loop Trail (Hike 21) to the left, also leading to Mount Si and various other connecting trails. Go loopy if you choose, or stay the course on the Mount Teneriffe Trail and continue climbing, up, up, and up!

At 2.1 miles, the trail passes the Teneriffe Connector Trail. If you haven't visited the falls, you could use this gorgeous trail to pop on over to them on your way down. For now, though, continue ascending on the old roadway-turned-trail as it switches back and forth, giving you a break at times with views and even a rocky bench!

At 4.1 miles, arrive at a signed map pointing toward the Mount Si Connector Trail to the road's left. This primitive, but frequently used, trail goes off and up toward the Mount Si area, giving you an alternative option to hike a circular route and visit more scenery. The world is yours to explore! But, set on seeing Mount Teneriffe's summit, continue following the old road, which eventually eases up the stout grade. The road-turned-trail passes a couple of other defunct roads, one to the right and one to the left, but it's easy to stay on the obvious main path as you wind around to the east. At 5.5 miles, the trail narrows and leaves the road for the comfort of the evergreens.

From here, the trail climbs steeply again, then reaches a forested knoll, which rolls down and up to ultimately reach the rocky summit of Mount Teneriffe at 6.5 miles. Be as sure-footed as the mountain goats that frequent this area when you pose for your pictures and break out your snack, as the summit is a bit narrow and precarious. Views on a clear day up here make you feel blissfully happy to be alive. Several Cascades volcanos are on display saying hi, and you feel like you could touch the summits of the local North Bend peaks on all sides, such as Rattlesnake Ridge, Mount Washington, and Mailbox Peak. Rest the quads and knees before creaking back the way you came or using any one of the connecting trails.

24 Teneriffe Falls

RATING/DIFFICULTY: ****/3
ROUNDTRIP: 6.2 miles
ELEV GAIN/HIGH POINT: 1650 feet/2510 feet
SEASON: Year-round

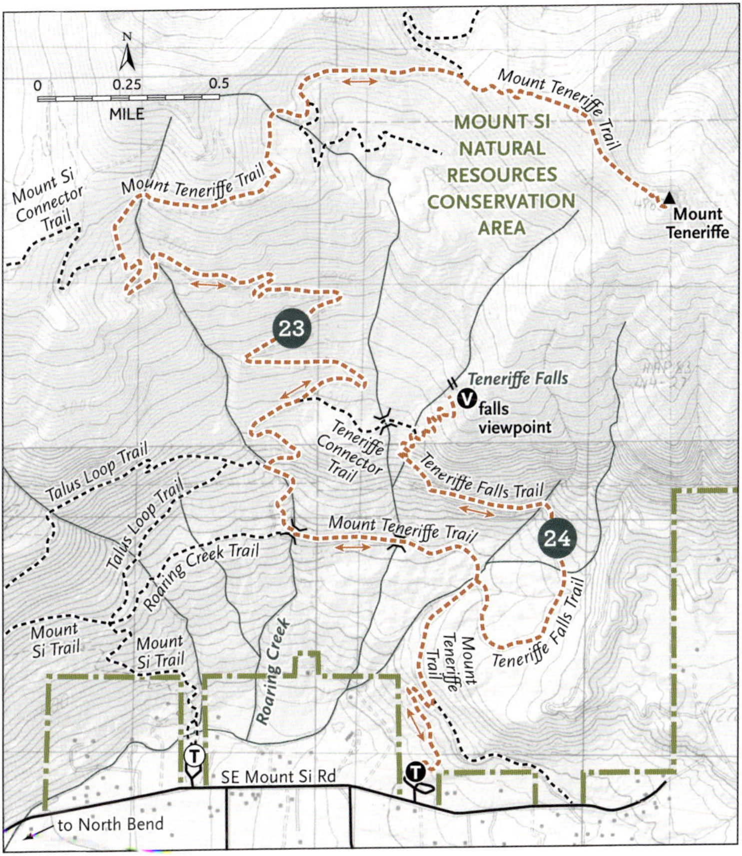

Maps: Green Trails Maps Mount Si NRCA No. 206S, Department of Natural Resources Mount Si NRCA Trail Map; **Contact:** Department of Natural Resources; **Notes:** Discover Pass required. Pit toilets at trailhead. Trailhead Direct bus (see Resources) is available most summers. The name of the waterfall was changed in recent years from Kamikaze Falls but may still appear this way on some maps and websites. The former trailhead was farther east on SE Mount Si Road and no longer serves as a parking area. Open to leashed dogs; **GPS:** N 47 29.207, W 121 45.599

Especially during snowmelt in spring, when the water is at its highest flow, the waterfall is a great place to visit and marvel at the roaring drops. Tucked deep into the forest, the whitewater cascades steeply through chunky rock with green, mossy edges, making for great photography options. There are two spots to see the falls—the lower and upper—and you'll want to visit them both on your trek. Even when it's not pumping, it's a peaceful place and a great workout to boot!

GETTING THERE

From I-90 near North Bend: Take exit 32 (436th Avenue SE) and head north. In 0.3 mile, take the second exit (to stay straight) at the roundabout. At 0.5 mile, take the second exit (going left) on SE North Bend Way. In 0.9 mile, turn right onto SE Mount Si Road. Continue, passing the trailheads for Little Si and Mount Si, until 3.9 miles, when you arrive at the large signed Mount Teneriffe trailhead to the road's left.

ON THE TRAIL

Walk toward the signed map kiosk and find the trail starting directly behind it. Pass through western hemlock, red alder, sword ferns, salal, and other native plants on a pleasant trail tread as you gently gain elevation. In 0.5 mile, reach a road-turned-trail at a signed junction and head left toward the falls.

A few social trails branch off the main trail, mostly to visit old stumps or the babbling creek to the left. Stay on the main trail until, at nearly 0.9 mile, you reach a signed intersection pointing you toward the falls to the right. The path you were following at this point goes to Mount Teneriffe's summit and other connecting trails along the way. Turn right and climb moderately for a couple hundred feet until the trail levels out. This, too, was a former logging road, and the grade becomes more mellow after the first little push.

At around 1.8 miles, peekaboo views to the left show off the valley below and Mount Washington across the interstate. These views will get better as you continue to climb, so unless you are aching to see them, hang tight—they get even better!

At almost 2 miles, the trail cuts back to the right on a switchback and loses the old road. From this point on, the trail is mostly rocky talus that will test even the most coordinated feet as it switches back and forth up the angled and somewhat precarious rocks. This area can also be a bit confusing, as social trails can accidentally lead you closer to the water on unofficial tread. If this happens, instead of continuing on the sketchy paths upward, go right, and eventually you'll run into the official trail, which is well-traveled and quite clear once you see it again.

The trail is steeper now, and the views open to the forested ridgelines of the Cedar River watershed and Mount Washington. Rattlesnake Mountain is visible, as is Truck Town in North Bend.

At 2.5 miles, arrive at the brand-new Teneriffe Connector Trail. The bridge, which is visible from the intersection, was installed in the fall of 2022, and the trail is now complete. If you want to make a loop and see a change of scenery on your way back, it's possible to use this trail. To do so, after seeing the falls, come back down to this trail and turn right here to reach the Mount Teneriffe Trail. Once there, turn left and follow the Mount Teneriffe Trail back to the trailhead. The whole distance

Teneriffe Falls is a purring ballet of mist, moss, and motion.

is roughly the same, and you'll be retracing 0.9 mile of trail after you pass the turnoff for Teneriffe Falls.

For now, more climbing continues until at 2.9 miles, a viewpoint to the left shows off the lower falls. The viewing areas are narrow, steep, and tight, so use caution as you visit. And if you choose to grab a snack, consider picnicking away from the viewing areas to give others the opportunity to see the sights.

You might be thinking this is the main event, but there's more!

Keep switching back, and arrive at a pullout where the upper falls is visible at 3.1 miles. It's a spectacular sight when it's really cranking, and you might even get misted. Some folks choose to drop down to cross the falls here and picnic on the other side, but use extreme caution should you decide to do that; it's slippery and could put a terrible ending on a great day.

In theory, the trail continues climbing above the upper falls and eventually, steeply and crudely, makes its way to Teneriffe summit. It's not approved for use by land managers because it is hazardous and unmaintained. It's best to use the Mount Teneriffe Trail to reach the top.

When you've loaded up your phone with great photographs, head back the way you came, or scoot off to the Teneriffe Connector Trail or other adjacent area trails to see something new.

25 Palouse to Cascades: Homestead Valley to Mine Creek Trestle

RATING/DIFFICULTY: **/2
ROUNDTRIP: 5.4 miles
ELEV GAIN/HIGH POINT: 550 feet/1470 feet
SEASON: Year-round

Maps: Green Trails Maps Mount Si NRCA No. 206S, Olallie State Park map; **Contact:** Washington State Parks; **Notes:** Discover Pass required. Pit toilets available at trailhead. As with many popular hikes, this one gets very crowded on weekends. Park only in allowable areas, and have a plan B hike if parking is full. The trailhead closes at dusk. Open to leashed dogs; **GPS:** N 47 26.507, W 121 40.331

Spend the afternoon wandering on an old railroad grade, passing a couple of high trestles, and enjoying the views of the Cascade foothills. Bring the whole

Where trains once roared, footsteps now whisper, crossing the trestles of time.

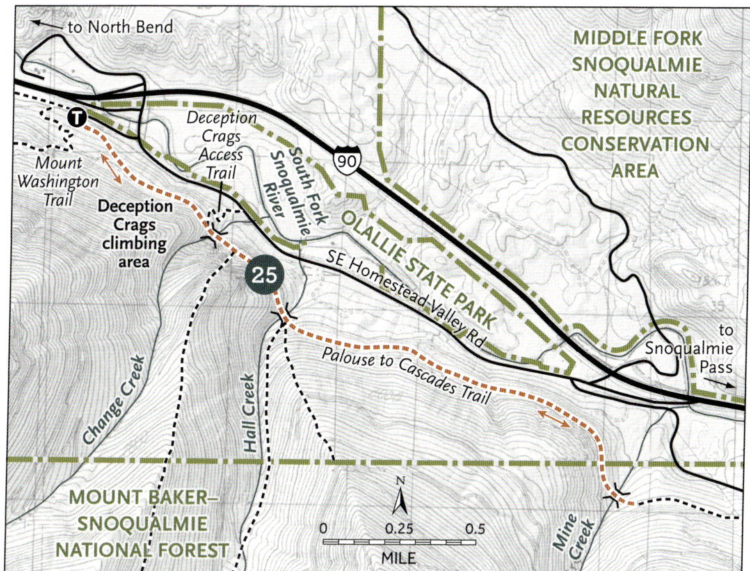

family on this one and make it as short or as long as you'd like—it's easy and enjoyable.

GETTING THERE

From I-90 near North Bend: Take exit 38 toward SE Homestead Valley Road. Turn right onto Homestead Valley Road and cross over the South Fork Snoqualmie River. At 0.1 mile from the exit, turn right into the driveway for Olallie State Park and find parking straight ahead.

ON THE TRAIL

Locate the steep connector trail between two boulders in the parking area's southwest corner, and follow it up for 0.1 mile to a service road. Follow the service road to the right to 0.2 mile to meet with the former Chicago, Milwaukee, St. Paul, and Pacific Railway path, now a wide gravel trail. Turn left and begin a much flatter walk.

The trains that used to run on this track connected the Milwaukee and Chicago areas to Seattle and the West Coast and carried a variety of cargo, from passengers to goods. With heavy snow, avalanches, and fire dangers ever looming, the trains continued to persevere. The original lines were established in the Pacific Northwest in 1909, and by 1917, the first electrified trains ran on these tracks—a breakthrough in technology at that point that allowed the trains to be more powerful against nature's elements. Throughout the decades, financial difficulty ensued until the trains finally quit their runs in 1980. By 1984, Washington State Parks had acquired the tracks with the intent of creating recreational opportunities. Today, the trains' legacy lives on, only now as a playground for muscle-powered sports. You can still see evidence of the train era in some antiquated railroad ties strewn here and there, and the former powerlines that once supported their efforts.

At 0.9 mile, a rock-climbing area known as Deception Crags is adjacent to the trail. In summer months, the clicking and clacking of carabiners against bolts and their gear stations are prevalent as the climbers make their way up the various sport routes. It's fun to stop and watch them gracefully move up rock like it ain't no thing. A port-a-potty and picnic areas are found here too. If you ever want to get up to this spot quickly, a spur trail connects down to the Homestead Valley Road at this location.

Immediately after the climbing area, the lofty Change Creek Trestle guides you across Change Creek and the thick vegetation below you. There is much to see as you enjoy the views of the creek and the peaks across I-90, such as Mailbox and Dirty Harrys.

At 1.2 miles, stop and enjoy the Hall Creek Trestle, another elevated structure carrying you high across the active creek far below. Imagine a fast train racing through these mountains over this high perch!

The walk continues with forested thickets followed by sweeping views across the I-90 corridor and pockets of wildflowers like coltsfoot and pearly everlasting.

At 2.7 miles, arrive at the Mine Creek Trestle, the third on our journey. The mountains around this bridge are welcoming with their forested shoulders and lingering high-country snow in springtime. Walk a bit farther to tag the trestle's far end if you wish, then meander back the way you came. If you haven't had enough walking, continue following the old railroad grade for as far and as long as you desire.

26 Palouse to Cascades: Cedar Falls to Iron Horse Falls

RATING/DIFFICULTY: **/1
ROUNDTRIP: 6.2 miles
ELEV GAIN/HIGH POINT: 280 feet/1210 feet
SEASON: Year-round

Maps: Green Trails Maps Mount Si NRCA No. 206S, Olallie State Park map; **Contact:** Washington State Parks; **Notes:** Discover Pass required. Pit toilets and picnic areas available near the trailhead. Alternative parking at the adjacent Rattlesnake Ledge trailhead (Hike 30). As with many popular hikes, this one gets very crowded on weekends. The trailhead closes at dusk. Open to leashed dogs, stock, bicycles; **GPS:** N 47 25.960, W 121 45.976

The journey is the destination as you wander through history on the former route of the Chicago, Milwaukee, St. Paul, and Pacific Railway. You can make this hike as long or as short as you wish, but a pleasant, easy goal is Iron Horse Falls, which drops effortlessly down Boetzke Creek.

GETTING THERE

From I-90 near North Bend: Take exit 32 for 436th Avenue SE and head south. The road becomes Cedar Falls Road SE in a short distance. Follow Cedar Falls Road for 3 miles, passing the signed Rattlesnake Lake Recreation Area to the right. Locate the signed Cedar Falls trailhead to the road's left at 3.1 miles, and find ample parking.

ON THE TRAIL

From the parking area, walk toward the restrooms and find the paved pathway. At 0.1 mile, an informational kiosk to the left shares

Iron Horse Falls plunges a dramatic 150 feet along the Palouse to Cascades Trail—a hidden marvel tucked into Washington's historic rail corridor.

details on the Chicago, Milwaukee, St. Paul, and Pacific Railway and also some helpful information on the surrounding area. Follow the arrow to the right and then proceed, passing a defunct forest road. In 0.2 mile, turn left at another arrow and follow the connector trail up to the obvious old railroad grade.

Make a left on the railroad grade and head east through mature evergreens and the occasional deciduous tree, such as bigleaf maple. A large, horizontal sign noting Cedar Falls sits to the left—a vestige from the substation that was once near this area.

At 0.8 mile, the trail crosses a small bridge over Boxley Creek (a peaceful dribble in the summer months), then reaches a signed junction to the right for Cedar Butte (see Hike 27). Peeks of Mount Si and Mount Teneriffe are visible through the trees as you make your way along the wide swath.

The Olallie Trail, along with a map kiosk, appears to the right at 2 miles. This trail climbs up through second-growth forest, until it eventually passes a cutoff for Mount Washington and dead-ends in 9 miles. While it's technically open to feet and hooves, it was built with mountain bikers in mind, with banked turns, tight switchbacks, and technical biking elements. Mountain bikers are the primary users and zip down this trail on knobby wheels, enjoying the heck out of the fast, flowy grade. Should you attempt to trail run or hike this trail, avoid headphones and keep on your toes.

Two bridges are up next, one at 2.6 miles and another 2.7 miles. Both have water trickles over wet areas, but neither are as impressive as the one up next—our destination! At 3.1 miles, reach a trestle over Boetzke Creek with the graceful, horsetail-shaped Iron Horse Falls to the right. In springtime during snowmelt, it's much more impressive than in summer months, as it drops a total height of 150 feet in cascading whitewater.

After viewing the falls, you can continue walking to your heart's content, or head back the way you came and call it a day.

27 Cedar Butte

RATING/DIFFICULTY: ***/3

ROUNDTRIP: 4.4 miles

ELEV GAIN/HIGH POINT: 980 feet/1873 feet

SEASON: Year-round

Map: Green Trails Maps Rattlesnake Mountain No. 205S; **Contact:** Washington State Parks; **Notes:** Discover Pass required. Pit toilets and picnic areas available near the trailhead. Alternative parking at the adjacent Rattlesnake Ledge trailhead (Hike 29). Open to leashed dogs, mountain bikes (to saddle junction), and stock (on railroad grade); **GPS:** N 47 25.960, W 121 45.976

Cedar Butte is like Rattlesnake Ledge's little brother, only without the crowds and giant views. The heavily forested trail leads to the summit where peekaboo views of Mount Si, Mount Teneriffe, and the bustling I-90 are showcased. It won't blow your mind with panoramas, but it's got good ambiance and is a decent place to get away from the masses if Rattlesnake is overwhelmed with visitors.

GETTING THERE

From I-90 near North Bend: Take exit 32 and head south. You are on 436th Avenue SE, though it becomes Cedar Falls Road SE in a short distance. Follow Cedar Falls Road for 3 miles, passing the Rattlesnake Lake

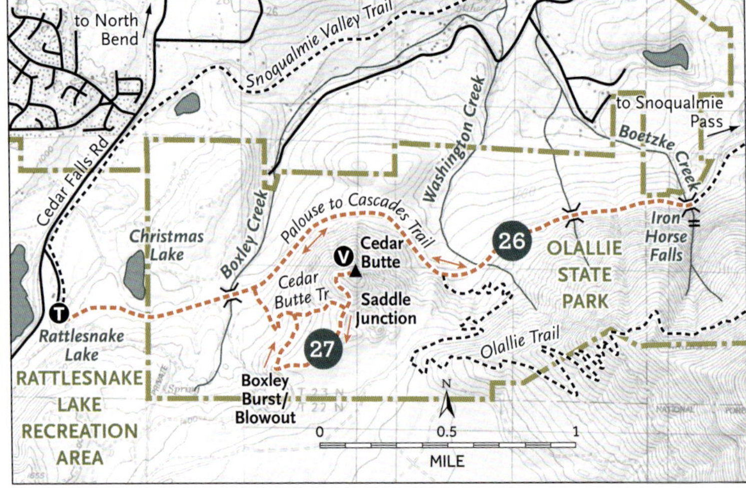

Recreation Area, until you arrive at the Cedar Falls trailhead on the left (also signed Palouse to Cascades Trail). Park here and don't forget to display your Discover Pass.

ON THE TRAIL

Locate the trailhead by walking northeast, toward the pit toilets and informational kiosks. A sign with a drawing of a hiker points to the right, 200 feet from the parking area. Turn right, cross an old forest service road, and continue up the wide trail, also a former forest road. In 0.1 mile, the trail switches back to the left, and in 0.2 mile it arrives at the Palouse to Cascades Trail. This used to be part of the Chicago, Milwaukee, St. Paul, and Pacific Railway from 1909 to 1980, but today it serves as a recreational wonderland. Turn left, heading east on the wide route, enjoying the gentle grade of the former railroad's route.

At 0.8 mile, cross a bridge over Boxley Creek and prepare to start looking to your right for the trail. The Cedar Butte Trail comes up on you quickly, but you'll know it when you see it, because a small tree holds a sign for the trail and an unmistakable single-track pathway leads up into the hinterlands. Once you see it, head right and start your climb.

At 1.2 miles, arrive at an unsigned Y junction. The path I'm outlining will lead you back to this spot toward the end of our journey, so make a mental note, but stay straight for now. Up, up, up you go, steeply at times, through salal at your feet and a mix of conifers and deciduous trees above you.

Just when you need to catch your breath, the trail levels out and arrives at what is known as Saddle Junction at 1.5 miles. A tree sign is a bit confusing, pointing to the summit (left) and blowout (right). We are headed to the summit but will come back to this spot once we've been to the top. So turn left and start toward the view. Another sign confirms you are going the right way, pointing to the fragile summit, which is off-limits to horses and bikes.

At 1.8 miles, arrive at a small viewpoint toward Rattlesnake Lake and its picturesque ledges. The top is only 0.1 mile away—keep on pushing!

Grab a snack at the top and enjoy the evergreen-framed views of the Middle Fork Snoqualmie River valley and the neighboring peaks. The metal geodetic survey marker (benchmark) attached to a rock at the top makes the ten-year-old in me snicker every time, as it says "Ceder Butt" (said her butt) instead of Cedar Butte. The National Geodetic Survey department of NOAA has it listed as Cedar Butte but recognizes that the embossed stamp says this. Someone from 1937 who put it there is still probably laughing at that one.

When it's time to go down, you might get a bit confused when you see an arrow on a tree pointing southwest. Long ago, this was a loop and a short way to get back to the summit trail you came up on, but over the years, the trail has dwindled and is hard to find. Some summers after a fair bit of traffic, it's obvious, but in the shoulder seasons it can be overgrown. If you aren't sure about it, simply trace your steps back down from the summit until you arrive at Saddle Junction again. You are now 2.4 miles from the trailhead and probably feel those good endorphins kicking in!

This time at Saddle Junction, point your boots toward the blowout and follow the trail southwest. This stretch of trail has some of the most gorgeous specimens of vine maples I've ever encountered. Some even bend across the trail as archways, as if to welcome you to a secret hiding spot. The lengthy, pliable vine

Though the leaves of vine maples steal the show in fall, winter reveals their moss-draped arms stretching over the trail near Cedar Butte.

maple stems were used by the Indigenous people for basket weaving, fish traps, bows, arrows, and even some hand tools.

In just shy of 2.8 miles, arrive at a few boot trails that head off to the left. The valley below you, now looking only like a sea of deciduous woods, is where the Boxley Burst—or Boxley Blowout—occurred in the early morning hours of December 23, 1918. Water from high rain volumes backed up behind a masonry dam and seeped into the ground, causing the land to be become unstable. That fateful December predawn morning, a surge of water caused half a million cubic yards of earth and gravel to pull off the hillside and sent the cementlike mixture down the valley into Boxley Creek. Picking up speed from runoff, the mixture turned into a 150-foot-wide river and made a beeline for the now extinct mill town of Edgewick. A diligent night watchman recognized the landscape changing and swiftly acted. He ran around screaming and blowing a whistle, waking up residents who scrambled for high ground in the darkness. By the time it was over, nearly every building in the town was destroyed and the logging operation had no hope of rebuilding and resuming operations.

With history swirling in your mind, follow the trail as it descends and arrives back at the unsigned Y junction where we were earlier in our trek, at 3.2 miles. Turn left here and descend back to the railroad grade. Once on the railroad grade, turn left, the way you arrived.

28 Twin Falls

RATING/DIFFICULTY: *****/2

ROUNDTRIP: 2.5 miles

ELEV GAIN/HIGH POINT: 760 feet/1340 feet

SEASON: Year-round

Maps: Green Trails Maps Mount Si NRCA No. 206S, Olallie State Park map; **Contact:**

Washington State Parks; **Notes:** Discover Pass required. Pit toilets available at trailhead. As with many popular hikes, this one gets full on weekends. Park only in allowable areas, and have a plan B hike if parking is not available. There are two trailheads for this hike—this hike description is from the lower trailhead. The upper trailhead closes at dusk. Open to leashed dogs; **GPS:** N 47 27.164, W 121 42.320

There are two ways to see this beautiful pair of foamy, cascading waterfalls—the upper approach and the lower approach. The lower, as described here, contains less elevation gain to the first viewpoint, a noble goal if you are hiking with wee ones. However far you decide to roam, you are sure to be in awe at the spectacular falls, the lower one being the tallest waterfall along the South Fork Snoqualmie River!

GETTING THERE

Main (Lower) trailhead: From I-90 near North Bend, take exit 34 for 468th Avenue SE and head south off the freeway. In 0.6 mile, turn left onto SE 159th Street. Continue to 1.2 miles, where you'll find the trailhead at the end of the roadway.

Alternative (Upper) trailhead: From I-90 near North Bend, take exit 38 toward SE Homestead Valley Road. Turn right onto Homestead Valley Road, cross over the South Fork Snoqualmie River, and in 0.1 mile, turn right into the driveway for Olallie State Park and find parking straight ahead. To get to the Twin Falls Trail from here, follow the steep connector trail that starts between two boulders to the parking area's southwest, and in 0.1 mile, go right at the T intersection on a service road. Follow the service road to the former railroad grade and continue on what

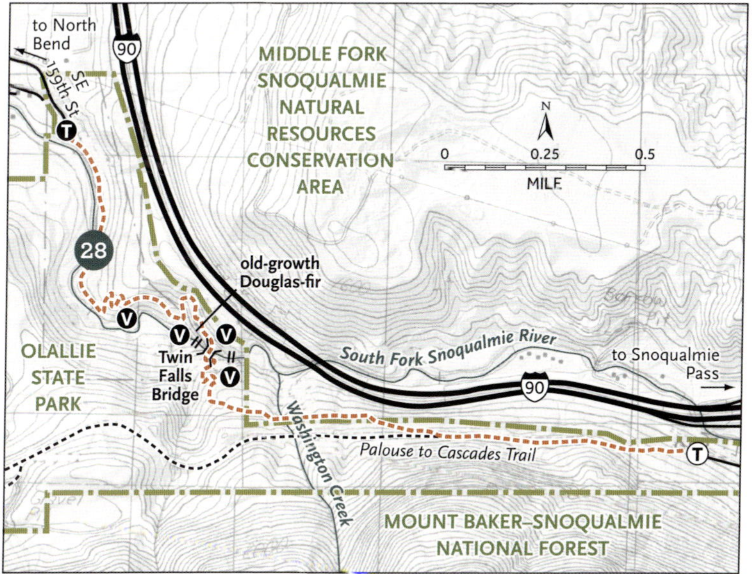

The tiered horsetails of falling water is one of the breathtaking sights on the Twin Falls Trail.

is now called the Palouse to Cascades Trail. Walk right (west) for 0.4 mile to find the Twin Falls Trail on your right.

ON THE TRAIL

The walk begins through a gorgeous smattering of mature Douglas-fir, western hemlock, and western red cedar. At your knees and feet, thimbleberry, goatsbeard, devil's club, and queen's cup show in spring and summer months.

The trail grade is mellow and the soundtrack the purring white noise from the South Fork Snoqualmie River, which is off to the right. As you continue, bigleaf and vine maple in the fall make this an earth-toned vision backed by the mossy green rocks near the water's edge.

In 0.5 mile, that gentle grade you have been following turns uphill and starts switchbacking to the first viewpoint. This climb can be tough if you aren't in good shape, gaining 200 feet in 0.3 mile to arrive at your first vista of Lower Twin Falls. If this is your turnaround spot, you should be quite happy with this glimpse—it's breathtaking even from this distance.

Once you've enjoyed the viewpoint, continue onward on a somewhat new stretch of trail, rebuilt after flooding washed it away in part in 2014. An ancient Douglas-fir, estimated to be between 400 and 600 years old, is an interesting feature to the right. The protective fencing has been in disrepair for a few years, so admire it from a distance and avoid stepping on its veins (roots).

From here the trail climbs again, gaining elevation until at 1 mile it reaches a junction to the right with a series of steps going down to a spectacular viewpoint of the lower falls. Though well-protected with wooden railings, in snowy winters or during heavy rains, these boards can be slippery, so watch your footing carefully. The tiered horsetails of the whitewater are roughly 15 feet wide and angled over 80 degrees in pitch as they hammer into a cliff band that has worn away with time. The 135-foot drop of this powerful water is awe-inspiring and slightly shivery all at once. Standing on the wooden platforms gets you a front-row seat to the magnificence.

What goes down must come back up, so plod back up the stairs, and head left to continue. The trail climbs up a bit, then drops on a series of trail steps to deliver you to a large, wooden pedestrian bridge between the two waterfalls at 1.2 miles. From here, you can get a view of the upper falls, a series of two drops falling 30 feet with sheer force and strength. Many people turn back here, but if the day is young and your energy is buzzing, continue uphill for another 0.1 mile to an upper falls viewpoint, behind a wooden support railing. It's less impressive than the other viewpoints but allows for a slightly better peek at the depth of the upper falls. Turn back when you've enjoyed all the fun . . . or read on for more options.

EXTENDING YOUR HIKE

If you're still full of vigor and want more of a workout, you could follow the trail as it ascends (and ends) at the railroad-turned-trail Palouse to Cascades Trail, 0.8 mile from the upper falls viewpoint. Walk either direction on the fairly flat Palouse to Cascades Trail and prolong your outdoor time. If you *really* want to kick your booty, head left and find the Mount Washington Trail (Hike 65) located off the Palouse to Cascades Trail to the south at 0.3 mile. Make sure you have a functioning headlamp, carry plenty of food and water, and are feeling like a champ before taking on a day like this . . . it's a killer of a day in the Cascades.

29 Bare Mountain

RATING/DIFFICULTY: ***/4
ROUNDTRIP: 8.3 miles
ELEV GAIN/HIGH POINT: 3180 feet/5353 feet
SEASON: Year-round

Maps: Green Trails Maps Mount Si No. 174 and Skykomish No. 175; **Contact:** Mount Baker–Snoqualmie National Forest, Snoqualmie Ranger District; **Notes:** Northwest Forest Pass or Interagency Pass required. Bring water shoes for crossing Bear Creek if the weather has recently been wet, or if you'd prefer to wade instead of crossing on logs or rocks. The drive to the trailhead is on a narrow dirt road with potholes—high clearance vehicles highly recommended. Allow an extra hour each direction for the rough road. Once you leave the town of North Bend, there are no more services or restrooms. Open to leashed dogs; **GPS:** N 47 38.381, W 121 31.725

This hike is in the boonies. In fact, when you look at a larger map, you'll see this peak is actually closer to Highway 2 than North Bend and is quite remote. So, what does that mean? Less crowds, more solitude, and probably a place you've never been. The road getting there is rough and you might shed a few tears on behalf of your vehicle if you don't go slowly enough, but once you get there you'll love the views, quietness, and tranquility. It's worth the effort!

GETTING THERE

From I-90 near North Bend: Take exit 31 in North Bend and head northwest toward town. You will now be on Bendigo Boulevard S. In just over 0.9 mile, go right on W. North Bend Way. At 1 mile, turn left on Ballarat Avenue N. Stay on Ballarat Avenue N. as it winds its way north and changes names to SE 108th Street and 428th Avenue SE and, finally, North Fork Road SE.

At just over 5 miles from the freeway, veer left on the poorly signed North Fork Road SE (Forest Road 57). The road is signed "Dead End in 24 Miles." At 5.7 miles, the pavement ends and the road narrows. Proceed on the rough gravel road until 23.2 miles, when the road makes a hard left and crosses over

Lennox Creek. Immediately afterward, take the next right and stay on FR 57 until you reach the trailhead to the road's left at 26.4 miles.

ON THE TRAIL

This trail is part of the Alpine Lakes Wilderness, so be sure to fill out your free wilderness-use permit before you hit the rocky trail. From 1905 to 1934, this pathway was an old road that carried mined minerals out of Bear Creek Mine, not far from here. Over the years, the slope has attracted water runoff and now is more of a rough, dry creek bed, but at least we don't have to bushwhack!

At 0.7 mile, reach a crossing with Bear Creek, which can be high after big rains or spring runoff. Usually, it can be crossed on a log or by rock-hopping with fancy footwork to keep dry shoes. If conditions are concerning, or you possess the coordination of a drunk wallaby, you might want to wade and save yourself the embarrassment of going in the drink.

After Bear Creek, the conditions get less rocky, and we can breathe a sigh of relief as we cross Bear Creek again, this time on a bridge. Perplexingly, Bare Mountain is our destination, but Bear Creek is the water source. Is this a mistake or intentional? The top of the peak is barren and filled with berries, which would naturally attract bears, so . . . hmmm . . . the mystery deepens.

The trail officially enters the Alpine Lakes Wilderness and an often-overgrown hillside traverse. Thimbleberry, goatsbeard, bracken fern, and other plants try to take over the pathway, so whack 'em back and help your fellow trail trodders.

Painting the landscape in seasonal splendor, fall colors line the trail near the summit of Bare Mountain.

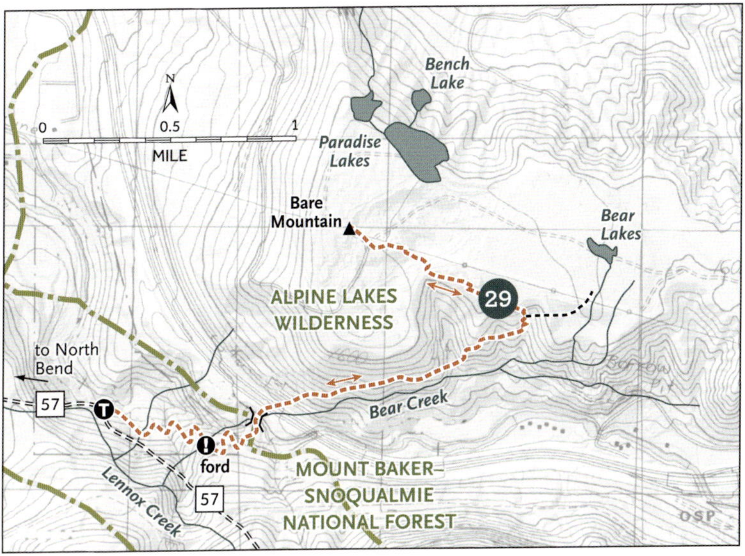

At 1.9 miles, the trail takes a hard left and begins switchbacking steeply up the slopes of Bare Mountain. Near this area, you're likely to see a faint boot path to the right leading up toward the old mining area and some remaining rusty equipment. It's an interesting place to wander if time permits, but be sure you have good navigational skills and can find your way back, since it's not obvious.

Views of Mount Rainier show up to the south and give you a good excuse to stop and snap a few photos without letting the others in your group know you really needed to stop because you are out of breath. For that pro tip, you're welcome. Beargrass, Sitka mountain ash, and rosy spirea make this area a vision in the summer. In the fall, autumn colors explode here!

As you near the top, a couple of vantage points look down onto the two Paradise Lakes in the valley to the north, and before you know it, you are on the summit at just over 4.1 miles! A classic L-4 fire tower stood on this peak from 1935 to 1973; its rusty metal supports still standing are a testament to its past. If the weather is crystal clear, Glacier Peak—one of the Pacific Northwest's most elusive volcanoes—can be seen, as well as distant peaks north into the Alpine Lakes Wilderness. Enjoy every sweet drop, then head back when you are ready to face the road again.

30 Rattlesnake Ledge

RATING/DIFFICULTY: *****/3

ROUNDTRIP: 4.6 miles

ELEV GAIN/HIGH POINT: 1160 feet/2080 feet

SEASON: Year-round

Map: Green Trails Maps Rattlesnake Mountain No. 205S; **Contact:** Seattle Public

Sometimes the cloudiest days make for the best sunsets on the three Rattlesnake Ledges.

Utilities; **Notes:** No passes required (subject to change). Privy available at trailhead. Especially weekends and summer days, parking is extremely challenging; obey all parking signs and barriers. Illegally parked vehicles will be cited and towed. Expect crowds year-round, with exception of early morning or late evening. Garbage and recycling available near trailhead. Be sure to tell others to avoid putting stickers and graffiti on posts, signs, bridges, and rocks (because we know you aren't doing this). Gate is open from dawn to dusk. Though this hike is usually lowland enough for year-round hiking, snow may be present in the winter, and shoe traction is sometimes necessary. Rules governing this park are changing soon; refer to the land managers for the most up-to-date information. Open to dogs under voice command (under review currently and subject to change, refer to posted signs); see map p. 124; **GPS:** N 47 43.475, W 121 76.878

If you want a massive payoff with views, without too much distance, this is the hike. Because the sweeping panoramic views of Chester Morse Lake, the Middle Fork valley, and the mighty peaks of the Cascades are so outstanding, it makes an incredible day hike—and word of that has spread. With over 300,000 visitors a year, you likely won't be by yourself on this jaunt. I hike this trail frequently, as I live around the corner, and being solo on the summit has only happened three times in over fifteen years. That said, smiling faces abound, as folks are beaming when they reach their lofty goal.

GETTING THERE

From I-90 near North Bend: Take exit 32 and head south. You are on 436th Avenue SE, though it becomes Cedar Falls Road SE in a short distance. At 2.4 miles, come to the signed Rattlesnake Lake Recreation Area to the right. Drive past the open gate and take your first left to find several large parking areas.

ON THE TRAIL

From the parking area, you can see Rattlesnake Ledge sticking out proudly, and it's almost hard to believe you'll be standing on top of that great prominence! To find the trail, locate the wide service road behind a gate to the lake's north. Follow the path as it curves around the northern tip of Rattlesnake Lake and arrives at the official trailhead, complete with toilets and an interpretive sign. The trail starts to the road's right at 0.3 mile from the parking area, but distance can vary depending on how far away you parked.

Thanks to Washington Trails Association, a trail facelift in the post-Covid era has made the trail wider, more sustainable, and better able to drain during wet weather.

In just under a mile, a small log bench appears to the right. It's sloped and not the most comfortable trailside perch but will do if you need to catch your breath or fish out your water bottle.

A keen eye will find tree markers along the path, indicating distance traveled since the trailhead. In just over a mile from the official trailhead, the grade steepens and the path crosses a small bridge over a seasonal dribble, which rages in the wet season. At 1.1 miles, the trail takes a hard switchback to the right, but some folks go off-trail and go straight ahead at this point because they hear an unnamed creek and expect a large waterfall. The small canyon that houses the water is deceitfully echo-y, and it's pretty disappointing to find it's just cascading water and not the big feature you expect. Stay on the trail and save your energy—there's more steep stuff ahead.

At 1.2 miles, arrive at a second bridge, again over a seasonal creeklet. Like the first, this bridge is flat and a nice reprieve from the climbing. All too soon, the huffing and puffing starts again, this time with only two long switchbacks left.

At 1.9 miles, arrive at a signed Y junction. Turn right and follow the magical wooden trail stairs another 0.1 mile as they lead high to Ledge 1. At the top, a large fissure in the rock can be tricky to get across, so many choose to walk to the right side of the rock and find a place to sit and enjoy. Brave ones hop it and find their roost on the other side. Whatever you do, please be careful. There is no guardrail, and lives have been lost up here over the years.

Enjoy the mountain and valley views. When you are done, head back to the signed Y junction and either go back down or follow the ridgeline northwest as it climbs steeply to more rocky ledges (Ledges 2 and 3) a half mile or so one way.

If you are really feeling motivated, continue on the trail to East Peak and a tower with a limited Snoqualmie Valley view, visiting the other peaks as you go. Checking out East Peak from Ledge No. 1 will cost you 5 miles roundtrip and 1350 feet more of elevation gain. Or . . . heck, hike across all of Rattlesnake Mountain (Hike 30). Whatever you decide, it's a great way to spend a day.

31 Rattlesnake Lake Pathway

RATING/DIFFICULTY: ***/1

ROUNDTRIP: 1.5 miles

ELEV GAIN/HIGH POINT: 100 feet/1010 feet

SEASON: Year-round

Map: Green Trails Maps Rattlesnake Mountain No. 205S; **Contact:** Washington State

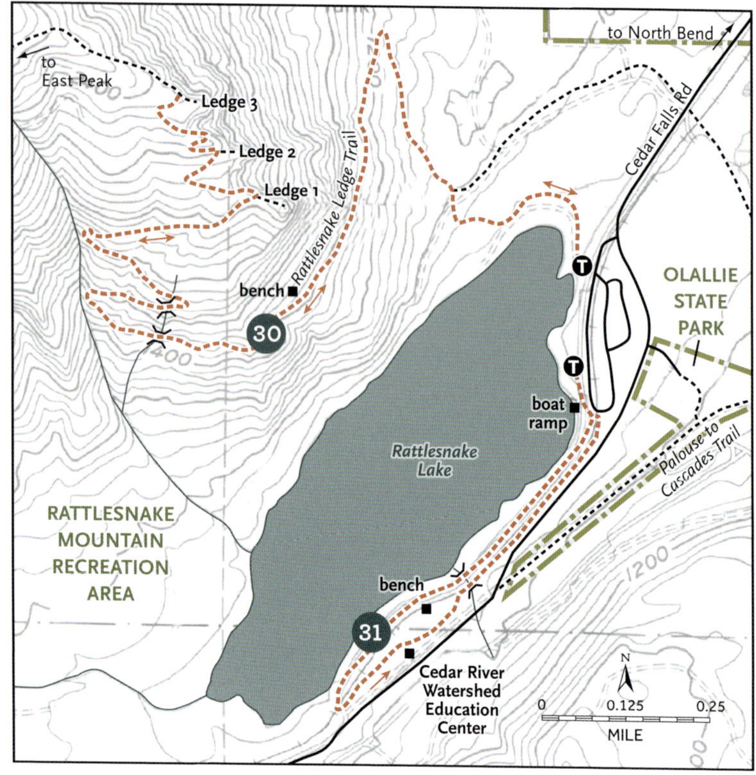

Parks; **Notes:** ADA-accessible trail. Pit toilets and picnic areas available near the trailhead. Cedar River Watershed Education Center open Thursday–Friday (12–4 PM) and Saturdays (10 AM–4 PM). Hours are subject to change; check website for hours (see Resources). Open to dogs, bicycles; **GPS:** N 47 25.996, W 121 46.162

This primarily paved pathway is ideal for sauntering, pushing a stroller or wheelchair, or riding bikes. Views from the pathway showcase the lake and the ledge, and the Cedar River Watershed Education Center is a good place to learn all about the water for the City of Seattle and environs. While this trail doesn't go all the way around the lake, it does make a nice loop that is doable for almost all abilities. What's more, the lake often drops low enough that you can divert off this pathway and walk around the lake's shoreline, if conditions are permissible.

GETTING THERE

From I-90 near North Bend: Take exit 32 and head south. You are on 436th Avenue SE, though it becomes Cedar Falls Road SE in a short distance. Continue for 2.8 miles, until you arrive at a large sign for Rattlesnake Lake and the Rattlesnake Ledge Trail. Go right and pass through the gate, noting the closing time (usually dawn to dusk) so you don't get stuck behind it. Park and walk toward the lake.

ON THE TRAIL

From the parking area, locate the pit toilets and informational kiosk, then turn left (southwest) and follow the paved trail as it wanders along the eastern edge of Rattlesnake Lake. It's tempting to visit the lake and snap pictures in this spot, so enjoy it to your heart's content, then continue walking the paved path when you're ready. In roughly 400 feet, arrive at the boat ramp where kayakers, fisherman, and stand-up paddle boarders are usually busy in the summer months.

At 0.2 mile, an educational sign shares how to spot wildlife. There are two bald eagles who nest in this area and are often hanging out in one of the tallest deciduous trees on the opposite side of the lake. Do you see them? They are hard to spot, so look closely or pull up your binoculars if you brought them.

A signed trail junction points toward the Cedar River Watershed Education Center to the left at 0.3 mile. We will return to this spot via this trail upon completing our loop. For now, stay straight on the paved pathway and continue the amble. Garbage cans and an outhouse are close by if you need them. Several small boot paths connect to the lake from the main trail and lure hikers down to get up close and personal with the lake; photograph it, touch it, feel it!

At 0.4 mile, arrive at a wooden bridge crossing an inlet creek from the Cedar River watershed. These cascades beg for a slow-motion video or a slow shutter speed, especially when they are really cranking. You'll also likely notice the bat boxes around the pathway. The thin boxes with narrow horizontal openings are perfect for protection, allowing bats to raise their young and keep warm or cool. Bats are highly beneficial to the ecosystem, as they keep insect populations in check, are great pollinators, and help keep the biodiversity of the natural world in balance. Fun fact: Bats aren't actually blind! While their vision isn't sharp, they have small, sensitive eyes that help them adapt to darkness. They also use echolocation and, through soundwaves, can find their way around quickly in complete blackness.

A well-placed bench for sitting and watching the world go by appears at 0.5 mile. This is a good point to stop and consider options. If you want to explore the whole lake and the waterline is low enough, you can drop down to the shoreline and walk the rocky lakeside perimeter. You'll have to hop across a couple of inlet creeks at the lake's far southwestern side, but it's usually possible to keep your shoes dry. If the lake is really low, you might even see the foundations of the former community of Moncton.

Long before Rattlesnake Lake was here, the community of Moncton took up this basin. Built not far from the rail line of the Chicago, Milwaukee, St. Paul, and Pacific Railway, workers (and their families) primarily in the industries of logging, railroad, and water services, took up residence here. A hotel, barbershop, saloon, restaurants, indoor

Pause, rest, and enjoy the view from this bench alongside the Rattlesnake Lake Pathway.

swimming pool, and a few stores provided services to those who lived in this mountain community. In May of 1915, with more than 200 people living in the town, the masonry dam upstream began to seep, and slowly, the town became flooded. By the end of that year, Rattlesnake Lake had formed, leaving the former town underwater. Thankfully, it happened slowly enough that residents were able to recover some personal items before they evacuated. Eventually they received compensation for their land. The lake remains today, hiding most evidence of the town, save for some bricks, driveways, and chimneys, evident in low-water times.

Immediately after the bench, two side trails to the left make shortcuts to the loop. If you feel the need to get there quicker, you can take one; otherwise, stay on the paved path and at 0.7 mile, arrive at an outhouse followed by a hairpin turn to the left.

Follow the hairpin turn and the paved pathway to reach the Cedar River Watershed Education Center at 0.9 mile. The green building and its collection of rain drums in the forest court are fun to see, as is the watershed exhibit (look up hours before you go). Restrooms are usually open at the center, even when the exhibits aren't.

Folks needing pavement for ADA or stroller access will be content turning back after they visit the watershed and retracing their steps. Otherwise, continue walking northeast until arriving at an unsigned crushed-gravel trail. Follow this trail as it descends, then crosses a wooden bridge over a waterway. At 1.3 miles, the gravel trail delivers you back to the paved trail to complete your loop. Head back the way you came, and maybe even consider a trip up to Rattlesnake Ledge (Hike 30) if time and vigor permit.

32 Rattlesnake Mountain

RATING/DIFFICULTY: ****/4
ONE-WAY: 10.7 miles
ELEV GAIN/HIGH POINT: 2670 feet/3415 feet
SEASON: Oct–May (year-round to Stans Overlook)

Map: Green Trails Maps Rattlesnake Mountain No. 205S; **Contact:** Department of Natural Resources and Seattle Public Utilities; **Notes:** Discover Pass required at Rattlesnake Mountain Snoqualmie Point trailhead. No passes required at Rattlesnake Ledge trailhead (subject to change). Two trailheads connect Rattlesnake Mountain—one on the west (Rattlesnake Mountain Snoqualmie Point trailhead) and one on the east (Rattlesnake Lake trailhead). This hike may use either trailhead for out and back, or make it a thru hike with two cars: one at each trailhead. This trail description starts at Rattlesnake Mountain Snoqualmie Point trailhead. Privy and picnic areas available at trailheads. Especially weekends and summer days, parking is extremely challenging; obey all parking signs and barriers. Illegally parked vehicles will be cited and towed. Gate is open from dawn to dusk at both ends. Rattlesnake Mountain Snoqualmie Point trailhead is a car-prowl hot spot; avoid leaving any valuables in vehicle. Roundtrip distances: Stans Overlook 4.1 miles, Grand Prospect 8.4 miles. Elevation gain: Stans Overlook 1030 feet, Grand Prospect 2110 feet. High points: Stans Overlook 2120 feet, Grand Prospect 3090 feet. Open to leashed dogs (mountain bikes and stock on adjacent trails); **GPS:** (Rattlesnake Mountain Snoqualmie Point trailhead) N 47 30.557, W 121 50.650, (Rattlesnake Ledge trailhead) N 47 43.475, W 121 76.878

You've no doubt heard about Rattlesnake Ledge, but did you know you could get there by starting from a western trailhead and traversing Rattlesnake Mountain? This hike makes a challenging day, so you may want to leave a car at each trailhead and do a thru hike if you decide to go the whole 10.7 miles to Rattlesnake Lake. But, you don't have to go all the way for views, workouts, and worthy destinations! Starting at the western side of Rattlesnake Mountain, you could climb up to Stans Overlook, where a couple of benches and a picnic table allow you hang out with a peekaboo view of the Snoqualmie Valley. Should you decide to continue, a viewpoint called Grand Prospect makes for a challenging and scenic goal—with even better views of the valley below and Mount Si to the north. Keep going through clear-cut lands with Rainier views until passing East Peak and eventually all three of Rattlesnake's ledges. Or turn back whenever you want for a good workout with far fewer crowds than the Rattlesnake Ledge approach.

GETTING THERE

Main trailhead (Rattlesnake Mountain Snoqualmie Point): From I-90 eastbound near North Bend, take exit 27, turn right on Winery Road, and continue for 0.3 mile. Turn right into the Rattlesnake Mountain Snoqualmie Point trailhead and find the large parking area straight ahead.

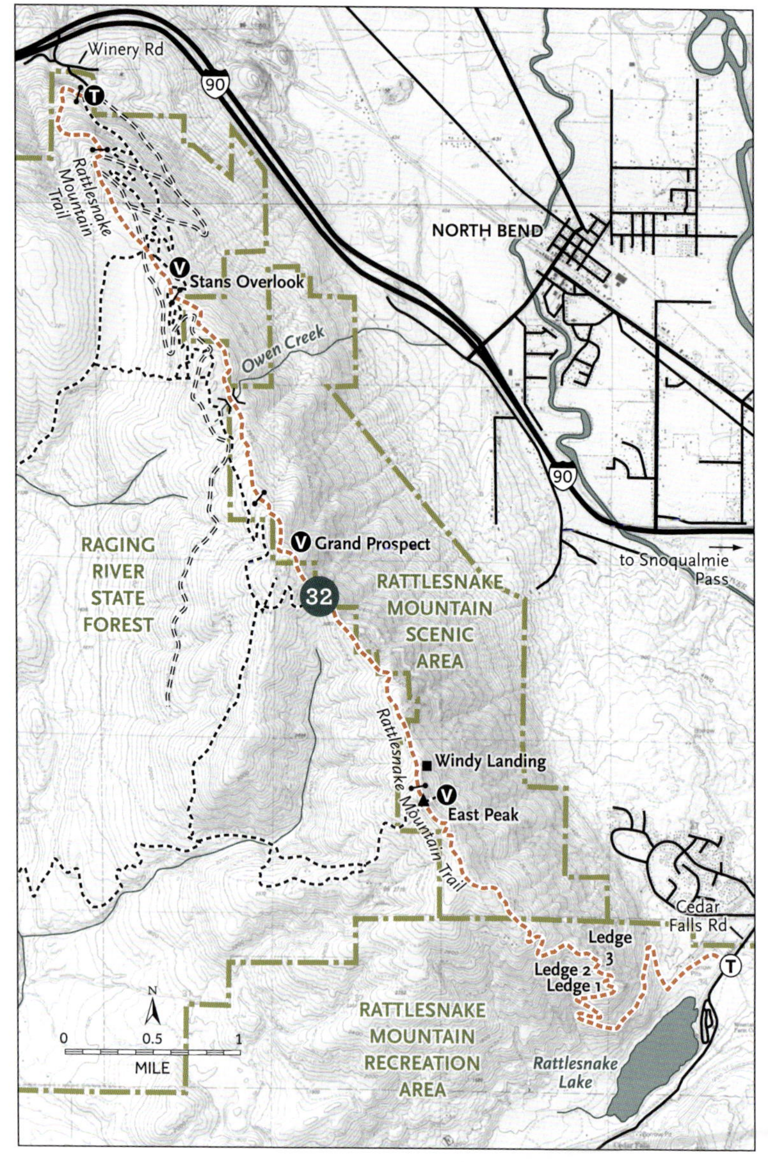

Winery Rd
90
Rattlesnake Mountain Trail
NORTH BEND
Stans Overlook
Owen Creek
90
Grand Prospect
to Snoqualmie Pass
RAGING RIVER STATE FOREST
32
RATTLESNAKE MOUNTAIN SCENIC AREA
Rattlesnake Mountain Trail
Windy Landing
East Peak
Cedar Falls Rd
Ledge 3
Ledge 2
Ledge 1
N
0
0.5
1
MILE
RATTLESNAKE MOUNTAIN RECREATION AREA
Rattlesnake Lake

Alternative trailhead (Rattlesnake Lake): From I-90 near North Bend, take exit 32 and head south. You are on 436th Avenue SE, though it becomes Cedar Falls Road SE in a short distance. Follow Cedar Falls Road for 2.4 miles to the signed Rattlesnake Lake Recreation Area to the right. Drive past the open gate and take your first left to find several large parking areas.

ON THE TRAIL

Head up the shared-use Trailhead Connector Trail, noting that mountain bikes and horses are free to use this path. In 450 feet, cross a gravel service road and find a kiosk for the Raging River State Forest Mountain Bike Trail System. The Department of Natural Resources has done a fantastic job of managing the safety of users in this area and has segregated hikers and bikers onto separate trails going to roughly the same places. The bikers go to the left just after the sign, but we continue through a pedestrian turnstile designed to remind all other users that this stretch is for hikers only. These turnstiles will pop up on both sides of all forest road crossings from this point onward. This area was steeped in logging efforts for years before it became part of Rattlesnake Mountain Scenic Area, so there are crisscrossing roads all over the place, and we will be passing many as we continue forward.

Begin your climb, alternating between moderate and steep grades, passing through vine and bigleaf maple, red alder, and western hemlock. At just over 1 mile, our trail crosses the service road again. The service road is lightly used for vehicles but receives a fair amount of use by cyclists, so do a double-check before crossing. Several more road crossings are in store, separated by deep emerald foliage, such as sword ferns, salal, and Oregon grape. The road sign here calls out 1.5 miles, but that's the road's distance, not ours. Onward you go!

The trail cuts through a powerline connector service road at 1.3 miles, with wires high above the path. Thanks to the clearing for this technology, the view opens a bit and gives you a reprieve from the thick foliage. The trail also flattens out somewhat here, letting your quads and your lungs take a much-needed break.

Another wooden turnstile followed by a road crossing appears at 1.6 miles, with a sign pointing out mileage and directions. At 2 miles, arrive at a crossing of a forest-road-turned-trail with signs aplenty. Once again, a kiosk points out the mountain bike trails, while other signs point out Stans Overlook and other trails. Mountain bikers and hikers converge on this spot and share the lookout, so don't be surprised to see the wheelers here.

To visit Stans Overlook, take a left and walk the short, level 200 feet to reach two benches, a picnic table, and a decent view of distant peaks such as Fuller Mountain as well as the northwestern part of North Bend. Stans Overlook was named after Stan Unger, one of the Issaquah Alps Trails Club hike leaders who helped pioneer the route of the original Mountains to Sound Greenway march from Snoqualmie Pass to the Seattle Waterfront. Many folks make Stans Overlook the goal for the day, but others choose to putter onward.

To keep the show rollin', walk back the short 200 feet from Stans Overlook to where you arrived and look across the road-turned-trail to find the now familiar pedestrian turnstile. Bikers also have a connecting trail here and it might be easy to take the wrong one if you aren't paying attention. By using the turnstile and the trail signage, you'll find your way.

The vista from Grand Prospect on Rattlesnake Mountain is a pleasant place to gawk at Mount Si looming large over the Snoqualmie Valley.

The trail then climbs into second-growth forest and has a peaceful ambiance through the evergreens as it gets you higher and higher onto the ridgeline. At 2.5 miles, the trail crosses another defunct logging road and continues with the forest promenade sprinkled with Sitka spruce, Douglas-fir, and western hemlock.

The ascent is moderate but not too leg-weary and even gives you a slight downhill for a couple hundred feet to cross the rippling Owen Creek on a weathered footbridge. There is one more swale to cross, this one without water, before you reach another pedestrian turnstile at 3.5 miles. This time, you are on what feels much more like a former logging road, with a wider path edged with scrappy stick trees sporting skinny trunks and spindly limbs. A sign with an arrow points to the left here, should it not be obvious.

At 3.8 miles, the forest road keeps going but is blocked off with logs and sticks to prevent you from missing the turn and wandering aimlessly. If you are mid-chat with a friend, you might neglect to see that the trail jogs left and turns into what feels more like a trail instead of old road. The junction signage has seen better days and was on the ground toppled over last time I visited. Be alert and, before you know it, find yourself passing through another wooden turnstile.

The single-track trail delivers you back to yet another former forest-road-turned-trail and spits you out with a bit of level ground at Grand Prospect, at 4.2 miles. Besides the Rattlesnake Ledges, this is the best viewpoint along the mountain, with breathtaking views of Mount Si and the sprawling Snoqualmie Valley. In winter, folks often use snowshoes or shoe traction to visit this spot. Gray jays—otherwise known as camp robbers, Canada jays, or whisky jacks—are frequent guests and may steal your unattended sandwich. Keep a close eye on your food and don't share—their faces are irresistible, but they need to learn to forage on a natural diet.

Grand Prospect is a praise-worthy undertaking, and turning back here makes a fantastically full day. Beyond here, the views aren't as favorable and the clear-cuts are plentiful until you get close to East Peak. But if you are a trail runner, have extra energy to burn, or are doing a thru hike with a car staged at the Rattlesnake Ledge trailhead, carry on!

The trail now goes through a working forest of clear-cuts, and the grade is deceiving at first. You might think that since you are past Grand Prospect, it's all downhill, but that's not the case. Trail crews have worked hard to reestablish the trail through the clear-cuts, at times climbing up, around, and over sad, log-strewn hillsides. The silver lining to tree culling is that now Mount Rainier pops up on the horizon, along with the Puget Sound and Olympic Mountains on a clear day.

At just shy of 5 miles, you'll want to pay close attention at a rather confusing junction. Straight ahead of you is a wooden turnstile that leads to a forest road. You might assume that since you've gone through so many, you should go through this one too, but not true here. The signed trail we are following turns to the left on this side of the barrier, but it isn't in-your-face obvious. The turnstile is reminding cyclists and horses on the opposite side of us that this trail is hiker-only and they should stay out on the forest road.

Continue along the trail until the clear-cut ends and you are once again in a healthy forest. At 5.9 miles, pass a sign for Windy Landing to the left. The signage would make you think this feature is something special, but don't be fooled, Grasshopper. The overgrown trees block any hopes of vistas, and following the spur trail will just lead to a big pile of prickly brambles with the foul scent of disappointment. Onward!

Pass through another wooden turnstile to arrive at a signed junction near a forest road at 6.2 miles. You are now in the area known as East Peak, and you have options. You can (A) park yourself on the bench tucked into the trees to the right prior to crossing the forest road, (B) walk the forest road 0.1 mile to the left up to visit a bench with a viewpoint of the valley and Mount Si, (C) take the forest road to the right roughly 100 feet to find the continuation of the Rattlesnake Mountain Trail, or (D) do all of the above.

Assuming you are continuing onward, at a minimum, perform option C, then afterward cross through yet another turnstile and carry on. From here forward, the trail is more of the same, crossing a couple of forest roads, all with turnstiles—déjà vu? But now we go downhill; hands in the air for the ride!

From Grand Prospect to East Peak, you generally won't see a lot of other hikers, but starting at East Peak, it's game on. The crowds get progressively denser the closer you get to Rattlesnake Ledge, but you've had your solitude, and by now, you might be too tired to do much more than smile at each one.

At 8.3 miles, arrive at an unsigned spur left to Rattlesnake Ledge 3 (Upper Ledge). Another 0.2 mile after that, another spur trail left takes you traipsing off to Ledge 2, and finally, the junction for the main Rattlesnake Ledge 1 comes at 8.7 miles. Head left to visit the final ledge, or tuck and roll all the way back to down to Rattlesnake Lake, arriving at the signed trailhead at 10.7 miles. Pit toilets, trash cans, and an information kiosk await at this spot. Turn left to walk another 0.3 mile to the parking area if you left a car, or tighten your laces and run back to the other trailhead where you started.

OPPOSITE: *Recreational opportunities are plentiful in the stunning Middle Fork Snoqualmie Natural Area.*

MIDDLE FORK SNOQUALMIE NATURAL AREA

NOT LONG AGO, THE MIDDLE FORK AREA was an illegal dumping ground, filled with widespread trash and criminal misuse. But then organizations like Mountains to Sound Greenway Trust stepped in to raise funds and create work projects in a shared effort to clean up the valley and open the area to sustainable recreation and environmental healing. These days, the valley is thriving, and the area has become a much-loved gem filled with new trailheads, river access, and recreationalists enjoying the beauty of the quiet forests and unique ecosystem. Some of the finest hiking trails in the area lie within its mountainous corridor.

33 Mailbox Peak

RATING/DIFFICULTY: ****/5
ROUNDTRIP: 10.2 miles
ELEV GAIN/HIGH POINT: 4090 feet/4822 feet
SEASON: May–Oct

Map: Green Trails Maps Middle Fork Snoqualmie No. 174SX; **Contact:** Department of Natural Resources (DNR); **Notes:** Discover Pass required. Pit toilets at trailhead. Many maps and online sources have the trail distance for this hike listed incorrectly. The gate to the upper parking area opens around 8:00 AM and closes at dusk. Weekends, like at most popular trailheads, are jam-packed and parking gets full quickly. Arrive early and choose weekdays if possible. Obey all posted no-parking signs and avoid parking at the Granite Creek Connector Trail, as it's not intended for Mailbox overflow parking (see Hike 35). Have a solid plan B if parking at both upper and lower Mailbox parking lots are full. Open to leashed dogs; **GPS:** N 47 28.049, W 121 40.458

As a truly definitive Northwest hike, Mailbox Peak's views of Mount Rainier, the Snoqualmie Valley, and the other rugged PNW peaks does not disappoint. However, you'll have to get to the summit first. Thanks to the newish, longer trail—built in 2014 after the old trail (Hike 34) ate the pride/abilities of too many hikers—the climbing is less steep and the trail tread pleasant. But that doesn't make it easy. The hike is one of the most difficult in the classic Cascade peaks due to the sustained pitch, which at times takes your breath away, along with the scenery. As a rather cruel joke, the hardest part is the final summit bid, which has you dragging your tired bones up 940 feet in a bit under 0.6 mile. Buckle up, it's a doozy.

GETTING THERE

From I-90 near North Bend: Take exit 34 and turn north on 468th Avenue SE, passing gas and dining options. In 0.6 mile, turn right on SE Middle Fork Road. At 1.5 miles, at the Y, bear right on the one-way SE Lake Dorothy Road. At 2.8 miles, the one-way road ends and officially becomes SE Middle Fork Road (Forest Road 56). Signage here announces you are entering the Middle Fork Snoqualmie River valley. Stay on SE Middle Fork Road until 3.1 miles and find the lower Mailbox Peak trailhead parking on both the left and right sides of the road. An upper parking lot with pit toilets is found by following a spur road beyond the open gate (see Notes) just 0.1 mile farther.

ON THE TRAIL

From the parking area, walk uphill to a white car gate (on some maps called Grouse Ridgeway) on a defunct forest road. Shimmy around the gate, and in 0.2 mile from the

Covered in stickers and packed with knickknacks, the famous mailbox kicks back at the summit of Mailbox Peak, living its best mountaintop life.

upper parking area (0.3 from the lower), locate the well-signed trail, along with a map kiosk to the road's left.

The trail kicks off with deciduous trees and brushy riparian foliage such as alder, maple, salmonberry, thimbleberry, and a variety of ferns. Several creeks, which are easy to hop, dribble across the trail, including a rather large one with a wooden pedestrian bridge 0.5 mile from the signed trail junction.

Another beautiful trail bridge, this one larger, arrives shortly after the first one. There is something kind of magical about these bridges, since the break in the evergreens makes it feel like you are in a terrarium with filtered light streaming down on the forest floor.

At 2 miles, the forest understory changes to be sparse and woody, thanks to the lack of light through the large conifers. As you continue uphill, there are some impressive old trees, including some mature western hemlocks, well over 200 years old. This rainy climate is a perfect home for them, and they provide plenty of shade on this climb for warm summer days.

A break from the forest comes at 3.9 miles, when the trail switches back across a rocky swale filled with slide alder, devil's club, and other usual PNW plant suspects. This break in the forest offers peeks of peaks such as Green Mountain across the Middle Fork valley, and you sense you are getting closer.

You'll want to admire the hard work of the puncheon bridges, rock walls, and turnpikes the volunteers and nonprofits so laboriously built, as you stop to catch your breath.

At nearly 4.5 miles, arrive at a curious unsigned intersection. Our path goes straight ahead on the same trail we've been following, but it's cut by the old trail, going downhill to the right, and uphill to the left. If you feel strong, you could shave 0.1 mile off the upcoming switchback by following the old trail (see Hike 34) uphill for 0.1 mile to connect with our trail, but the grade is steeper, so pick your poison.

If you aren't dripping in sweat or slightly chafed, stand by for the fun. The final push to the summit is through exposed talus and loose, rocky soil, climbing a whopping 940 feet in just under 0.6 mile. Snort, drool, and mumble as you pull your exhausted corpse up the final steep pitch until, finally, there it is . . . the mailbox!

The mailbox itself was schlepped up here on July 4, 1960, by Seattle postman Carl Heine who intended it to be a fun summit register for youth campers at a nearby summer retreat. Since then, it's been replaced over fifteen times and has become more of a summit shrine than a registry. Stickers coat the outside, and people leave all kinds of oddities near or inside it. Stuffed animals, confession letters, toys and trinkets, flags, bandanas, pictures, jewelry, coins, and adult beverages are just some of the items left behind. A team of volunteers and DNR staff periodically haul out the loot so that the summit avoids looking like a rummage sale.

When you've recovered your quads and your lungs, head back the way you came. You could take the old trail down, but I don't recommend it. It's wicked steep with a lot

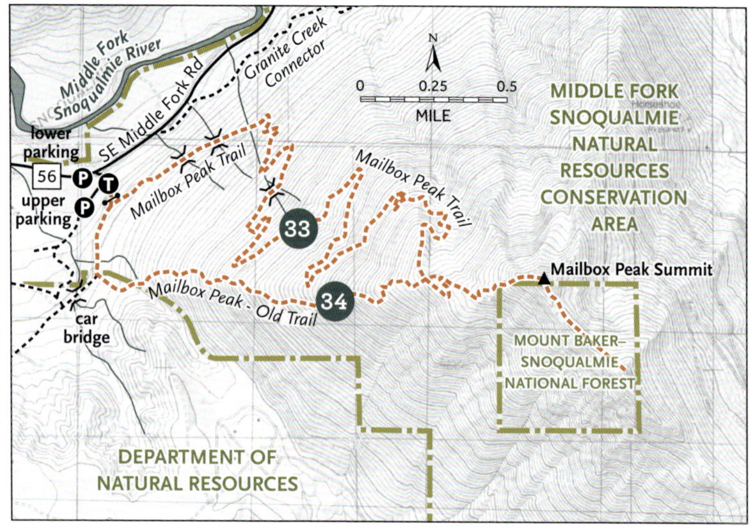

of slippery roots where tired feet can trip and send you sailing. It's best served as an approach trail if you get the gumption to give it a go next time.

34 Mailbox Peak: Old Trail

RATING/DIFFICULTY: ****/5
ROUNDTRIP: 6.6 miles
ELEV GAIN/HIGH POINT: 4000 feet/4822 feet
SEASON: May–Oct

Map: Green Trails Maps Middle Fork Snoqualmie No. 174SX; **Contact:** Department of Natural Resources; **Notes:** Discover Pass required. Pit toilets at trailhead. The gate to the upper parking area opens around 8 AM and closes at dusk. Weekends, like at most popular trailheads, are jam-packed and parking gets full quickly. Arrive early and choose weekdays if possible. Obey all posted no-parking signs, and avoid parking at the Granite Creek Connector Trail, as it's not intended for Mailbox overflow parking (see Hike 35). Have a solid plan B if parking at both upper and lower Mailbox parking lots are full. Open to leashed dogs; **GPS:** N 47 28.049, W 121 40.458

Gluttons for punishment unite! With a beautiful "new" trail (2014, Hike 33) guiding you back and forth more gently, why would you want to huff up the narrow, rough, old one? Well, because of its wildly difficult, unforgiving reputation, of course! The feather in your cap is climbing inclines ridiculously steep with hands and feet at times, through thick snaking roots, loose soil, and gnarly boulders so that you'll reach the summit in much less distance than the wise souls on the other trail who don't suffer this pain. And when you have accomplished the formidable, strenuous beast, you'll pat yourself on your ringing-wet back in proud achievement, knowing you are better because you challenged every cell in your body to show up and fight. Think twice if you are in poor shape or are inexperienced; Search and Rescue gets called here a lot, and having your name in the nightly news is downright embarrassing.

GETTING THERE

From I-90 near North Bend: Take exit 34 and go north on 468th Avenue SE, passing gas and dining options. At 0.6 mile, turn right on SE Middle Fork Road. At 1.5 miles, at the Y, bear right on the one-way SE Lake Dorothy Road. At 2.8 miles, the one-way road ends and officially becomes SE Middle Fork Road (Forest Road 56). Signage here announces you are entering the Middle Fork Snoqualmie River valley. Stay on SE Middle Fork Road until 3.1 miles and find the lower Mailbox Peak trailhead parking on both the left and right sides of the road. An upper parking lot with pit toilets is found by following a spur road beyond the open gate (see Notes) just 0.1 mile farther.

ON THE TRAIL

From the parking area, walk uphill to a white car gate (on some maps called Grouse Ridgeway) on a defunct forest road. Shimmy around the gate, and in 0.2 mile from the upper parking area (0.3 mile from the lower), pass the new trail to the road's left. Keep rolling to 0.4 mile, reaching a kiosk and an obvious trail to the road's left just prior to the car bridge.

The trail starts off gentle enough, with a narrow straightforward tread, even coming close to a dribbling creek. *This isn't bad*, you think. Beautiful old stumps serving as nurse

Fancy footwork is required for those hardy souls making the challenging grunt up Old Mailbox Peak.

logs are living museums of the logging efforts of yesteryear. Then, a maelstrom of rooty challenge smacks you right in the schnoz. In the first mile, you'll gain over 730 feet, and in most sections, you'll have to decide whether to follow the boot path straight up the natural ladder or follow the slightly less challenging steep switchback; both are tough, so you do you. There are so many braided trails on this path that your head might spin, but most go to the same place; up.

Beg for your body's forgiveness as you make your way higher and higher up the heavily forested slopes, clinging to wet roots and moss-covered rock. White triangles stuck to trees guide the way through a particularly steep stretch at 1.7 miles from where you parked. Keep your eyes up on the trees, but stop when you do, because you need to watch your feet as you pick your way through the rigorous incline laden with massive amounts of tripping hazards. Type 2 fun really is fun; but that comes later and usually with a good story.

At 2.4 miles, the trees start looking smaller as the path breaks out into beargrass, huckleberries, and other familiar Cascade foliage—the first sign besides your wobbly legs, that you are getting somewhere! Oh, happy day. The trail reaches a four-way junction at 2.6 miles with the new trail. To the left and right is the new trail, but straight ahead is more punishment with the last of the old trail—a switchback shortcut. If you are tired and ready for a slightly easier grade on a wider trail, you can take the new trail to the right and follow as it switches back, but this costs you an extra 0.1 mile. Hard call, right? Listen to your lungs, Linda.

Either way, you'll be climbing the new trail in a short distance and rocking through the boulder field near the top, pretending you aren't in pain; you are surviving this absurd challenge, though you might be questioning your sanity.

At 3.3 miles, stand on the top with the mailbox front and center while rivers run down your humbled, raspberry face. You did it! Be sure to check and see if anyone sent you love letters before turning back. If you delight in suffering, you could go down what you just came up, or you could take the new trail for a change of scenery and a change of pace. In the end, the craziest memories are the ones that leave you soggy, exhausted, and pushing limits you didn't know existed. Usually, this is accomplished by those with a mad grit and fierce moxie. I bet I just described you, didn't I?

35 Granite Lakes

RATING/DIFFICULTY: ****/3
ROUNDTRIP: 8.4 miles
ELEV GAIN/HIGH POINT: 2320 feet/3150 feet
SEASON: late May–Oct

Map: Green Trails Maps Middle Fork Snoqualmie No. 174SX; **Contact:** Department of Natural Resources (DNR); **Notes:** Discover Pass required. There are technically two parking areas that connect to Granite Lakes. One is the Granite Creek Connector trailhead, which is a roadside pullout with room for only about three or four cars, and the other, the large, new Granite Creek trailhead with room for about forty-five cars. This trail description starts at the main Granite Creek trailhead, but should

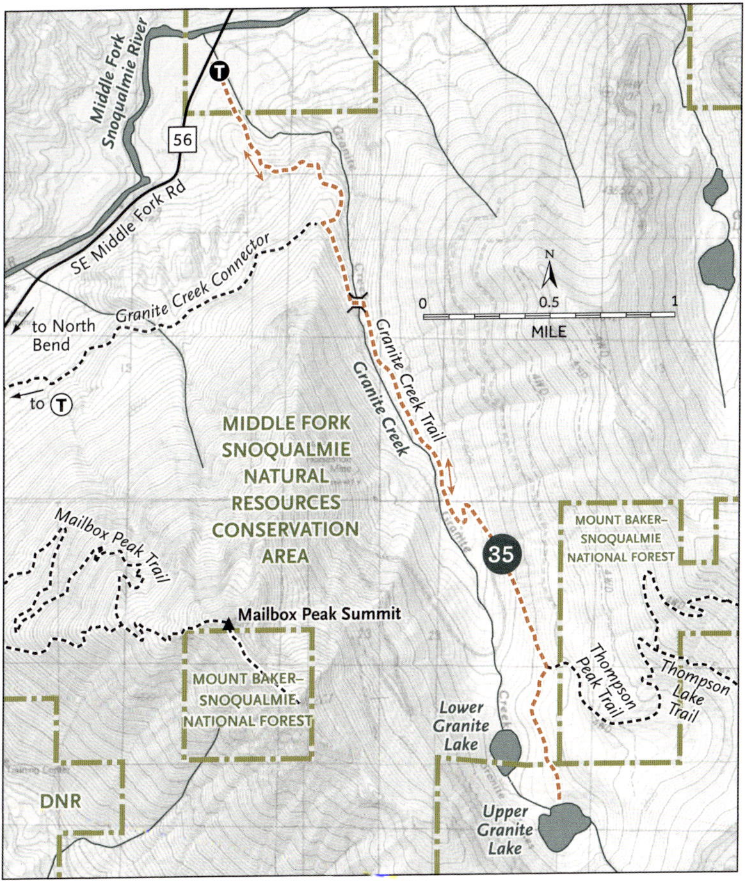

Upper Granite Lake lies shallow and clear in its idyllic basin tucked beneath rocky ridges.

you choose to use the other, signs along the way will guide you. Pit toilets available at trailhead. This trail can be done year-round but in winter is often slick and requires snowshoes or shoe traction. If you choose to do this trail in winter, understand avalanche risk and be prepared with lifesaving backcountry snow gear. Open to leashed dogs; **GPS:** N 47 29.557, W 121 38.386

Years ago, getting to these lakes required a bushwhack, a hazardous creek ford, and good navigation skills. Thankfully, these days, with the efforts of Washington DNR and several outdoor nonprofits, a scenic, well-used, and maintained trail now allows us to visit the upper lake and enjoy all the bounty in this peaceful backcountry setting.

GETTING THERE

From I-90 near North Bend: Take exit 34 and go north on 468th Avenue SE, passing gas and dining options. In 0.6 mile, turn right on SE Middle Fork Road. At 1.5 miles, at the Y, bear right on the one-way SE Lake Dorothy Road. At 2.8 miles, the one-way road ends and officially becomes SE Middle Fork Road (Forest Road 56). Signage here announces you are entering the Middle Fork Snoqualmie River valley. Stay on SE Middle Fork Road, passing the Mailbox Peak trailhead, and locate the Granite Creek Connector trailhead at 3.4 miles. This is the alternative parking area, should you need a backup or want to take this connecting, alternative start to the hike. Otherwise, keep going and find the Granite Creek trailhead on the right at 5.6 miles.

ON THE TRAIL

Locate the trailhead to the northeast of the parking area and pause to look at the informational kiosk, complete with a map. Give your quads the customary pep talk, because even though this trail follows the course of an old logging road, this puppy is punchy and gains 870 feet in the first 1.3 miles. Thankfully, it does so with the help of a couple of benches, which give you an opportunity to stop and recover your lungs if you are in need. The evergreen canopy above you sways in the winds, and a few large boulders are showcased along the way. Despite the upward grunt, the trail tread is pleasant without too many rocks or roots, and overall, the ambiance has a good vibe.

Reach the Granite Creek Connector junction at 1.4 miles, and turn left, now on a much easier grade. If you decided to park at the alternative trailhead (Granite Creek Connector), you will connect with us at this point, after hiking 2.5 miles from your car to this spot.

The trail takes on a riparian feel, with sword ferns, devil's club, salmonberries, and thimbleberries sometimes trying to grow over the trail. The grade makes for a hiking good time, and at 1.9 miles, you arrive at a sturdy wooden bridge over the bouncing whitewater of Granite Creek. You can't help but stop here and enjoy the peaceful soundtrack of the playful cascades.

From here, the trail narrows and begins a brushy gradual incline that lasts nearly all the way to the upper lake. During spring and summer, this trail gets slightly overgrown with slide alder and salmonberries, which try to grab you with their outstretched arms. Do some trail maintenance and give 'em a whack with your pole, or carefully break the bully bushes until they understand their pecking order.

Trickling creeks drain across the trail—some small, some large, but in most months, they are rock- or log-hoppable while keeping dry shoes.

At 3.5 miles, arrive at a signed Y junction. The Granite Creek Trail goes right here toward Granite Lakes, while Thompson Peak Trail (see Extending Your Hike) is to your left. Although the trail is called the Granite *Lakes* Trail, the path only leads to the Upper Lake, not lakes plural as the name implies. Getting to the lower lake requires a difficult bushwhack with thorny plants and slippery rocks and isn't done often. Yet there are two, so plural it is.

Bear right and continue on the narrow spur, crossing a fairly wide, flowing creek. In early season or after big rains, this creek is a shoe-wetter, but in mid- to late summer, you can rock-hop across it.

At 4.2 miles, find yourself on one of the many game trails that lead to the water's edge. This lake isn't one with a wide flat beach, so you'll have to find a spot along boot paths to call your own while you visit.

EXTENDING YOUR HIKE

If time and energy are in your favor, you could extend your hike and visit Thompson Lake. At the signed junction near Granite Lakes, head east and follow an old logging-road-turned-trail to a ridge, before steeply descending into the Thompson Lake basin and shoreline. This extension is a roundtrip distance of 4.7 miles with 1890 feet of elevation gain.

36 South Bessemer Mountain

RATING/DIFFICULTY: ***/4
ROUNDTRIP: 13.4 miles
ELEV GAIN/HIGH POINT: 4090 feet/5011 feet
SEASON: late July–Oct

Map: Green Trails Maps Middle Fork Snoqualmie No. 174SX; **Contact:** Mount Baker–Snoqualmie National Forest, Snoqualmie Ranger District, Department of Natural Resources; **Notes:** Discover Pass required. Pit toilets across the road at Oxbow Loop trailhead (see Hike 46). A new trailhead has been proposed; check with land managers for parking changes. Open to leashed dogs, stock, mountain bikes; **GPS:** N 47 30.976, W 121 36.773

You might be discouraged to hear that this hike follows a logging road for the entirety of the climb. But there are good things to be found en route, including quietness and a great workout. If you see anyone, you'll probably be happy to stop and chat, since they might be the only person you see all day. Wildlife is common here too, including beautiful black bears who also enjoy seclusion and scamper off when they see you. Oh, and did I mention the gorgeous views from the top?

Rugged mountains form a backdrop to blooming fireweed near South Bessemer Mountain.

GETTING THERE

From I-90 near North Bend: Take exit 34 and go north on 468th Avenue SE, passing gas and dining options. In 0.6 mile, turn right on SE Middle Fork Road. At 1.5 miles, at the Y, bear right on the one-way SE Lake Dorothy Road. At 2.8 miles, the one-way road ends and officially becomes SE Middle Fork Road (Forest Road 56). Signage here announces you are entering the Middle Fork Snoqualmie River valley. Stay on SE Middle Fork Road, passing various trailheads, and at 7.8 miles, park by a closed gate to the road's left. Please do not block gate access; private land requires access. If full, find parking in designated areas along SE Middle Fork Road and walk. Do not park in unauthorized spots.

ON THE TRAIL

Walk around the gate at Bessemer Road and head up the primitive roadway. In 0.1 mile, cross an in-need-of-repairs car bridge over Big Blowout Creek. It's creaky and tired, but it will allow for a safe crossing when you select your steps correctly. At 0.2 mile, pass a wide turnaround spot that is rumored to serve someday as the new trailhead.

The road-turned-trail continues, climbing gradually until, at 1.1 miles and just over 350 feet of elevation gain, you arrive at a signed junction with the CCC Trail and a large new bridge to the left. Turn right here and follow the roadway as it meanders through the forest. At 1.4 miles, arrive at another gorgeous new CCC bridge, which rests off to the road's right to take recreationalists across a large washout. We keep to the road, though you may want to check out the bridge just for fun. At 1.7 miles reach an active quarry where there might be a bit of confusion, since they've made a couple of driveways into the area. Continue straight ahead here, on the same trajectory you've been following. If you go the wrong way, you'll end up in a gravel pit and quickly realize your mistake.

The road switches back and forth, and at 2.6 miles, with nearly 1000 feet of elevation gain under your feet, the road meets Switchback Falls—part of the east fork of Big Blowout Creek—and crosses underneath it. During high flows, this crossing can be hazardous, and it's best to turn back if you don't feel safe. In late season, though, the water is passable, even with dry feet if you are good on your toes.

After another switchback, an additional waterfall, this one called Gossamer Falls, is purring to the left. This time, the water flowing from its drop is much easier to cross and you hop across—no fancy footwork required. The road continues ascending, crossing another creek's trickle with a rock-hop at 3.3 miles.

At 4.4 miles, after 2120 feet of elevation gain, look to the right for a rock stack (cairn), and turn right on what appears to be a single-track trail. In a few steps, you realize it's not a single track but rather another former forest road. The road tread gets substantially rockier and becomes ankle-twisty if you aren't watching your feet. Stick with it—the reward awaits!

At 5.3 miles, views open to the right, including those of the tippy top of Mount Rainier and the Middle Fork Snoqualmie Valley below you.

At 5.5 miles, ignore another former forest road heading left and continue climbing on the main road you've been following. Shortly after that, a different former logging road goes right—bear left and continue climbing up hill.

At 6.2 miles, after climbing 3460 feet, a wide, flat area that was a former road junction (now just a gravel area with wildflowers trying to take over) offers a place to rest if you need a break. But completing this hike is foremost in mind now, so why stop here? You are only 0.5 mile from the top!

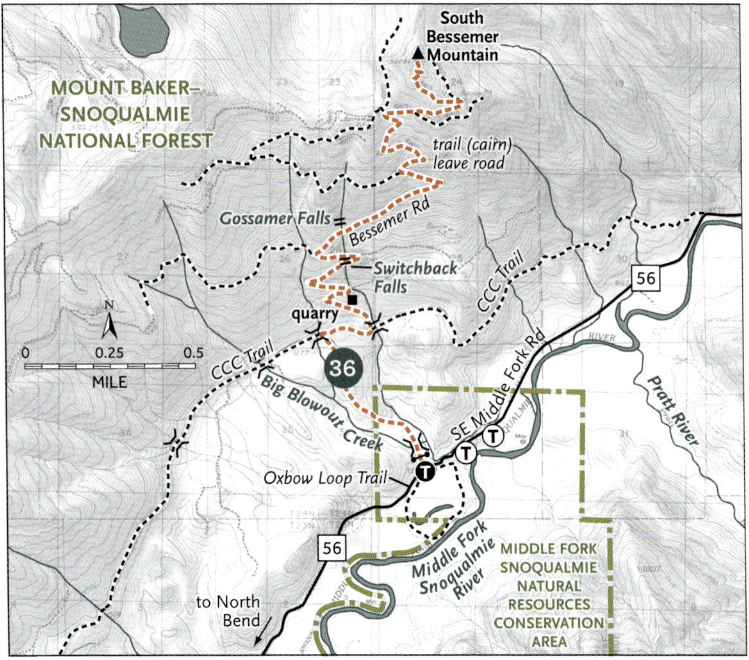

Follow the cairns as the road starts to peter out, and arrive at the summit of South Bessemer with a mind full of victory and legs full of strength. This place is gorgeous—and the views are outstanding. Mount Rainier stands proud in the distance, and the Middle Fork peaks, such as The Pulpit, Garfield, and Burnt Boot Peak, are front and center. Moolock Mountain is your neighbor to the west, and the main summit of Mount Bessemer—only attainable with rock climbing equipment—is to the northeast. Pearly everlasting, columbine, rosy spirea, fireweed, and the occasional garter snake hang out near the summit. It's a world away from the life below this peak—enjoy every quiet moment before turning back.

37 Lower CCC Trail

RATING/DIFFICULTY: **/2
ROUNDTRIP: 6.9 miles
ELEV GAIN/HIGH POINT: 740 feet/1580 feet
SEASON: Year-round

Map: Green Trails Maps Middle Fork Snoqualmie No. 174SX; **Contact:** Mount Baker–Snoqualmie National Forest, Snoqualmie Ranger District, and Department of Natural

Resources; **Notes:** Discover Pass required. Pit toilets across the road at Oxbow Loop trailhead (see Hike 46). A new trailhead has been proposed as well as a trail reroute in the future. Open to leashed dogs, stock, mountain bikes; **GPS:** N 47 30.976, W 121 36.773

In the next few years, this trail and trailhead may look very different. For starters, there is talk of more parking and a proper trailhead allowing easier access. As of this book's publication date, two large, beautiful metal bridges have been installed over the angrier waterways, but there are more bridges slated for the future. The trail will also get rerouted at the end so you can connect from this trail to Teneriffe trailhead (see Hikes 23 and 24) and make it a thru hike or extend your day. But today we are experiencing what future-you will refer to as "back in the day." The hike these days is along the quiet former CCC road, complete with a lot of dribbling creeks, gentle breezes, views, and solitude. It's a good place to reconnect with others, or yourself.

GETTING THERE

From I-90 near North Bend: Take exit 34 and go north on 468th Avenue SE, passing gas and dining options. In 0.6 mile, turn right on SE Middle Fork Road. At 1.5 miles, at the Y, bear right on the one-way SE Lake Dorothy Road. At 2.8 miles, the one-way road ends and officially becomes SE Middle Fork Road (Forest Road 56). Signage here announces you are entering the Middle Fork Snoqualmie River valley. Stay on SE Middle Fork Road, passing various trailheads, and at 7.8 miles, park by a closed gate to the road's left—please do not block gate access. This is Bessemer Road, though it's not signed as either a road or an official trailhead. If full, find parking in designated areas along SE Middle Fork Road and walk. Do not park in unauthorized spots.

ON THE TRAIL

Start the hike by walking around the gate at Bessemer Road and up the primitive roadway. In 0.1 mile, arrive at an in-need-of-repairs car bridge over Big Blowout Creek, followed by a turnaround spot that is rumored to be the intended new trailhead. Will it happen? Time will tell.

The road's elevation gain is most of the huff and puff you'll have for the day, so embrace the ascent and consider it your workout. Years ago, this road was paved, but the pavement has crumbled away and now it's mostly gravel under your feet.

At 1.1 miles, arrive at a signed junction with the CCC Trail. Our hike goes left and crosses one of the brand-new metal bridges that spans Big Blowout Creek. Like most of the structures in the backcountry, this bridge was recently placed via helicopter drop in this picturesque location so that we can get across without wet shoes or a twisted ankle. Thank you, crews!

Just after the bridge, ignore the built-without-permission extreme mountain bike trail that heads off into the forest. Instead, follow the gentle contours of the old road. Sword ferns and moss have landscaped the edges of the narrow pathway on what was once the obvious road grade. Countless mellow creeks and frisky waterways are crossed with a rock-hop in most seasons as you make your way along the peaceful path.

The Civilian Conservation Corps was founded as a means of work relief for young men between the ages of eighteen and twenty-five who were struggling with

A metal bridge spans a playful creek along the Lower CCC Trail.

employment during the Great Depression. As part of President Franklin D. Roosevelt's New Deal program, they put their skills to work, creating infrastructure such as bridges, roads, and fire towers on public lands. What's more, they planted 3.5 billion trees. Nearly 100 years later, their work is still visible, and this road—built between 1936 and 1939 for logging efforts—is one of their creations.

With history bouncing in your head, arrive at the second brand-new metal bridge at 2.2 miles. Equally impressive as the first, it's a welcome blessing and makes this trail feel loved.

In another 0.1 mile, cross a small gorge with a creek using its powerful water chisel to chip away the banks. I suspect a bridge will span this creek before long, but it's an easy crossing now.

Views get better and better and, at 3 miles, decent peeks of Mailbox Peak and other prominent mountain molars show up to the left. When you get here, you have options—stay a while and drop your sit pad for a snack, calling this the end, or carry on another 0.4 mile to visit the mossy, rocky Brawling Creek before heading back.

EXTENDING YOUR HIKE

After Brawling Creek, keep going 0.5 mile to reach the unsigned Green Mountain Trail to your right (Hike 38). Turn right and scoot up to Far Enough Promontory or Last Chance Promontory if time and motivation allow. At 4 miles from your starting point, just past the Green Mountain Trail junction, you'll come across a newly built trail that offers an alternative to the muddy, freshly-logged double track. This scenic route winds through the forest and leads all the way to the Mount Teneriffe area. The new stretch of trail is approximately 4 miles in length, with a gentle elevation gain of around 300 feet, making for a pleasant and immersive thru hike to extend your day.

38 Last Chance Promontory on Green Mountain

RATING/DIFFICULTY: **/4

ROUNDTRIP: 12.5 miles

ELEV GAIN/HIGH POINT: 2230 feet/2990 feet

SEASON: Year-round

Map: Green Trails Maps Middle Fork Snoqualmie No. 174SX; **Contact:** Mount Baker–Snoqualmie National Forest, Snoqualmie Ranger District, Department of

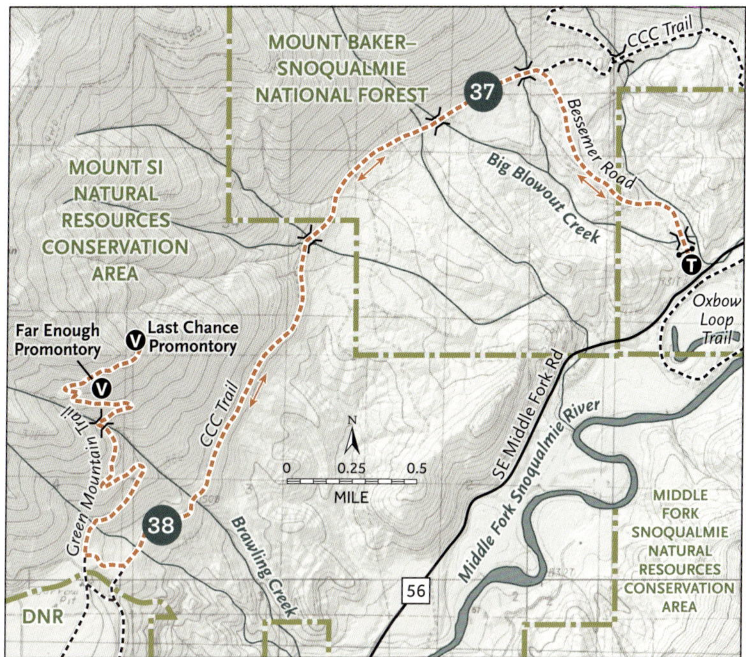

Natural Resources (DNR); **Notes:** Discover Pass required. Pit toilets across the road at Oxbow Loop trailhead (see Hike 46). A new trailhead has been proposed. Please do not use the approach of the Sitka Spruce Trail, which occasionally appears on maps, as DNR wishes it to be decommissioned. CCC Road open to leashed dogs, stock, mountain bikes; Last Chance Promontory Trail open to leashed dogs; **GPS:** N 47 30.976, W 121 36.773

This trail is one of the few around North Bend where you can hike on a weekday—and maybe even a weekend—and have the whole place to yourself. It follows roads-turned-trails for most of it, but it's peaceful and serene. It's not a summit, but an outcropping with a pleasant view of the Middle Fork Snoqualmie River valley and its rugged mountains, where you can sit and ponder the wonders of nature, or simply eat your lunch on a well-earned vista.

GETTING THERE

From I-90 near North Bend: Take exit 34 and go north on 468th Avenue SE, passing gas and dining options. In 0.6 mile, turn right on SE Middle Fork Road. At 1.5 miles, at the Y, bear right on the one-way SE Lake Dorothy Road. At 2.8 miles, the one-way road ends and officially becomes SE Middle Fork Road (Forest Road 56). Signage here announces you are entering the Middle Fork

Gorgeous mountain views across the valley are on display from Last Chance Promontory on Green Mountain.

Snoqualmie River valley. Stay on SE Middle Fork Road, passing various trailheads, and at 7.8 miles, park by a closed gate to the road's left—please do not block gate access. This is Bessemer Road, though it's not signed as either a road or an official trailhead. If full, find parking in designated areas along SE Middle Fork Road and walk. Do not park in unauthorized spots.

ON THE TRAIL

Walk around the gate on Bessemer Road and up the primitive roadway. In 0.1 mile, cross a car bridge over Big Blowout Creek. The road ascends gradually, and at 1.1 miles, arrives at the CCC Trail. Head left here and cross one of the new metal bridges spanning Big Blowout Creek. This beauty is just one of the many improvements recently made by DNR to the recreation of this area. Hats off to them!

The road you are following, now with a single track running down its center, was created by the CCC, or the Civilian Conservation Corps. President Franklin D. Roosevelt's "green army," as they were nicknamed, were a group of men ages eighteen to twenty-five who were put to work during the Great Depression building structures and improvements on public lands. This road was built between 1936 and 1939 as a logging road.

At 2.2 miles, reach the second brand-new bridge, equally as beautiful as the first. It feels a little like you are all alone on this abandoned old road, then voilà, a beautiful new bridge is once again front and center, reminding you that this trail is loved by many.

At 2.3 miles, cross a small gorge with a lively creek. I suspect a bridge will span this creek before long, but it's a straightforward crossing now and can be done in most seasons without wet shoes, though hiking poles are helpful.

Views across the valley are visible through the trees to the left as you continue along the old roadway. At 3.4 miles, reach Brawling Creek, which soon will be spanned by another beautiful new bridge. For now, it's a rock-hop requiring a bit of coordination for dry shoes.

In the next 0.5 mile, keep your eyes peeled to the right for our trail. It's quite obvious, and has recently been rerouted and improved, but presently is unsigned. Look for the spindly evergreen bases with the discernable path running through them and take it.

From here, the trail follows an old logging road up through a mixed evergreen and deciduous forest, passing the occasional large relic stump with springboard marks—a testament to the logging that happened years ago. At 5.3 miles, at what feels like a place few people ever visit, you get a surprise! Another brand-new wood-and-metal bridge appears over Brawling Creek. It feels unexpected and novel amid the history of logging and the relative isolation of this pathway. People were here and worked very hard—recently!

Continue climbing after the bridge, and at 6.1 miles, the road-turned-trail levels out and reaches a peekaboo view in a break from the trees, known as Far Enough Promontory. It's unsigned and not an obvious spot, so you might be wondering if you are there—but if you have a view without trees, you've reached it. Keep going for another 0.1 mile for the final push to Last Chance Promontory, or as it's also known, Absolute Last Chance Promontory. If you haven't gotten the point via the name, this is the final outcropping and our destination for the day. Pull out a sit pad along the former roadway near a large talus field and enjoy a snack before heading back.

As a side note, this road does continue but becomes difficult to follow with plenty of blowdowns, as it's not often used. You might also notice a rock cairn on the upper talus field above the road. Avoid this route if you aren't an experienced mountaineer, as it's a sketchy, hard-to-follow climber's scramble for a mile to the actual summit of Green Mountain; getting down is hazardous and navigationally difficult. Be safe out there, friends!

39 Middle CCC Trail

RATING/DIFFICULTY: **/2
ROUNDTRIP: 6.2 miles
ELEV GAIN/HIGH POINT: 890 feet/1310 feet
SEASON: Year-round

Map: Green Trails Maps Middle Fork Snoqualmie No. 174SX; **Contact:** Mount Baker–Snoqualmie National Forest, Snoqualmie Ranger District; **Notes:** Northwest Forest Pass or Interagency Pass required. Pit toilets 2 miles farther northeast at Middle Fork trailhead. Parking gets full on weekends and holidays—have a plan B. Open to leashed dogs, stock, mountain bikes; **GPS:** N 47 30.242, W 121 34.635

This hike is perfect for those who want a leisurely stroll or a woodsy walk without the crowds. You'll be walking along a former roadbed built by the Civilian Conservation Corps, President Franklin D. Roosevelt's "green army" of young men, which functioned from 1933 to 1942. Over time, the road has taken on a primitive feel and is now becoming more trail-esque—a good place to rest the soul in a crazy world.

The journey is the reward on the moss-lined CCC Trail.

GETTING THERE

From I-90 near North Bend: Take exit 34 and go north on 468th Avenue SE, passing gas and dining options. In 0.6 mile, turn right on SE Middle Fork Road. At 1.5 miles, at the Y, bear right on the one-way SE Lake Dorothy Road. At 2.8 miles, the one-way road ends and officially becomes SE Middle Fork Road (Forest Road 56). Signage here announces you are entering the Middle Fork Snoqualmie River valley. Stay on SE Middle Fork Road, passing various trailheads, and at 10.1 miles, find a signed parking area for the CCC Trail, for roughly six vehicles, to the road's left.

ON THE TRAIL

The trail gently swoops uphill from the parking area and begins a gradual climb along the CCC Trail. Creeklets drip in from the hillside to the right, all rock-hoppable.

In 0.4 mile, the trail passes the unsigned turnoff for Pratt Balcony (Hike 40), then at 0.5 mile, crosses a washout and a fumble-foot crossing on scree and talus. Thankfully, it's passable without too much unexpected dancing and you continue walking the former road. To the left, just after the washout, a beautiful nurse log, complete with mature, thriving trees, is visible. Nurse logs, or decaying stumps, are a perfect nursery for seedlings, complete with nutrients and light to harbor the new growth and protect them from pathogens and other harmful funguses. Thanks to death, new life springs forth. What a gift!

In the shoulder season, countless creeks and wet drips, some with micro waterfalls, are crossed by a big step or a jump. By late summertime, far fewer are flowing, but the area still bears evidence of the copious amounts of rain, upward of 90 inches per year, that dumps into these mountains. Sword ferns grow heartily, as do a variety of sedge, moss, algae, and lichen.

Mossy cliff bands are visible to the road's right as it gradually gains elevation. At 2 miles, a viewpoint to the left showcases the spectacular mountains of the Middle Fork, including the lofty Russian Butte. You could plunk down a sit pad, bust out a picnic, and call it a day, or continue onward, still exploring the former roadway.

After the valley views, the trail begins a gradual descent until it reaches a large washout at 2.8 miles. Logs and boulders are strewn about, and prior to 2023, you might have stood here and dreaded the crossing, but now a stunning rust-colored bridge guides those who travel here across the former mess and, immediately afterward, places you at the Bessemer Road junction, where you turn left.

For a good final destination, follow the road to the left and wander another 0.3 mile until you reach a junction where Bessemer Road takes a hard left and winds down to the Blowout Creek trailhead (see Hike 37). Continue on the CCC Trail, now the lower portion, to another new metal bridge over Big Blowout Creek at 3.1 miles. The shoulders of the new bridge have several boulders that make good sit spots to relax before heading back.

40 Pratt Balcony

RATING/DIFFICULTY: ****/2

ROUNDTRIP: 2.4 miles

ELEV GAIN/HIGH POINT: 610 feet/1570 feet

SEASON: Year-round

Map: Green Trails Maps Middle Fork Snoqualmie No. 174SX; **Contact:** Mount Baker–Snoqualmie National Forest, Snoqualmie Ranger District; **Notes:** Northwest Forest Pass or Interagency Pass required. Trail is unmaintained and unofficial; travel at your own risk

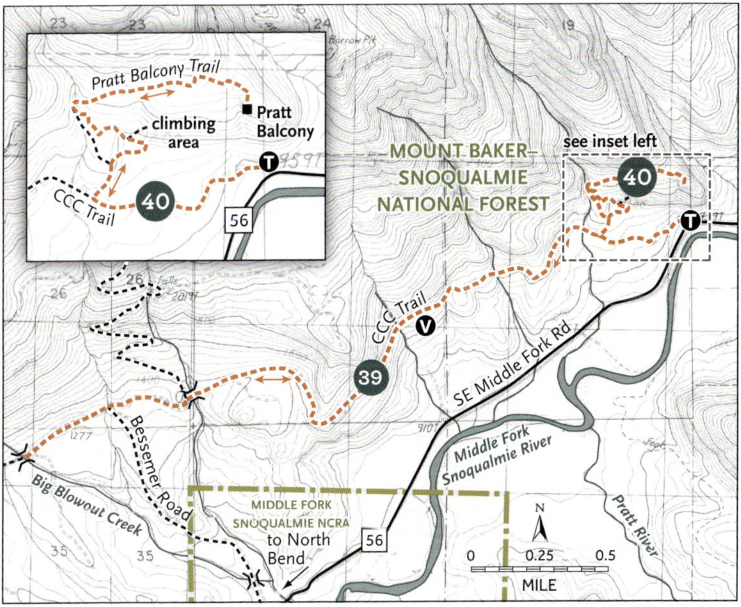

The author and her rough collie, Scout, enjoy the fading sunshine at day's end from Pratt Balcony.

and have a good map. Avoid posting signs or creating cairns; no campfires. Pit toilets 2 miles farther east at Middle Fork trailhead. Open to leashed dogs; **GPS:** N 47 30.242, W 121 34.635

I hemmed and hawed about whether to put this hike in this guidebook. For years, it was a find-it-yourself destination, free from the crowding and pressure, but in recent years, the internet and mapping apps have guided many new folks to this spot, so the secret is out. This short, somewhat steep little path arrives at a huge visual payoff with spectacular views over the Middle Fork Snoqualmie River in the shadow of the looming Russian Butte.

GETTING THERE

From I-90 near North Bend: Take exit 34 and go north on 468th Avenue SE, passing gas and dining options. In 0.6 mile, turn right on SE Middle Fork Road. At 1.5 miles, at the Y, bear right on the one-way SE Lake Dorothy Road. At 2.8 miles, the one-way road ends and officially becomes SE Middle Fork Road (Forest Road 56). Signage here announces you are entering the Middle Fork Snoqualmie River valley. Stay on SE Middle Fork Road, passing various trailheads, and at 10.1 miles, find a signed parking area for the CCC Trail for roughly six vehicles, to the road's left.

ON THE TRAIL

Follow the signed CCC Trail to the west, crossing a couple of dribbles and seasonal creeks as you meander. In 0.4 mile, look to the right and find an unsigned, obvious pathway behind an odd gravel pile and a few scattered boulders. Just behind the boulders, the trail is clear. The CCC Trail goes straight ahead at this junction, so if you reach a large boulder-filled water washout near a seasonal creek, you've gone too far.

This is a good time to mention that the Forest Service has limited crews to maintain or improve this trail, so it's our job to keep it as pristine and unobtrusively trodden as possible. Please do not put up trail signs, flagging, reflectors, or other markers. Please *do* pack out all your trash. In other words, leave no trace.

Once you pass the boulders, the trail begins a forested climb on an obvious single track. In 0.5 mile, reach an unsigned junction. There are two approaches to get to the same spot farther up the trail; however, the one to the left shoots up a steep, rocky stretch with surrounding briars and is more difficult than staying straight. In fact, sometimes, it's blocked off with sticks to remind you that staying straight is a better option for both trail tread and forest aesthetics.

From here, the obvious trail cruises through the mossy western hemlocks and western red cedars, and switches back to the left to get you higher on your quest. You might hear the clicking and clanking of rock climbers' gear from a couple of large walls adjacent to this trail, known on some maps as the Lower Pratt climbing area. Their primitive boot path scoots off to the right at 0.6 mile, while ours continues straight ahead.

At 0.8 mile, reach the intersection where the rocky shortcut trail meets up with ours. A small side trail leads to West Bessemer Creek and provides a spot for the pup to grab water if you brought him, or just a pretty place for a splash in summer months.

The trail takes a hard right and follows a rocky former logging road as it winds up to the viewpoint. At 1.2 miles, the obvious trail guides you to the right, where you'll find perfect spots to sit and views that might melt you into a puddle. If you brought kids or dogs, hold little hands and make sure the leash is secure—this is a fairly steep cliff. Refrain from building a fire here, since water isn't close by if a large spark takes flight.

Lastly, there must be at least one remaining find-it-yourself, right? Those who enjoy a challenge can hunt for a roughed-in boot path leading you up to a view of Mount Garfield, complete with a log for sitting and dreaming. That is, until the boot path gets worn in. Hints: Look for the series of cut logs on your way back, roughly 100 feet from the balcony viewpoint.

41 Upper CCC Trail

RATING/DIFFICULTY: ***/2
ROUNDTRIP: 6.8 miles
ELEV GAIN/HIGH POINT: 940 feet/1280 feet
SEASON: Year-round

Map: Green Trails Maps Middle Fork Snoqualmie No. 174SX; **Contact:** Mount Baker–Snoqualmie National Forest, Snoqualmie Ranger District; **Notes:** Northwest Forest Pass or Interagency Pass required. Pit toilets at trailhead. Picnic areas available. As a thru-hiking option, park a second car at the Middle CCC trailhead (see Hike 39). Open to leashed dogs, stock, mountain bikes; see map, page 156; **GPS:** N 47 32.888, W 121 32.194

This hike showcases one of the Middle Fork Snoqualmie River valley's most stunning rainforests, complete with a variety of mosses, lichen, and algae. The deep-emerald, moss-draped trees and dripping creeks are proof that this area's cool, wet climate is perfect for these organisms. What's more, the hike is not difficult, and nearly all who set foot on the pathway can enjoy seeing all or part of this gorgeous, second-growth forest.

GETTING THERE

From I-90 near North Bend: Take exit 34 and go north on 468th Avenue SE, passing gas and dining options. In 0.6 mile, turn right on SE Middle Fork Road. At 1.5 miles, at the Y, bear right on the one-way SE Lake Dorothy Road. At 2.8 miles, the one-way road ends and officially becomes SE Middle Fork Road (Forest Road 56). Signage here announces you are entering the Middle Fork Snoqualmie River valley. Stay on SE Middle Fork Road, passing various trailheads, for 12.7 miles to a

The high precipitation the Middle Fork area receives is revealed in the mossy understory.

large sign to the road's right for Middle Fork trailhead. Parking is plentiful.

ON THE TRAIL

From the parking area, walk toward the road and locate the trail, directly across the street. Immediately, you know this place is special. Sword fern carpets span in nearly all directions, and tall, healthy western hemlocks and western red cedars guide you through the forest along a narrow, gentle pathway.

In 0.3 mile, arrive at a wooden boardwalk over a wetland. Roughly midway through the boardwalk, a signed trail junction arrives from the right, a cutoff to the campground. Onward you go through more brilliant forest until the trail climbs to the old road-turned-trail, where a signed junction guides you to the left at 0.4 mile.

From this point on, the trail has an identity crisis as to whether it's still an old roadbed, at times being wide and open, sometimes narrow, then grown in tightly with the typical PNW cast of moisture-loving characters. Moss lines the edges of the trail as if it were planted intentionally for the perfect landscaping border. It feels like someone dropped you into a fairy tale as you wander through the tall, lichen-covered trees amid filtered sunlight, while Pacific wrens sing their long, complex songs. A moment of "All is right in the world" might even hit you when all this natural bounty comes together at fortuitous junctures.

You might snap back from your daydream when you hit the first washout crossing at 1.1 miles. The rocky crossing is straightforward and thankfully not an ankle twister. The trail continues with the occasional boardwalk and wooden footbridge guiding you over wet, marshy areas. Creeks trickle and trip, some across the trail, but they are easy to hop over.

The road-turned-trail was built by the Civilian Conservation Corps, a voluntary government work-relief program for unemployed, unmarried young men who, on the heels of the Great Depression, had given up on a promising future.

At 2.3 miles, the trail crosses a beautiful wooden bridge over a brushy creek and wet area. Tip your hat to the trail builders and nonprofits who work to put these features en route and make our hike much more pleasant.

Just following the bridge, a short boot path leads to a survey marker to the right. Cadastral survey markers are often used to delineate or triangulate property boundaries and management areas. Nothing to see here folks; carry on!

Two more landslide washouts, these much bigger than the first, start at 3.1 miles. Both have a trickling creek but are passable without wet shoes. They might, however, require some tricky hopping and a little shimmy to get across the boulders, but it's nothing to write home about.

The last little push shows off a couple of sneak-peek-through-the-trees views of jagged peaks across the valley before the trail descends and delivers you to SE Middle Fork Road. Technically, you could walk the road to the left back to your car (2.2 miles), but I wouldn't recommend it. Most drivers out here are hopped up on endorphins and might be too gleefully blissed-out to notice you there on the narrow-if-at-all shoulder. Walk back on that gorgeous trail instead, or hop in the vehicle you left as part of your thru hike.

42 Garfield Ledges

RATING/DIFFICULTY: ****/2

ROUNDTRIP: 2.1 miles

ELEV GAIN/HIGH POINT: 620 feet/1700 feet

SEASON: Year-round

Map: Green Trails Maps Middle Fork Snoqualmie No. 174SX; **Contact:** Mount Baker–Snoqualmie National Forest, Snoqualmie Ranger District; **Notes:** Northwest Forest Pass or Interagency Pass required. Pit toilets at trailhead. Picnic areas available. Open to leashed dogs; **GPS:** N 47 33.350, W 121 32.133

In 2019, this scenic new trail opened, giving hikers an opportunity to enjoy a sweeping panorama of the Middle Fork Snoqualmie River valley and surrounding

An interpretive sign at Garfield Ledges' panoramic viewpoint offers information about the valley below.

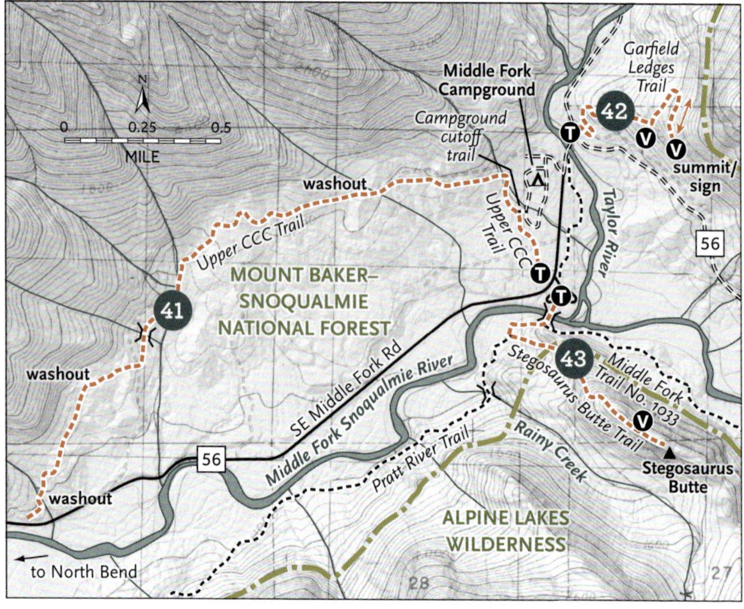

peaks. It's consistently steep, but it's short and pays off with views for days.

GETTING THERE

From I-90 near North Bend: Take exit 34 and go north on 468th Avenue SE, passing gas and dining options. In 0.6 mile, turn right on SE Middle Fork Road. At 1.5 miles, at the Y, bear right on the one-way SE Lake Dorothy Road. At 2.8 miles, the one-way road ends and officially becomes SE Middle Fork Road (Forest Road 56). Signage here announces you are entering the Middle Fork Snoqualmie River valley. Stay on SE Middle Fork Road, passing various trailheads, river points, and landmarks (including the Middle Fork Campground and Middle Fork trailhead) until the signed end of the county road and, sadly, the end of the pavement at 12.7 miles. Tell your car you love it and you are very sorry for the rough road ahead; thankfully, it's only 0.1 mile beyond this point to get to the parking area. Gently proceed through the potholes, crossing the Taylor River on a sturdy bridge, until you reach the parking area on the other side. You can park anywhere, but the closest access to the trailhead is near the pit toilets.

ON THE TRAIL

The trailhead is just to the right of the pit toilets, so once you've found it, head on up. In less than 80 feet, a kiosk shares a map, leave-no-trace reminders, and some natural history.

Sword ferns, salal, Oregon grape, and heaps of spongy moss coat the forest floor, while above you, second-growth western hemlocks and Douglas-firs shimmy in the wind. At 0.2 mile, the way levels off just a bit, giving you a chance to catch your breath before it climbs again.

Volunteers and trail crews did a fantastic job with this build, and at 0.5 mile, you reach your first set of trail stairs, placed strategically on a steep, rocky section. Just after them, a rocky outcropping lacking good views allows you to step off the trail if you need to grab water or put away a jacket.

The trail tread ebbs and flows between compact dirt and stony tread, with more trail stairs here and there. Listen for barred owls along the way at sunset—a nesting location isn't far off!

At 1 mile, you pop out of the trees and there you are—on the ledges! An interpretive sign tells how the valley below you formed, but you'll have a hard time reading it at first because all your eyes want to do is stare at that impressive vista. The sprawling river valley below you was cut from glaciers, and this overlook allows you to see exactly where they were. Bold peaks such as Stegosaurus Butte, Preacher Mountain, and others show off their rocky shoulders, while in the far distance, Rattlesnake Mountain comes to the pretty party.

Find a perch, enjoy a snack, and snap some pics before turning back.

43 Stegosaurus Butte

RATING/DIFFICULTY: **/4
ROUNDTRIP: 2.4 miles
ELEV GAIN/HIGH POINT: 1150 feet/2070 feet
SEASON: July–Sept

Map: Green Trails Maps Middle Fork Snoqualmie No. 174SX; **Contact:** Mount Baker–Snoqualmie National Forest, Snoqualmie Ranger District; **Notes.** Northwest Forest Pass or Interagency Pass required. Pit toilets at trailhead. Picnic areas available. Trail may be muddy, especially during shoulder seasons—avoid trail during this period. Trail is unmaintained and primitive; use at your own risk and discretion. Open to leashed dogs, stock (on Pratt River Trail); **GPS:** N 47 32.888, W 121 32.194

This hike isn't for everyone. It's unmaintained and unofficial, though it's on almost all maps and is well-known in the hiking community. It's rugged and so ridiculously steep in places that you may need to use your hands along with your feet to pull yourself up the slopes. When muddy, it can be a slippery slide. But if conditions and stamina are in your favor, it treats you to lovely views of Mount Garfield and the mountains to the southwest, such as Preacher and The Pulpit. Expect a primitive trail and you'll get exactly that.

GETTING THERE

From I-90 near North Bend: Take exit 34 and go north on 468th Avenue SE, passing gas and dining options. In 0.6 mile, turn right on SE Middle Fork Road. At 1.5 miles, at the Y, bear right on the one-way SE Lake Dorothy Road. At 2.8 miles, the one-way road ends and officially becomes SE Middle Fork Road (Forest Road 56). Signage here announces you are entering the Middle Fork Snoqualmie River valley. Stay on SE Middle Fork Road, passing various trailheads, for 12.7 miles to a large sign to the road's right for Middle Fork trailhead. Parking is plentiful.

ON THE TRAIL

The Middle Fork trailhead is often busy and buzzing, but most folks are here to hike other trails. Rest assured, you'll soon be free from

Mount Garfield looms over Stegosaurus Butte—brothers carved by time.

the crowds and wriggling up the slopes of Steg B. From the parking area, walk southeast toward the pit toilets and mapped kiosk, then follow the trail as it wanders toward the bridge.

The bridge is a fantastic architectural feature, and some folks come out here just to stand on its midspan and feel tiny amid the giant evergreens and rushing emerald water of the Middle Fork Snoqualmie River. Once across, at 0.1 mile, arrive at a T junction signed for Middle Fork Trail No. 1033 (see Hike 47) to the left. Head right here on what is now the Pratt River Trail. Several boot-beaten social trails head down to the river, but ours continues along a wide path sporting mossy rock walls and forested hillsides.

At 0.25 mile, keep your eyes peeled to the left. The trail junction is not signed, and you'll walk right by it if you aren't paying close attention. But, if you are focused on finding it, you'll do that move where you stop, smile widely, and do a double-take in disbelief! There it is: a well-traveled but hard-to-see dirt pathway—jackpot! If you end up at the big bridge over Rainy Creek, you've gone too far.

Turn left onto the Stegosaurus Butte Trail and start your slog, which climbs slowly at first, then gets busy making elevation gain. A few souvenirs of the logging efforts some years back are found in the form of rusty, frayed logging cables to the right.

The trail switches back on steep, tight grades as it makes its way uphill. Big roots and rocky steps make it feel like stairs sometimes as you step up and pull yourself along. Trekking poles are extremely handy for this trail, not only for the uphill, but for the knee-twisting downhill that will soon enough be your fate. You can almost see the top, though it's still dense forest—this climbing must stop, right? And it does.

At 0.9 mile, the trail levels out and gives your lungs a break. Just shy of 1 mile, it shows you to a well-used viewpoint to the left. This is the best view of Mount Garfield and its ledges and steep walls of almost anywhere in the area. Far below, the jade Middle Fork Snoqualmie River is visible—a marvel considering you were just right next to it! This is the perfect picnic spot, but you'll also want to check out the viewpoint to the southeast, in another 0.3 mile. To do that, continue following the trail, which is even more primitive now, as it descends briefly to a saddle. From the saddle, the trail climbs up and delivers you to an obvious, trodden lookout where a few rocky perches allow you to sit and take it in. The white noise you hear is the turbulent Rainy Creek deep in the valley. Rugged landscapes are front and center, and you might want to spend some time searching the hills for wildlife such as mountain goats or grazing bears.

You might be tempted to keep going on the boot trails beyond the final lookout, but they eventually dead-end in bushwhacks. After you've enjoyed the natural rewards of this area, retrace your steps back.

44 Pratt River Trail and Big Tree

RATING/DIFFICULTY: ***/3

ROUNDTRIP: 8.8 miles

ELEV GAIN/HIGH POINT: 1390 feet/1280 feet

SEASON: Year-round

Map: Green Trails Maps Middle Fork Snoqualmie No. 174SX; **Contact:** Mount Baker–Snoqualmie National Forest, Snoqualmie Ranger District; **Notes:** Northwest Forest Pass or Interagency Pass required. Trail to the Big Tree is unmaintained and difficult to follow—be prepared with a good map and navigation skills if you choose to visit. Pit toilets at trailhead. Picnic areas available. Open to leashed dogs, stock; see map, page 162; **GPS:** N 47 32.888, W 121 32.194

The mysteriously picturesque Pratt River Trail is a great pick for a rainy-day lowland hike, when other trails are snowy or when you want something that's not too difficult. The path bobs and weaves along the Middle Fork Snoqualmie River, passing rushing waterfalls, mossy outcroppings, and peekaboo mountain views until it reaches the Pratt River confluence. You can make this day shorter by turning back at this point, or keep going on a much more primitive grade to one of the biggest Douglas-firs in the valley.

GETTING THERE

From I-90 near North Bend: Take exit 34 and go north on 468th Avenue SE, passing gas and dining options. In 0.6 mile, turn right on SE Middle Fork Road. At 1.5 miles, at the Y, bear right on the one-way SE Lake Dorothy Road. At 2.8 miles, the one-way road ends and officially becomes SE Middle Fork Road (Forest Road 56). Signage here announces you are entering the Middle Fork Snoqualmie River valley. Stay on SE Middle Fork Road, passing various trailheads, for 12.7 miles to a large sign to the road's right for Middle Fork trailhead. Parking is plentiful.

ON THE TRAIL

Locate the trailhead near the pit toilets and large map kiosk on the southwestern side of the parking lot, then follow it past a large interpretive sign on invasive plants. Tip

Misty forests frame the emerald waters of the Middle Fork Snoqualmie River near the Pratt River Trail.

your hat in appreciation to the conservation groups who work to remove them, especially prickly Himalayan blackberries, ouch!

The trail goes through a large healthy forest before it arrives at the wood-and-steel Gateway Bridge, a stunning piece of architecture spanning the Middle Fork Snoqualmie River. The bridge itself is reason to come here because from its midspan, the sight is gorgeous; the river looks a deep jade color as it surrounds itself with matching evergreens. In the distance, Garfield Mountain and Ledges (Hike 42) are visible to the northeast. You'll want to linger, but the trail awaits!

After the bridge, the trail arrives at a signed T with the Middle Fork Trail. If you want to go left at some point, check out Hike 47, but for now, turn right and start down the Pratt River Trail. Almost immediately, a spur trail heads down to the river. You'll see several of these on your hike, so take them to visit the water if you please; otherwise stick to the main, well-traveled path. Just after the spur, a sign on a tree to the right reassures you that you are on the right path.

A few creeklets drip in from the left, some large enough to rock-hop, some small and charming as they drip through the thick moss on the trailside boulders. This whole place is like a giant sponge, especially in the rainy shoulder seasons. At 0.5 mile, arrive at a wooden bridge set over the waterfalling cascades of Rainy Creek. Western hemlock and western red cedar, as well as sword and deer fern line the creek's edges, and lime-colored moss covers nearly all the non-submerged boulders, making your eyes see so much green, it practically hurts. This is true Northwest glamour! If you have kids with you, mobility limitations, or simply not much time, this is a good turnaround spot. Otherwise carry on!

The trail continues, with spectacular large boulders to the left and impressive river and mountain views as the gentle trail makes its way along the river. Thanks to the efforts of the new construction around 2010, trail features such as stairs and wetland bridges help you make good time. At 1.4 miles, a recent washout forces you to pick your way through the rocky, sandy debris field. It's not hard to find your way, but use care not to roll an ankle as you look up to see where the rubble came from.

Moss, ferns, wetlands, root rocks, and evergreen and deciduous trees take you farther downstream through a variety of interesting microclimates, until at 3 miles, you reach an unsigned junction. Straight ahead, a spur makes its way to the riverbank and a campsite where most people revel in the beauty and declare the end of their hike. From this point on, the trail gets much more primitive, muddy, and bushwacky, especially after you turn off to see the big tree; continue if you are ready for more adventure!

The trail takes a gradual left turn and heads up the Pratt River valley, though you can't see the Pratt River at this point. You are near the area where the North Bend Timber Company had a logging operation as late as 1941, complete with a railroad, though signs of it are mostly gone now. The trail, now much narrower and in need of drainage work, begins a sloppy, wet climb for the next mile. Even in summer months, drips and runoff keep puddles and mud in places, so use care not to spin out. Salmonberries try to overtake the trail in a few spots, but it's not hard to keep on the path where routefinding is straightforward.

At 4 miles, reach a signed junction pointing toward the Big Trees to the right and the Trail to the left. Head right, though it's false advertising, since there is only one truly big tree and several larger-than-most trees. Now the true adventure begins; don't say you weren't warned. There are blowdowns to crawl over and bogs to walk through along the next 0.4 mile, but the faint trail is always evident. The trail drops down some and before you know it, you are standing in front of a behemoth Douglas-fir, along with a log for sitting and a small clearing indicating you've reached your goal. Pat yourself on your clammy back for a job well done and wander back to the trailhead when you've marinated enough in green.

45 Camp Brown

RATING/DIFFICULTY: **/1
ROUNDTRIP: 0.5 mile
ELEV GAIN/HIGH POINT: Negligible/1020 feet
SEASON: Year-round

Map: Green Trails Maps Middle Fork Snoqualmie No. 174SX; **Contact:** Mount Baker–Snoqualmie National Forest, Snoqualmie Ranger District; **Notes:** Northwest Forest Pass or Interagency Pass required. This trail is ADA accessible, but blowdowns are common and the surface is crushed gravel. Contact ranger station or search recent online trip reports for current updates. Pit toilets at trailhead. Picnic areas along route with barbeque grills. River access possible. Open to leashed dogs; **GPS:** N 47 32.768, W 121 32.706

This short, nearly all level, ADA-approved loop laden with postcard-worthy picnic spots is a wonderful place to stop and enjoy life. Not only is the interpretive loop accessible for those with disabilities, but it is also a great place to take toddlers, elders, those recovering from injury, or anyone who wants to breathe deeply and sit by the river basking in the sweetness of nature.

GETTING THERE

From I-90 near North Bend: Take exit 34 and go left north on 468th Avenue SE, passing gas and dining options. In 0.6 mile, turn right on SE Middle Fork Road. At 1.5 miles, at the Y, bear right on the one-way SE Lake Dorothy Road. At 2.8 miles, the one-way road ends and officially becomes SE Middle

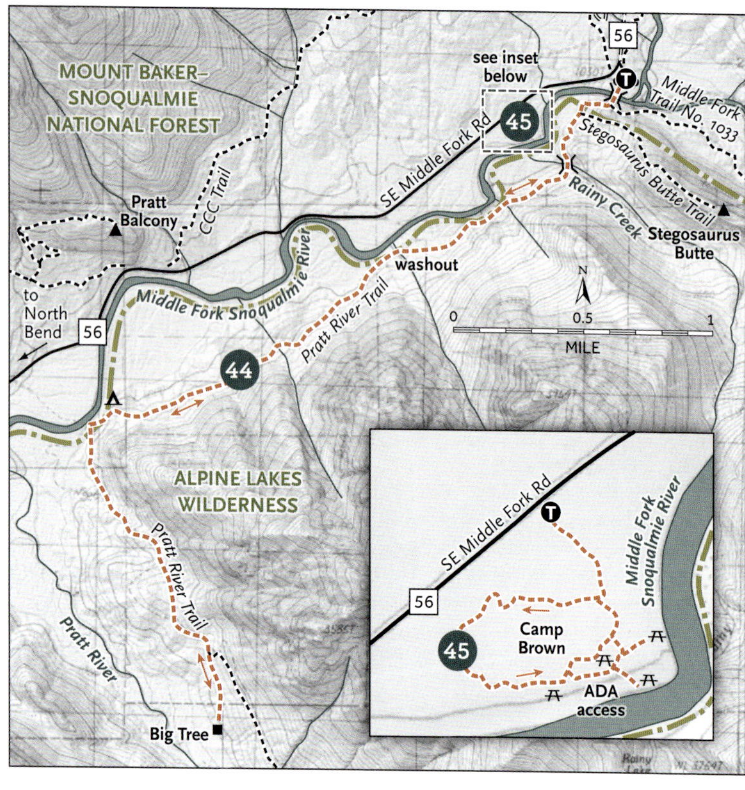

Fork Road (Forest Road 56). Signage here announces you are entering the Middle Fork Snoqualmie River valley. Stay on SE Middle Fork Road, passing trailheads for Mailbox Peak and Oxbow Loop, until you reach the signed Camp Brown Trail to your right at 11.8 miles.

ON THE TRAIL

Pass the informational kiosk, stopping if you wish to read it. You will be walking near the former Camp Brown, which served as the North Bend Timber Company's logging camp from 1929 to 1937. The signage helps you understand how the valley has changed from both human and natural influences.

In just under 350 feet, arrive at your first junction, where a spur straight ahead leads to a picnic spot and river viewpoint. It's a breathtaking view of Stegosaurus Butte and surrounding peaks showing off their rocky prominence. Visit if you wish, or bear right for your first of several interpretive signs on natural history.

Almost immediately after the sign, the trail loop begins. You can go right or left, but

Lunch with a view—river songs and mountain shadows at Camp Brown

most tend to walk right, so I'll assume we are headed that way. Along the way, there are several nooks with picnic tables and grills, including some of the best picnic spots in this whole valley. The river's purr is the primary soundtrack, save for the occasional bird, such as the knocking of the hairy woodpecker or single note of the varied thrush. You are buried in a spectacular forest with tall evergreens above your head and mossy understory near your feet.

At 0.3 mile, arrive at a signed ADA river bar access that contains a ramp down to the shoreline for another peek. Those interested in stair access can continue walking a short distance along the loop to find log steps leading to the same destination. More wonderful picnic viewpoints appear and, if you didn't bring the spread this time, make a mental note to come back—maybe next time throw in a book and a comfy chair for a day of complete perfection.

When the loop completes, turn right and retrace your steps back to the parking area.

46 Oxbow Loop

RATING/DIFFICULTY: ***/1
ROUNDTRIP: 1.4 miles
ELEV GAIN/HIGH POINT: 70 feet/940feet
SEASON: Year-round

Map: Green Trails Maps Middle Fork Snoqualmie No. 174SX; **Contact:** Department of Natural Resources; **Notes:** Discover Pass required. Pit toilets at northeast trailhead. Park in designated spots and not along the roadway. While there are two trailheads, this description starts at the beginning of the loop. If you park at the trailhead to the northeast, with the pit toilet, add 0.4 mile roundtrip and 10 feet of elevation gain to the hike. Some of the Middle Fork valley is Department of Natural Resources land, which requires a Discover Pass, while the other part is managed by the Forest Service, which requires a Northwest Forest Pass or an Interagency Pass. If you venture farther up the road and decide to stop for a picnic or another hike, be prepared with both passes. Open to leashed dogs; **GPS:** N 47 23.870, W 121 29.196

Built between 2018 and 2019, this newish, relatively level trail is a wonderful option for anyone who wants a mellow walk around a scenic waterway. Those with kids, physical disabilities, aging dogs, or other challenges will also appreciate the grade and the work that was performed to create this masterpiece. According to the nonprofit Mountains to Sound Greenway, more than 12,000 hours of contractor, crew, and volunteer time (an equivalent of 500 days), along with 220 tons of gravel and one 80-foot bridge delivered by helicopter were required to create this trail. Hiking with that knowledge makes you appreciate and enjoy it even more.

Though wrapped in forest, Oxbow Loop still offers glimpses of mountain majesty worthy of a photo stop.

GETTING THERE

From I-90 near North Bend: Take exit 34 and go north on 468th Avenue SE, passing gas and dining options. In 0.6 mile, turn right on SE Middle Fork Road. At 1.5 miles, at the Y, bear right on the one-way SE Lake Dorothy Road. At 2.8 miles, the one-way road ends and officially becomes SE Middle Fork Road (Forest Road 56). Signage here announces you are entering the Middle Fork Snoqualmie River valley. Stay on SE Middle Fork Road, passing trailheads for Mailbox Peak and Granite Creek, until you reach the first Oxbow trailhead at 8 miles from I-90. If this is full, a second trailhead with a pit toilet is found 0.1 mile farther up the road.

ON THE TRAIL

You can take this loop in either direction—both are equally beautiful with similar views. I prefer going right, maybe because I'm right-handed and left feels a little foreign to me. Off the start, bigleaf maples shimmer in passing breezes, and birds such as golden-crowned kinglets, varied thrushes, and Pacific wrens sing and call in the limbs above.

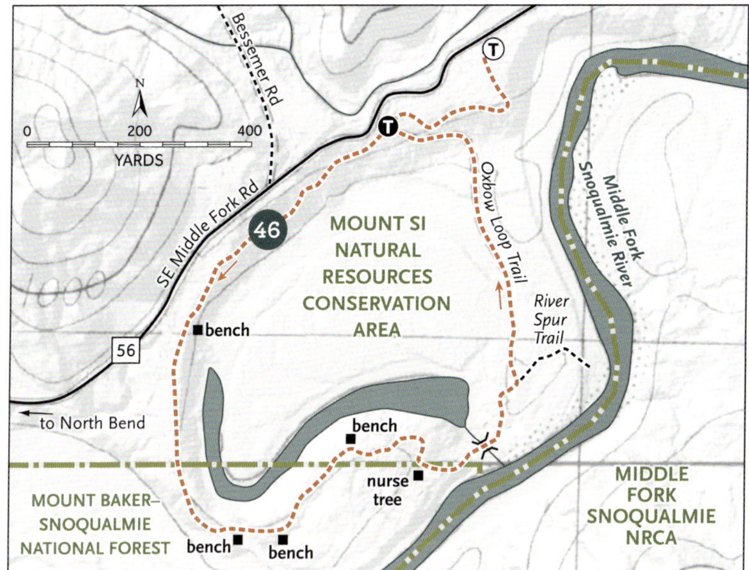

At 0.3 mile, an official viewpoint offers the first of four log benches you will encounter on this hike. Because this area receives so much rainfall, the benches are usually a bit wet, so a sit pad will keep your rear dry and comfortable if you intend to hang out on them.

Tens of thousands of years back, the Vashon Glacier formed an ice dam and subsequent lake, which later melted and sent glacial flooding and mineral deposits deep into this valley. The Middle and South Fork Snoqualmie Valleys with their wandering waterways, side channels, and swamps are all left over from the flood. This oxbow is a wetland of wonder that has become separated from the river, providing calm water for aquatic birds such as common goldeneyes, Canada geese, American coots, and ruddy ducks. Challenge your kids with bird IDs as you walk. There are wonderful smartphone apps, such as BirdNET, Merlin Bird ID, and eBird for education on calls and visual identification.

At 0.4 mile, look to the left through the foliage and spy one of many evergreens covered in bearded lichen. The stringy strands—which drop more than three feet in places—make these trees look like they have hair. The hike exhibits a mossy understory as you continue wandering past three more benches with viewpoints of the oxbow and the colorful hillsides of Bootalicious Peak to the northwest. The last bench appears at 0.7 mile.

The trail makes a hairpin turn at 0.9 mile and showcases a fantastic nurse tree to the right, where several evergreens have taken advantage of the stump's generous nutrients and grown into tall spectacles themselves. Immediately after the nurse tree, the trail crosses a wooden bridge over the oxbow's former outlet.

At 1.1 miles, the trail arrives at a junction where a short, rocky trail heads right, down to the banks of the Middle Fork Snoqualmie River. An out-and-back from this point will add 0.1 mile roundtrip, should you want to check it out. If not, bear left at this junction and wander back through deciduous trees until reaching the trailhead, completing your loop. With kids, dogs, and adults all piled back in the vehicle, continue exploring the Middle Fork valley, or head back for treats or lunch in North Bend.

47 Middle Fork Trail

RATING/DIFFICULTY: ***/3
ROUNDTRIP: 12.5 miles
ELEV GAIN/HIGH POINT: 1670 feet/1380 feet
SEASON: Year-round

Map: Green Trails Maps Middle Fork Snoqualmie No. 174SX; **Contact:** Mount Baker–Snoqualmie National Forest, Snoqualmie Ranger District; **Notes:** Northwest Forest Pass or Interagency Pass required. Pit toilets at trailhead. Picnic areas available. Trail may be muddy, especially during shoulder seasons. The road to Dingford Creek trailhead is extremely rough and is only recommended for high-clearance vehicles. Open to leashed dogs. Open to mountain bikes on odd-numbered calendar days June 1–Oct 31. Open to stock July 15–Oct 31; **GPS:** N 47 32.888, W 121 32.194

The forests of the Middle Fork Snoqualmie River valley are luxuriously mossy, lichen laden, perpetually damp, and brimming with wild and unwieldy vegetation. They are so thick and lush that the outstanding scenery almost feels like someone dropped you in a fable and at any moment a tiny fairy might whiz by. This hike is about a deep forest and wetlands—where the journey is the destination.

GETTING THERE

Middle Fork (main) Trailhead: From I-90 near North Bend, take exit 34 and go north on 468th Avenue SE, passing gas and dining options. In 0.6 mile, turn right on SE Middle Fork Road. At 1.5 miles, at the Y, bear right on the one-way SE Lake Dorothy Road. At 2.8 miles, the one-way road ends and officially becomes SE Middle Fork Road (Forest Road 56). Signage here announces you are entering the Middle Fork Snoqualmie River valley. Stay on SE Middle Fork Road, passing various trailheads, for 12.7 miles to a large sign to the road's right for Middle Fork trailhead. Parking is plentiful.

Dingford Creek Trailhead (alternative trailhead, only recommended for AWD or 4x4 and high-clearance vehicles): Follow the directions above, but continue past the Middle Fork trailhead for another 0.1 mile to reach a right turn at the signed junction for Dingford Creek trailhead. Follow this soul-sucking, nightmare-evoking road for 6 miles to the road's end, where you'll find the trailhead.

ON THE TRAIL

From the Middle Fork trailhead parking area, walk toward the pit toilet and large map kiosk and begin your hike. The vivid green limbs of the hushed forest welcome you as you walk toward Gateway Bridge, spanning the Middle Fork Snoqualmie River. The bridge itself is a remarkable piece of architecture, and the sights from midspan are a treat for the eyes. The river is a deep jade color with distant mountains such as Garfield, with jagged peaks and ridgelines. This view will get even

Another masterful bridge over rushing, icy waters—built by dedicated volunteers and trail crews who make the wilderness safer for us all

better on the hike, so snap a few pictures, then continue onward.

Beyond the bridge, arrive at a signed T-junction. The right branch heads off to the Pratt River Trail (Hike 44), and our trail goes left. From here it traverses a narrow stretch of trail just above the river, where outstanding views of Garfield Mountain towering above the babbling river will make you pause and gawk. As you'd expect, a couple of small boot paths cut through the forest and down to the riverbank, the larger at 0.2 mile.

Lichen, moss, and algae grow with such reckless abandon here, they've almost taken over every surface, including even the trees themselves. Mosses—including stair-step, rock, cat's tail, Lyell's bristle, lanky, and sphagnum—are found along this trail, and it's not uncommon to see many varieties growing side by side in just one square foot. One of their main functions is to be an anchor for rocks, soil, or tree matter to prevent erosion. They are tough, adaptable plants and have been known to survive in high heat, low temperatures, and even when they get dried out. And since they don't have roots, they can grow just about anywhere, such as steep hillsides, slick rocky outcroppings, and even in water. Instead of roots, they have tiny hairlike structures with which they draw nutrients and photosynthesize. Because they are so adaptable, they live on every continent on Earth and can survive in environments like damp, dark caves or arid deserts. What's more, they've been around a long time—even dating back 500 million years. Tuck those wild knowledge feathers in your hat and keep walking.

At 1.3 miles, arrive at a curious new sign about the next 1000 feet being steep, narrow tread and reminding equestrians and bicyclists to use caution. This stretch of trail was rebuilt after a washout made a mess of things several years ago. The reroute is a

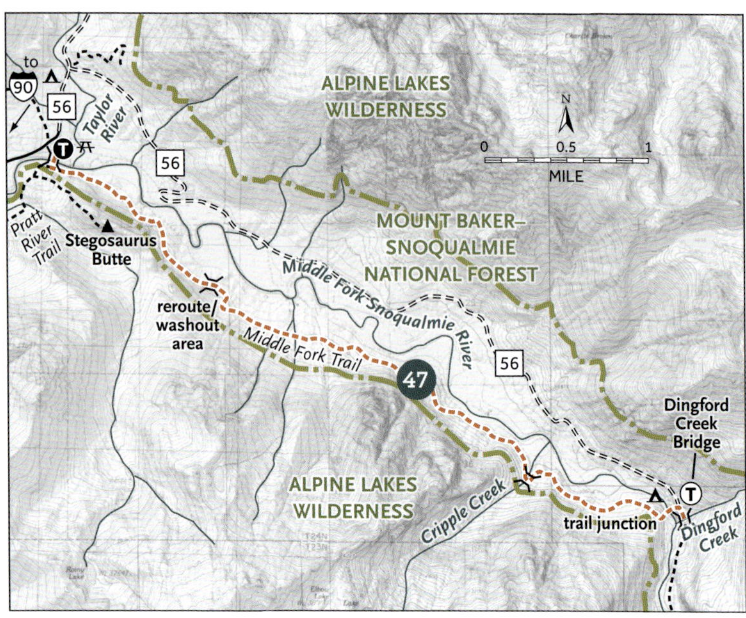

more sustainable, long-term solution, climbing up and over the jumble and utilizing the hillside above it for the traverse. Since most of this trail contains gentle ups and downs, the new part feels a bit grueling, but at least it's short. It ascends on pleasant trail tread before descending on the other side, a total distance of 0.5 mile.

Trail building along this whole trail is impressive, since structures are imperative in places for drainage control and wetland protection, especially as this trail is open to bike tires and horse hooves. Trail builders use various structures such as turnpikes and puncheon bridges to help users get through the most damage-prone areas. Turnpikes are elevated surfaces usually bordered by logs that keep the trail higher than the natural contour to help with drainage. Puncheons are like boardwalks and are near the ground, keeping the trail out of bogs and wetlands. If you are interested in joining a trail crew and learning more about how trails are constructed, along with how much hard work is involved, volunteer opportunities abound (see Resources).

At 3 miles, rock-hop across a washed out, open area. Your shoes will stay dry, and navigation is straightforward. After crossing, you head back into the enchanted, fairy-tale forest and ramble on.

At 4.2 miles, the path leads you down to the river's edge and continues near its banks. The river isn't spitting rapids or twisting and turning in fury at this spot, but rather flowing slowly and tranquilly, providing an excellent spot for a quiet break or peaceful meditation. The hangout spots are limited, but there are a couple of areas where you could bust out a sit pad and relax. Perhaps this is your goal for the day? If not, carry on.

The next feature arrives at 5 miles, where a large bridge in need of a few railing repairs gets you over the roaring Cripple Creek. A waterfall above the bridge is a little tough to see, thanks to some boulders and fallen logs, but you'll see some of it and hear it churning.

At 5.9 miles, campsites are visible near the riverbank down a hill to the left. A signed trail junction points them out, should you want to hang out there for a picture-perfect lunch break. You are just shy of 6 miles from the trailhead where you started but close to the Dingford Creek trailhead, so it's not too surprising to see developed camps and other hikers coming in this way. This area feels a world away from civilization, but you are just a bridge crossing and a short walk away from cars! The road leading to Dingford Creek trailhead is loaded with car-swallowing potholes and water erosion problems and is only recommended for high-clearance vehicles. It's best to walk back on the trail instead of thru-hike, unless you have a capable vehicle and friends willing to do a two-car shuttle.

Our destination for the day is the lovely Dingford Creek Bridge, near the confluence of Dingford Creek and the Middle Fork Snoqualmie. To find it, continue walking past the campsites, and at 6.1 miles, arrive at a signed trail junction dropping a short distance down to its span. Don't miss the giant old-growth western red cedar to the right, just before the junction!

Once on the bridge, admire the aquamarine rapids churning through boulders below your feet before heading back.

EXTENDING YOUR HIKE

You can continue following the Middle Fork Trail (instead of turning off toward the Dingford Creek Bridge) for as long as you'd like. Hiking the whole trail is a huge day, fit for trail runners or brawny day hikers with ample gumption and boundless energy. The biggest challenges by far are the multiple hazardous water fords, which are swift, slick, and powerful, especially in spring and early summer. Waiting to hike this until late summer is the safest option. The other challenge is navigation, as Mother Nature's water chisels have made a mess of trail finding, especially near Burnt Boot Creek. Be prepared to turn back, and don't get yourself in a pickle if things look sketchy.

Should you decide to hike the Middle Fork Trail's upper section, and all goes well, it parallels the Dutch Miller Gap Trail (FR 56, Hike 51) on the other side of the valley. Loops, thru hikes, or overnights are possible by connecting the Middle Fork Trail with the Dutch Miller Gap Trail.

48 Marten Lake

RATING/DIFFICULTY: ****/5
ROUNDTRIP: 9 miles
ELEV GAIN/HIGH POINT: 1960 feet/3020 feet
SEASON: July–Oct

Map: Green Trails Maps Middle Fork Snoqualmie No. 174SX; **Contact:** Mount Baker–Snoqualmie National Forest, Snoqualmie Ranger District, Department of Natural Resources; **Notes:** Northwest Forest Pass or Interagency Pass required. Pit toilets at trailhead. Picnic areas available. Distance can vary slightly depending on which braided social trail you take. Avoid creating more social trails or cairns. Trail can be slick and hazardous when wet and muddy. Open to leashed dogs; **GPS:** N 47 33.652, W 121 31.931

The shoreline of Marten Lake rests in quiet harmony as fall drapes the forest in warm, glowing hues.

You might be looking at the hike stats and thinking it sounds moderate, but this hike is definitely not for rookies or anyone who is looking for a classic, straightforward trail. The first 2.8 miles are exactly that on a road-turned-trail, but afterward the trail darts into a steep maze of unimproved, unmaintained trails with navigational challenges and a jumble of roots and rocks, requiring, at times, hands-and-feet climbing. Add some mud, water diversion issues, and overgrown salmonberries to the mix and you have a trail made for only those who are well-prepared for this adventure. Know your limits and choose a different hike if this sounds overwhelming. This is a day-hiking book, but I'd be remiss if I didn't tell you that there is only one campsite at this lake and it's also the day-use area, so best to plan the overnight elsewhere.

GETTING THERE

From I-90 near North Bend: Take exit 34 and go north on 468th Avenue SE, passing gas and dining options. In 0.6 mile, turn right on SE Middle Fork Road. At 1.5 miles, at the Y, bear right on the one-way SE Lake Dorothy Road. At 2.8 miles, the one-way road ends and officially becomes SE Middle Fork Road (Forest Road 56). Signage here announces you are entering the Middle Fork Snoqualmie River valley. Stay on SE Middle Fork Road, passing various trailheads, river points, and landmarks (including the Middle Fork Campground and Middle Fork trailhead) until the official signed end of the county road and, sadly, the end of the pavement at 12.7 miles. Tell your car you love it and you are very sorry for the rough road ahead. Gently proceed through the frequent huge potholes, crossing the Taylor River on a sturdy bridge. Continue another ponytail-wiggling, tummy-jiggling 0.5 mile to reach the dead end at the Snoqualmie Lake trailhead.

ON THE TRAIL

From the Snoqualmie Lake trailhead, cross the Taylor River on a sturdy car bridge, only with your feet. This road-turned-trail was closed to cars in the late 1980s, but recent private land claims up near Quartz Creek have opened the way to commercial vehicles, so it very much feels like a roadway again. The vehicles are few and far between, so don't worry your sweet head about becoming a hood ornament. Instead, enjoy gawking at the trailside campsites, located right next to the river.

In 0.4 mile, pass the junction for the Quartz Creek Trail, where the wide newer road-turned-trail veers left. Our trail goes straight ahead, now more of a single track.

The gentle grade of the former roadbed helps you keep a steady pace, and at 0.6 mile, it arrives at your first creek crossing. This one is a rock-hop in most seasons, so even the most uncoordinated among us can usually get through with dry shoes. With the sheer number of wide creek crossings, trekking poles come in extremely handy all along this hike.

Almost immediately after the creek, Mount Garfield's west peak is visible to the right; framed like a portrait through the trees. What a wild, wonderful place!

Hop over a couple more creeks and creeklets before, at 2.8 miles, you arrive at an easy-to-miss, unsigned but obvious pathway heading off into the forest to the left. If you get to the large, wooden bridge over the churning Marten Creek, backtrack 0.1 mile and look closely for the trail (now to the right). If you find the trail without visiting the bridge, make a note to jog a little farther along the path on your way out to visit it. The waterfall and splendor of it all are not to be missed.

If you found the trail to Marten Lake, congratulations! Your first mission is complete. Now the climbing and challenge begin. Pick your way up the slope, climbing over large blowdowns and cruising up through giant hemlocks, with multiple options for pathways. Over the years, folks have tied pink ribbons to the trees or built cairns in attempts to be helpful, but this is frowned upon by land management, so please don't do it. Most of the braided trails eventually lead to the same place: up!

To your right along this stretch is the gorgeous Marten Creek, which drops in tiers to audible waterfalls along the trail. There are at least three viewpoints for the cascading rumbles, so be sure to step over to the water's edge and check it out. Use caution when you do so, as this area can be muddy and slippery when wet.

After 0.5 mile of steep, challenging climbing on the Marten Lake Trail (3.3 miles from the trailhead), the path diverts around a gigantic erratic boulder left over from the ice age, before continuing a narrow, sometimes muddy, wet climb up the valley.

At 3.6 miles, the trail crosses a shrubby swale where you play whack-a-bush with your trekking pole. Salmonberries, bracken fern, vine maple, and slide alder try to trip you up, but you are a champion, and they are no match for your skill and dexterity. Smack 'em!

Almost immediately after the brushy hillside, the type 2 fun begins. You thought this was already type 2 fun? Buckle up. Next up, the steep gets steeper and the rough gets rougher. Make your way up through roots, vines, and loose dirt using the occasional pull-up maneuver and walrus flop as you attempt to exhibit grace and poise in your forward progress.

Eventually, you reach a relatively flat stretch where your calves start to forgive you before the trail descends toward the lake. After 4.4 miles, the trail shows you to a campsite along the lake's shoreline. If it's occupied, you'll have to apologize for the intrusion, as it's one of the only places to sit and enjoy the shore. A primitive trail is found to the left of the lake and pops up at a few spots, but it's overgrown and there isn't much opportunity for shoreline access save for a rock or two that are sketchy at best. To the lake's right is a logjam, which can sometimes be crossed if you have twinkle toes, but it isn't optimal either. Wander around and explore, burning a few more calories before finding your landing spot.

Be safe, be careful, and remember, what goes up must come down. Save some energy for the precarious maneuvers you'll need to perform to get back to the Snoqualmie Lake Trail. Once there, remember to pop over to the bridge to see Marten Creek in all its glory before heading back to your car on a trail that, thankfully, is much more mellow.

49 Otter Falls and Lipsy Lake

RATING/DIFFICULTY: ****/3
ROUNDTRIP: 10.1 miles
ELEV GAIN/HIGH POINT: 840 feet/1760 feet
SEASON: Apr–Oct

Map: Green Trails Maps Middle Fork Snoqualmie No. 174SX; **Contact:** Mount Baker–Snoqualmie National Forest, Snoqualmie Ranger District, Department of Natural Resources; **Notes:** Northwest Forest Pass or Interagency Pass required. Pit toilets at trailhead. Picnic areas available. Open to leashed dogs, stock, mountain bikes; **GPS:** N 47 33.652, W 121 31.931

The defunct Taylor River Road serves as the pathway that guides you over a few buzzing creeks to reach the turnoff to the marvelous Otter Falls. Lipsy Lake catches the waterfall in its peaceful little basin and is the perfect place to park yourself when you want to enjoy the tranquility of the natural surroundings.

GETTING THERE

From I-90 near North Bend: Take exit 34 and go north on 468th Avenue SE, passing gas and dining options. In 0.6 mile, turn right on SE Middle Fork Road. At 1.5 miles, at the Y, bear right on the one-way SE Lake Dorothy Road. At 2.8 miles, the one-way road ends and officially becomes SE Middle Fork Road (Forest Road 56). Signage here announces you are entering the Middle Fork Snoqualmie River valley. Stay on SE Middle Fork Road, passing various trailheads, river points, and landmarks (including the Middle Fork

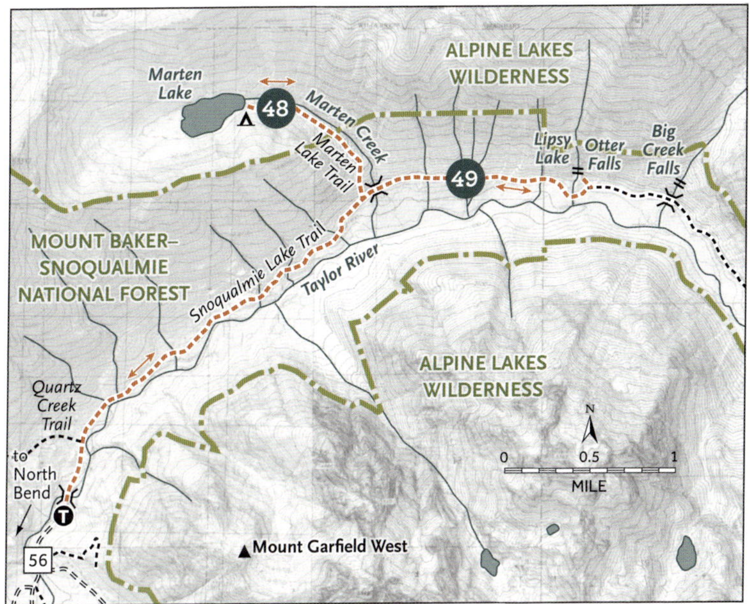

Campground and Middle Fork trailhead) until the official signed end of the county road and, sadly, the end of the pavement at 12.7 miles. Tell your car you love it and you are very sorry for the rough road ahead. Gently proceed through the frequent huge potholes, crossing the Taylor River on a sturdy bridge. Continue another ponytail-wiggling, tummy-jiggling 0.5 mile to reach the dead end at the Snoqualmie Lake trailhead.

ON THE TRAIL

The trail kicks off from the Snoqualmie Lake trailhead by crossing Taylor River on a bridge that once held a lot more than feet, thanks to logging and mining efforts in this area. These days, shoes instead of tires follow this road-turned-trail, and the powerful cascading water beneath the bridge makes you pause. Campsites are abundant to the right, down by the creek, and make a great place to visit if you want to just enjoy the river's shoreline.

In 0.4 mile, pass the junction for the Quartz Creek Trail heading off to the left, which, thanks to private land stakes, is a large, gravel road. Our trail goes straight ahead and now resembles a single-track pathway.

The gentle grade of the former roadbed helps you keep a steady pace, and at 0.6 mile, it arrives at your first creek crossing. This one is a rock-hop in most seasons, so even the most uncoordinated among us can usually get through with dry shoes. With the sheer number of wide creek crossings, trekking poles come in extremely handy all along this hike.

Otter Falls cascades into the scene as a happy hiker soaks in the beauty at Lipsy Lake.

Almost immediately after the creek, Mount Garfield's west peak is visible to the right, framed like a portrait through the trees. The Middle Fork can't help but be gorgeous and seems to be most humble about it.

The Taylor River was named for William Taylor, who was responsible for platting the townsite of North Bend. He was a true pioneer and was instrumental in the community, taking on the role of county commissioner, school board representative, general store owner, conservationist, and bridge builder and land designer, among other contributions. Even the park where the North Bend Trail Depot is located bears his name. Photos show him with an epic handlebar mustache, so obviously, he was also a man of distinguished grooming and exquisite taste. He passed away in 1941, at age eighty-eight, after living a long, productive life, and is buried not far from Mount Si.

Hop over a couple more creeks and creeklets before, at 2.8 miles, an obvious unsigned trail heading up to Marten Lake appears to the left (Hike 48). A short 0.1 mile beyond that trail, a gorgeous wooden thank-goodness-it's-there bridge crosses the turbulent Marten Creek, where a mandatory picture and maybe even video, must be taken.

A few more seasonal creeks are jumped across, and a beautiful camp shows up to the right, followed by a wide creek at 3.9 miles. With luck and an abundance of teeter-tottering on rocks, you might be able to get across this one without waterlogged kicks—but slips happen, and only you know the intimate dialogue between your brain and your feet. Don't go in the drink unless you intend to. If you do, pretend you wanted that to happen and own it like a boss. Nothing to see here folks, carry on.

More forest travel follows, allowing you to catch up on chitchat with trail pals, until at 4.7 miles, it's you versus the water again. The granddaddy of all water crossings is upon you—saving the best for last. If you are here in springtime, you might get your feet wet, but it really depends on your balancing abilities and the water's run rate. Early on a warm day, you might be able to get over this wet wonder with some cunning skills and sturdy shoe placement. However, if the winter snowpack is colliding with the heat of the day, you might be surprised to see those same rocks covered in water on your return. In mid- to late summer, you can usually get across without soaked toes. If not, maybe just submit to wet footwear (or use water shoes) and use all the judgment your mama gave you so you don't twist an ankle with your unexpected slips.

In less than 0.2 mile beyond the big water crossing, arrive at a signed junction to Otter Falls heading off to the left. The sign is small and without much fanfare, considering this trail is so popular. Turn left and take the braided spur up through the spindly forest. Several trails lead to the same place, made by confused folks looking for the "main" one, which doesn't really exist. If you are going up, you are going the right way. And you can see the falls, so navigation is obvious.

In a hair over 5 miles, arrive at the main feature—the awe-inspiring Otter Falls, which flows into the itty-bitty, puddle-like Lipsy Lake. A small pebble beach waits for you to enjoy its quiet nooks. The best time to view the waterfall is from April to late June because in late summertime, it turns to more of a trickle. A whopping 502 feet are visible from this angle, but if you can imagine it, there are 1200 feet of falls coming down to this drainage—over double what we can see! Head back the way you arrived when you are done enjoying this gorgeous place.

EXTENDING YOUR HIKE

When you are done enjoying the falls, head back to the main trail via the spur, and, if time permits—turn left to visit Big Creek Falls. It adds 1 mile roundtrip and 70 feet of elevation gain to your day. The old road feels very much like a trail so far up this valley, so it's almost shocking to come across the old car bridge that covers the falls. During the height of spring runoff, the waterfall here rages with a fury so fierce, it nearly makes you quake.

50 Hester Lake

RATING/DIFFICULTY: ****/4
ROUNDTRIP: 11.4 miles
ELEV GAIN/HIGH POINT: 2660 feet/3850 feet
SEASON: July–Oct

Map: Green Trails Maps Middle Fork Snoqualmie No. 174SX; **Contact:** Mount Baker–Snoqualmie National Forest, Snoqualmie Ranger District; **Notes:** Northwest Forest Pass or Interagency Pass required. Pit toilets at trailhead. Picnic areas available. Trail may be muddy, especially during shoulder seasons. The road to Dingford Creek trailhead is extremely rough and is only recommended for AWD or 4x4 vehicles with 8 inches or more of clearance. The last 6 miles of driving directions will take forty-five minutes to an hour each way. Please plan accordingly. Water crossings during early summer or after large rains may get shoes wet—bring water shoes or slop through it. Open to leashed dogs, stock; **GPS:** N 47 31.056, W 121 27.226

Hester Lake naps beneath alpine ridges—perfect for those craving solitude.

Once you've braved the road to the trailhead, the rest is gravy. Okay, maybe more like mashed potatoes *and* gravy when you add the elevation gain and water crossings, but the reward is well worth it. You'll be standing on the shoreline of a peaceful and rarely visited alpine lake with plenty of solitude and views.

GETTING THERE

From I-90 near North Bend: Take exit 34 and go north on 468th Avenue SE, passing gas and dining options. In 0.6 mile, turn right on SE Middle Fork Road. At 1.5 miles, at the Y, bear right on the one-way SE Lake Dorothy Road. At 2.8 miles, the one-way road ends and officially becomes the SE Middle Fork Road (Forest Road 56). Signage here announces you are entering the Middle Fork Snoqualmie River valley. Stay on SE Middle Fork Road, passing various trailheads. At 12.7 miles, pass the Middle Fork trailhead and immediately slow down; your vehicle might get swallowed whole otherwise, thanks to potholes. Thankfully they get repaired periodically. Here, the road turns to gravel and crosses the Taylor River on a sturdy bridge. Reach the picnic area/trailhead for Garfield Ledges at 12.8 miles and turn right toward the Dingford Creek trailhead on FR 56 just before the pit toilets. Follow this hot mess of a washed out, potholed, bad-word-evoking road until roughly (and I mean rough-ly) 18.8 miles, where your vehicle and your kidneys stop bouncing and you arrive at the Dingford Creek trailhead.

ON THE TRAIL

From the parking area, hop onto the well-signed Dingford Creek Trail and begin your climb. The trail wastes no time rocketing you into the forest with an incline that will test your fitness level. Thankfully in roughly a mile, it eases, so lean into the burn. Dingford Creek purrs with white noise like the soundtrack of a relaxing day spa as your breathing gives you rhythm.

In 0.8 mile, reach the Alpine Lakes Wilderness boundary, announced by a tree sign to the right. At 1 mile, the trail crosses Pumpkinseed Creek and its adjacent falls, which pitch themselves over a granite slab into a pool below. When the snow is melting in the high country, this waterfall is quite pretty and worth a picture—you may even want to swap into water shoes if you brought them, since you'll have to pick your way across. By late summer or early fall in most years, it's possible to access Hester Lake with dry shoes by rock-hopping all the bigger water crossings. But in early to midsummer, prepare for slopping through some wetness.

Drippy creeks and the occasional muddy patch make the trail a perfect representation of the Pacific Northwest, as it guides you through the understory of plants such as salmonberry, snowberry, queen's cup, vanilla leaf, Oregon grape, deer fern, and trillium.

At 2.1 miles, Goat Creek—near a large swath of giant, erratic boulders left over from the ice age—crosses the trail. In early summer, you might have to wade to get across safely, unless you are coordinated enough to tap dance across the slick rock tops.

After 3.3 miles, arrive a signed intersection with options. Straight ahead is Myrtle Lake

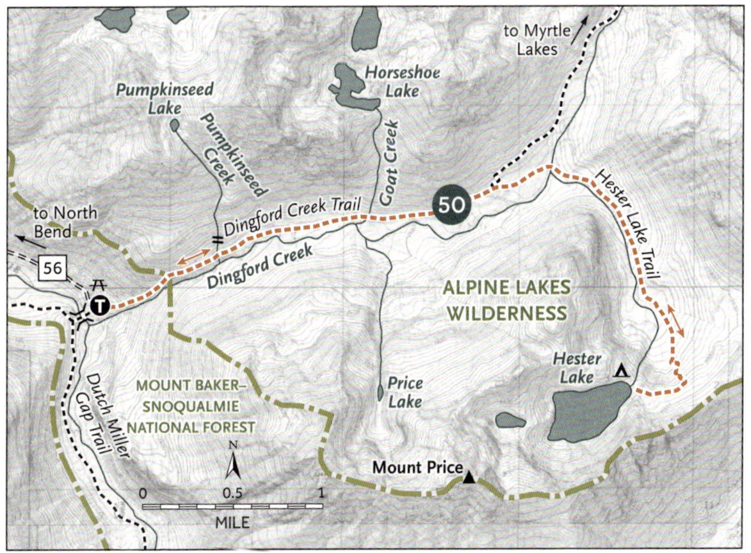

(see Extending Your Hike), and to the right is our trail to Hester. You are some distance from civilization at this point, but after that crazy drive, you feel even farther away from development. This intersection feels like a magical stop in the forest—even though you've been following a trail, you feel almost like no one has been here, yet there's a welcoming sign on a purposely placed post in a small clearing in a thick forest.

Turn right, and almost immediately after the sign, cross another creek where springtime rains and snowmelt will have your shoes and socks soaked. From this point onward, there are several back-and-forth crossings of this creek, an unnamed tributary to Dingford. Each time, the trail is either obvious, or a cairn (rock stack) is located at an opposing bank. Washouts change these crossings each year, so a good map and some navigation skills will come in handy.

At 3.7 miles, admire the work of trail crews who have placed split log crossings over wet marshy areas—well done, folks! This might be a good time to mention that work crews are often volunteers with organizations such as Washington Trails Association or Mountains to Sound Greenway, who donate time simply for the love of trails. If you are moved by this, perhaps you'd want to consider volunteering or donating some dollars? It's a good way to give back to the places you love (see Resources). Speaking of love, wait until you see this lake!

At 4 miles, the trail takes a reroute to avoid its former path through a fragile meadow. The work of trail crews is once again evident, as the rocky surface has a cobblestone effect in places. Elk are frequent users of this meadow, so keep your voices and your footsteps quiet for the best shot at seeing them.

Marshy bogs and more creeks pop up as you continue your journey toward Hester Lake. Stick with it—it feels much longer than it really is due to narrow trail tread and, at times, tricky toe taps.

Eventually, the trail takes a steeper turn and pushes up to a ridge where it levels off and passes a shallow pond on the left—so close now! At 5.5 miles, cross a log jam over the lake's outlet, using caution with your steps. The logs are firm and sturdy, but shifts in water below their resting place can cause them to be slippery. After the log jam, the trail sort of peters out, but if you walk toward the water's edge on the logs, you will find a trail to the lake's shoreline, which houses several tent sites. Your options for relaxing include the solid camps on terra firma or the logs themselves, which provide ample views of the lake. A couple of small rocky outcroppings are found by following the lake's shoreline to the northwest, making ideal places to snap some pictures of the serene lake with Mount Price in the background. There is a peacefulness here that soaks through your skin. Take it with you as you head back to wherever you live.

EXTENDING YOUR HIKE

If you have the time and energy, you might enjoy a side trip to peaceful Myrtle Lake, a 4.2-mile roundtrip excursion from the signed junction. The 2.1-mile access is fairly brushy, and in early summer, mud pockets show up in the wet areas, but the path is generally easy to follow. From the intersection, you'll climb another 885 feet to arrive at the placid lake under the shoulders of Little Bulger Mountain, surrounded by forest. This lake isn't visited as often as others in the Alpine Lakes region, so you'll feel like you have the whole place to yourself. You can also continue onward to Little Myrtle Lake, just shy of 1 mile one way and another 480 feet in elevation gain up the trail.

51 Dutch Miller Gap Trail

RATING/DIFFICULTY: ***/3
ROUNDTRIP: 10.2 miles
ELEV GAIN/HIGH POINT: 790 feet/2080 feet
SEASON: Apr–late Oct

Map: Green Trails Maps Middle Fork Snoqualmie No. 174SX; **Contact:** Mount Baker–Snoqualmie National Forest, Snoqualmie Ranger District; **Notes:** Northwest Forest Pass or Interagency Pass required. Pit toilets at trailhead. Picnic areas available. Trail may be muddy, especially during shoulder seasons. The road to Dingford Creek trailhead is extremely rough and is only recommended for AWD or 4x4 vehicles with 8 inches or more of clearance. The last 6 miles of driving directions will take forty-five minutes to an hour each way. Please plan accordingly. Hike is described to Goldmyer Hot Springs, but shorter or longer distances are possible. Open to leashed dogs, mountain bikes, stock; **GPS:** N 47 28.929, W 121 23.049

If you have a high-clearance, off-road vehicle and don't mind a road that's more like a boulder-filled riverbed than a forest road, you will make it to this trailhead with minimal grief and probably really enjoy this hike along an old road-turned-trail. But why visit with such a bad road? Well for starters, it's the only way to see the raging Dingford Creek Falls, unless you hike the Middle Fork Trail down to Dingford Creek trailhead and walk the old

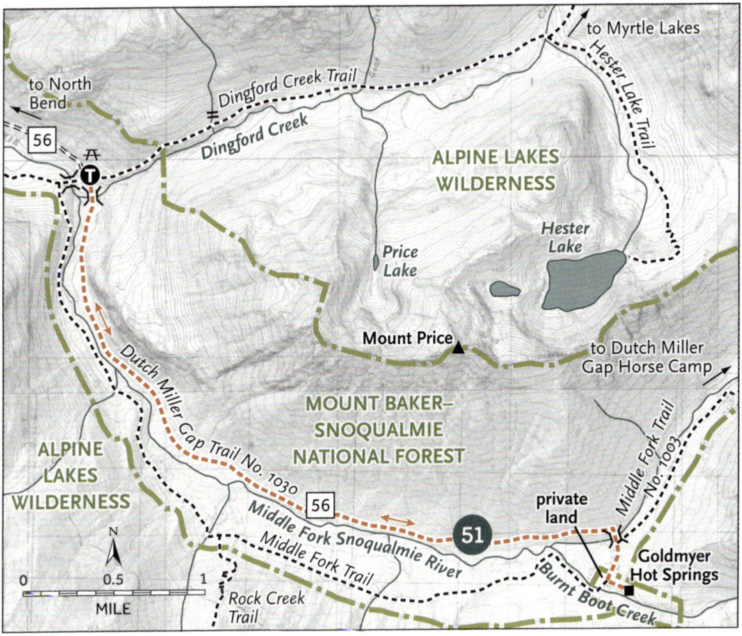

The Dutch Miller Gap Trail follows an old roadway, gradually climbing alongside the river as it makes its way up the valley.

road. Additionally, there are spots to stop and enjoy the river with ample solitude and beautiful mountain views as you get farther up the valley. Furthermore, it's the most direct route to the private Goldmyer Hot Springs, which is an interesting spot and a perfect turnaround destination. You'll have to make a reservation to soak, and you can't *see* the hot springs unless you have a soaking reservation, but it's interesting to at least visit the caretaker's cabin deep in the forest. Finally, if you trail run or enjoy long days and want to lose yourself in woodsy bliss, you can get to the end of the road where it dives back into single track and makes its way to a number of backcountry destinations.

GETTING THERE

From I-90 near North Bend: Take exit 34 and go north on 468th Avenue SE, passing gas and dining options. In 0.6 mile, turn right on SE Middle Fork Road. At 1.5 miles, at the Y, bear right on the one-way SE Lake Dorothy Road. At 2.8 miles, the one-way road ends and officially becomes SE Middle Fork Road (Forest Road 56). Signage here announces you are entering the Middle Fork Snoqualmie River valley. Stay on SE Middle Fork Road, passing various trailheads. At 12.7 miles, pass the Middle Fork trailhead and immediately slow down; your vehicle might get swallowed whole otherwise, thanks to potholes. Thankfully they get repaired periodically. Here, the road turns to gravel and crosses the Taylor River on a sturdy bridge. Reach the picnic area/trailhead for Garfield Ledges at 12.8 miles and turn right toward the Dingford Creek trailhead on FR 56 just before the pit toilets. Follow this hot mess of a washed out, potholed, bad-word-evoking road until at roughly (and I mean rough-ly) 18.8 miles your vehicle and your kidneys stop bouncing and you arrive at the Dingford Creek trailhead.

ON THE TRAIL

Divert around the gate and begin your enjoyable walk up the defunct road, still called FR 56 on some maps, and on others, Dutch Miller Gap Trail No. 1030. Though this road is seldom used for vehicles, don't be shocked to see them. Mining claims and private land still are part of this valley, and landowners and caretakers are provided access. Also, the occasional Forest Service personnel doing research, maintenance, or surveys still come and go.

In less than 0.2 mile, arrive at a car bridge crossing Dingford Creek Falls, a whitewater sensation in the springtime. These steep, tiered cascades plunge one after the other for a total height of 100 feet, with an average width of 15 feet. The visible portion of the falls from the bridge thunders into 25-foot and 50-foot horsetails pounding through granite bedrock and rocky outcroppings. In late summer into early autumn, the falls slows down substantially and, though not a dribble, isn't nearly as impressive.

The road-turned-trail peacefully cuts through western hemlock, western red cedar, and Sitka spruce, with salmonberries, sword ferns, coltsfoot, and large-leaved avens near your feet. With the Middle Fork Snoqualmie River near the roadway, fine photos can be made of the blue-green water in the foreground and distant craggy peaks keeping watch from above. When the mercury rises, a splash in a calm stretch of water is a good way to cool down and enjoy complete solitude surrounded by the idyllic soundtrack of dancing water.

In just under 2 miles, the road splits. The left branch is an effort to make a smoother ride for vehicles; the right one is slightly less distance, but they both end up in the same place. Choose your adventure!

The road continues with more of the same, until at 3 miles, it angles upward and gently climbs away from the river valley. At 4.5 miles, arrive at a signed Y junction, with the right branch pointing toward Goldmyer Hot Springs. As with so many trails, you have options! At this point, most folks visit the hot springs cabin and call it a day, adding 1.2 miles roundtrip from this junction.

To do that, turn right, drop down to the river, and admire it once again on a sturdy pedestrian bridge. From there, wander toward Goldmyer Hot Springs on the well-signed path to check out the caretaker's cabin and learn more about the hot springs. Soaking is by reservation only, and you aren't permitted to see the clothing-optional hot springs soaking pools from the caretaker's cabin, but the natural beauty alone is worth the trip. Ancient forests surround the property, including some trees up to 900 years old! What's more, the landscape is draped in a cloak of enchanted moss and lichen, a testament to the wet weather in this valley.

EXTENDING YOUR HIKE

Trail runners or those with gumption, time, and perhaps overnight gear might want to keep going another 3 miles (one way) up the road, passing the terminus of the Middle Fork trailhead until it arrives at what is known as

Dutch Miller Gap Horse Camp. From here, the road ends and a single track appears, taking you up toward Williams Lake, Dutch Miller Gap, and more beautiful backcountry destinations. Bicycles are no longer permitted after the horse camp. Loops are possible by connecting the Middle Fork Trail with the Dutch Miller Gap Trail (FR 56) at the trailhead, near Goldmyer, or at the far end near Dutch Miller Gap Horse Camp.

Middle Fork Trail No. 1003 (see Hike 47) is also found off Dingford Creek trailhead. To find it, head south from the parking lot near the toilets and cross the beautiful pedestrian bridge spanning the river. Head up the other side and turn left, following the signs for the Middle Fork Trail.

Note: The Middle Fork Trail has a few challenges. Water crossings can be tough, hazardous, and impassable in spring or early summer, especially near Thunder Creek and Burnt Boot Creek. You may also find navigational challenges near Burnt Boot Creek, since flooding has damaged the area; know your limitations and turn back if you aren't comfortable.

OPPOSITE: *Fall bursts into earth-toned wonder underneath the summit of Granite Mountain (Hike 61).*

SNOQUALMIE PASS

THE SNOQUALMIE PASS AREA HOLDS some of the most scenic hikes in this book—no matter which hike you choose, you can't go wrong. For easier reference, I've split the hikes into three areas: West, Summit, and East, referring to where the hikes lie in relationship to the summit itself. The ones toward the eastern side lie just over the Cascade Crest, where you might find slightly drier conditions and different varieties of foliage than those to the west.

SNOQUALMIE PASS WEST

52 Annette Lake

RATING/DIFFICULTY: ****/3
ROUNDTRIP: 7.2 miles
ELEV GAIN/HIGH POINT: 1750 feet/3620 feet
SEASON: late June–Oct

Maps: Green Trails Maps Snoqualmie Pass No. 207 and Snoqualmie Pass Gateway No. 207SXL; **Contact:** Mount Baker–Snoqualmie National Forest, Snoqualmie Ranger District; **Notes:** Sno-Park Pass required Dec–Mar; Northwest Forest Pass or Interagency Pass required Apr–Nov. Pit toilet at trailhead. This area is prone to avalanche hazards, so avoid in the case of heavy snowfall. Ongoing trail work closes trail periodically, so check with Forest Service or online sources prior to departure. Open to leashed dogs; **GPS:** N 47 23.561, W 121 28.443

This is one of the more popular hikes along the I-90 corridor, and once you visit, you'll see why. This shimmery 18.4-acre lake sits in an oasis under the towering Abiel and Silver Peaks. No sugar coating here—the hike is challenging, but mostly because it's a consistent grade until you get to the lake. It's worth every grunt to get there.

GETTING THERE

From I-90 near North Bend: Drive east for 16 miles, take exit 47, and turn south on Asahel Curtis Road. In approximately 0.1 mile, turn left at the stop sign onto the gravel Tinkham Road (Forest Road 55). At 0.5 mile, find a large parking area to the road's right. This also serves as the Asahel Curtis Nature Trail parking area.

ON THE TRAIL

The Asahel Curtis Nature Trail and the Annette Lake Trail start from the same area, but the signed Annette Lake Trail is closest to the parking area. Asahel Curtis is a good warmup if you go the wrong direction or if you deliberately want to check it out (Hike 53). Otherwise, head on up the Annette Lake Trail and start your forest frolic.

At just shy of 0.2 mile, the trail crosses a wooden bridge over the spirited Humpback Creek, which flaunts its animated whitewater cascades. After doing so much hiking across the country where resources are limited, I feel so much gratitude for our trail crews, volunteers, and nonprofits such as Mountains to Sound Greenway and Washington Trails Association that work to make these trails so enjoyable and safe. Notice the craftsmanship and effort it took to place this bridge here, and admire the work that's been done recently on this trail to make it sustainable for the increased use. The improvement project included reconstructing, re-excavating, and elevating the trail and installing 330 feet of crib ladder step to help with erosion and runoff. Tip your hat and maybe your credit card if it's possible.

When the wind is still, Annette Lake perfectly mirrors the trees and clouds.

From here, continue through the conifers, crossing over a defunct logging road and under some powerlines where wildflowers like fireweed and pearly everlasting join the party.

At 1.1 miles, the trail crosses the former railroad, now the Palouse to Cascades Trail, and then continues on the other side. From here to the lake, you'll be treated to some large, healthy western red cedars, western hemlocks, and Douglas-firs, mixed with a couple of creek hops to take your mind off the burn of the constant ascent. Thankfully, switchbacks help you with the steepest parts.

The final push makes a long traverse on the side of a slope, where avalanche chutes make this stretch dangerous during elevated avalanche forecasts come winter. In the summer, you'll hardly notice and it's easy to keep a good pace, since the trail grade eases up. At 3.4 miles, reach a signed junction with a spur trail that goes left and climbs to a primitive box-style privy.

Now it's just a hop, skip, and a jump to the lake's shoreline, where the trail delivers you to the north side. You can go either direction around the lake—either left toward some forested tent sites and sitting nooks, or right, where a boot path offers some shoreline access and hangout alcoves.

Lake Annette was named for a teenager named Annette Wiestling, who, along with three other people, went for a hiking adventure on May 17, 1913. She was invited on the trip by her friend of a similar age, Elizabeth Wright. Elizabeth's dad, George Wright (a member of the Mountaineers Club) and his buddy Hugh Caldwell (also a Mountaineer and future Seattle mayor) thought it would be a good character builder to bring the girls along. Annette wore brand-new elk-hide hiking boots, a long, woolen ankle-length skirt, and a large-brimmed hat; you know . . . practical attire. Since it was May, everything was snowy and, of course, there was no trail to the lake, so they bushwhacked up the slopes of Humpback Creek, accidently grabbing the prickly devil's club to pull themselves along. When they got to the lake, they roped up to attempt to walk onto the frozen lake. George Wright was in front, followed by Annette, then Elizabeth, then Hugh Caldwell. As Annette stepped out onto the lake, her father joked that Annette was probably the first Caucasian female ever to be on that lake, though that was not proven. When they returned home, George Wright wrote the US Geologic Survey and requested the lake be named in her honor. And, from that point on, it became Annette Lake.

Before heading back, absorb the spectacular views and immerse yourself in the

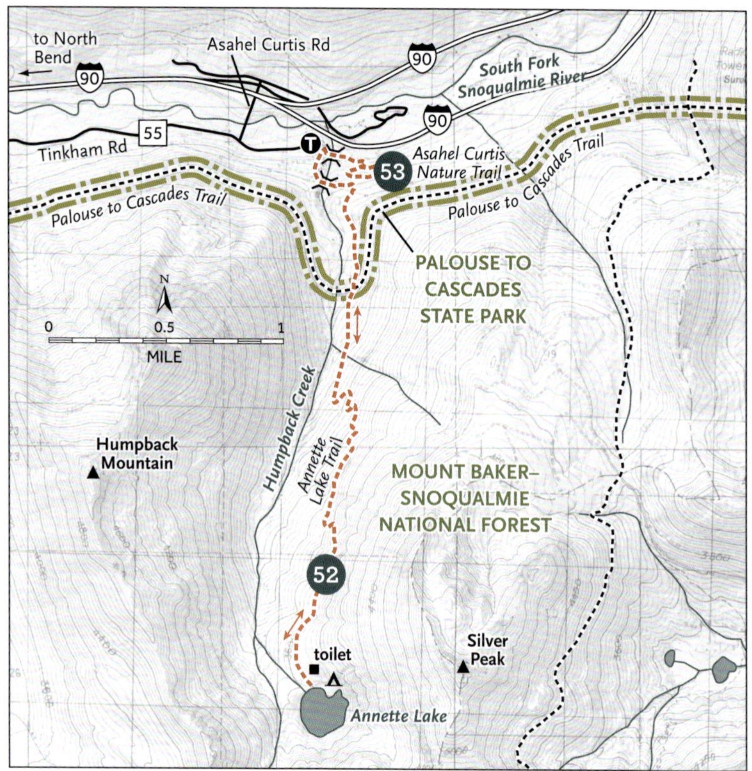

turquoise water, which is clear enough to see the rocks and logs at the bottom.

53 Asahel Curtis Nature Trail

RATING/DIFFICULTY: ***/1
ROUNDTRIP: 0.8 mile
ELEV GAIN/HIGH POINT: 230 feet/2150 feet
SEASON: Apr–Nov

Maps: Green Trails Maps Snoqualmie Pass No. 207 and Snoqualmie Pass Gateway No. 207SXL; **Contact:** Mount Baker–Snoqualmie National Forest, Snoqualmie Ranger District; **Notes:** Sno-Park Pass required Dec–Mar; Northwest Forest Pass or Interagency Pass required Apr–Nov. Pit toilet at trailhead. This area is prone to avalanche hazards, so avoid in the case of heavy snowfall. Ongoing trail work closes trail periodically, so check with Forest Service or online sources prior to departure. Open to leashed dogs; **GPS:** N 47 23.561, W 121 28.443

For taking small kids, stretching legs, or warming up before embarking on the Annette Lake Trail, this hike can't be beat. Beautiful wooden bridges over the thunderous Humpback Creek, gorgeous varieties of old-growth trees, and interpretive signage give this hike a deep-woods, magical feeling even though you can still hear the buzz of I-90.

GETTING THERE

From I-90 near North Bend: Drive east for 16 miles, take exit 47, and turn south on Asahel Curtis Road. In approximately 0.1 mile, turn left at the stop sign onto the gravel Tinkham Road (Forest Road 55). At 0.5 mile, find a large parking area to the road's right. This also serves as the Annette Lake trailhead.

ON THE TRAIL

From the parking area, walk toward the signed map kiosk and then follow the well-signed trail past the Annette Lake Trail (Hike 52) to the Asahel Curtis Nature Trail.

In 275 feet, arrive at the first of two poetic wooden bridges framed like a storybook in a forest of drapy western red cedar and vine maple. Take a few pics, and let your mind wander back in time to the late 1800s and early 1900s when cameras were rare and it took mad skills to take and develop images. Not only would you have to have the money to afford a large-scale camera, but you'd also have to know how to fuse chemical solutions,

Trail stairs guide nature enthusiasts toward the educational signage nestled among firs and ferns.

develop glass-plate negatives, and capture images that were centered and focused, without electronic guidance.

Asahel Curtis, Seattle photographer and mountaineer, established a career of photographing Washington State back in those days, taking shots of mining and farming operations, Seattle urban areas, presidential visits, and natural landscapes, among other subjects. He also had a lengthy backcountry résumé, including being the first to ascend Mount Shuksan, guiding trips up Mount Rainier, organizing work parties for trail building, and being one of three founders of the Mountaineers Club. He photographed many of his outdoor pursuits, which today are archived as historic records. The trail you follow is a tribute to him, and you'll want to keep the snapshots coming as you cross the second bridge across the braided Humpback Creek.

Signage guides you through the walk, helping you learn conifer names and interesting natural facts. At 0.2 mile, arrive at the start of the nature loop, which can go either direction. One of the best features of the loop is found about halfway through and is known as the Parade of Giants. Here, one of the last groves of old-growth forest still stands, including behemoth Douglas-fir, western red cedar, western hemlock, and Pacific silver fir.

Understory plants such as skunk cabbage, ferns, vanilla leaf, trillium, yellow violet, and huckleberries populate the area with healthy foliage. Benches are scattered along the route to stop and take it in, should you want to pause.

At just over 0.6 mile, the loop is complete. At this point, follow the path you came in on, back over Humpback Creek and to the parking area.

54 Bandera Mountain

RATING/DIFFICULTY: ***/4
ROUNDTRIP: 7 miles
ELEV GAIN/HIGH POINT: 2950 feet/5140 feet
SEASON: July–Oct

Maps: Green Trails Maps Bandera No. 206 and Snoqualmie Pass Gateway No. 207SXL; **Contact:** Mount Baker–Snoqualmie National Forest, Snoqualmie Ranger District; **Notes:** Northwest Forest Pass or Interagency Pass required. Potholes on access road. Busy trail and trailhead; avoid weekends or get to the parking area early. Pit toilets and picnic areas at trailhead. Obey all posted no-parking signs. Open to leashed dogs; see map, page 192; **GPS:** N 47 25.487, W 121 35.006

Since the true summit of Bandera is in a viewless forest, most people will shoot for what is known as Bandera West or Little Bandera and call that their destination. The top is impressive, with panoramic views of many of the Cascade peaks such as Mount Rainier and McClellan Butte, along with the strips of asphalt known as I-90 in the valley below. It's a tough hike, to be certain, but the views are worth the workout!

GETTING THERE

From I-90 near North Bend: Drive east for just over 14.5 miles, take exit 45, and turn north. Follow the road as it turns back to the west and becomes dirt and gravel. In 1 mile, stay straight at a fork in the road, marked as Forest Road 9031 (a.k.a. Mason Lake Road) with signage pointing toward the Ira Spring Trail. Find the large parking area at the road's end.

Beargrass bursts into full bloom along the steep, sunlit slopes of Bandera Mountain.

ON THE TRAIL

The hike starts on the Ira Spring Trail, which also goes to Mason Lake and other Alpine Lakes Wilderness destinations. Ira Spring and Harvey Manning were northwest hiking legends and some of the first hiking guidebook authors (Mountaineers Books) in the Pacific Northwest. Their humorous, occasionally snarky, well-honored writing style introduced many backcountry dreamers and outdoor lovers to quiet places to rest the soul. To follow in their huge footprints is my challenging task, and I do my best to uphold their memories and dedication as I write.

The old roadbed-turned-trail starts out as a fairly level, straight westbound walk, then makes a hard right and in 0.5-mile, climbs past two waterfalls, one a trickle in late season, the other an impressive cascade leaping over boulders. A log bridge carries you safely across the second one as you continue your ascent.

At 1.5 miles, the path leaves the roadbed and grinds upward through the forest, across the talus slopes, and along brushy avalanche gullies, until, soon, you reach a large boulder field with views of the valley and Mount Rainier to the south. At 2.9 miles, reach a signed junction with Bandera Mountain Trail. Instead of continuing to Mason Lake to the left, follow the signs toward Bandera, going straight uphill.

This path is much more primitive than the one you've been following. In fact, you are now retracing the steps of firefighters as they created the most direct path up this mountain to attempt to contain a 1958 fire. A slash burn created by loggers had sent a spark into the wind, and it lit up this dry hillside in a hurry. Over sixty-five years later, the mountain still hasn't recovered. Their rustic path to the top is ridiculously steep—so much so that in places, you might be tempted to use your hands as well as your feet to pull yourself along. Now imagine them carrying firefighting gear up these slopes. Ouch! Feel that burn; you'll gain just over 1000 feet in a mere 0.5 mile.

Due to the open slopes, beargrass, lupine, fireweed, paintbrush, huckleberries, bracken fern, and other acid-loving, sun-craving wildflowers and plants display their coloration and healthy leaves. Stop for a lot of plant pictures if you don't want your friends to notice if you're out of shape (though something tells me they might notice anyway). Big boulders, requiring giant step-ups at times, get you up higher, where views of Mason Lake and Mount Defiance are sublime. Continue following the path until you arrive at the dirt and boulder-scattered summit of Little Bandera, also called Bandera West. Sweeping panoramas from this relatively flat area (along with the thought that you must go back down those steeps) make this the destination of the day for most folks. Head back once you've had some recovery time and start getting chilled from the brisk wind hitting your sweaty core.

EXTENDING YOUR HIKE

You've seen the best views up here, but some people may still want to bag the official summit (elevation 5240 feet) to say they've done it. A boot-beaten game trail continues along the ridgeline eastbound, going up and down to reach a forested, viewless summit. The trail is dicey in places and can be tough to follow. If you have mad coordination and sick navigation skills, go for it! This adds 1.6 miles roundtrip and nearly 420 feet cumulative elevation gain.

55 Mason Lake

RATING/DIFFICULTY: ****/3
ROUNDTRIP: 6.8 miles
ELEV GAIN/HIGH POINT: 2450 feet/4310 feet
SEASON: July–early Nov

Map: Green Trails Maps Snoqualmie Pass Gateway No. 207S; **Contact:** Mount Baker–Snoqualmie National Forest, Snoqualmie Ranger District; **Notes:** Northwest Forest Pass or Interagency Pass required. Pit toilets and picnic area at trailhead; backcountry privy at lake. Potholes on access road. Busy trail and trailhead; avoid weekends or get to the parking area early. Obey all posted no-parking signs. Open to leashed dogs; **GPS:** N 47 25.487, W 121 35.006

Climbing up to Mason Lake is a bit grueling, as the trail's pitch sustains a steep grade most of the hike, only easing to drop into the lake basin. But once you expend the sweat equity to get there, it's

Nestled in the Alpine Lakes Wilderness, tranquil Mason Lake is a popular destination.

a gorgeous lake set in a rustic mountain setting with plenty of places to sit, enjoy a picnic, and immerse in the magnificent vibe of the Pacific Northwest backcountry.

GETTING THERE

From I-90 near North Bend: Drive east for 14.5 miles, take exit 45, and turn north. Follow the road as it turns back to the west and becomes dirt and gravel. In 1 mile, stay straight at the fork in the road, marked as Forest Road 9031 (a.k.a. Mason Lake Road) with signage pointing toward the Ira Spring Trail. Find the large parking area at the road's end.

ON THE TRAIL

The trail starts off on an old roadbed-turned-trail, called the Ira Spring Trail after the legendary photographer, mountaineer, and Pacific Northwest hiking advocate. Ira Spring and Harvey Manning co-authored many of the 100 Hikes series books for this publisher (Mountaineers Books) and kicked off the backcountry dreams of so many folks through their useful guides.

In just over 0.5 mile, the trail passes two waterfalls, one a mere trickle in late season, the other more impressive, warranting a log bridge over its bouncing cascades. Grab the camera for a snap or two before continuing your uphill pump. Trailside alders abound, as do a few talus fields where pikas—members of the rabbit family—sound their squeaky alarms.

In 1.5 miles, the path leaves the road's pleasant grade and begins a steeper incline intended to take you high into the environs without wasting much time. Switchbacks help

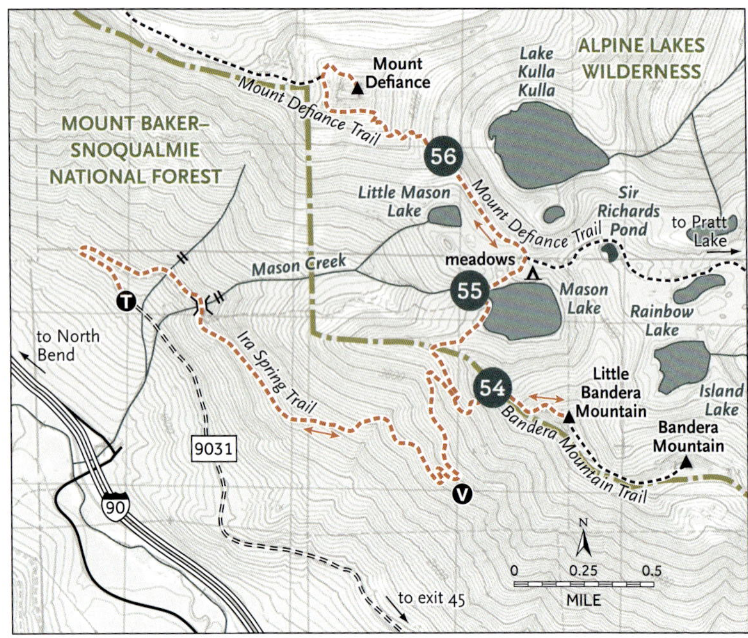

with the grade as you focus on your breathing, and before you know it, you reach a large boulder field offering views of Mount Rainier to the south, along with the buzzing band of interstate deep in the valley below you.

The uphill grunt continues until, at 2.9 miles, you arrive at a junction with Bandera Mountain Trail (Hike 54), which goes straight ahead. Our path switches back to the left toward Mason Lake and cruises up to the western edge of the ridgeline, where it reaches a high point before dropping into the lake basin. The trail cruises around the lake's western shore, then arrives at a rock-hop across an outlet stream just prior to reaching the northern side. Countless social trails form a web of paths to tent sites and shoreline viewpoints. A backcountry toilet is found in this area as well. The Forest Service has installed a few tree signs to help you find your way in the network of trails and forest. Reverse your path back to your car when you are done, or carry on, wanderers!

EXTENDING YOUR HIKE

You can extend your hike another 3.4 miles roundtrip (with 700 feet more cumulative gain) and visit even more lakes. To do so, head northeast from Mason Lake on the main trail as it heads northeast. In 0.3 mile from the lake, reach a signed junction. Turn right here, signed toward Pratt and Island Lakes. At 0.8 mile, reach Sir Richards Pond to the right, followed by Rainbow Lake (1.2 miles). At 1.4 miles, reach a signed junction for Island Lake. From here it's 0.6-mile roundtrip to see Island Lake. There are even more hiking options, such as going past Island Lake's junction and dropping into the Pratt Lake basin. From there, the sky's the limit!

56 Mount Defiance

RATING/DIFFICULTY: ****/4
ROUNDTRIP: 10 miles
ELEV GAIN/HIGH POINT: 3800 feet/5584 feet
SEASON: July–late Oct

Map: Green Trails Maps Snoqualmie Pass Gateway No. 207S; **Contact:** Snoqualmie National Forest, Snoqualmie Ranger District; **Notes:** Northwest Forest Pass or Interagency Pass required. Pit toilets at trailhead; backcountry privy at Mason Lake. Potholes on access road. Busy trail and trailhead; avoid weekends or get to the parking area early. Obey all posted no-parking signs. Open to leashed dogs; **GPS:** N 47 25.487, W 121 35.006

Those looking to sit on top of the one of the Cascades' tippy-top peaks, without the crowds of Mount Si, will enjoy the vista and ample reward for the consistent climbing. Thankfully, the uphill is broken up with a visit to the Mason Lake basin, where you can rest to make the adventure a little less strenuous.

GETTING THERE

From I-90 near North Bend: Drive east for 14.5 miles, take exit 45, and turn north. Follow the road as it turns back to the west and becomes dirt and gravel. In 1 mile, stay straight at the fork in the road, marked as Forest Road 9031 (a.k.a. Mason Lake Road) and signage pointing toward the Ira Spring Trail. Find the large parking area at the road's end.

ON THE TRAIL

The trail starts off on the Ira Spring Trail, an old road-turned-trail at this point. The grade is very easy and pleasant until it makes a hairpin turn to the right and starts its ascent.

In just over 0.5 mile, the trail passes two waterfalls, one larger than the other and housing a log bridge over its playful whitewater. The PNW is a gorgeous place; people from other places would hike far and wide just to see this, and yet it's just a mere stop on our way! Take a few pics and continue your uphill prod.

Trailside alders abound, as do a few talus fields where pikas—members of the rabbit family—often scamper about.

At 1.5 miles, the trail departs the old road and becomes a steep single track climbing up, up, and away through a couple of winter avalanche chutes filled with Cascade mountain ash, slide alder, and other plants attempting to secure the soil.

A couple of switchbacks appear to help you with the grade while guiding you higher. Mount Rainier is visible now on the southern horizon and will stay with you all the way until you drop into the Mason Lake basin.

The uphill grind, now bobbing and weaving through a boulder field, continues until, at 2.9 miles, you arrive at a junction with the Bandera Mountain Trail (Hike 54), which goes straight ahead. Our path switches back to the left toward Mason Lake and cruises up to the western edge of the ridgeline, where it reaches a high point before dropping into the lake basin. From here, the trail swings around an outlet stream where you do some rock- and log-hopping before being delivered to the teeming shores of Mason Lake.

It gets a bit confusing in here, since social trails seem to run in every direction. Thankfully, the Forest Service has installed some

Hikers make their way across the bright, flower-strewn slopes of Mount Defiance's broad shoulders.

signs on trees, helping to guide us along the main trail and away from the tent sites, back-country privy, and day-hiking hangouts. The trail is now gentle as it works its way through the evergreens and arrives at a signed Y junction at 3.7 miles. To the right the sign points to Pratt and Island Lakes, but our path—signed for Mount Defiance—is to the left.

The path gets steeper as you go left and climb toward the summit. Thankfully, it keeps you in the trees for a little bit, which is pleasant on a hot, sunny day. At 4.4 miles, the trail breaks out of the forest and traverses an open slope laden with seasonal wildflowers and the buzzing insects that pollinate them. Paintbrush, lupine, rosy spiraea, pearly everlasting, Sitka valerian, beargrass, columbine, aster, and other favorites explode into a carpet of colors when you hit it right, usually late July or early August. The views of the surrounding mountains are outstanding from here and will just keep getting better.

Continue through the meadow until the trail levels out slightly and you come upon an unsigned but well-used boot path to the right at 4.8 miles. Go right here and start up a steep, primitive, and somewhat loose path toward the summit. The rustic trail through rocks, juniper, and heather clumps and loose pebbles feels like it shoots you straight into the sky, and you huff and puff your way up it. Graciously, it's short, and at 5 miles, find yourself on the rocky summit of Mount Defiance.

Park yourself on a rock, break out a snack, and let those views hit you! Both Lake Kulla Kulla and Mason Lake are visible to the southeast, and Bandera and Granite Mountains are both detectable in roughly the same direction. Mount Rainier, your ever-present companion, is still front and center to the south, and a clear day will even reveal Mount Adams far in the distance. The peaks and views here are boundless, and you'll want to stay up here all day, provided the insects aren't too bad. But what goes up must go down, so head back when your soul is full.

57 Denny Creek to Keekwulee Falls

RATING/DIFFICULTY: ****/3
ROUNDTRIP: 4 miles
ELEV GAIN/HIGH POINT: 970 feet/3100 feet
SEASON: July–Oct

Maps: Green Trails Maps Snoqualmie Pass No. 207 and Snoqualmie Pass Gateway No. 207S; **Contact:** Mount Baker–Snoqualmie National Forest, Snoqualmie Ranger District; **Notes:** Northwest Forest Pass or Interagency Pass required. Pit toilets at trailhead. This trailhead also serves the Franklin Falls Trail. The road to the trailhead closes seasonally; double-check with rangers before going. Denny Creek can be high during melt-off; use caution with crossing, and avoid swimming during large flows. Open to leashed dogs; **GPS:** N 47 24.860, W 121 26.364

The shallow pools and natural waterslides of Denny Creek are a great place to splash around when the mercury rises. The path to the creek is easy, and once there, you can continue by climbing to Keekwulee Falls, a spectacular 171-foot waterfall where viewpoints showcase the dropping tiers.

GETTING THERE

From I-90 near North Bend: Take exit 47 and turn north, crossing over the freeway. Go right at the T intersection onto Forest Road 58. In 0.3 mile, turn left to remain on FR 58, passing the Denny Creek Campground, until you reach a large parking area to the road's right, just shy of 3 miles from the T intersection. Note: The old trailhead used to be located to the left before the new parking area was built, but the spur road leading to it is now closed. The trailhead for Franklin Falls Trail is also located near here, along with a pit toilet and ADA parking.

ON THE TRAIL

From the parking area, follow the trail as it heads down toward a couple of ADA parking spots and crosses the road. Wander toward the Franklin Falls trailhead, where more ADA spots are located. One last pit toilet awaits if you forgot the piddle stop. From here, walk around the gate at the car bridge, cross over

Keekwulee Falls rewards every visitor with a stunning cascade and serene forest backdrop.

the river, and continue walking up the road, passing several vacation cabins. Reach the official trailhead for Denny Creek Trail, along with the permanently locked bathroom, 0.3 mile from where you parked.

Dive into the second-growth forest and begin your hike surrounded by large hemlocks, sword fern, devil's club, and other foliage so green it hurts. This area would be quite perfect, were it not for the constant hum of the freeway, along with the occasional deep rumbling of big-rig compression brakes.

At 0.6 mile from the parking area, a narrow, well-crafted pedestrian bridge spans a shady forested stretch of Denny Creek, while the typical PNW plant players, such as Cascade huckleberries, vine maples, and thimbleberries, thrive in the riparian zone.

At 1.2 miles, the trail crosses under a freeway overpass, which feels a little intimidating as you look up and see the traffic buzzing high above you. You'll soon forget you are near civilization as you cross into the Alpine Lakes Wilderness, then reach Denny Creek in 1.2 miles, and 460 feet of elevation gain, from the trailhead. In 2009, the bridge that spanned this creek gave way and went tumbling downstream. During snow melt-off or after heavy rains, use caution with both crossing and swimming, as the current can be quite strong and the stepping stones can be wet and slick. If you get lucky, there will be a log over the crossing, but if it's not there, it's better to get wet shoes than to risk a broken ankle.

When the weather is warm, nothing beats the heat than to hang out here. The waterslide, which gently flows over smooth rocks into calm pools, makes a perfect place to take a ride on a natural slide, provided the water is flowing enough to push you down the slab. Enjoy your time at the water's edge and turn back if that's enough for the day, or keep rolling.

After the creek, the route gains elevation under a forest canopy until it breaks out onto an open talus field along a ravine that is, at times, quite steep. The rocky slope showcases the small evergreens that are trying to grow in this spot, despite the winter snowslides. Sunlight infiltrates the shrubs and wildflowers—such as red columbine, scarlet paintbrush, Sitka valerian, and tiger lily—helping them produce blooms.

Watch your footing carefully now that Keekwulee Falls is coming into view at 1.7 miles. What a vision! There are a couple of viewpoints along the way where you can stop and peer over the edge—just use extreme care in these places, as one slip means a very bad day. The word *Keekwulee* translates from Chinook Jargon, a pidgin trading language, to "to fall down"—and fall down this water does! While the total height of the falls is 171 feet, with two dropping tiers, the one we see here is the longest at 142 feet.

Wander as far as you want, even up to Melakwa Lake (Hike 58) if you please, or turn back here and call it a day.

58 Melakwa Lake

RATING/DIFFICULTY: *****/4
ROUNDTRIP: 8.8 miles
ELEV GAIN/HIGH POINT: 2750 feet/4600 feet
SEASON: July–Oct

Maps: Green Trails Maps Snoqualmie Pass No. 207 and Snoqualmie Pass Gateway No. 207S; **Contact:** Mount Baker–Snoqualmie National Forest, Snoqualmie Ranger District; **Notes:** Northwest Forest Pass or Interagency Pass required. Pit toilets at trailhead. This trailhead also serves the Franklin Falls Trail.

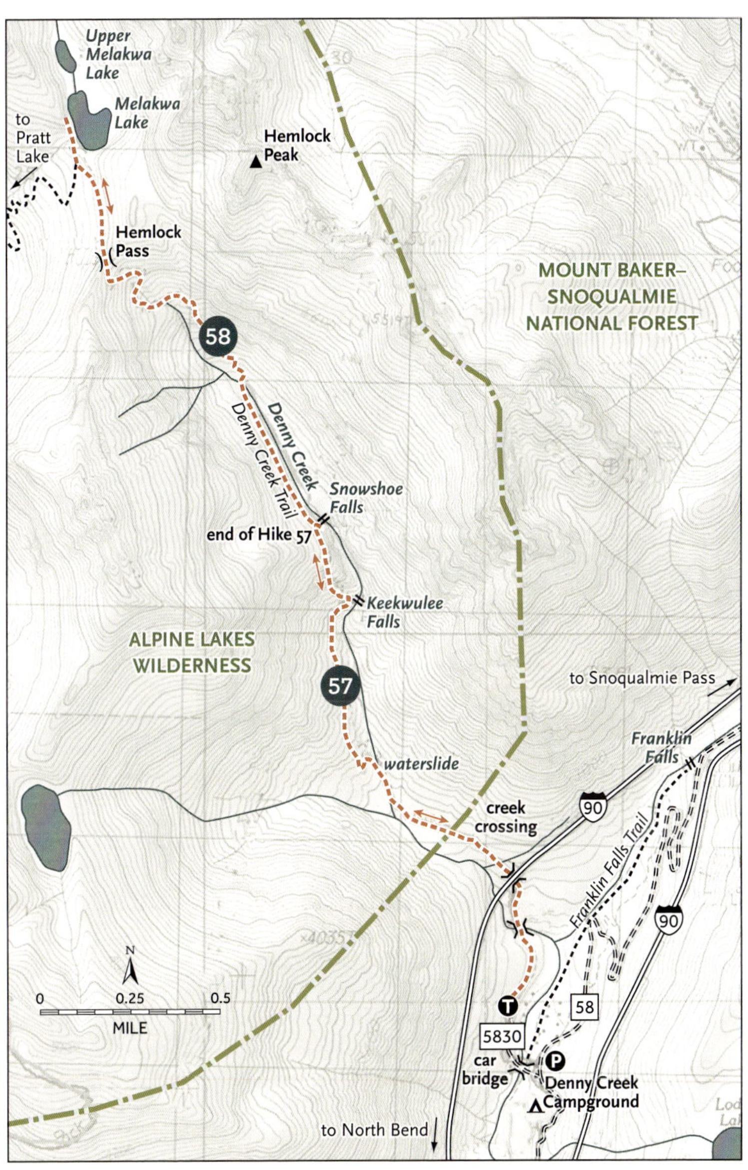
Upper
Melakwa
Lake
Melakwa
Lake
to
Pratt
Lake
Hemlock
Peak
Hemlock
Pass
MOUNT BAKER–
SNOQUALMIE
NATIONAL FOREST
58
Denny Creek
Denny Creek Trail
Snowshoe
Falls
end of Hike 57
Keekwulee
Falls
ALPINE LAKES
WILDERNESS
57
to Snoqualmie Pass
Franklin
Falls
waterslide
creek
crossing
90
Franklin Falls Trail
90
0
0.25
0.5
MILE
58
5830
car
bridge
Denny Creek
Campground
to North Bend

The road to the trailhead closes seasonally; double-check with rangers before going. Denny Creek can be high during melt-off; use caution with crossing, and avoid swimming during large flows. Open to leashed dogs; **GPS:** N 47 24.860, W 121 26.364

With sparkling water surrounded by rugged mountain majesty, this lake and the basin in which it sits are a true Northwest showpiece. You'll work hard to get up there, but the scenic natural features along the way, such as the impressive Keekwulee Falls, will help you forget about the huffing and puffing.

GETTING THERE

From I-90 near North Bend: Take exit 47, and turn north, crossing over the freeway. Go right at the T intersection onto Forest Road 58. In 0.3 mile, turn left to remain on FR 58. Continue, passing the Denny Creek Campground, until you reach a large parking area to the road's right, just shy of 3 miles from the T intersection.

ON THE TRAIL

From the parking area, follow the trail as it heads down toward a couple of ADA parking spots and crosses the road. Wander toward the Franklin Falls trailhead, where more ADA spots are located and a pit toilet is found. Keep walking the road, across the car bridge and around the gate. Several vacation cabins are tucked into the woods around the area: lucky ducks! Reach the official Denny Creek Trail, along with the former trailhead and the permanently locked bathrooms, 0.3 mile from where you parked.

The trail starts with a wooded cruise through tall hemlocks and Douglas-firs, with the usual PNW foliage, such as sword fern, salal, and Oregon grape near your feet. The mossy understory is evidence of the damp, humid climate. Were it not for the rumble of large trucks and freeway echo, this area would be serene and tranquil.

At 0.6 mile from the trailhead, a narrow, well-crafted pedestrian bridge spans a shady forested stretch of Denny Creek, while the typical PNW plant players, such as Cascade huckleberries, vine maples, and thimbleberries, thrive in the riparian zone.

A freeway overpass above you in 1.2 miles is a bit of a distraction, since you are hiking through a sublime, hopefully sunlit forest and the structure feels out of place. Those vehicles are so far up there, and what if . . . never mind. Carry on and leave the cares behind.

Pass into the Alpine Lakes Wilderness, then reach the inviting Denny Creek at 1.2 miles. Years ago, the bridge in this location was carried off by avalanche debris, so now it's either a rock-hop, log-totter, or ford in summer when the creek is high.

When the weather is warm, nothing beats the heat better than hanging out here. The waterslide, which gently flows over smooth rocks into calm pools, makes a perfect place to take a ride on a natural slide, provided the water is flowing enough to carry you downhill. Folks flock here in the summer months to enjoy the slide and sit in the shallow pools—nature's perfect waterpark.

Once across, begin a climb through evergreens until the path breaks out into a rocky, open ravine. Steeply at times, the route gains elevation and displays much smaller trees trying desperately to grow and survive winter snowslides. Shrubs, trees, and wildflowers such as vine maple, slide alder, rosy spirea, scarlet paintbrush, Sitka valerian, and pearly everlasting enjoy the direct sunlight and reflected rock warmth.

Tucked beneath rocky mountain ledges, Melakwa Lake shimmers—an alpine vision.

Keekwulee Falls, translated from Chinook Jargon, a pidgin trading language, means "to fall down," and you might do that if you aren't watching your feet when you see the gorgeous falling water. According to a recent survey, the total height of the falls is 171 feet, with two dropping tiers, the longest at 142 feet. You'll follow the waterfall and its white noise soundtrack as you continue up the stone-laden ravine.

At just over 2.3 miles, arrive at what I like to call the false pass, because your brain gets super excited about a relatively level area and thinks you are close. Sad trombone—you are still 1.8 miles to the actual top of the climb, officially known as Hemlock Pass. But at least it's beautiful and a bit of a reprieve from the climbing. Rock-hop across Denny Creek again and continue your ascent through talus fields until you start a series of steep switchbacks that feel particularly grueling because of their pitch. Keep at it . . . reward is coming! At 4.1 miles, reach the oh-thank-goodness-I'm-finally-here Hemlock Pass, which is flat and welcoming. Grab a log if you need to catch your breath, or power through, knowing you are almost to the lake.

At 4.4 miles, bear right toward the signed Melakwa Lake. This junction is slightly confusing because it is also signed Melakwa Lake Trail No. 1011, heading left downhill toward Pratt Lake. Just hug the right side of this junction and you'll get to your destination. A wee bit of climbing happens now, but you are nearly there . . . just a few more steps—then BOOM.

The lake's outlet is the first thing that greets you with a logjam that looks intimidating but is quite stable. Balance across the jam, then reach a day-use area complete with a backcountry privy and plenty of spots to hang out and enjoy the lake and surrounding basin.

If you still have gumption, you can follow a boot-beaten trail over the boulders from the day-use area around to the lake's left (western side). Keep walking until you come to Melakwa's northern outlet. Walk north and discover Upper Melakwa Lake only 0.2 mile from its big sibling. Quiet campsites with rocks for picnics and resting are found on the lake's eastern shore. Enjoy all that you came for and head back the way you arrived when time is up.

EXTENDING YOUR HIKE

Remember that signed junction you passed for Melakwa Lake Trail No. 1011? On your way back, you could take it to descend to Lower Tuscohatchie Lake. You'll need to climb back up the hill you go down, so be sure to save some energy. Visiting this lake basin and coming back will add 4 miles and about 1200 feet of elevation gain.

Or you could do a thru hike with a two-car shuttle, leaving one vehicle at Pratt Lake trailhead. The total hike is 14 miles and 3800 feet of elevation gain. If you don't have a second vehicle, you could always walk Forest Road 58 back to your vehicle at the trailhead. Doing the road walk adds 3 miles and roughly 450 more feet to the above numbers. It's a huge day, but if you are a trail runner or superhero, it's within the sunup-to-sundown timeframe, provided you're okay with starting early and finishing late.

59 Dirty Harrys Balcony

RATING/DIFFICULTY: ***/3
ROUNDTRIP: 4.5 miles
ELEV GAIN/HIGH POINT: 1610 feet/2610 feet
SEASON: July–Oct

Maps: Green Trails Maps Mount Si Natural Resource Conservation Area No. 206S and Bandera No. 206, Dirty Harrys Peak Department of Natural Resources (DNR) Map; **Contact:** DNR; **Notes:** Discover Pass required. Avoid weekends or get to the parking area early. Pit toilets at trailhead. Open to leashed dogs; **GPS:** N 47 25.868, W 121 37.948

For years, the trail to this area existed mostly as a fun play area for climbers, not the well-traveled, well-signed hiking destination it is now. In 2017, Mountains to Sound Greenway partnered with Washington Trails Association and DNR to improve this formerly primitive trail and make it a gem with rewarding views along the I-90 corridor. The hike to Dirty Harrys Balcony is perfect for an after-work workout.

GETTING THERE

From I-90 near North Bend: Take exit 38, turn south onto SE Homestead Valley Road, and cross over the South Fork Snoqualmie River. Continue eastbound 1.8 miles, then turn left (signed "Fire Training Academy") and follow the road back under the freeway. Find the trailhead just 0.2 mile after crossing under the freeway.

ON THE TRAIL

From the parking area, locate the large kiosk with the trail kicking off to its right. This is the main trail, but in 0.1 mile, it delivers you back out to the paved road, where you'll turn left and walk on pavement for a couple hundred feet, crossing over the Middle Fork Snoqualmie River. Just beyond the river, give a look to your right and find the signed trail again near the guard rail, darting back into the forest.

Since this trail is shared with rock climbing areas, there are a lot of signed junctions cruising off the main route toward the rocky outcroppings. Our trail is well marked, often saying Dirty Harrys Peak Trail or just DHPT, so look for the signs if you get confused. The tread is rocky and thick with heavy roots,

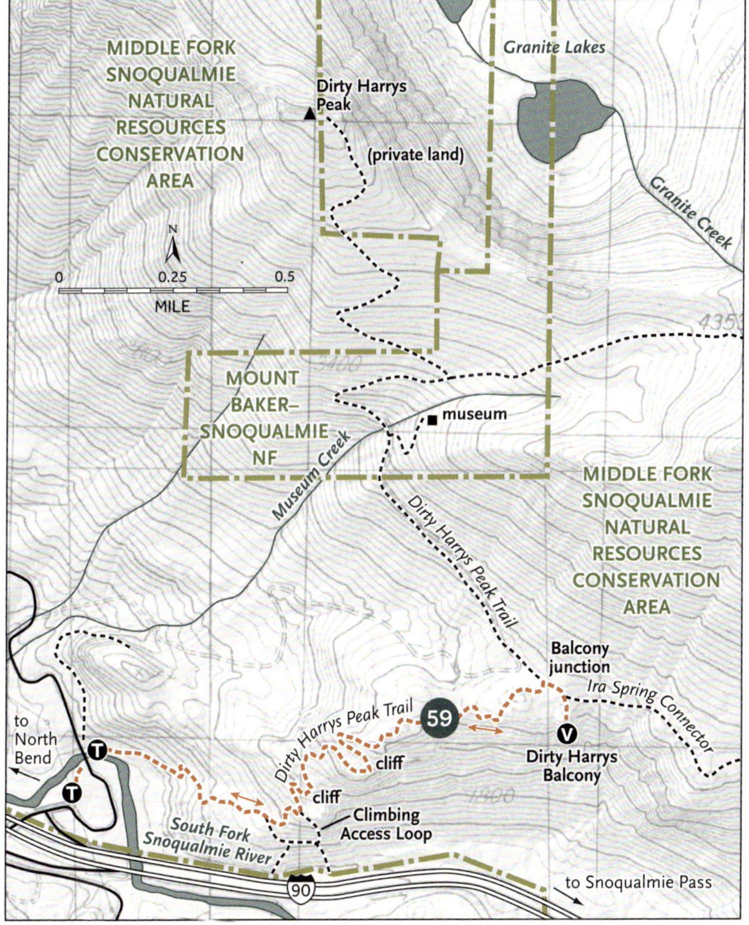

Ribbons of Interstate 90 buzz through the valley far below Dirty Harrys Balcony.

which, when wet, can cause some unanticipated shimmies. The forest is dense and the trees spindly and close together. Little light hits the forest floor in most places, so the understory is much thinner than many other PNW trails. The seeds that do sprout must fight to find enough soil to feed their roots among the rocks.

Most of the climbing spur trails are obviously not the main path, but at 0.8 mile, the one signed Climbing Access Loop intersects the main trail on a similar trajectory and can easily make you follow it. If you are deep in conversation or not paying attention, you might unexpectedly take a wrong turn.

Several side peekaboo areas near rocky outcroppings offer views of Mount Washington and Rattlesnake Ridge as you climb higher and higher. Other social trails in the area lead to cliffs, making you wonder if they might be the actual Dirty Harrys Balcony, but rest assured, our destination is well-signed and farther up. At 1.6 miles, the path flattens out a little, giving you a break from climbing. It doesn't last long before you are back to ascending, but you get the sense you are finally getting somewhere.

The peak you are hiking is named after the notorious logger Harry Gault, who performed some questionable and environmentally destructive logging practices in the 1940s. The man was known for pillaging even the steepest of mountains, dismantling all the trees in hopes that he could make a profit. Because of the nature of the wet, often decaying wood, it was rumored only 25 percent of what he cut was worth selling.

After 2.1 miles, reach a wide junction signed for Dirty Harrys Balcony and turn right. In another couple hundred feet, reach another junction. This one is signed for the Ira Spring Connector Trail to the left and Dirty Harrys Balcony to the right. Despite the sign and well-traveled look to the Ira Spring Connector Trail, it's a primitive boot path traversing the mountain with a couple of side trails and no signage. This trail leads over to the Ira Spring Trail (see Hikes 54, 55, and 56), and a good map is required if you decide to explore it. For now, continue to the right, following the well-used pathway another 0.1 mile to the rocky outcropping known as Dirty Harrys Balcony. You are high above the swarming traffic along the strips of I-90, and the rugged peaks all around you—such as McClellan Butte and Humpback Mountain—flaunt their mighty summits. Turn back or keep going!

EXTENDING YOUR HIKE

There is much to explore in this area! Did you know that some of the old logging equipment used by Dirty Harry himself still rests near here? An unofficial trail heads up to what is now known as Dirty Harrys Museum. To find it, retrace your steps from the balcony out to the main trail (Dirty Harrys Peak Trail) and turn right at the balcony junction instead of left back toward your car. Continue your uphill trod, this time on a much more obvious old roadway; a slash cut in the middle of a mountain. Who would have thought you could ever drive up here? In 0.6 mile beyond the balcony turnoff, just prior to what is informally known Museum Creek, a large burbling creek, look to the right for a boot path heading up next to the water. Sometimes, a cairn or two is located near the turnoff, but you must be paying attention or you might walk right by it. This detour to the museum adds 0.4 mile roundtrip from DHPT, give or take for walking around the area. Follow this path as it climbs up to another defunct rocky road where you'll go right, then hairpin back to the left. Before you know it, you are staring at . . . a truck and many more artifacts.

The old truck, known as a GMC CCKW, a Jimmy, or a G-508 (built between 1941 and 1945) was a military-issued truck like those used in the Normandy invasion of WWII. Dirty Harry managed to acquire the truck, a super powerful and capable off-road vehicle, to help with his shady logging. The one here is tailored with a logging boom. The truck's tires are half buried, and the old thing is riddled with bullet holes from people who didn't know better. On that note, I'm sure I don't need to say this, but for formality's sake, please don't remove or disrupt any of the historic relics.

Follow your steps back out to the main trail and continue for as long as your legs will carry you. If you want to continue on to Dirty Harrys Peak, it's nearly 1.5 miles from here (one way). Be advised, it gets wicked steep and challenging near the top. What's more, it crosses private property, though it's not signed as such. Have a good map and know where to turn back to avoid trespassing.

60 Franklin Falls and Wagon Road Trail Loop

RATING/DIFFICULTY: ****/2
ROUNDTRIP: 2.3 miles
ELEV GAIN/HIGH POINT: 480 feet/2650 feet
SEASON: May–Oct

Maps: Green Trails Maps Snoqualmie Pass No. 207 and Snoqualmie Pass Gateway No. 207S; **Contact:** Mount Baker–Snoqualmie National Forest, Snoqualmie Ranger District; **Notes:** Northwest Forest Pass or Interagency Pass required. Pit toilets at trailhead. In winter, the parking area becomes an official Sno-Park, with Sno-Park permits required. If you visit during winter, wear shoe traction for

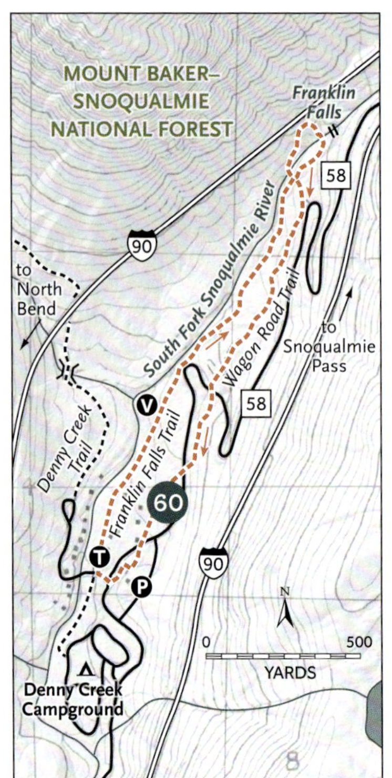

icy surfaces. Open to leashed dogs; **GPS:** N 47 24.860, W 121 26.364

This gorgeous waterfall is a crowd favorite for obvious reasons; it's a short hike accessible by most, and it's quite a spectacle to observe. The falls is just below the large westbound I-90 overpass, but its roar often overpowers the noise of the freeway and will draw your eyes away from anything manmade. For a change of scenery, take the Wagon Road Trail back through the forest to make a loop.

GETTING THERE

From I-90 near North Bend: Take exit 47 and turn north. Go right at the T intersection onto Forest Road 58. In 0.3 mile, turn left to remain on FR 58. Continue, passing the Denny Creek Campground, until you reach a large parking area to the road's right, just shy of 3 miles from the T intersection.

ON THE TRAIL

From the parking area, head downhill on the gravel walkway. Cross the road and arrive at pit toilets, a handicapped parking area, and the signed kiosk and official trailhead for Franklin Falls heading off to the right. Straight ahead, behind the closed car gate, is the Denny Creek trailhead (see Hike 57). The South Fork Snoqualmie River purrs and whirls, making you even more excited to see the falls, so turn right at the sign.

A few private cabins, along with private property, are scattered in the trees. Those lucky folks get to enjoy this area from their own personal havens! In 0.3 mile from the trailhead, access to the river shows up via a small spur trail and a great sitting log to the left. Use caution if you have small kids, dogs, or balance issues and decide to stick your toes in the river. During early summer, this river shows no mercy with its ferocity.

At 0.5 mile, a viewpoint to the left allows you to see the cascading creek, which spits and bubbles through a slot canyon almost the whole way to Franklin Falls. Erosion-preventing trail stairs guide you up areas that can be muddy after rainfall or snow melt.

Giant western red cedars, along with a couple more viewing pullouts, grace the trail to the right and left after 1 mile. At 1.1 miles, arrive at a signed junction with the Wagon

Road Trail coming in from the right. To make a loop, we will visit the falls, then come back to this spot and turn to follow the Wagon Road Trail back to the car.

For now, continue following the pathway to reach the falls and the often wet rocky ledges serving as the viewing areas at 1.2 miles. The whitewater of Franklin Falls, bordered by cliffs and evergreens, drops in three tiered plunges with a total height of 151 feet, though we can only see 85 feet of it from this viewpoint. But 85 feet is enough to feel the rumble of the powerful water in your chest and feel the delicate mist as it falls into the pool below.

Spray from the falls might cover your camera's lens if you are visiting after a big rain or during late spring or early summer, so wipe it with a cleaning cloth for the best pictures. Use care during cold spells, as this area gets icy and will send you heinie over tea kettle without proper shoe traction.

When you've enjoyed the falls, turn back on the trail and reach the Wagon Road Trail junction you passed earlier. From here, you can retrace your steps on the Franklin Falls Trail. Or for a change of scenery, turn left on the Wagon Road Trail and follow it through the forest, reaching a map kiosk at 1.4 miles. Straight ahead of you, FR 58 is visible, along with a spur trail to reach it, but bear right to stay in the forest. From here, the trail guides you through some large healthy conifers and over a handful of new wooden footbridges, until at 1.9 miles, it crosses FR 58 for the first of three times. Each time it crosses, the trail is obvious on the other side of the road. As you get closer to the parking area, you could walk the road, but the forest continues to be a pleasant walk and it's easy to get back either direction.

The author and her dog, Scout, visit Franklin Falls on a late spring day.

At 2.3 miles, arrive back at the signed junction just 250 feet from the parking area to the left. At this point, follow your previous steps back to your waiting vehicle, content with your adventure.

61 Granite Mountain

RATING/DIFFICULTY: ****/5
ROUNDTRIP: 8.5 miles
ELEV GAIN/HIGH POINT: 3800 feet/5629 feet
SEASON: July–Oct

Maps: Green Trails Maps Snoqualmie Pass No. 207 and Snoqualmie Pass Gateway No. 207S; **Contact:** Snoqualmie National Forest, Snoqualmie Ranger District; **Notes:** Northwest Forest Pass or Interagency Pass required.

Tarns make a perfect spot to pause for a snack of seasonal huckleberries on the way to Granite Mountain.

Pit toilets and picnic tables at trailhead. Trailhead break-ins common; take valuables with you. As with all I-90 corridor hikes, this one is crowded and parking fills up quickly, especially on weekends. Obey all no-parking signs. Open to leashed dogs; see map, page 209; **GPS:** N 47 23.870, W 121 29.196

This hike is for those who love big views and don't mind a tough, grueling climb to see them. If you've hiked Mount Si and thought it was a doozy, Granite is equally demanding, if not more so. Thankfully, sweeping views, grand subalpine landscape, and a classic L-4 lookout tower take your mind off your crunchy knees and fiery quads. Reward is plentiful on this classic I-90, hafta-do-it hike.

GETTING THERE

From I-90 near North Bend: Take exit 47. At the stop sign, turn north and proceed over the freeway. When the road comes to a T intersection, turn left and follow it a short distance to the Pratt Lake trailhead. The parking area is limited to thirty-five to forty cars and fills up quickly; however, roadside parking is permitted.

ON THE TRAIL

From the beginning, the trail, called the Pratt Lake Trail at this point, welcomes you under the arms of evergreens such as western and mountain hemlocks, western red cedars, and Douglas-firs. The thick canopy is a beautiful representation of a healthy Pacific Northwest forest as you climb along well-used trail. In 0.5 mile, the trail switches back, dabbling with the edges of a bushy avalanche chute on the turn, before delivering you back to the forest.

At 1.2 miles, the intersection for Granite Mountain Trail shows up on a hard turn to the right. If you are deep in conversation with your hiking pals, you might walk right past it and mistakenly continue on the Pratt Lake Trail, so keep your eyes open and ready.

Once on the Granite Mountain Trail, the real climbing begins. Back and forth you go on switchbacks higher and higher into the hinterlands. Avalanche swales containing vine maple, Sitka mountain ash, red elderberry, and other foliage make their home in these challenging areas, doing their best to hold down the soil in the summer months.

The higher you go, the tighter the switchbacks, until, at 3.5 miles, the grade eases and you find yourself high above I-90. Mount Rainier peeks up from the south, and the hillside above you is abundant with beargrass, spirea, heather, and in late summer, some of the most abundant and delicious huckleberries in all the land. This place is gorgeous in fall too, when the foliage turns shades of burgundy, sienna, and saffron and makes the ground look like an earthy quilt.

A couple of small, relatively flat areas of parkland, with big boulders, small tarns, and flitting butterflies provide a place to rest and grab a snack if you are worn out from the climb. Just a little more up and you'll be there! The final push comes by crossing a grassy meadow, then picking your way through a talus field where pika—guinea-pig-sized members of the rabbit family—squeak like dog toys, sounding alarms at your presence.

The top will make you grateful for those strong legs that carried you here! Below you, the busy I-90 corridor hums, while Mount Rainier stands proudly on the southern skyline. Behind you to the north are Crystal and Tuscohatchie Lakes and Mount Stewart on the distant horizon. For more than one hundred years, the top of this peak has had some sort of structure. The first was a primitive cabin; the present L-4 tower was built and is maintained by volunteer efforts. If it's staffed during your visit, you are welcome inside to check it out; otherwise, consider it off-limits, but enjoy its deck and novelty.

When you have sucked in all the beauty and are high on endorphins, make your way back to the car, the way you came. Then, for the love of Peter, Paul, *and* Mary, go to North Bend and scare up some ice cream. You earned it and then some.

62 Pratt Lake

RATING/DIFFICULTY: ****/4
ROUNDTRIP: 13 miles
ELEV GAIN/HIGH POINT: 3450 feet/4140 feet
SEASON: July–Oct

Maps: Green Trails Maps Bandera No. 206, Snoqualmie Pass No. 207, and Snoqualmie Pass Gateway No. 207S; **Contact:** Mount Baker–Snoqualmie National Forest, Snoqualmie Ranger District; **Notes:** Northwest Forest Pass or Interagency Pass required. Pit toilets and picnic tables at trailhead. Trailhead break-ins common; take valuables with you. As with all I-90 corridor hikes, this one is crowded and parking fills up quickly, especially on weekends. Two approaches are available to this hike—one via the Ira Spring Trail (Hike 55) and the other as listed here. Open to leashed dogs; **GPS:** N 47 23.870, W 121 29.196

Pratt Lake hides under the broad shoulders of Pratt Mountain and nameless ridgelines. Getting to it requires some work, but when you drop into that lake basin, there is a quietness away from the hum of I-90 and a true feeling of backcountry that you don't get on every hike.

GETTING THERE

From I-90 near North Bend: Take exit 47. At the stop sign, turn north and proceed over

Cradled by ridges and wrapped in forest, Pratt Lake is one of nature's quiet masterpieces.

the freeway. When the road comes to a T intersection, turn left and follow it a short distance to the Pratt Lake trailhead. The parking area is limited to thirty-five to forty cars and fills up quickly; however, roadside parking is permitted. Obey all no-parking signs.

ON THE TRAIL

On the Pratt Lake Trail, follow the switchbacks up the forested slope, crossing the occasional cool, clear creek by jumping rocks. A peekaboo view of an avalanche path comes into view in 0.5 mile, followed by a signed intersection with the Granite Mountain Trail to the right at 1.2 miles. Continue straight ahead on your forest ramble.

Over the next couple of miles, the trail continues climbing at a steady grade, passing more dribbling creeks and dipping into wet ravines. All the waterways are easily crossed with dry shoes, even in the wettest weather.

After 3 miles, a signed junction for Talapus Lake Trail appears to the left. This trail cruises over to Talapus and Olallie Lakes (Hike 63) and is a unique approach for a visit. In fact, if you have time and want to bust over to Olallie Lake, it's 1 mile and 200 feet of cumulative elevation gain from this spot. If not, keep pushing onward and upward.

A viewpoint down onto Olallie Lake's basin comes up next, at 3.9 miles. The break in the trees is also a welcome reprieve from the monotony of the so-green-it-hurts forest, and you might find yourself wanting to balance a hindquarter on a pointy rock near the vista. Just beware the grey jays (a.k.a. whisky jacks, Canada jays, camp robbers), whose sweet dark eyes are hard to resist as they brazenly beg for nibbles. Sweet as they look, they've been known to grab a whole bar or sandwich out of one's hand, so hold on tightly to your snacks.

At 4.1 miles, reach the top of the climb along a forested ridge. A signed trail junction points toward Pratt and Melakwa Lakes to the right and Island Lake (Hike 64) straight ahead. Follow the signs toward Pratt Lake, dropping down through a series of talus slopes under the rocky summit of Pratt Mountain high off to the left. It feels steep going down, but somehow it doesn't feel quite as bad going back up. Maybe that's because when I usually do it, it's after a belly full of chocolate at the lake.

At 5.1 miles, the path levels out in a wet, mossy forest, with pretty creeklets dancing and dripping through the duff. You are getting close! Before you know it, you pop out on the hillside above the southern end of Pratt Lake.

At 5.9 miles, the trail finally dips down to meet up with the northern tip of Pratt Lake, where you arrive at a couple of signed junctions—the first for a backcountry privy, and the second for two connecting trails, Melakwa Lake Trail, and a few steps down it, the Pratt River Trail (also knowns as the Pratt River Connector Trail on some maps). Wander down toward the lake's shoreline for some rocky sit options, or bear right and find a beautiful campsite near the water's edge to drop your pack (provided the camp isn't occupied). It's a big, beautiful day, and you earned the sites and views—soak it in before turning back.

63 Talapus and Olallie Lakes

RATING/DIFFICULTY: ***/3
ROUNDTRIP: 6.8 miles
ELEV GAIN/HIGH POINT: 1300 feet/3880 feet
SEASON: June–Oct

Maps: Green Trails Maps Bandera No. 206 and Snoqualmie Pass Gateway No. 207SXL; **Contact:** Mount Baker–Snoqualmie National Forest, Snoqualmie Ranger District; **Notes:** Northwest Forest Pass or Interagency Pass required. Free wilderness-use permit at trailhead most years (though it's been down during timber harvest). Pit toilet at trailhead. Avoid weekends or holidays for crowds. Obey all posted no-parking signs. Road to trailhead

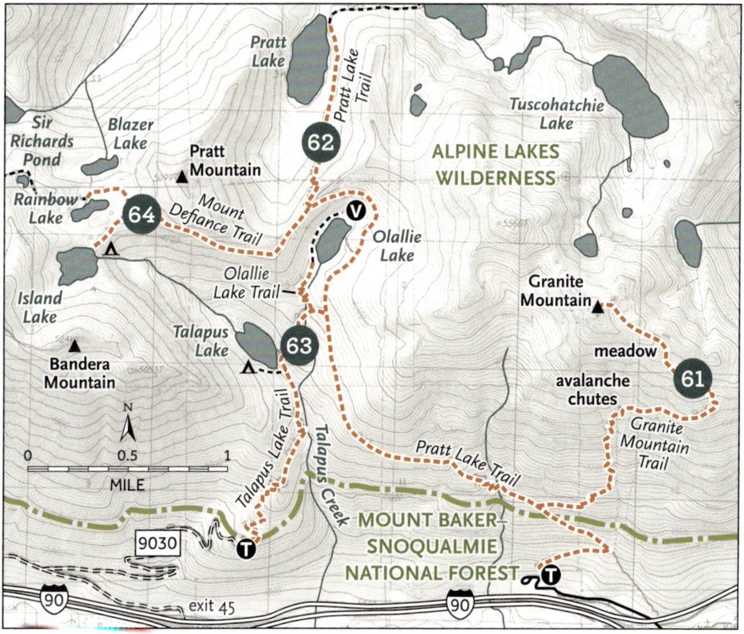

The iced-over Olallie Lake is a contrast to the warm shoreline sunshine on an early summer day.

can be rough, but most years, passenger cars will make it by going slowly. Open to leashed dogs, stock; **GPS:** N 47 24.077, W 121 31.094

Two spectacular mountain lakes, ringed by forest-green conifers, await your presence. Between the ease of the grade and the location of these lakes off the I-90 corridor, this trail can be a busy buzz. But if you can carve out weekday time or hike it on a slightly off-weather day, you will usually have some moments of quiet reflection. No matter when you go, these lakes are true PNW treasures and make a perfect destination for newbies and seasoned hikers alike to experience those soul-easing backcountry vibes.

GETTING THERE

From I-90 near North Bend: Take exit 45, and turn north on Forest Road 9030. Follow the road as it turns back to the west and becomes dirt and gravel. In 1 mile, stay right at a signed junction for Talapus Lake Trail No. 1039. At 3.3 miles, reach the end of the road, where you'll find the parking area and trailhead.

ON THE TRAIL

From the trailhead, pass the kiosk and notice recent forest-thinning activity. In 2022, 175 acres of timber were harvested and sold in order to thin the dense conifers and create forest openings for other growth opportunities. A nearby sign offers more information if you're interested. The harvesters were kind enough to leave thin swaths of trees for our trail as we make our way up the obvious path.

In 0.3 mile, reach the Alpine Lakes Wilderness boundary and the official end of the timber harvest. The western red cedars, western hemlocks, and Douglas-fir trees proudly display their limbs above your head as you start to moderately switchback up the trail. A couple of peeks of Talapus Creek, which flows through peppy cascades, is visible to the left as you make your way up the slope.

At 1.6 miles, reach a trail junction with a kiosk and a map of the Talapus Lake basin tent sites, toilet, day-use area, and regulations. You have options for visiting the lake—left via a spur trail to the southwestern shoreline, or right on the main trail to the northeastern. Since you are here, why not check them both out? As this spot, turn left and follow the spur trail through the forest to a few woodsy camps where photo opportunities and shoreline access await. Doing an out-and-back from the Talapus basin sign junction will be 0.4 mile, or even less if you turn around on the spur trail before its dead end.

After you see that side of the lake, retrace your steps to the kiosk for Talapus Lake basin and continue along the main trail. Now, turn right at the sign and cross a narrow footbridge with log hand railings over the lake's outlet. A series of puncheon bridges/ boardwalks over a wetland are next, taking you over the drips and dips to reach a signed intersection for the day-use area to the left. The log-strewn shoreline is a must-visit, with plenty of spots to drop your pack, fish out your gorp, and grab a camera. Across the trail to the right is a spur trail leading to a campsite as well as a boot path to a primitive box-style privy. Those with small kids, senior dogs, or other worthy reasons might decide that Talapus Lake is their destination for the day and relish this lake basin before heading back. Assuming you visited the other side of the lake, it's 2.2 miles to the day-use area, give or take your steps.

If your boots are ready to keep walkin', follow the main trail north past Talapus Lake as it wanders through the conifers and passes a couple more tent sites to the left. Ascend higher with the occasional switchback, until at 3.3 miles, you pass a signed trail junction for the connecting path to the Pratt Lake Trail coming in from the right. To learn about approaching this hike from that trailhead, check out Hike 62

Keep 'er rolling to find the southwestern end of Olallie Lake and the day-use area to the right, just 0.1 mile farther. The day-use area is a great spot to experience the lake and replenish some calories. Watch out for the grey jays (a.k.a. camp robbers, whisky jacks, Canada jays), darling birds with a name crisis who prey on the kind-hearted hikers seeking their pictures. They have been known to aggressively steal whole sandwiches right out of hands without so much as a charitable offer. Avoid feeding these rascals!

If you want to check out more tent or sit spots and get the gold star for visiting the whole area, continue for another 0.3 mile until the trail narrows and becomes harder to follow. There are two signed privy spur trails in this basin, both to the main trail's left after the day-use area. Congratulations on a day well spent!

64 Island and Rainbow Lakes

RATING/DIFFICULTY: ***/4
ROUNDTRIP: 11.8 miles
ELEV GAIN/HIGH POINT: 3310 feet/4580 feet
SEASON: July–Oct

Maps: Green Trails Maps Snoqualmie Pass No. 207 and Snoqualmie Pass Gateway No. 207S; **Contact:** Mount Baker–Snoqualmie National Forest, Snoqualmie Ranger District; **Notes:** Northwest Forest Pass or Interagency Pass required. Pit toilets and picnic tables at trailhead. Trailhead break-ins common; take valuables with you. As with all I-90 corridor hikes, this one is crowded and parking fills up quickly, especially on weekends. Obey all no-parking signs. Two approaches are available to this hike—one via the Ira Spring Trail (Hike 55) and the other as listed here. Open to leashed dogs; see map, page 209; **GPS:** N 47 23.870, W 121 29.196

A challenging, peaceful climb through the evergreens leads to a forested ridgeline. From there, a descent drops you to a couple of backcountry lakes with nooks and crannies to enjoy some peaceful scenery and have a nibble.

GETTING THERE

From I-90 near North Bend: Take exit 47. At the stop sign, turn north and proceed over the freeway. When the road comes to a T intersection, turn left and follow it a short distance to the Pratt Lake trailhead. The parking area is limited to thirty-five to forty cars and fills up quickly; however, roadside parking is permitted. Obey all no-parking posted signs.

ON THE TRAIL

The Pratt Lake Trail escorts you up the forested slope with a couple of switchbacks and creeks that soothingly chatter on their way down to the Snoqualmie River. They are all easily crossed with rock-hops and add to the ambiance of the area.

In 1.2 miles, reach the signed intersection with the Granite Mountain Trail, which comes in from the right. Our trail continues straight ahead, climbing steadily and passing even more creeklets, some dipping into small ravines. Trail builders have created a few split-log boardwalks in the wettest places to get you across with dry feet and protect the fragile mountainside runoff.

At 3 miles, arrive at a signed junction for Talapus Lake Trail, off to the left (Hike 63). If time permits, you can jog over to visit Olallie Lake, which is 1 mile roundtrip and 200 feet of cumulative elevation gain from this point. Otherwise, keep on pushing uphill.

At 3.9 miles, reach a break in the trees with a viewpoint down into the Olallie Lake basin to the left. If you stop here, you might be surprised to see the unnaturally tame grey jays (a.k.a. Canada jays, camp robbers, whisky jacks) that beg from tree limbs with their shamelessly cute faces. They have learned how to take snacks directly from your hands, so hold on tight if you decide to whip out food.

Just beyond the viewpoint, at 4.1 miles, the top of the ridge is obtained. A signed junction points the way to Pratt and Melakwa Lakes to the right, and straight ahead to Island Lake. Continue onward, now on the Mount Defiance Trail, following the sign toward Island Lake. The trail leads slightly uphill, then starts dropping into the lake basin. Huckleberries in this area—all the way through the lakes—are sweet, plentiful, and delicious when they are in season. Eat your fill and restore some energy, as you'll have to climb back up this hill on the return.

At 5.4 miles, a signed junction with Island Lake appears to the left. Turn left and follow the spur trail, passing a couple of lily-pad-laden ponds to the left and right, as well as a signed trail spur left for a primitive backcountry privy. Wander off to it if you need a bio-break; otherwise, stay on course to arrive at the lake at 5.7 miles. A few boot paths lead around the lake's edges to good sitting rocks and tent sites for relaxing. When you've experienced the lake, retrace your steps back to where you turned off for Island Lake and go left (west). Rainbow Lake is found in another

A mosaic of rock, brush, and water—nature's palette at Island Lake.

0.2 mile, this time right next to the trail. It, too, has spots near its edges for reflection both figuratively and literally. In the autumn, foliage in this spot can be spectacular as it mirrors rich earth tones into the water. Turn back when time is up, or explore, explore, explore some more!

EXTENDING YOUR HIKE

Beyond Rainbow Lake, you can find a scenic little body of water known as Sir Richards Pond. This is a good goal if you feel like pushing a little bit farther but don't have a ton of time or vigor. Visiting the pond and returning to Rainbow Lake is 0.8 mile roundtrip with roughly 210 feet of cumulative elevation gain. If you want to go farther, you have options of visiting Mason Lake or Mount Defiance—and beyond! In fact, you could make a thru hike from Pratt Lake trailhead to the Ira Spring trailhead if you did a two-car shuttle, visiting Sir Richards Pond and Mason Lake on your way. Doing this would be approximately 11.1 miles with 3430 feet of elevation gain. Having options is freedom!

65 Mount Washington

RATING/DIFFICULTY: ***/4
ROUNDTRIP: 8.6 miles
ELEV GAIN/HIGH POINT: 3110 feet/4395 feet
SEASON: June–Oct

Maps: Green Trails Maps Middle Fork Snoqualmie No. 174SX and Bandera No. 206; **Contact:** Washington State Parks; **Notes:** Discover Pass required. Pit toilets available. As with many popular hikes, this one gets very crowded on weekends. Trailhead closes at dusk. Open to leashed dogs; **GPS:** N 47 24.529, W 121 40.695

As with many hikes in the I-90 corridor, the steepness will test your fitness prowess. To throw in some type 2 fun, the trail tread is filled with ankle-rolling rocks for much of the way. Thankfully, the top is well worth the struggles, and the views into the Cedar River watershed are outstanding.

GETTING THERE

From I-90 near North Bend: Take exit 38 toward SE Homestead Valley Road. Turn right onto SE Homestead Valley Road and cross over the South Fork Snoqualmie River. In 0.1 mile, turn right again into the driveway for Olallie State Park and find parking straight ahead.

ON THE TRAIL

Follow the steep trail connector trail between two boulders to the parking area's southwest and in 0.1 mile, bear right at the T junction on a service road. Follow the service road for another 0.1 mile to the former railroad grade that is now the Palouse to Cascades Trail, then head right (west). Keep your eyes open

Shaped like a giant scoop of vanilla ice cream, Mount Rainier rises on the horizon from the final ridgeline of Mount Washington.

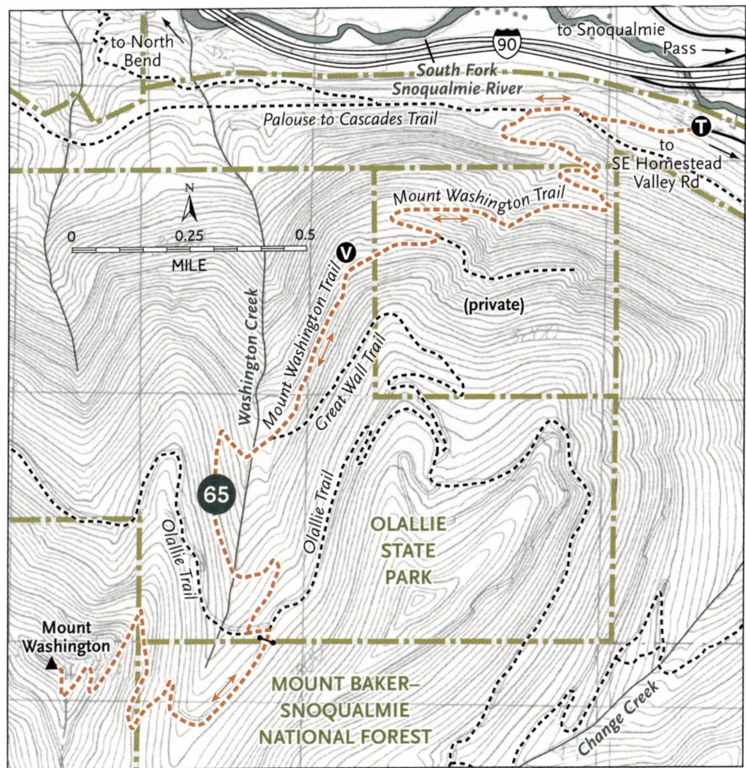

for an obvious side trail to the left at 0.3 mile. This is the Mount Washington Trail, though the sign is often missing.

Climbers use this area, and spur trails to rock walls dart here and there starting only a few steps in. Thankfully the main trail is wider and more obvious, so it's not hard to navigate. At 0.7 mile, another climbers' trail heads left, while we continue our uphill grind. A few muddy pockets with seasonal dribbles make for a mess in wet weather.

At 1 mile, a beautiful spring shoots straight out of the side of the rock to the left. Maidenhair ferns with their soft fronds and black stems are almost as cool as the water, which sounds like someone left the faucet on. Mother Nature is magical.

For the next 0.8 mile, the trail is grueling, with a steep pitch on what feels like a riverbed at times. Heck, people trail run here . . . so just remember that as you drag your bones up, up, and away. You got this!

At 1.6 miles, a trail arrives from the left, heading up to another climbing area. A handwritten, wooden sign points to the right, helping guide you along the main trail if you get confused. Not long after that, the trail levels out, and the worst of the uphill climbing is over. Of course, it's not over until you are standing at the summit, but the sustained pitch at least bobs and weaves, giving you a bit of reprieve now and again.

A viewpoint of Rattlesnake Mountain pops out at 1.8 miles, on what used to be known as Owl Hike Spot—a popular goal for folks who just wanted to reach a vista before turning back. These days, the vista is a bit overgrown and not swoon-worthy, but it still provides an enjoyable break from the trees and cliffs.

At 2.2 miles, and after over 1700 feet of climbing, the trail reaches a signed junction with Great Wall Trail to the left as it climbs through a brushy, often overgrown stretch. The trail carries you up to intersect an old logging road known as the Olallie Trail, 3 miles from where you started. This intersection throws folks off, since our trail disappears into the road and it's not clear whether to go left or right—a good guidebook to the rescue! Turn left, and in roughly 315 feet, find the continuation of the trail, with a badly weathered sign pointing uphill to the right. Go through the pedestrian turnstile and continue for another 1.3 miles, passing another defunct logging road before arriving at a ridge leading to the top of the peak, 0.1 mile farther.

The view from the summit isn't as panoramic as the one from the ridge, but you'll want to touch it and at least peek at I-90 far below you. Head back down toward the ridge for a few rocky perches on which to enjoy the views. On a clear day, Mount Rainier, Chester Morse Lake, Puget Sound, and even the Olympics on the far horizon are visible. Enjoy the birds, the breeze, and the tranquility of this gorgeous hill before returning to the real world.

66 McClellan Butte

RATING/DIFFICULTY: ****/5
ROUNDTRIP: 11.6 miles
ELEV GAIN/HIGH POINT: 3710 feet/5162 feet
SEASON: July–Oct

Maps: Green Trails Maps Snoqualmie Pass No. 207 and Snoqualmie Pass Gateway 207SXL; **Contact:** Mount Baker–Snoqualmie National Forest, Snoqualmie Ranger District; **Notes:** Northwest Forest Pass or Interagency Pass required. Pit toilets at trailhead. This area is prone to avalanche hazards, so avoid in the case of heavy snowfall. Open to leashed dogs; **GPS:** N 47 24.727, W 121 35.350

A few notable summits are profiled along the I-90 corridor, and McClellan Butte—with its rocky pinnacle—is one of those. The climbing is consistent to get to the rocky saddle near the top. From there, it's a relatively exposed scramble to the true summit, where a fire lookout cabin once stood. If the scramble gives you jitters, the rocky saddle is still worthy of those sublime views.

GETTING THERE

From I-90 near North Bend: Take exit 42 for Tinkham Road. Turn south and cross a bridge over the Snoqualmie River. Pass the Department of Transportation building and a couple of private residences. In 0.2 mile, the road turns to gravel, then at 0.3 mile, it reaches a signed spur road pointing right for the McClellan Butte trailhead. Head up the spur road and find the large parking lot and turnaround loop at 0.5 mile from the freeway.

ON THE TRAIL

From the parking area, climb gently through the hemlocks, firs, and spruces until at 0.4

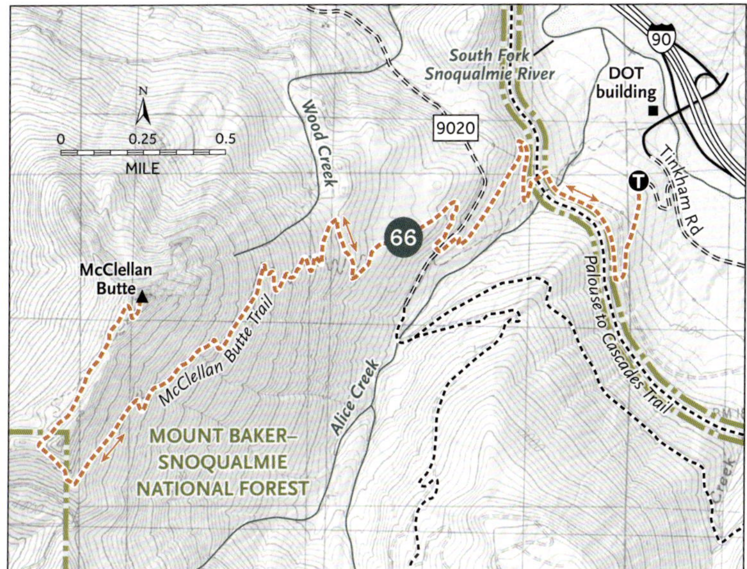

mile, the trail makes a hard right on an old forest-road-turned-trail. It's easy to miss, since there is also a trail going straight ahead. Note: If you miss the turn and go straight, you'll end up on the Palouse to Cascades Trail in 0.1 mile. From there, turn right and follow it for under 0.5 mile to a signed junction with the McClellan Butte Trail to the left.

After the hairpin turn, continue your gentle climbing until intersecting with the Palouse to Cascades Trail (the former Chicago, Milwaukee, St. Paul, and Pacific Railway) 1 mile from the trailhead. The signed continuation of our trail is directly across the former tracks.

Onward and upward you go, passing some lingering old-growth trees that somehow didn't fall victim to the logging efforts of yesteryear. The trail tread is relatively easy, with cushioned evergreen needles and plenty of shade as you make your way up.

At 1.8 miles, the trail crosses an unsigned former logging road (Forest Road 9020). Some folks use this old road as an access point for this trail, but this approach is not encouraged by the Forest Service or by your cherished vehicle. The forest road to this point is rough, and the official trailhead listed in the directions is the preferred method of getting you on the peak.

After 2.4 miles, the trail gets steeper, narrower, and rockier, with shorter switchbacks to get you higher, faster. As you continue, views of the I-90 valley with neighboring peaks such as Bandera and Granite are visible to the northeast. A few creeks in rocky ravines are crossed with big steps as you traverse hillsides through brushy avalanche-prone slide zones. Each year, tiny landslides take out more and more material in these gullies, so watch your footing,

Those who brave the final, rocky climb to McClellan Butte's summit are met with expansive views from the former home of a fire lookout.

especially in early season before the path across them really gets worn in.

In just after 3.5 miles, the trail wraps around the base of some rocky ledges where mountain goats often hang out in the notches and nooks.

At 4.8 miles, the trail reaches a horseshoe bend underneath an unnamed peak and turns you from a southwestern direction to a northwestern pursuit. It feels good to be turning and feeling like the top is close! The trail wraps again to complete the horseshoe bend at the edge of the Cedar River watershed. This final traverse—through huckleberries, lupine, vanilla leaf, and a variety of other classic PNW foliage—opens up the slopes to the northwestern direction. A tiny tarn a few paces downslope provides a welcome watering hole in the spring for a variety of birds and small mammals but usually dries up by midsummer.

A rocky ridgeline is obtained at 5.3 miles, the final push before the summit scramble. If you aren't comfortable moving up the exposed stone face to the summit, this makes a fine place to call the top. You'll have to get somewhat creative on where to put your sit pad, but you'll find a spot, even though it maybe not be perfectly level. Views of neighboring I-90 peaks and multiple mountain layers in all directions are outstanding from this perch too.

Those with decent balance who are comfortable with exposure can continue up the straightforward, somewhat vertical scramble to the tippy top. It's best to play it safe and avoid this final bit if snow or rain makes the rocks slippery. A few obvious steps and handholds have been blasted into the rocks here and there, so watch for them and move deliberately. If you get off course, stop and look around to find the more polished path; it stays mostly to the left near the ridgeline. The rock is chunky, and the holds are bold, so the climbing is more mental than physical.

After 5.8 miles, stand on the mostly level summit! In the 1930s, a fire lookout cabin was built on this spot, but little is known about it, save for the rusty metal reinforcements and hooks and twisted cables that still have a strong hold deep in the rock. The tops of these high Cascade peaks are so freeing, with bird's-eye views as far as you can see. Enjoy every minute, then be sure to use caution on your descent.

SNOQUALMIE PASS SUMMIT

67 Commonwealth Basin to Lundin Peak

RATING/DIFFICULTY: ****/4
ROUNDTRIP: 9.8 miles
ELEV GAIN/HIGH POINT: 2910 feet/5700 feet
SEASON: July–Oct

Maps: Green Trails Maps Snoqualmie Pass No. 207 and Snoqualmie Pass Gateway No. 207S; **Contact:** Mount Baker–Snoqualmie National Forest, Snoqualmie Ranger District; **Notes:** Northwest Forest Pass or Interagency Pass required. Free wilderness use permit required, available at trailhead. Pit toilets and picnic area at trailhead. Trailhead break-ins common; take valuables with you. Avoid weekends, if possible, as parking at this trailhead can be challenging. Have a plan B if parking is full. Commonwealth basin is a popular winter snowshoe destination. Open to leashed dogs (stock on PCT only); **GPS:** N 47 25.676, W 121 24.813

Considering this hike is along the I-90 corridor, you'd expect more crowds, but this one hides quietly in the depth of thick forest and streams that pour through the basin. And if you want a bit more than a sea of green, pump up the quads to hit Lundin Peak and find a peaceful perch to

Red Pond is a scenic diversion to check out on your way to Lundin Peak viewpoint.

unpack your worries—and maybe even leave them behind when you return.

GETTING THERE

From I-90: Take exit 52 for Snoqualmie Pass West. Turn north at the end of the exit ramp. Turn right in roughly 100 yards onto a dirt road signed for the Pacific Crest Trail (PCT), and drive into the parking area. The trailhead is on the east side of the parking area.

ON THE TRAIL

Follow the well-signed PCT past the picnic area and begin your switchbacking ascent. Views open up to Guye Peak to the west, and at 1.8 miles, the trail enters the Alpine Lakes Wilderness, as noted by a tree sign. A talus field near here often contains little squeaking pikas, which look like tiny guinea pigs, though they are members of the rabbit family. They busy themselves making piles of grasses and

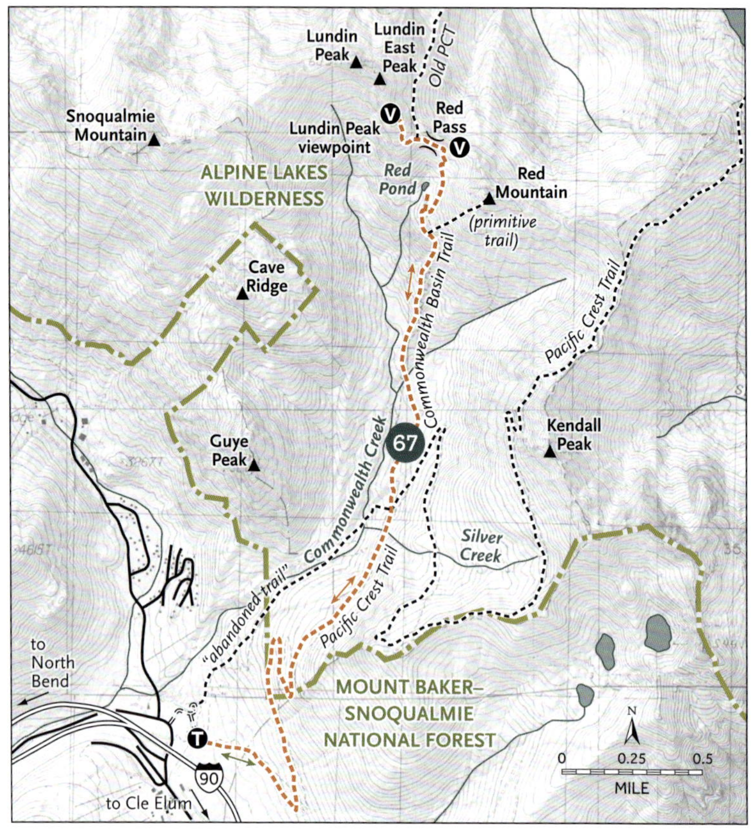

wildflowers known as haystacks to eat during the long winter months.

After huffing puffing for 2.4 miles, reach a signed junction with Commonwealth Basin Trail, which splits off to the left at this point. Follow it and in roughly 300 feet, the trail delivers you to a junction. To the left is a sign with the word "abandoned," but the trail is quite well-traveled and obvious. This is a good time to mention that on the way down, you could follow this abandoned trail back to the parking area; however, be forewarned. The abandoned trail, while frequently used, has several crisscrossing branches and alternative routes, so good navigation skills and an up-to-date map are key, should you decide to explore.

For now, follow the signs pointing toward Commonwealth Creek and Red Mountain, and experience this thick riparian zone, buried under sturdy western hemlock and Douglas-fir boughs. At 2.8 miles, cross Commonwealth Creek on logs and rocks, and find an open break spot near the creek just after the crossing. This makes a good turnaround point if you aren't interested in making a longer trek and the mosquitoes are sucking out all your hemoglobin.

From here, the trail climbs through thickets of shrubs such as huckleberry, mountain ash, and vine maple and steeply climbs up the ridgeline, giving way to views of Red Mountain just above the ridge and behind you to the ski area across the valley. As you get higher, the area feels subalpine, with more talus and low-growing bushes such as mountain heather and dwarf huckleberries. At 3.9 miles, the trail splits to an unsigned Y. To the left is a viewpoint, and to the right is the continuation of our trail. Walk a few steps to the viewpoint to admire the surrounding hills and valley, then retrace your steps and continue following the main trail.

In about 30 feet, notice a faint trail heading off to the right and one continuing straight ahead. The one to the right is an unmaintained trail leading up Red Mountain. While it's only 0.4 mile one-way to the top from this spot, it gains over 1000 feet in that distance, and the second half is a quite precarious hands-and-feet scramble with potential fall hazards. Only take this detour if you are comfortable with heights, risk, and exposure.

Continue on the main trail to 4 miles and find yourself at another unsigned, not obvious, junction. In fact, if you aren't really paying attention here, you might blow by it without realizing that there are two boot paths—one going straight and one heading slightly to the right.

Going straight for another 0.1 mile gets you to what is known as Red Pond, a shallow body of water without an official moniker. You'll want to return to this trail spot after visiting the pond, so make a mental note of where you are standing. In fall, when the bushes turn vibrant earth tones and the slopes above are also sprinkled with colors, it's quite picturesque. A boot-beaten path follows the pond's curve to the left before it peters out with just enough space for you to snap some pictures.

After visiting the pond, return to the last junction, where your mental note was taken. If you lost track, you've come 4.2 miles from the trailhead. This time, take the other branch of the junction, which now is heading uphill toward Lundin Peak. A talus slope under the sturdy shoulders of Red Mountain welcomes you, and at 4.8 miles, reach a small saddle, unofficially called Red Pass, where a series of rocky outcroppings offer views of Thomas

Mountain and others across the valley. What a spot! But wait, there's more!

Continue onward to find yourself passing an old PCT blaze along with a barely visible sign noting that the trail is abandoned. But this isn't the PCT, so you might scratch your head in wonder. Long ago, when the PCT was known as the Cascade Crest Trail (CCT), this trail was created to get hikers down the other side into the Middle Fork valley near Burnt Boot Creek. Because of its pitch and orientation, the other side of this ridge was dangerous for travel until the snow melted, which was sometimes well into August. What's more, it was hazardous for stock. In the 1970s, the trail was rerouted to Snow Lake, using the Rock Creek route as an alternative access to the Middle Fork valley, but that wasn't optimal either, as some suggested it should be higher along the ridges. Finally, in 1979, the trail was rerouted to its current location near Kendall Peak after the creation of the Kendall Katwalk. Near the blaze, the faint former trail that drops over the ridge is still visible with a keen eye, though it's rarely used and is more of a bushwhack these days. Give yourself a high-five for finding the old blaze; cool, right?

Continue along the ridge as it climbs up an obvious path toward the summit of Lundin Peak. At 5 miles, reach a viewpoint and the informal top of Lundin Peak, where a rocky protrusion prevents you from reaching the technically true summit. That's okay—this is a victory, and you can stake the imaginary flag anyway. From here, the views on a clear day are outstanding, with the peaks of the Central Cascades proudly bragging. You might feel like you are a long way from the trailhead, but the return trip is just a hop, skip, and a jump, especially since you'll save the 0.2-mile side trail to the pond. Congratulations on a day well spent.

68 Silver Peak

RATING/DIFFICULTY: ****/4
ROUNDTRIP: 5.6 miles
ELEV GAIN/HIGH POINT: 2070 feet/5605 feet
SEASON: July–Oct

Maps: Green Trails Maps Snoqualmie Pass No. 207 and Snoqualmie Pass Gateway No. 207SXL; **Contact:** Okanogan-Wenatchee National Forest, Cle Elum Ranger District; **Notes:** Road to trailhead rough the last 0.2 mile, though most vehicles will make it. No facilities available. Hike is somewhat technical near the top, not for those with a fear of exposure. Open to leashed dogs, stock (on PCT); see map, page 225; **GPS:** N 47 22.392, W 121 26.814

Silver Peak has a rough trail to the top, and though it's well-used, it isn't officially maintained. Because of its rough-and-tumble nature, and because the top is primarily a large, steep scree field requiring hands-and-feet climbing, it can be a bit intimidating for those with a fear of heights or who aren't used to exposure. If that's you, probably best to skip it, but if you are comfortable with rugged, sketchy trails and peak-bagger-style primitive summits, this is your jam.

GETTING THERE

From I-90 east of Snoqualmie Pass: Take exit 54, signed for Hyak and State Route 906, and turn southwest onto Hyak Drive. Stay straight past two stop signs. The road passes by houses and winds to the left, where it becomes Hyak Drive E. At 0.6 mile, pass through an open gate, and shortly after, the road turns to gravel and is signed for Forest Road 9070. Stay on FR 9070, ignoring all side roads, until 5.5 miles and the easy-to-miss trailhead to the left, where the road begins to flatten out. Find limited roadside parking near the PCT trailhead.

ON THE TRAIL

The Pacific Crest Trail (PCT) crosses FR 9070 in an area known as Windy Pass, going both north and south at this intersection. To get to Silver Peak, take the PCT south, which was to the left of the roadway as you drove in. The trail is marked with a tall, skinny brown sign holding the PCT symbol and icons indicating the allowed users.

Cruise past a small pond in a clear-cut area before dipping into the conifers. The grade is gentle to moderate at times, the trail tread decent—known in the circles as PCT grade. A couple of creeks and dribbles are near the trail but may dry up in late season or warm summers. At just shy of 1.7 miles, keep your eyes wide open for the easily missed, unsigned side trail to Silver Peak to the right. If you don't have a fitness watch or GPS helping you with distance, the best advice I can give you is to look for it just beyond a series of descending switchbacks. Usually a cairn (rock pile) marks the turnoff, but you must be scanning or you'll likely walk right by it.

Lingering snow often clings to the slopes of Silver Peak well into early summer.

Once you've found the Silver Peak Trail, follow it right as it steeply climbs almost 400 feet in just 0.3 mile on a narrow tread. As your quads cry out for help, reach a saddle where a few primitive side trails meet up. Our path to Silver Peak goes right here, and before long, you've got the summit in view!

This high-country open hillside wrought with stones, heather, and juniper helps gauge your progress, since your summit is *right* there. The sheer pitch and the wobbly-ankle footwork can be a bit of a mental challenge, but you got this . . . just keep on keeping on. The top of the peak has a few dicey sections that will have you doing some light scrambling (think class 2 or 3 at most), so if you are woozy or dubious, call wherever you end up the goal for the day. Otherwise, power through the tough spots and stand on the top of the peak as a champion, 2.8 miles from where you started.

The views from the top on a clear day are outstanding. Mount Rainier towers over the skyline behind you, while Mount Catherine (Hike 70) is to your northeast, along with countless others. Below you twinkles Annette Lake, another pleasant hike in this book (Hike 52).

69 Cold Creek Loop

RATING/DIFFICULTY: ****/3
ROUNDTRIP: 6.6 miles
ELEV GAIN/HIGH POINT: 1850 feet/4400 feet
SEASON: July–Oct

Map: Green Trails Maps Snoqualmie Pass No. 207; **Contact:** Okanogan-Wenatchee National Forest, Cle Elum Ranger District; **Notes:** Open to leashed dogs (stock on PCT only); **GPS:** N 47 21.788, W 121 25.344

If you are looking for a less crowded option on a weekend, this is a good hike. There are two lakes: a tiny one not accessible by the trail, and a larger one, which is the main destination. The big Twin Lake is shallow, peaceful, and set in a quiet mountain drainage with buzzing dragonflies and the occasional lily pad around its perimeter. It's a good destination for kiddos if you turn back at the lake and don't make the full loop. Others will want to keep going, seeing it all without doing the same trail. To mix things up, you could even extend the distance by visiting Mirror Lake, Silver Peak, or Mount Catherine, which are all easily accessible along the route.

Stillness reigns at the foot of the mountains at big Twin Lake.

GETTING THERE

From I-90 east of Snoqualmie Pass: Take exit 54, signed for Hyak and State Route 906, and turn southwest onto Hyak Drive. Stay straight past two stop signs. The road passes by houses and winds to the left, where it becomes Hyak Drive E. At 0.6 mile, pass through an open gate, and shortly after, the road turns to gravel and is signed for Forest Road 9070. Stay on FR 9070, ignoring all side roads, until arriving at a hairpin turn to the right at 3.5 miles. Look for the large roadside pullout to the road's right here and ensure your vehicle is well off the roadway. The trail is located across the road and slightly downhill from the parking area.

ON THE TRAIL

The trail hides a bit out of view of the road, but it's obvious once you find it in the roadside brush. A few steps in, it reassures you with a sign declaring you are on Cold Creek Trail No. 1303. Just after the sign, hop your way across a dribbling creek, then arrive at a viewpoint that looks down onto the little canyon holding Cold Creek.

The trail is dense with western hemlock and western red cedar, which attracts sweetly calling birds such as the Pacific wren and the varied thrush. In 0.7 mile, reach a signed junction with Mount Catherine Trail No. 1348 heading off to the right. You can do the loop in either direction, but either way you go, this is where you'll return. For now, continue straight ahead and reach the big Twin Lake at 0.8 mile. A couple of tent sites are sprinkled around, and a few social trails walk down to the lakeshore, so be sure to visit. If you brought the wee ones or those who aren't used to hiking, you could call this spot your destination and be content with the accomplishment. Otherwise, onward!

The main trail takes a hard left turn at the lake and crosses the lake's outlet on a large downed log. Use caution, as the log can be slick as a slug's bottom when it's wet. From here the trail climbs steeply up a brushy swale adjacent to the lake's southern shoreline and shows off views of both Twin Lakes.

The shrubs, especially in late summer after a hardy growing season, can be dense and prickly, making it hard to see your feet. Thankfully, this stretch goes quickly and at 2.3 miles, you arrive at a signed junction with the PCT. If you want to add on a visit to Mirror Lake from this spot, go left and follow the PCT to the lake's shoreline. The detour is 4 miles roundtrip with a cumulative elevation gain of 1675 feet.

Otherwise, turn right and follow the PCT on a much gentler grade as it crosses through an area with marshy bogs and tarns. This can

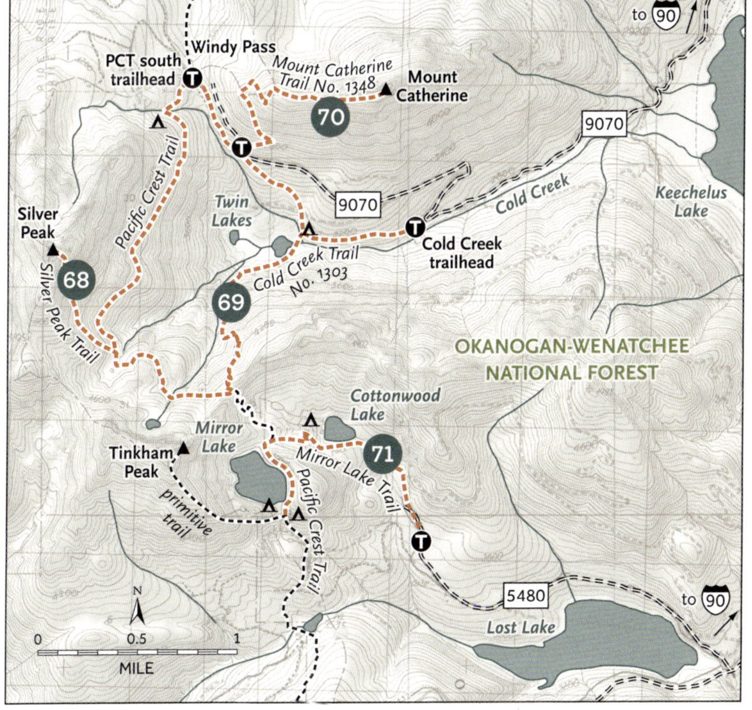

be a mosquito factory in early summer, but in fall, the insects thin out and the area lights up with earth-toned landscaping near the trail's edges.

At 3.1 miles, you are likely to walk past the cairn to the left, marking the unsigned path toward Silver Peak (Hike 68), a popular destination for scramblers and peak baggers. If you are comfortable with exposure and trails that are rough and tumble, you may want to take a detour to the top of this peak. Doing so will be an extra 2.2 miles roundtrip with roughly 1330 cumulative feet of elevation gain. If you aren't fond of scrambles or haven't done much peak bagging, but you still want to summit something along this route, I recommend Mount Catherine, which is coming up!

Continue hiking the PCT with gentle ups and downs, passing a couple of dribbling creeks that dry up by late summer. At 4.8 miles, the trail delivers you to FR 9070 in an area known as Windy Pass. This is the same road where you left your vehicle, only you are farther northwest of where you parked. Turn right and walk the road, using care to watch for the light traffic, until an unsigned junction with Mount Catherine Trail No. 1348 shows up to the road's left, just shy of 5.1 miles. Usually, a cluster of cars and trucks will be lining the road's shoulders in this area, which is a clue you are getting close—Mount Catherine is popular (see Hike 70)! If you want to scoot to the top, the trail detour is approximately 2.8 miles roundtrip with 1270 feet of elevation gain.

Technically, you could take the road all the way back to your vehicle, but the trail is safer and more enjoyable. To find the return trail, look to the right just short of 0.1 mile after the Mount Catherine Trail and find what appears to be an unsigned trail ducking off into the forest. A few steps in, a tree sign notes you are on the Mount Catherine Trail and points toward Twin Lakes, assuring you of the correct path.

After periods of rain, this part can be muddy, so you may need to hop a few bogs or creeklets and whack a few bushes back where they are overgrown, but routefinding is straightforward. At 5.9 miles, arrive at an area that should look familiar—this is where you started the loop earlier in the day. Turn left here and retrace your steps on the Cold Creek Trail back to your waiting vehicle.

70 Mount Catherine

RATING/DIFFICULTY: ***/3
ROUNDTRIP: 2.8 miles
ELEV GAIN/HIGH POINT: 1290 feet/5052 feet
SEASON: July–Oct

Maps: Green Trails Maps Snoqualmie Pass No. 207 and Snoqualmie Pass Gateway No. 207SXL; **Contact:** Okanogan-Wenatchee National Forest, Cle Elum Ranger District; **Notes:** No facilities available. Popular winter sports destination. Open to leashed dogs; see map, page 225; **GPS:** N 47 21.208, W 121 26.669

The climbing is steep but short, so most folks will do some heavy huffing and puffing along the way. But once at the top, the views are outstanding!

GETTING THERE

From I-90 east of Snoqualmie Pass: Take exit 54, signed for Hyak and State Route 906, and turn southwest onto Hyak Drive. Stay straight past two stop signs. The road passes by houses and winds to the left, where it becomes Hyak Drive E. At 0.6 mile, pass through an open gate, and shortly after, the

From the summit of Mount Catherine, sweeping views reveal the peaks lining the Interstate 90 corridor.

road turns to gravel and is signed for Forest Road 9070. Stay on FR 9070, ignoring all side roads, until the easy-to-miss trailhead shows up to the road's right at 5.3 miles. Find limited roadside parking near the trailhead.

ON THE TRAIL

A wide, rocky former logging-road-turned-trail greets you, and in about 300 feet, a tree sign to the left confirms you are on Mount Catherine Trail No. 1348. Pearly everlasting, a perennial plant with beautiful white flowers, grows in the pockets of sunlight underneath western hemlocks. Grand and Pacific silver firs tower above your head as you switchback up the at times rather steep slopes. Back and forth you go on the now narrow trail, passing by huckleberry bushes, where the berries tempt you in late summer.

At 0.8 mile, the path flattens out slightly on a ridgeline and takes a much straighter trajectory to the east through the forest. Just prior to the summit, views open, with a couple of heave-ho spots that might require both hands and feet to hoist yourself up through a few rocky protrusions.

At 1.4 miles, arrive at the top of the peak, where a narrow rocky outcropping gives way to views all around. Be prepared to share the top—it gets pretty crowded during peak times, as space is limited. Below you to the east, Keechelus Lake twinkles with a deep denim blue, while behind you, Mount Rainier hovers with her big vanilla ice cream top. Silver (Hike 68) and Tinkham Peaks are visible much closer to the southwest. Of course, the well-loved peaks of the Snoqualmie area, such as Mount Margaret, are also popping out to the north.

Remnants of a former airway beacon found in the form of rebar, cables, bolts, and bits and pieces of steel are unassuming to most who visit. These airway beacons, which had a large blinking flame, were primarily built in the 1920s and '30s to allow old-timey aviators to navigate from Montana to Seattle on the Transcontinental Airway, like a sky freeway. A metal tower under the structure would have housed the fuel, a colorless acetylene gas that powered the burning signal. Like fire tower lookouts, most were decommissioned and removed, though a couple remain. If you want to see one that still is sitting peacefully, albeit without the flame, check out Hike 81 in this book!

Return to your vehicle the same way you arrived, and maybe check out another hike in this area, since this one was short. Or not . . . A brewery isn't far away.

71 Cottonwood and Mirror Lakes

RATING/DIFFICULTY: *****/2

ROUNDTRIP: 3 miles

ELEV GAIN/HIGH POINT: 710 feet/4220 feet

SEASON: July–Oct

Map: Green Trails Maps Snoqualmie Pass Gateway No. 207SXL; **Contact:** Okanogan-Wenatchee National Forest, Cle Elum Ranger District; **Notes:** Northwest Forest Pass or Interagency Pass required. No facilities at trailhead. Open to leashed dogs, stock; see map, page 225; **GPS:** N 47 20.542, W 121 25.356

The hike to Mirror and Cottonwood Lakes is a wonderful payoff for a short, fairly easy trail. Cottonwood Lake is serene, tucked into a natural drainage underneath a couple of unnamed peaks. The destination, and almost twice as big as Cottonwood, is Mirror Lake, which sits under Tinkham Peak and, on a windless day, reflects the mountain in its calm waters, as its name suggests.

GETTING THERE

From I-90 east of Snoqualmie Pass: Take exit 62, signed for Stampede Pass and Kachess Lake. Turn southwest and follow Forest Road 54 for 1.1 miles. Turn right onto the gravel FR 5480, signed for Lost Lake. At 5.3 miles, arrive at a three-way junction; continue straight ahead and pass Lost Lake on the road's left. At 7.3 miles, find parking along the roadside and in a couple of obvious pullouts. The road continues another 0.3 mile to a parking area to the road's right, but it's extremely rough and narrow, not suitable for most vehicles.

ON THE TRAIL

Walk the road the final 0.3 mile until it curves back to the right to the parking area, and find the Mirror Lake Trail to the road's left. The trail is obvious as it meanders along the forest floor under a canopy of hemlocks and cedars.

Several easy creek crossings are hopped, skipped, and jumped as you wander along, gaining elevation. In 0.6 mile, arrive at a signed trail spur to the right, taking you

The hike to scenic gem Mirror Lake offers big rewards with minimal effort.

toward Cottonwood Lake. Follow the spur to a couple of pleasant, forested tent sites adjacent to the lake's shoreline—a perfect place to stop and take it in. Perhaps most peculiar is that the lake is lined in assorted deciduous shrubs with a backdrop of evergreens and not a cottonwood in sight. Maybe cottonwood seedpods float this way when spring arrives? And the plot thickens.

Back on the main trail, continue your trek, now gaining more elevation until, at 1.3 miles, you reach a T junction with the Pacific Crest Trail. If you are visiting during thru-hiker season, you might see some resilient northbound folks who have made their way here all the way from Mexico. Give them a fist bump and plenty of good vibes for the rest of their journey—they are only a couple of weeks away from the finish line.

Turn left at the PCT junction and follow the trail as it winds its way around Mirror Lake's edges. There are several spurs that drop down to visit the twinkling, teal-colored lake, so stop where you please, or follow the trail to the lake's far eastern shore to a large tent site with a lot of logs for sitting. Some folks may even want to cross the lake's outlet on a cluster of logs and find even more shoreline nooks before turning back.

EXTENDING YOUR HIKE

If you are surefooted, comfortable with exposure, and willing to put in some extra sweat and possibly a few tears, you may want to continue following the lake around the outlet to the south. From there, follow a well-used but unmaintained trail as it wanders west and climbs the at times ridiculously steep, rustic trail toward the top of the rocky Tinkham Peak. The views of neighboring peaks and the lake far below are simply outstanding, but the pointy, clumps of rocks near the summit aren't great places to flop down, so tag it, catch your breath, and head back. This detour will be approximately 1.8 miles roundtrip from the large camp spot at the southern end of Mirror Lake, with a cumulative gain of nearly 1120 feet. Talk about a burner.

72 Gold Creek Pond Loop

RATING/DIFFICULTY: *****/1
ROUNDTRIP: 1.3 miles
ELEV GAIN/HIGH POINT: Negligible/2610 feet
SEASON: late June–Oct

Maps: Green Trails Maps Snoqualmie Pass No. 207 and Snoqualmie Pass Gateway 207S; **Contact:** Mount Baker–Snoqualmie National Forest, Snoqualmie Ranger District; **Notes:** Northwest Forest Pass or Interagency Pass required. Pit toilets at trailhead. This trail is also very popular in the winter for snowshoeing—if you choose to go then, a different parking pass is required. Picnic areas available at the pond. No fishing, paddling, watercrafting, or swimming permitted at the pond. ADA-accessible paved pathway around pond; however, use caution with wheelchairs, as some of the pavement is uneven. Access road has 0.4 mile of large potholes, but most passenger cars make it by going slowly. Open to leashed dogs; **GPS:** N 47 23.804, W 121 22.761

Check the contacts above before you go to Gold Creek Pond, as it will be closed periodically for the foreseeable future for a much-needed environmental facelift. There are only a few trails in the region that are this flat and easily accessible with such amazing mountain views! This trail checks all the boxes for scenery, ease of grade, and overall good vibes. Kids, those with physical challenges, and pretty much everyone else, will love the paved pathway around the pond that allows to you get some fresh air, while not being difficult or long.

GETTING THERE

From I-90 east of Snoqualmie Pass: Take exit 54 signed for Hyak and State Route 906. Head north and proceed 0.1 mile to Forest Road 4832, signed for Gold Creek. Turn right and in 1 mile, turn left on FR 142, signed for Gold Creek. The road is unpaved and rough with potholes for the next 0.4 mile. Reach a Y and bear left, where it's signed for Gold Creek Pond (the right-hand branch is gated). The pavement returns, and you find yourself on the loop for parking with the obvious trailhead and pit toilet.

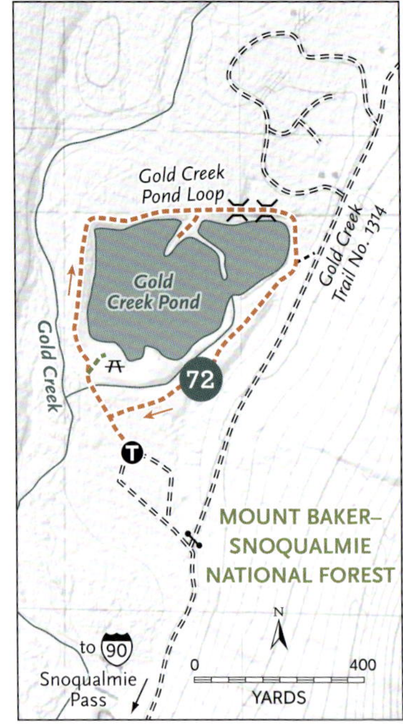

Little explorers, big reflections—Gold Creek Pond mirrors the mountains and their wonder.

ON THE TRAIL

The signboards at the parking area provide information on restoration and history of the area and have a fee box for those who don't have a Northwest Forest or Interagency Pass and need to pick up a day-use pass for parking. Follow the trail as it wanders through riparian brush and evergreens that hide the pond until it arrives at the signed junction for Gold Creek Pond Loop. You can go either direction at this spot, but most folks are eager to see the pond and the views, so they head left and take the quickest route.

In 250 feet from the trailhead, reach some interpretive signage on kokanee salmon and water diversions, both key to this area. I'll let you read the signs instead of giving you the summary—such a fascinating place!

In another 200 feet, arrive at the main picnic area with the pond and the views of the Alpine Lakes Wilderness front and center. Far, far in the distance, the Pacific Crest Trail traverses those mountains, and one can use their imagination on where it crosses. This is one of the best picture spots in the valley, so be sure to snap away—there's your Christmas card!

Conifers line the paved trail's edges, while birds such as Steller's jays squawk from their boughs. At 0.2 mile from the trailhead, reach a bench along with an interpretive sign about the damage historical logging did to this area and how restoration efforts are helping put things back to a healthy natural environment. Another bench and interpretive sign follow in another 0.1 mile. This sign shares interesting information about how the pond is actually manmade, a former mining area for gravel with which I-90 was constructed.

At 0.5 mile, an interpretive sign to the right discusses how the mining efforts in the 1970s still affect the area. Be sure to check out the spur trail near the sign, which starts out paved and then turns to dirt and explores the 0.2 mile out-and-back peninsula, to see the pond more closely.

Back on the path, the trail introduces a couple of wooden bridges over seasonal creeks before it arrives at a junction with Gold Creek Trail No. 1314, coming in from the left, at 0.6 mile. Sadly, this trail hasn't been given much love and becomes difficult to follow as it wanders up the Gold Creek valley.

Your around-the-pond romp continues until you arrive back at the loop's signed start, 0.9 mile from the Gold Creek Trail junction. Turn left to walk the short distance back to the parking area, or go right, to revisit the picnic area and feast on the PB&Js that you brought for just such an occasion.

73 Palouse to Cascades: Snoqualmie Tunnel

RATING/DIFFICULTY: ****/1
ROUNDTRIP: 5.4 miles
ELEV GAIN/HIGH POINT: Negligible/2630 feet
SEASON: late June–Oct

Map: Green Trails Maps Snoqualmie Pass No. 207; **Contact:** Washington State Parks; **Notes:** Discover Pass Required. Picnic areas and pit toilets at trailhead and at tunnel entrance and exits. Tunnel open weather dependently May 1–Nov 1. Formerly known as Iron Horse Tunnel along the John Wayne Trail—may still be listed as such on some maps. Headlamps or illumination are necessary in the tunnel's darkness. Open to leashed dogs, bikers, stock; **GPS:** N 47 23.483, W 121 23.552

Constructed between 1912 and 1914, but abandoned now for over forty-five years, this 2.3-mile-long tunnel used to guide the Chicago, Milwaukee, St. Paul, and Pacific Railway through mountains near Snoqualmie Pass. These days, as part of the Palouse to Cascades Trail, it guides hikers, bikers, and horses through the chilly, drippy darkness, making a spooky but fun experience for all ages.

GETTING THERE

From I-90 east of Snoqualmie Pass: Take exit 54 signed for Hyak and State Route 906 and turn southwest at the exit ramp stop sign. Arrive at a second stop sign and turn left (SR 906), following the sign toward Iron Horse State Park (though this may be updated to the new name, Palouse to Cascades State Park at some point). In another 0.4 mile, turn right

Step into the Snoqualmie Tunnel with a headlamp to light your way and a jacket to fend off the cold, even in summer.

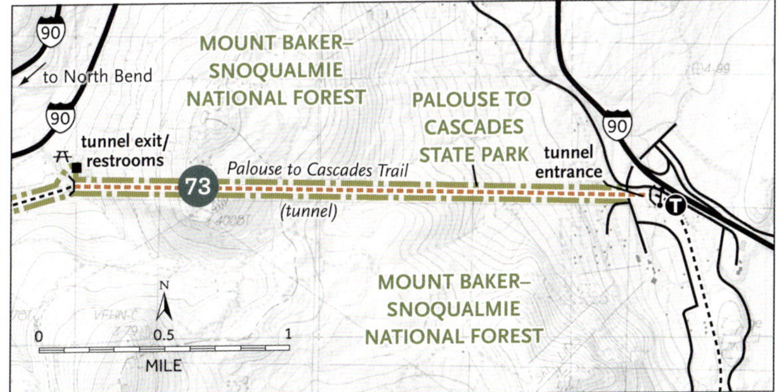

again (also signed for the state park), then keep looking right one more time and find the well-signed trailhead and gated parking area in another 0.1 mile. The parking area is quite large; the closest parking spots to the tunnel are on the far western side.

ON THE TRAIL

From the parking lot, find the large trailhead sign calling out Iron Horse State Park by walking west to the large gravel rails-to-trails path. Turn right (northwest) at the sign and begin your hike. In 0.1 mile, walk around a closed gate, designed to keep motorized traffic out. The former railroad grade continues straight ahead before curving slightly to the left and entering the tunnel at 0.4 mile. Stop here and pull out your headlamp or flashlight, and get the jacket handy before you lose the light.

Immediately you notice the cold! The deep tunnel under the mountain is like a refrigerated tube, making your nose cold and your cheeks rosy. If you are visiting on a chilly day, you may even want gloves, a hat, and hand warmers. But in the hot summer, it feels like a giant air conditioner and serves as a good place to escape the heat.

The next sensory experience is the mild scent of wet earth and the muskiness of dank concrete, which makes it feel like a murky cave. You might get a bit nervous about the safety of the structure, especially because deep inside it's hard to see many details, but rest assured it's safe. In July 2011, the tunnel was reopened after a $700,000 two-year renovation that reconstructed the walls, ceilings, and pathway ensuring the tunnel's structural integrity. What's more, it's larger and wider than most caves, so you and others you pass will have plenty of room to walk or ride bikes.

Water drips from tiny holes and joints inside the tunnel, causing puddles here and there, so watch where you step and expect to get hit occasionally with a drop. The drips echo off the walls, which after big rainfalls sound much bigger than they are. The sounds of people talking or kids playing reverberate too, and there are usually plenty of voices to be heard; somehow, making noise in the dark space lends a sense of comfort. Kind of like singing in a lifeboat.

Headlamp beams wiggle as you walk, but part of the fun is watching the consistent light at the opposite end get bigger until it eventually delivers you to the outside world again. The western side offers a pit toilet, picnic tables, and interpretive signage for creature comforts. Appreciate the light and warmth before going back through the tunnel, or continue discovering the Palouse to Cascades Trail to your heart's delight.

74 Kendall Katwalk

RATING/DIFFICULTY: ****/4
ROUNDTRIP: 12.5 miles
ELEV GAIN/HIGH POINT: 2810 feet/5480 feet
SEASON: July–Oct

Maps: Green Trails Maps Snoqualmie Pass No. 207 and Snoqualmie Pass Gateway No. 207S; **Contact:** Mount Baker–Snoqualmie National Forest, Snoqualmie Ranger District; **Notes:** Northwest Forest Pass or Interagency Pass required. Free wilderness use permit required, available at trailhead. Pit toilets and picnic area at trailhead. Trailhead break-ins common; take valuables with you. As with all I-90 corridor hikes, this one is crowded; avoid weekends if possible. Open to leashed dogs, stock; **GPS:** N 47 25.676, W 121 24.813

The gem of this hike is the trail-building marvel called the Kendall Katwalk, a sheer rock-face-turned-hiker-friendly shelf blasted out of the granite with dynamite back in the '70s. Its goal, which it does with ease, is to guide hikers safely across the rock face on a pathway fit for cruising, while showcasing some mind-blowingly beautiful sights all along the way. What's more, you'll dip your toes in the pool of the Pacific Crest Trail (PCT) and maybe even strike up your interest to do all of it, or at least all of the Washington section at some point. As luck would have it, I have a book for that too (*Hiking the Pacific Crest Trail: Washington*). Kendall Katwalk is a bucket-list I-90 hike for sure!

Though photos make it look like a nerve-wracking edge walk, the Kendall Katwalk is much wider and more comfortable in person.

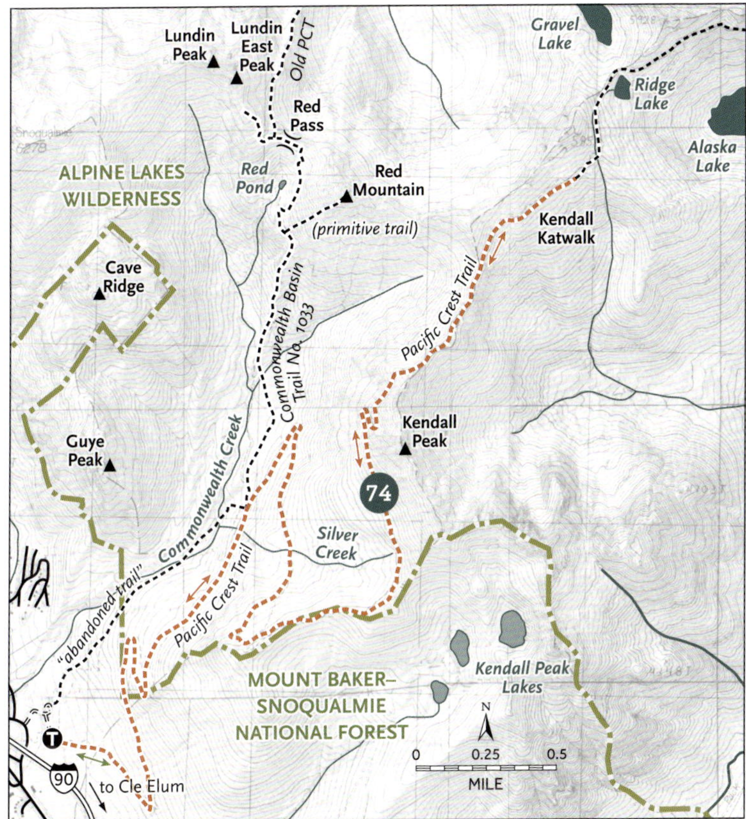

GETTING THERE

From I-90 east of Snoqualmie Pass: Take exit 52 for Snoqualmie Pass West. Turn north at the end of the exit ramp. Turn right in roughly 100 yards onto a dirt road signed for the PCT, and drive into the parking area. The trailhead is on the east side of the parking area.

ON THE TRAIL

Do your high kicks and a few squats (behind the pit toilets so you don't embarrass yourself) to warm up your muscles—you're going to be gaining elevation at a steady clip! In the first two hundred feet, ignore the less-used trails coming in from the left, a horse parking connector, and the Old Commonweath Trail. The PCT is basically a freeway here from so much traffic—you can't mistake the main path.

In no time, find yourself ascending under the strong limbs of Douglas-firs, while plants such as salmonberries, devil's club, queen's cup, vanilla leaf, and Cascade huckleberry decorate the trail near your legs. Arrive at the Alpine Lakes Wilderness boundary, announced with a trail sign, at 1.7 miles.

At 2.3 miles, Silver Creek comes in as a reliable water source in most summers. If you brought the pup, he'll probably appreciate lapping up some of that cold, clear drink, while you enjoy nibbling salmonberries or huckleberries in the vicinity.

Immediately after the creek, a junction with Commonwealth Basin Trail No. 1033 shows up (see Hike 67), and it's tempting to bear left and follow it, as it seems to be going slightly downhill! No such luck—our trail keeps climbing and bears right through the evergreens.

At 3.2 miles, Silver Creek shows up again, more reliable water if you need to top off. A few avalanche chutes follow, along with a couple of tributary creeklets trickling in from above. Slide alder, salmonberries, thimbleberries, and green corn lily try to take over in these spots, securing the ground, at least temporarily, until the next snowslide knocks them down. Eventually, the path gains a forested ridge before it pops out into a series of rocky, open hills with great views, including those of Red Mountain, with its cinnamon color taking your mind off your pumping heart.

Wildflowers such as Sitka valerian, lupine, and fireweed along with shrubs such as elderberry and rosy spirea are colorful in summer months, and the occasional mountain goat can be seen on the shoulders of Kendall Peak to your right. The ski slopes of the Summit at Snoqualmie are visible to the south, along with the bustling traffic of I-90.

The rock garden continues as the PCT crests the ridge and drops over the other side, where you get your first good look at the Kendall Katwalk, which starts 6 miles from the trailhead.

In the late 1970s, a trail crew suspended themselves on ropes and placed dynamite into sheer granite to blast this route—an impressive feat and an impressive stretch of trail! The best pictures are crafted from the Katwalk's northern side, looking back to the south. The shots show off the sheer walls and imposing scale of their pathway, making it look scarier than it is. Follow the Katwalk as far as you wish, or turn back when you've soaked it all in.

EXTENDING YOUR HIKE

If there is still fuel in your tank, you could keep rolling along this ridgeline for 2 miles roundtrip with 300 feet of cumulative elevation gain to reach two lakes, Ridge Lake directly to the trailside right (southeast) and Gravel Lake to the left (northwest). If you don't make it to the lakes, there are plenty of great rocky spots to pull out, devour your lunch, and decompress from the cares of life.

75 Kendall Peak Lakes

RATING/DIFFICULTY: ***/3
ROUNDTRIP: 8.4 miles
ELEV GAIN/HIGH POINT: 1890 feet/4450 feet
SEASON: July–Oct

Maps: Green Trails Maps Snoqualmie Pass No. 207 and Snoqualmie Pass Gateway No. 207S; **Contact:** Mount Baker–Snoqualmie National Forest, Snoqualmie Ranger District; **Notes:** Northwest Forest Pass or Interagency Pass required. No facilities at trailhead, though options are close by at Snoqualmie Pass. Popular snowshoe route. Open to leashed dogs; **GPS:** N 47 23.890, W 121 23.666

If you're up for a quieter mountain lake experience, this route leads to often uncrowded shorelines.

There are three lakes at the end of this hike, though one is more of a shallow marsh and another is tough to reach. The goal is the healthy, stunning middle lake, where you might be sitting solo on a summer day only a stone's throw away from some of the most crowded hikes in the state. To get here, you'll have to walk a former forest road, then take a short jaunt on a single-track trail, but the forest road is well graded, with some views along the way to keep up your interest.

GETTING THERE

From I-90 near Snoqualmie Pass: Take exit 54 signed for Hyak and State Route 906. Head north and proceed 0.1 mile to Forest Road 4832, signed for Gold Creek (FR 142). Parking is in the pullout straight ahead or along the roadside at this intersection. The trail begins straight ahead (northeast), past a vehicle barrier for the former road.

ON THE TRAIL

Walk around the vehicle barrier for the former roadway, and immediately shimmy your way through the skeletal remains of the old car bridge over Coal Creek. The badly eroded stretch seems to get worse each year, so use fancy footwork to ensure your safety, and watch dogs and kids closely in this spot. It's stable (for now) but narrow.

In 0.3 mile, another series of concrete barriers confirm that the road is closed. Had you been able to bust through the other concrete barriers with a tank, you'd have gone in the drink anyway, but now we have confirmation if there was any doubt.

Onward we roam, finding a bit more reprieve from the freeway noise the higher we get. This is a good hike for folks who want to catch up on conversation, because the path is easy to follow while deep in dialogue, and the moderate grade still allows most hikers to talk and breathe comfortably.

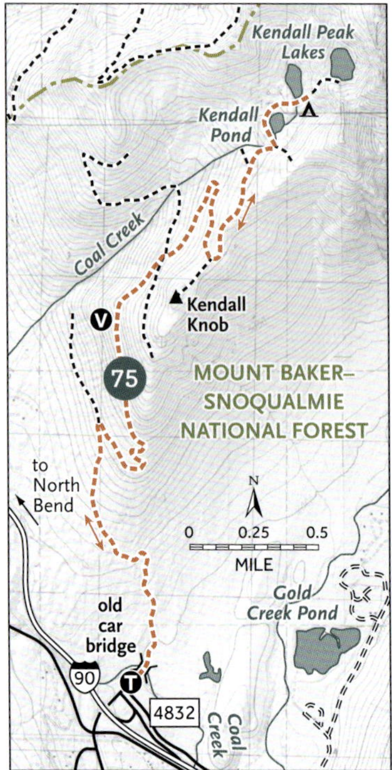

Periodically you'll pass side spurs from former logging efforts, which are now obsolete and overgrown, but the main road is well-traveled and obvious. At nearly 2.3 miles, the road opens to the left to exhibit the ski slopes and bustling traffic on I-90. It's a good place for a break if you need one at this point.

At 3.4 miles, the trail flattens out some and turns left in a wide swath. To the right is a boot-beaten spur leading up to the top of Kendall Knob, should your curiosity and extra energy guide you there. The detour will be about a half-mile roundtrip with an elevation gain of 100 feet. The path to the top isn't signed, but the trail is obvious.

Continue following the main road, and at 3.8 miles, reach a slightly confusing intersection where the main road-turned-trail goes right, though it's brushy and some folks instinctively get pulled straight ahead instead. This right-hand turn is key because it means we are getting close to where we need to catch the unsigned single track to the lakes. At 3.9 miles, start looking to your left for a trail ducking into the woods. There is no sign, but sometimes folks build arrows with sticks, or create cairns to indicate its presence. If you look, you'll find it even without homemade indications.

Follow the single track through the former logging area and reach the first body of water, Kendall Pond, at 4 miles. This lake is shallow, marshy, and an ideal mosquito nursery. If you are visiting in early summer, you will be tempted to hose yourself down with bug goop, walk fast, and beg for mercy. Though you have reached a goal, it's not an ideal place for lunch or a break, so keep following the trail as it jogs around the left side of the pond and reenters the forest. From here, the trail climbs some, but it's short and sweet, and at 4.2 miles, find yourself standing near the shore of the bigger, deeper, and much more scenic option for lunch, the most accessible of the two Kendall Peak Lakes. Follow the lake's shoreline to the right to find a couple of tent sites that provide good spots to drop packs and grab pictures and nibbles before heading back.

EXTENDING YOUR HIKE

The second of the Kendall Peak Lakes is challenging to find, as the trail peters out and it requires some off-trail bushwhacking. Wander off to locate it only if you have a good map and feel confident in your navigation skills. To get there, follow the shoreline of the first lake past the tent sites and continue around its southern edge to cross the outlet on a series of logs. From here, make your way northeast, steeply at times, to the second lake, for 0.4 mile roundtrip and 310 feet of cumulative elevation gain.

76 Lake Lillian and Twin Lakes

RATING/DIFFICULTY: ***/4
ROUNDTRIP: 9.2 miles
ELEV GAIN/HIGH POINT: 3060 feet/4490 feet
SEASON: July–Oct

Maps: Green Trails Maps Snoqualmie Pass No. 207 and Snoqualmie Pass Gateway No. 207S; **Contact:** Okanogan-Wenatchee National Forest, Cle Elum Ranger District; **Notes:** Northwest Forest Pass or Interagency Pass required. No facilities at trailhead. Open to leashed dogs; **GPS:** N 47 21.834, W 121 21.500

Though you aren't far from the busy I-90 corridor, as you get closer to Twin Lakes, this hike feels miles away from civilization. Since the trail takes you over rises and vales, it's a good place to explore the backcountry without having the classic, straight-up-and-straight-down hike, as it's more of a ramble. Yet, you'll get a fantastic workout.

GETTING THERE

From I-90 near Snoqualmie Pass: Take exit 54 signed for Hyak and State Route 906. Head north and proceed 0.1 mile to Forest Road 4832, signed for Gold Creek. In just over 2 miles, the road narrows and parallels I-90, then at 2.7 miles it turns to gravel. At 4 miles, continue following FR 4832 as it bears right; avoid going straight. At 4.1 miles, bear left (straight), following what is now FR 4934, and avoid heading right. Then, at 4.5 miles, just prior to a sharp turn right,

Twinkling cobalt waters of Lake Lillian contrast with the warm palette of fall foliage on the hillsides.

go straight ahead to the parking area and signed trailhead.

ON THE TRAIL

Most trails leave directly from the trailhead, but not this one. To find the trail, walk back out to the road on which you arrived (FR 4934) and head east (uphill). In 0.1 mile, after roughly 40 feet of elevation gain, take a left on a rarely used, narrow forest road.

At 0.7 mile, find a signed junction to the road's left with a picture of hikers and an arrow. This is our path (Lake Margaret Trail No. 1332.1), so turn left and follow the rocky and somewhat loose trail through former logging clear-cuts, which open up views to surrounding peaks. At 1.1 miles, the trail crosses a former logging road and continues on the other side, getting higher with each step.

Near the top of the ridge, a more mature forest welcomes you, and at 2.2 miles, reach a rather flat plateau with a signed junction and arrows pointing toward Lake Lillian Trail No. 1332 and Margaret Lake (see Hike 77). Turn left and continue your backcountry promenade.

At 2.6 miles, the trail passes an unsigned junction with the unmaintained trail to the top of Mount Margaret (see Hike 77). This narrow, user-created trail scoots off to the right, and these days it's almost more heavily traveled than the one we are on. In fact, when I was doing research for this book, someone must have thought that the Lake Lillian Trail was only there for Mount Margaret access, and they had placed logs across the path, seemingly directing all traffic toward Mount Margaret's summit.

Our trail does, in fact, continue and at 2.9 miles, it reaches a pass before dropping down toward the Twin Lakes basin. The area isn't dense forest now but rather smaller shrubs, such as huckleberry and elderberry, that give the area a meadowy feeling and allow vistas to Rampart Ridge's Southeast Peak.

The sparkling, tranquil Twin Lakes are just one lovely lake and a neighboring little hiccup filled with water. Social trails scoot off to the lake's shoreline, with a few spots to sit and soak it in before continuing onward.

After leaving Twin Lakes, pass a marshy pond to the left before ascending again to crest a forested ridge. From the ridge, the trail drops down through a boulder field before reaching an unsigned junction at 4.2 miles. From this point on, things can get confusing, as there are plentiful social trails and little to no signage. Bring a reliable map if you want to explore the area further. To the left at this intersection is the trail that leads to Lake Laura and the backdoor approach to this trail system. Lake Lillian is to the right, after climbing through some steep, loose terrain. At 4.4 miles, pop out at Lake Lillian's south shore. The charming lake is nestled into the strong arms of rocky protrusions mixed with conifers and sunlit meadows, and the lake has great ambiance, though hangout areas aren't plentiful. You'll need to get a bit creative with your resting spot, maybe even backtracking into the forest for a nibble after snapping some pictures. Return the way you came or keep exploring!

EXTENDING YOUR HIKE

This area is full of unmaintained trails that connect to other areas and roads, making it a mecca of enjoyment for good navigators and those comfortable on lightly used, hard-to-follow, sometimes sketchy, user-built trails.

From Lake Lillian, you can make your way around to the lake's east side on a somewhat exposed trail to reach Rampart Ridge, Rampart Lakes, and several tarns and ponds.

From Rampart Lakes, you could even take the trail over to summit Alta Mountain and visit Lila Lake basin (eyes on you, trail runners). Mileage and elevation gain vary based on your wanderings, but from Lillian Lake to the first Rampart Lake, you'll be at 2.8 miles roundtrip and an elevation gain at over 1200 feet.

The backdoor approach: You can also approach Lake Lillian and Lake Laura by

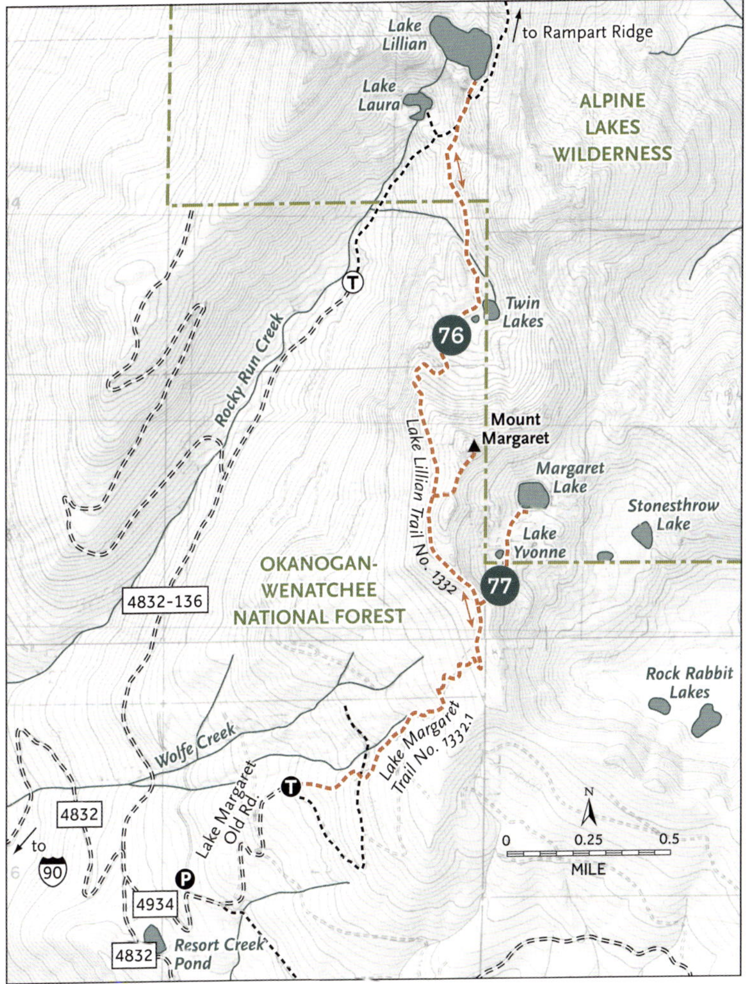

using a different forest road and hiking up the unofficial, unmaintained approach. This trail is comically steep in places, and the final forest road might voluntarily offer "Montana pinstriping" to your car thanks to overgrown branches. To get there, follow the same driving directions as above, except at 4 miles, go straight (instead of bearing right) on Forest Road 4832-136. At 5.2 miles, bear right to stay on the same road. Find parking in pullouts and on the roadside at the road's dead end, 5.9 miles from leaving I-90.

You can access both Lake Laura and Lake Lillian on this get-the-dessert-before-eating-dinner route, which is only 1.6 miles roundtrip. Short it is, but sweet it is not, as it gains over 1160 feet in a steep, pull-yourself-up-on-branches-style hike. Those who crave adventure with fitness aplenty will purr over this rough-and-tumble wonder.

77 Margaret Lake and Mount Margaret

RATING/DIFFICULTY: ***/3
ROUNDTRIP: 7 miles
ELEV GAIN/HIGH POINT: 2370 feet/5585 feet
SEASON: July–Oct

Maps: Green Trails Maps Snoqualmie Pass No. 207 and Snoqualmie Pass Gateway No. 207S; **Contact:** Okanogan-Wenatchee National Forest, Cle Elum Ranger District; **Notes:** Northwest Forest Pass or Interagency Pass required. No facilities at trailhead. Open to leashed dogs; see map, page 241; **GPS:** N 47 21.834, W 121 21.500

You can visit either the lake or the peak or both! If you have less time and have to pick only one of the two, visiting the lake is the better option, as the trail is maintained and it's slightly easier. But if time is on your side and you aren't opposed to a rough, user-made trail, Mount Margaret is a great workout leading to a panoramic vista.

GETTING THERE

From I-90 near Snoqualmie Pass: Take exit 54 signed for Hyak and State Route 906. Head north and proceed 0.1 mile to Forest Road 4832, signed for Gold Creek. In just over 2 miles, the road narrows and parallels I-90, then at 2.7 miles turns to gravel. At 4 miles, continue following FR 4832 as it bears right (avoid going straight). At 4.1 miles, bear left (straight), following what is now FR 4934, and avoid heading right. Then, at 4.5 miles, just prior to a sharp right turn, go straight ahead to the parking area and signed trailhead.

ON THE TRAIL

This trail doesn't leave from the parking lot but rather sends you on a little warm-up before it. To find the trail, walk back out to the road on which you arrived (FR 4934), and head east (uphill). In 0.1 mile, after roughly 40 feet of elevation gain, take a left on a rarely used, narrow forest road.

At 0.7 mile, find a signed junction to the road's left with a picture of hikers and an arrow. Lake Margaret Trail No. 1332.1 heads off here, so turn left and follow the path up through the former logging area. At 1.1 miles, cross a former logging road and continue with the loose, rocky trail on the opposite side.

The clear-cut area is growing back with berries and mini timbers, but thankfully a more mature forest welcomes you before reaching the top of the ridge. At 2.2 miles, a plateau on the ridgeline greets you with a signed junction. An arrow pointing left guides hikers toward Lake Lillian Trail No. 1332 (Hike 76). Also in this direction, though not signed as such, is Mount Margaret. An arrow also points to Margaret Lake, which is straight head. If you intend to visit Mount Margaret at this point, you'll want to turn left and skip forward three paragraphs. However, if you are planning on visiting Margaret Lake first, or only Margaret Lake, continue reading.

Cross over the ridge and begin your descent toward the Margaret Lake basin. The way drops rather steeply, switchbacking downhill to ease the knees, until it levels out some and passes Lake Yvonne to the left. This lake isn't a destination but rather a shallow pond serving as a prime mosquito incubator—run! Continue descending much more gradually to a basin that holds onto its winter snowpack and is usually the very last patch in the area to melt in early summer. At 2.8 miles, arrive at the shores of Margaret Lake. The calm, azure water is perfect for a swim on a hot day, or just to dip your toes. Head right for the best pack-drop spots.

When you've enjoyed the lake and its surrounding glory, retrace your path, climbing back out of the basin to gain the roughly 345 feet that you lost on the way down. At the top, arrive back at the signed intersection with Lake Lillian Trail No. 1332.

Go right (north) at this intersection. In 0.4 mile from this signed junction, look closely for an unsigned, primitive trail to the right, heading into the forest. Turn right and submerge yourself in the somewhat vertical user-built trail through the conifers. Expect some loose soil, big roots, and a few gymnastics with blowdowns. Overall, it's not as bad as some in the area (I'm looking at *you*, old Mailbox Peak Trail). At the summit, just 0.3 mile since you started the rustic trail, outstanding views are found all the way from

Like so many pristine alpine lakes, Margaret Lake is a soothing balm for the spirit.

Mount Rainier to Mount Stuart. Of course, Margaret Lake is visible in the basin along with Stonesthrow Lake and a smattering of unnamed potholes. What a place!

Work your way back down, still purring from the panoramas, then boogie your way back to the trailhead.

EXTENDING YOUR HIKE

If you haven't had enough foot time . . . check out the hike to Twin Lakes and Lake Lillian (Hike 76).

78 Lodge Lake

RATING/DIFFICULTY: ****/2
ROUNDTRIP: 3.8 miles
ELEV GAIN/HIGH POINT: 850 feet/3490 feet
SEASON: late June–early Nov

Maps: Green Trails Maps Snoqualmie Pass No. 207 and Snoqualmie Pass Gateway No. 207S; **Contact:** Mount Baker–Snoqualmie National Forest, Snoqualmie Ranger District; **Notes:** Northwest Forest Pass or Interagency Pass required. No facilities at trailhead, though options are close by at Snoqualmie Pass. Open to leashed dogs, stock; **GPS:** N 47 25.639, W 121 25.286

The magic of the Pacific Crest Trail (PCT) has enticed hikers for years, and this is the perfect short sampling. A relatively easy trail leads hikers to a pretty lake tucked behind the ski hills near Snoqualmie Pass.

GETTING THERE

From I-90 east of Snoqualmie Pass: Take exit 52 for Snoqualmie Pass West. Go south and proceed roughly 100 yards to a direct road leading to the ski area's westernmost parking lot. The trailhead and large PCT signs are found at the parking area's western dead end.

ON THE TRAIL

Head up the PCT westbound, and at less than 340 feet, switchback to the left to start a long traverse first through the forest and then across the barren ski slopes. While this is a developed ski area, it's amazing how much wildlife is around here, especially toward dusk. It's one of my favorite haunts for quick evening walks, and I've seen black bears, bald eagles, black-tailed deer, and red-tailed hawks along these ski slopes before Beaver Lake. Keep your eyes out for wildlife, and enjoy every minute if you get the chance to see some.

A joyful hiker casts her arms into the wind, offering silent thanks to the wild beauty of Lodge Lake.

The trail crosses a couple of ski-lift access roads for this ski area known as Summit West, but the trail on the other side is always obvious. In 0.7 mile, reach the top of the climb in a small saddle between two high knobs. You'll see the view behind you on your return, but it's worth spinning around and looking at the beauty spread out like a postcard. Denny Mountain, Alpental Point, Guye Peak, Red Mountain, and others reach their lofty summits toward the sky, while brushy plants such as salmonberries, goldenrod, mountain ash, and fireweed outline the trail's edges.

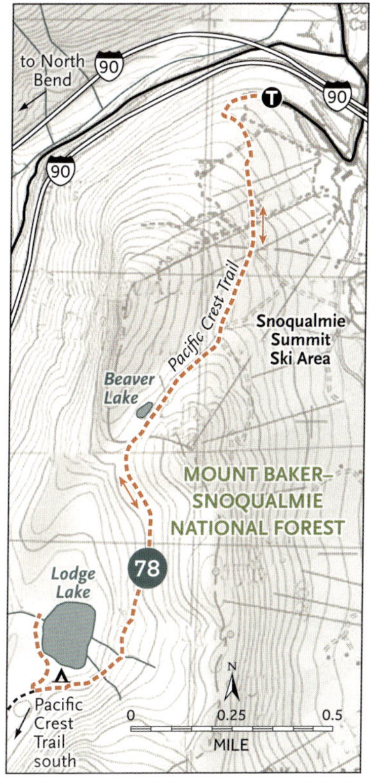

The trail descends slightly to reach Beaver Lake to the path's right, which is more like a pretty pond with birds flitting around its shrubby banks. The area is serene, so snap a few pictures and soak in that beauty before ducking back into the forest for your descent toward Lodge Lake. The mature forest of Douglas-firs, western hemlocks, and western red cedars accompanies you as you make your way through the damp, mossy forest. At 1.5 miles, rock-hop your way across a hardy creek with a quaint little waterfall before continuing to reach a signed junction at 1.8 miles, pointing toward Lodge Lake. Follow the spur trail, passing through a couple of forested tent sites to reach its shoreline.

Contrary to popular belief, this lake was not named due to its proximity to the ski lodges of the Summit at Snoqualmie. In fact, its moniker started before the ski area was ever established. In 1914, the Mountaineers Club volunteers constructed a gorgeous log lodge almost entirely out of trees found on the site. The structure sat on a knoll 0.3 mile southwest of Lodge Lake and featured a kitchen as well as dorms for men and women. There was no plumbing or electricity, but that wasn't uncommon back in those days. For years, the lodge housed organized outings of climbers, hikers, skiers, and snowshoers and also hosted an annual snowshoeing carnival. At night, they would dance to the music of the wind-up Victrola and tell stories by the big stone fireplace. But sadly, like so many buildings during that era, this one met with disaster. On a warm September day in 1944, as a caretaker was burning trash in the large fireplace, a spark went up the chimney and hit the roof, igniting a fire that burned the lodge to the ground. No evidence of any structure is found near the lake today—just the twinkling waters, which beg you to grab your camera.

The hill you came down to get to the lake isn't too bad going back up—plus, you get to pass Beaver Lake again as a bonus on your way back.

EXTENDING YOUR HIKE

If you want to make your trip longer, follow the PCT past Lodge Lake to the south to your heart's content, or, well . . . Mexico.

79 Snow Lake

RATING/DIFFICULTY: ****/3
ROUNDTRIP: 6.8 miles
ELEV GAIN/HIGH POINT: 1650 feet/4400 feet
SEASON: July–Oct

Maps: Green Trails Maps Snoqualmie Pass No. 207 and Snoqualmie Pass Gateway No. 207SXL; **Contact:** Mount Baker–Snoqualmie National Forest, Snoqualmie Ranger District; **Notes:** Northwest Forest Pass or Interagency Pass required. As of the 2026 season, the Summit at Snoqualmie requires advance registration and fees for overnight parking in some lots (see Resources). Parking lot can fill up on weekends. Expect crowding on all days. Pit toilet at trailhead and services at Snoqualmie Pass near trailhead. This area is prone to avalanche hazards, so avoid in the case of heavy snowfall. Open to leashed dogs, stock (on PCT); **GPS:** N 47 26.723, W 121 25.408

As one of the most scenic and accessible lakes in the area, in the summer months this place becomes a human anthill, complete with a food truck in the parking lot—true story. But crowds just mean more people to care and protect the trails from threats, and truly, if everyone had a chance to feast

Snow Lake draws a crowd, but its beauty is generous—there's more than enough wonder for everyone.

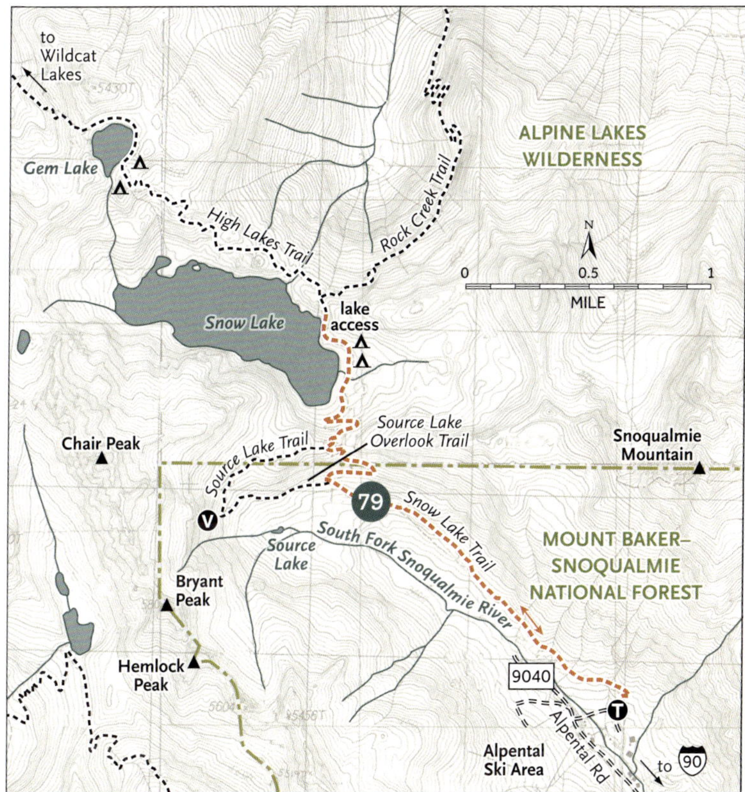

their eyes on this glory, the world would be a better place. Pack your patience and expect to see me, you, and half the zoo. If you want more solitude, simply go past Snow Lake to Gem Lake, where you start to lose the herd. Those that can swing an even longer hike will enjoy going even deeper into the hinterlands to Lower and Upper Wildcat Lakes, where beauty abounds so you can fill up the soul's cookie jar.

GETTING THERE

From I-90 east of Snoqualmie Pass: Take exit 52 for Snoqualmie Pass West. Go north and cross under the freeway. Stay right at the junction with Forest Road 58 and follow the road known as Erste Strasse as it winds northbound, passing homes and condominiums, until you arrive at a large parking area for Alpental Ski Area to your left at 1.6 miles. Find the trailhead across the road to the northeast.

ON THE TRAIL

A pleasant ramble kicks off the hike as you gain elevation gently for the first 1.7 miles, save for a few steep trail steps right off the get-go. Views of the Alpental Ski Area to the left are visible, and you can use your imagination to picture this place buzzing with skiers flying down the slopes in winter. As you make your way northwest, the trail mixes evergreen forests with talus fields and brushy avalanche swale while crossing a few seasonal trickles.

At 1.7 miles, the trail takes a hard right at a signed junction with the Source Lake Trail (see Extending Your Hike). From here, the trail switches back in through vegetated talus slopes, offering inspiring views of Chair Peak to the west. Though you aren't far from the parking lot, it feels a world away. The last bit of climbing is the steepest, so grit your teeth and grind up it until you reach a ridgeline and catch your breath.

From the saddle, the trail descends toward Snow Lake, which sparkles in deep blue in the basin below you. It's hard to walk down to it and not want to stop every other step for a postcard-perfect photo; now you see why it's so popular. Pika—small rabbit family mammals that look a little like guinea pigs—squeak in the talus as you walk by. Reach the lake at approximately 3.4 miles. The Snow Lake basin has several designated backcountry tent sites, along with a primitive toilet and a couple of areas with beachy spots to sit, swim, and soak in the day. If the areas are crowded, keep walking—there are several nooks to hang out in. Turn back the way you came or extend your hike!

EXTENDING YOUR HIKE

From Snow Lake, follow the trail around the lake's northeastern shore and pass a junction for the Rock Creek Trail heading off to the right, signed for Middle Fork Road. Gem Lake is signed with an arrow pointing the same direction you've been traveling. Follow the arrow toward Gem, and climb up through huckleberries and heather meadows mixed with talus pockets to the peaceful shoreline of Gem Lake, 2.8 miles roundtrip and 1400 feet elevation gain in addition to your Snow Lake trek. If trail brain is not wanting to do math, that's a total of 9.6 miles and 3050 feet of elevation gain on the day—give or take—depending on how much exploration you are doing.

If you've had a strong cappuccino today, you may even want to keep going! Wind around the northeastern side of Gem Lake to a signed junction for Wildcat Lakes at the top of a rise. The arrow points the way as the trail heads north and then steeply descends on switchbacks through a rocky tread for nearly 800 feet—a big drop! Wild Dare Peak to the north is visible on the horizon, as are several towering walls and unnamed ridgelines. Several creeks with strong, year-round water flows give the pup a chance to drink and you a chance to filter if need be. At 1.9 miles after Gem Lake, reach Lower Wildcat Lake, the less impressive of the two. The lake is set in a forested basin, and in season, the berries around here burst with varieties and flavors. Continue onward as the trail climbs up a somewhat steep but short hillside to reach the more alpine and scenic Upper Wildcat Lake, just 0.4 mile from the last. Campsites to the north provide places to sit and chill out. Going from Snow Lake trailhead to Upper Wildcat and back totals about 14 roundtrip miles and about 4330 feet of elevation gain.

Another option for a hike extension is to visit Source Lake overlook. At 1.7 miles from the trailhead, prior to reaching Snow Lake, head west at the signed junction until you see the lake in the basin below. There is no trail to the small, shallow lake, so most folks are content to stay high above it, reaching a boulder field with the unofficial overlook at 0.5 mile from the junction.

80 Stirrup Lake

RATING/DIFFICULTY: ***/2
ROUNDTRIP: 2.3 miles
ELEV GAIN/HIGH POINT: 480 feet/3560 feet
SEASON: late June–Oct

Map: Green Trails Maps Snoqualmie Pass No. 207; **Contact:** Okanogan-Wenatchee National Forest, Cle Elum Ranger District; **Notes:** Rough road in places; high-clearance vehicles recommended. No facilities at trailhead. This trail can be reached via the Pacific Crest Trail (PCT), and by continuing on Forest Road 5483 for 0.8 mile past the directions noted here, and then turning left onto FR 5483-118 for another 0.8 mile. Once there, head south on the PCT. Open to leashed dogs; **GPS:** N 47 18.147, W 121 24.281

The shallow but lovely Stirrup Lake is almost completely ignored when folks think of short hikes and scenic destinations. This is likely because the road in is long and rough. But if you can hang for the potholes, the hike is easy, short, and rewarding, with the shallow, scenic lake sitting under Meadow Mountain.

GETTING THERE

From I-90 near Snoqualmie Pass: Take exit 62 toward Stampede Pass and Kachess Lake and head southwest. Pass the Crystal Springs Sno-Park, and at 1.1 miles, near a white firehouse building, turn right onto FR 5480 (signed for Lost Lake). At 2.7 miles, turn left immediately after crossing Meadow Creek Bridge, on the signed FR 5483.

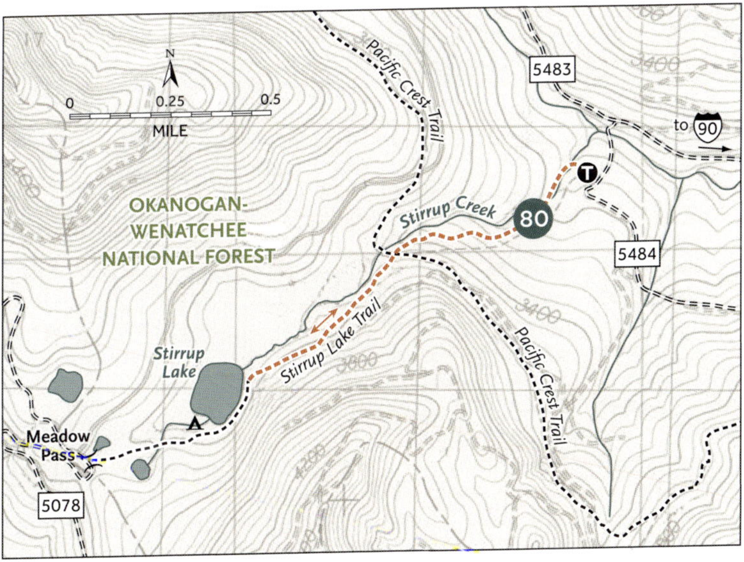

Cradled in a serene mountain basin, Stirrup Lake offers a tranquil escape.

At 4.3 miles, the road reaches an unsigned intersection. Bear left (remaining on FR 5483) and bob and weave through potholes. At 5.5 miles, reach another unsigned intersection and turn left on FR 5484. This road is brushy, narrow, and bumpy, but thankfully, you won't have to go far. Reach the trailhead on the right, in 0.2 mile, noted by a primitive, wooden, handwritten sign on a tree. Parking is either at the campsite to the road's left, which can fit a couple of cars (please park with courtesy), or along the roadside wherever you can squeeze.

ON THE TRAIL

From the parking area, the trail ducks into the forest and begins a gradual ascent up a ridge above Stirrup Creek. Keep your eyes open near your feet for the delicate petals of purple or white western wood anemone in late spring and early summer. Vanilla leaf, large leaf avens, and huckleberries grow trailside with health and vigor. If you are visiting in midsummer, you'll probably be stopping occasionally to pop a few berries in your mouth.

The trail gains most of its elevation in the first 0.7 mile before it reaches a signed junction with the Pacific Crest Trail. Turn right for about 10 to 12 steps before finding the unsigned trail continuing on the left: a tiny zigzag. From here, it's just over 0.4 mile to the lake, and it goes quite quickly, as the trail does its best to deliver you there without too much climbing.

The trail carries you to the lake's shoreline, which has even more huckleberries for nibbling. There isn't a large beach or area to spread out too much, but it's enough to get a feel for the place and take a few pictures. Turn around and return the same way you came in, with a couple of mosquito bites as souvenirs.

EXTENDING YOUR HIKE

To get a few bonus steps, follow the lake's shoreline trail to the southwest and find a tent site on a side spur trail in 0.3 mile. This area's shoreline stays muddy and wet until about midsummer, and the mosquitoes can be voracious, so move quickly or hose yourself with bug goop. If you follow the main path to its end, it delivers you rather uneventfully to Forest Road 5078 and an area known on maps as Meadow Pass, 0.6 mile from where you arrived at the lake.

SNOQUALMIE PASS EAST

81 Kachess Ridge to Kachess Beacon

RATING/DIFFICULTY: ***/3
ROUNDTRIP: 6.4 miles
ELEV GAIN/HIGH POINT: 2190 feet/4620 feet
SEASON: May–Oct

Map: Green Trails Maps Alpine Lakes East Stuart Range No. 208SX; **Contact:** Okanogan-Wenatchee National Forest, Cle Elum Ranger District; **Notes:** Northwest Forest Pass or Interagency Pass required. No facilities at trailhead. Open to leashed dogs, mountain bikes, stock; **GPS:** N 47 16.049, W 121 10.447

You've hiked to fire tower lookouts, but what about former airway beacon towers? Early aviators relied on the towers as visual aid with lights and letter-number combinations to help them navigate, and here on Kachess Ridge, you have a chance to see transportation history up close.

GETTING THERE

From I-90 near Easton: Take exit 70 for Easton and Sparks Road and head northeast. Eastbound travelers will cross back over the freeway. Turn left onto W. Sparks Road, and in 0.6 mile, arrive at Kachess Dam Road and go right. Kachess Dam Road becomes Forest Road 4818 and in a short distance, turns to gravel. At 1.5 miles, turn right onto FR 4818-101. Proceed on the dirt road to 2.1 miles, where the road dead-ends at the undeveloped trailhead signed for Trail Nos. 1212 and 1315. Parking is limited to a few pull-in and roadside spots, so use care not to block turnarounds or access.

ON THE TRAIL

Follow the obvious trail behind the signs, and in 250 feet, arrive at a junction. To the left, a clear trail is signed for Kachess Ridge Trail No. 1315. Follow this path as it climbs steeply at first, then rewards you with a less aggressive angle. In just under 0.5 mile, the trail displays some craggy peaks and ridgelines to the right, which have a rugged, wild beauty and make you want to stop for photos. This couldn't come at a better time—catch your breath as you snap away. There is an

Trail's end meets aviation history: Kachess Beacon still watches over the ridgeline.

open atmosphere of light though the trees, with peekaboo views.

Pass through a scree field and under some impressive cliffs before, at 1.3 miles, the trail switches back and nears Silver Creek. The pocket water sings and dances over stones and makes a great place for birding. Where there is water, there is life!

At 2.1 miles, reach a signed junction with Beacon Ridge Trail 1315.3, pointing to the left. This is us! Turn left and follow the narrower trail as it climbs up the final push to the beacon. This trail doesn't get the same attention as Kachess Ridge, so be prepared to do a few gymnastics over blowdowns.

At 3.2 miles, reach the old beacon, set along a picturesque ridge with views of Kachess Lake and Lake Easton, and Manastash Ridge. The old beacon was part of the Transcontinental Airway, which was essentially a sky freeway that aviators followed to make their way through the Cascades between the Pacific Northwest and Montana. Most of these towers were built between 1920 and 1935 for civil aviation and governmental airmail needs and contained a large blinking light. This light, illuminated using acetylene gas—a colorless flammable fuel—burned all hours of the day and night and was approximately 30,000 lumens. To give you an idea of the brightness, a fully lit room is roughly 6000 lumens. The metal cabin underneath the tower would have housed the fuel tanks that fed the burning glow. With advancements of more efficient navigational tools, most of the airway beacons were decommissioned by the mid-1960s. Like fire towers, many have been removed, but not all, of course. We are lucky to have the fragments of human history still around so we never forget what life was like before technology changed us so dramatically.

When you are ready to depart, note that there is a faint trail leading southeast. The Forest Service has been trying to decommission this game trail, so please retrace your steps instead of following this sketchy, former one.

82 Easton Ridge

RATING/DIFFICULTY: ***/4
ROUNDTRIP: 6.9 miles
ELEV GAIN/HIGH POINT: 2340 feet/4490 feet
SEASON: late May–Oct

Map: Green Trails Maps Alpine Lakes East Stuart Range No. 208SX; **Contact:** Okanogan-Wenatchee National Forest, Cle Elum Ranger District; **Notes:** Northwest Forest Pass or Interagency Pass required. No facilities at trailhead. Open to leashed dogs; **GPS:** N 47 16.049, W 121 10.447

The bottom part of this trail is steep and dusty, but eventually it reaches the ridge and changes to gentle ups and downs. The views are gorgeous of Mount Baldy, French Cabin, and several lakes, including Kachess, Easton, and Cle Elum, in valleys below. Spreading phlox, larkspur, balsamroot, and others, such as the rare calypso orchid, can be found along the trail when you take the time to look. Overall, it's a killer workout with good vistas.

GETTING THERE

From I-90 near Easton: Take exit 70 for Easton and Sparks Road and head northeast. Eastbound travelers will cross back over the freeway. Turn left onto W. Sparks Road, and in 0.6 mile, arrive at Kachess Dam Road and go right. Kachess Dam Road becomes Forest

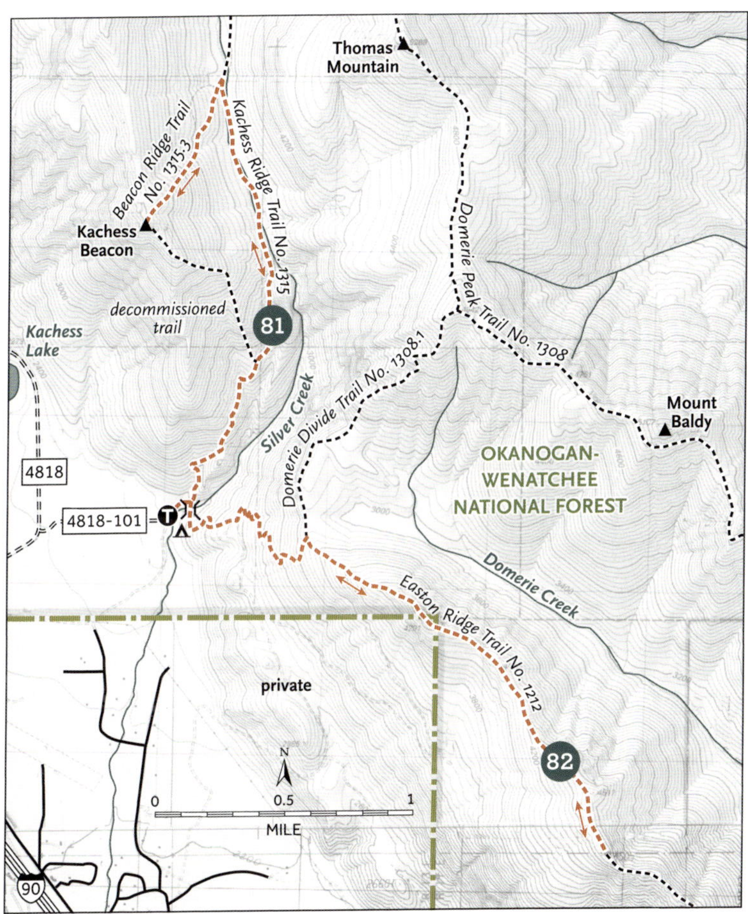

Road 4818 and in a short distance, turns to gravel. At 1.5 miles, turn right onto FR 4818-101. Proceed on the dirt road until 2.1 miles, where the road dead-ends at the undeveloped trailhead signed for Trail Nos. 1212 and 1315. Parking is limited to a few pull-in and roadside spots, so use care not to block turnarounds or access.

ON THE TRAIL

Follow the obvious trail behind the signs, and in 250 feet, arrive at a junction. To the left is a sign for Kachess Ridge Trail No. 1315 (Hike 81), but instead, follow the unsigned trail to the right. This trail winds us down toward the creek and passes a large tent site to the right before crossing a wooden bridge over Silver

A rugged stone outcropping signals the trail's end on Easton Ridge.

Creek. A beautiful artificial waterfall over a retaining wall begs for a picture or two before the climbing begins.

Now it's up, up, up, and up! Look closely for calypso orchids in the springtime as you start uphill. As one of only a handful of orchids in the Pacific Northwest, they conceal themselves well in the understory and are often hard to spot. Soil fungi and disturbances damage their ability to reproduce, so use care not to interrupt their habitat when you find one.

You'll huff and puff in the dusty soil as you make your way up the ridiculously steep grade. Over your shoulder when you stop, give a look out to see Kachess Lake twinkling bright blue down in the valley. Rocky hillsides on the shoulders of Kachess Beacon to the north beg for a mountain goat, though I've never seen one on them. Maybe you'll get lucky.

At 1.5 miles, after 1130 feet of climbing, reach a signed junction with Domerie Divide Trail No. 1308.1 heading to the left. Our trail goes right and continues the grueling climb on a how-is-it-even-possible-to-be-steeper grade. Groan your way up, stopping occasionally to breathe, until at 2 miles you reach the ridge and begin your ramble. Slight ups and downs at this point pose no comparison to what you just came through and are enjoyable, as they showcase Mount Rainier's summit to the south along with the ribbons of I-90. The trail stays close to the ridge, with a few social trails popping up intermittently to show off mountains such as Mount Baldy and the French Cabins to the left. Cle Elum Lake is also visible, along with the cabin-filled private lands and forest landscapes on its neighboring hills.

Oscillating between forest thickets filled with huckleberry bushes and open flower-filled hillsides, the trail cruises along until it reaches a large rocky outcropping across the trail, signifying the end. The trail once continued but ends on private land, so going beyond is not recommended. There are several scenic vistas with perfect perching locations along the ridge, should you not have time or energy to go all the way to the end. If you feel tired, you may just want to find one of those and call it a day, since the end is often windy and cold, and the views aren't too much different. Whatever you decide, head back the same way you arrived when you've soaked in all the views.

83 Lost and Manastash Lakes

RATING/DIFFICULTY: ****/4
ROUNDTRIP: 8 miles
ELEV GAIN/HIGH POINT: 1160 feet/5150 feet
SEASON: late June–Oct

Maps: Green Trails Maps Cle Elum No. 241 and Manastash Lake No. 273; **Contact:** Okanogan-Wenatchee National Forest, Cle Elum Ranger District; **Notes:** Northwest Forest Pass or Interagency Pass required. Pit toilets at trailhead. Seasonal closure to motorized use Oct. 15–June 15, snow dependent. Open to leashed dogs, stock, mountain bikes, motorcycles; **GPS:** N 47 01.519, W 120 56.340

Although the lakes are open to motorcycles, on a quiet early October day, I saw no one. Of course, that's not always the case, but occasionally the cards work in your favor and you have the whole trail to yourself. This gentle path leads to a couple of conifer-lined lakes that are great any time, but particularly in the autumn when larch trees show off their gilded needles.

GETTING THERE

From I-90 near Thorp: Take exit 101 for Thorp Highway and turn south on the highway. In 2 miles, turn right on Cove Road and follow it for 4 miles. At 6.1 miles, go right on Manastash Road, which becomes Forest Road 31, then reaches a signed junction for the Manastash Lake trailhead at 16.7 miles. Bear left at the junction onto Forest Road 31-114, and in 0.4 mile more (17.1 miles), locate a large parking area near the pit toilets.

ON THE TRAIL

From the parking area, walk west and locate the signed Manastash Lake Trail No.1350 trailhead. The gentle, single-track trail grade takes you past groves of pines, larches, and firs to reach a crossing of an unsigned road-turned-trail, Plantation Trail 1350.2, at 0.1 mile. The trail crosses this road-turned-trail again in another 0.1 mile as you continue making your way up through a light and airy forest.

At 0.6 mile, reach a small spur trail to a viewpoint to the left, which pops out on a rocky bluff. From here, views of neighboring treed ridgelines are visible, a perfect place for a quiet moment or a quick break.

At 0.7 mile, reach a signed junction of trail 1350.2. Turn left here and continue ascending through the forest, which occasionally opens

Golden western larches light up the shoreline of Lost Lake.

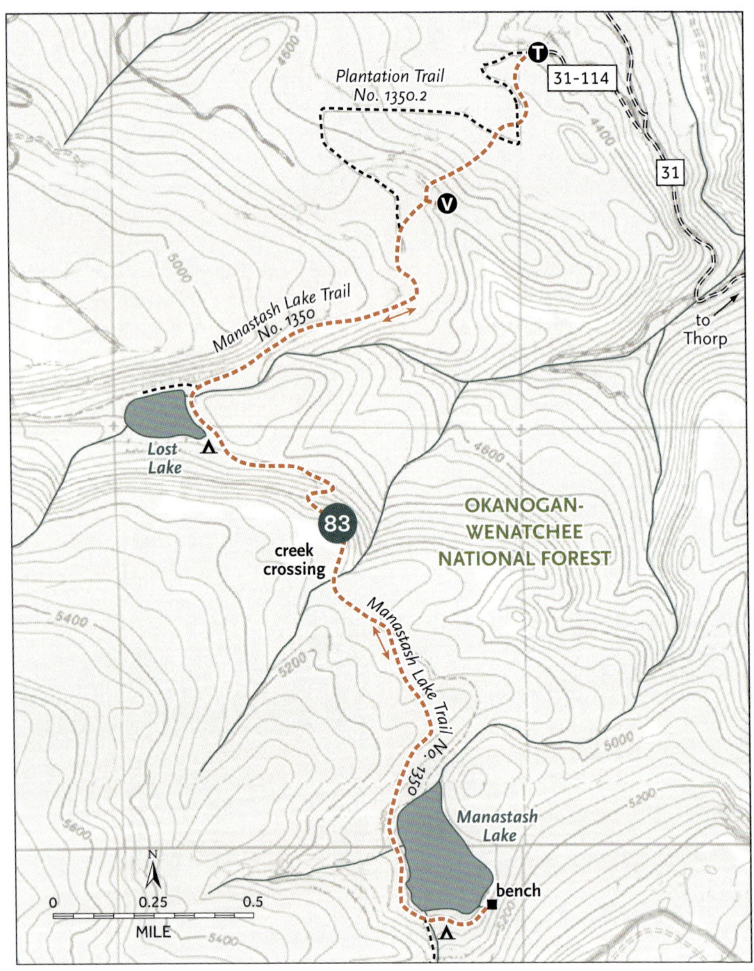

to sunlit meadows and provides different perspectives of unnamed distant ridges and valleys.

At 1.5 miles, reach Lost Lake and find yourself being pulled toward its shoreline via a spur trail straight ahead. A large log has fallen in this area and provides an ideal spot to sit and relax as you experience the peaceful water. Once you've taken it in, retrace your steps from the spur trail back to the main trail and turn right (south), where more views are found near a large camping area.

From Lost Lake to Manastash Lake, the trail goes up and down like the stock market, climbing steeply at times, then dropping down to gullies and climbing back up again. Compared to other PNW trails, this one is still forgiving and mellow, but you'll be ready for a break when you peek through the trees and see Manastash Lake at 3.5 miles.

Follow the trail around to the lake's southern end to 3.8 miles and find a large camping area, along with a primitive box-style privy. You may want to plop down on a log for a break at this point, or continue around to the southeastern side to a lovely surprise. At 3.9 miles, an Adirondack-style bench with two distinct chairs has been constructed on the lake's shoreline. The bench is signed with a plaque honoring the life of someone named John Bostick, who passed in 2006; clearly the area meant a lot to him or his family to leave such a beautiful memorial for all to enjoy. Sit, take a load off, and watch the world go by in his honor.

Technically, the trail continues by heading away from the lake to the south not far from the camping area and connects to a maze of older forest roads and off-road vehicle areas, but for those on feet, it's best to return the way you came.

84 Rachel Lake and Rampart Ridge

RATING/DIFFICULTY: ****/4
ROUNDTRIP: 10.6 miles
ELEV GAIN/HIGH POINT: 2200 feet/4650 feet
SEASON: July–Oct

Map: Green Trails Maps Snoqualmie Pass No. 207; **Contact:** Okanogan-Wenatchee National Forest, Cle Elum Ranger District; **Notes:** Northwest Forest Pass or Interagency Pass required. Pit toilet at trailhead. Open to leashed dogs, stock; **GPS:** N 47 24.049, W 121 17.015

This is one of those places that sticks with you long after you visit, thanks to its outstanding beauty. Set in a rocky bowl surrounded by huckleberry and heather bushes, Rachel Lake sparkles as it catches the light. Above it, Rampart Ridge offers more lakes and tarns, and you could wander for hours to visit them all. You may even want to climb up the lofty wildflower ridges near Alta Mountain to complete the day.

GETTING THERE

From I-90 between Snoqualmie Pass and Cle Elum: Take exit 62 and turn north toward Kachess Lake. Stay on this road for 5.6 miles, passing the Kachess Campground. Bear right on Forest Road 4930, signed for Rachel Lake. Follow signs for Rachel Lake until the road dead-ends in a parking loop for the trailhead, just over 9 miles from the freeway.

ON THE TRAIL

From the parking area, head north and locate the trailhead and its informational signage. Off you go, cruising up the trail to the soundtrack of the babbling Box Canyon Creek, which coos along to the left. The cruising is straightforward and mellow for the first 2.7 miles, but after that, the climbing launches like a rocket up, up, and away. Roots, rocks, mud bogs, rocky slabs, and water drainages cause scrambling at times, with a hand here and there to help you heave-ho. No one said this hiking thing was easy, but hey, it's beautiful when you get to the destination, so bear with it.

At 3.5 miles, the trail kindly levels out and gives you a break near a scenic waterfall.

Rock-hop across the water's outlet and take a break if you need an excuse to stop and catch your breath. The last push to Rachel Lake feels like you are on a stair stepper, so you arrive all sweaty, with endorphins making you smile. A primitive box-style toilet is found to the right, just prior to reaching the lake.

Pay attention to the flat area you cross as you head toward the lake, as it's the area where the trail continues up to Rampart Ridge. For now, continue straight ahead, with the lake drawing you to its shoreline. A couple of rocky perches offer places to crash and recharge before you decide what's next. For some, this is a fantastic destination for the day. Complete with superb views, Rachel Lake is just the type of scenery you dreamed of when you planned this hike. Ending here earns you worthy calorie burn with approximately 8 miles (roundtrip) and 1650 feet of elevation gain. But if you are still feeling hardy at the party, keep rolling. There's more!

The main trail toward Rampart Ridge can be a little hidden, so you'll want to look closely. Walk back the way you arrived, and in approximately 150 feet, when you hit that flat spot again, look to the left (north) for a narrow and well-traveled path. Go northwest on this trail, circling the lake's northern edge before coming up a steep hill above Rachel Lake. In 0.3 mile beyond Rachel Lake, arrive at a T junction. Go left here to reach Rampart

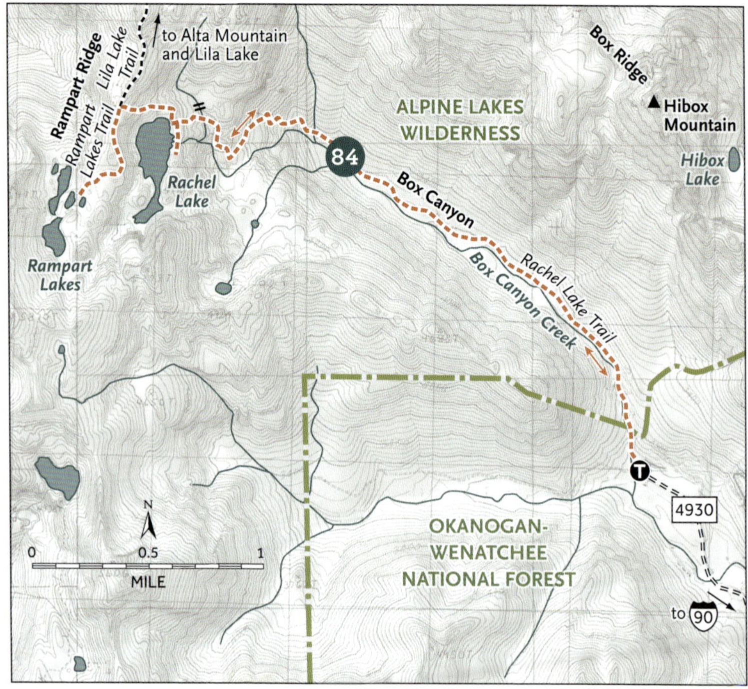

The exploration possibilities are endless at Rampart Lakes.

Ridge and the many lakes and connecting waterways in 1 mile. Boot paths go in every direction around the lakes, so pick your spot.

EXTENDING YOUR HIKE

If you go right at the T, you have options of visiting either Alta Mountain or the Lila Lake basin or both. From the T junction, a roundtrip visit to Alta Mountain is 2.6 miles (1300 feet elevation gain), or skip Alta and hit Lila Lake and it's 1.6 miles (620 feet elevation gain). Do them both and add 3.6 miles (1920 feet elevation gain). It's hard not to find yourself doing some cross-country in the alpine landscape, which adds a little more distance to your day.

85 Lake Easton Loop

RATING/DIFFICULTY: **/2
ROUNDTRIP: 5.8 miles
ELEV GAIN/HIGH POINT: 440 feet/2310 feet
SEASON: late May–Oct

Maps: Green Trails Maps Alpine Lakes East Stuart Range No. 208SX, Washington State Parks Map (see Resources); **Contact:** Washington State Parks; **Notes:** Discover Pass required. Pit toilets, beach area, picnic area, and kids' playground near trailhead. Open to leashed dogs, bicycles; **GPS:** N 47 15.235, W 121 11.858

Scout takes a moment to check out Lake Easton from a stony ridge.

If you don't mind a road walk through the tiny hamlet of Easton, you can put together a pleasant loop around the whole lake. Park trails guide you to the Palouse to Cascades Trail, which takes you through the town and back. A peaceful forest, a novel tunnel along the old railway, and a wonderful rocky viewpoint of the lake await!

GETTING THERE

From I-90 near Easton: Take exit 70 for Easton and Sparks Road. Turn right at the stop sign at the end of the off-ramp, and in 0.4 mile, turn right at the sign for Lake Easton State Park. Pass through the park entrance and take a right at the first stop sign (signed for the beach, boat launch, amphitheater, and picnic areas). Pass the picnic areas and boat launch, and at 1.5 miles from the freeway, go straight ahead at a stop sign into a large day-use area with ample parking.

ON THE TRAIL

From the parking area, follow the paved trail toward the beach and bear right at the kids' play area. The trail is noted with a picture of a hiker and ascends a small hill to the campground. Follow the trail through the campground, passing the restrooms on your left, before the trail arrives at US Highway 10, an old road that gets little use, 0.2 mile from where you parked. Turn left at the road and follow to its dead end at a large metal gate. Walk around the gate and find yourself on a former car bridge, now used for fishing and recreation.

Continue straight ahead on the old road and at 0.6 mile, reach a signed junction pointing you left for the Palouse to Cascades Trail. You are now in a little maze of mostly unsigned park trails, so stay on the widest, most-used path, which is even a slightly different color tread than the others. At 1 mile, arrive at a Y junction with a sign pointing you to the right toward the Palouse to Cascades Trail. At 1.3 mile, reach the signed Palouse to Cascades Trail and turn left.

The gentle former railroad grade then crosses the Yakima River on a sturdy trestle and begs you to stop for a view of both the river and the lake. Once across, a picnic table offers a place to stop and grab a snack or adjust gear if need be.

At 2 miles, the trail crosses through the short (roughly 280 feet) Easton tunnel. Unlike some tunnels along the Palouse to Cascades Trail, this one is bright enough to not warrant a flashlight or headlamp, though it's still tall and magnificent. Trains along the Chicago, Milwaukee, St. Paul, and Pacific Railway chugged through this narrow passage from 1909 to 1980, carrying

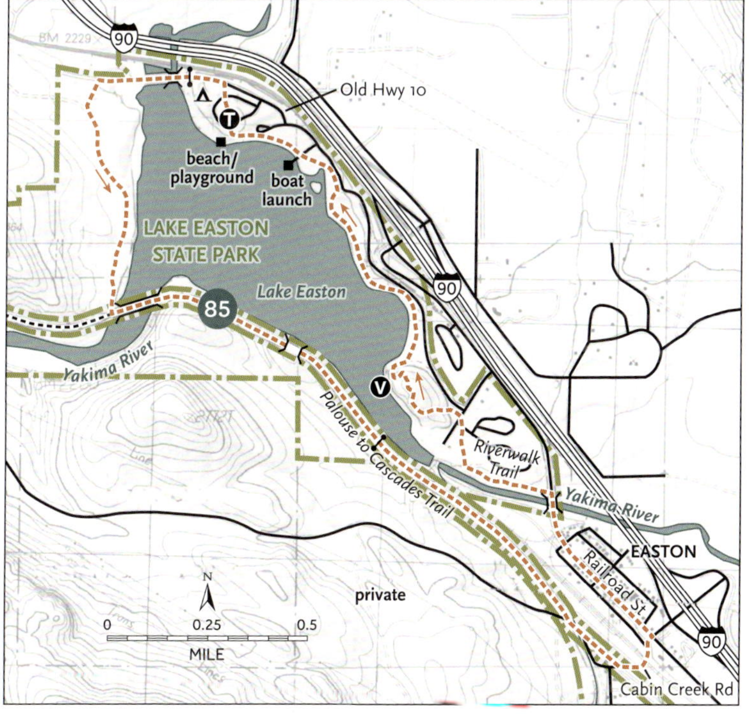

passengers and freight from Tacoma to Chicago. Marvel at the engineering wonder built so long ago but thankfully reinforced for our safety.

Walk around a large metal gate, and at 2.4 miles, pass the Easton Diversion Dam to the left. The unsightly metal fencing that prevents entry to the canal area is a bit of a buzzkill after all the beauty you've just enjoyed, but stay with it—it gets better when we get back to the park.

At 3.3 miles, the Palouse to Cascades Trail reaches Cabin Creek Road in the town of Easton. Turn left and begin your road walk, following the street as it wraps around to the left, over the railroad tracks, and down to intersect Railroad Street. Turn left onto Railroad Street, noting the tiny post office with the A-frame entrance; this sleepy town is so unique! Follow Railroad Street as it passes through the blink-and-you'll-miss-it settlement until the street crosses a car bridge over the Yakima River. At 4 miles, immediately after the bridge, follow a rather unassuming trail heading off to the left. In 200 feet, the trail reaches a T and is signed for the Riverwalk to the left and campsites to the right. Officially back in the park, turn left and follow the Riverwalk Trail, which can be brushy in spring and early summer, as it guides you through riparian brush and healthy forest near the Yakima River.

Continue straight ahead when you reach a park road at 4.5 miles, and in about 100 feet, look to the left for a trail signed with a picture of a hiker. Follow this path as it winds through the forest and up a knoll—the most elevation gain we've seen yet, but hardly worth a mention compared to most PNW hikes. Near the top, a rocky protrusion with views down onto the lake makes a perfect place to stop, enjoy a snack, and snap some pictures. From the viewpoint, the trail descends and winds its way around the lake, entering two picnic areas before arriving at the paved parking area for the boat launch. Walk toward the boat launch and look for the trail's continuation to the right, with a sign stating that motorized vehicles are prohibited. This wide path follows the lakeshore, returning you to the day-use area where you started, for a full loop.

OPPOSITE: *Cathedral Rock salutes the deep blue sky as it is mirrored below in the quiet tarn.*

CLE ELUM AND SALMON LA SAC

The Cle Elum and Salmon La Sac areas to the east of the Cascade Crest have slightly better weather than the hikes on the wet coastal side. It's a good place to escape for a change of scenery too, as many of the hikes in this region have larch trees, which turn a brilliant golden color in the fall, and balsamroot, which displays a gorgeous deep-yellow flower in the springtime. Whenever you hike, you're sure to find some solitude.

86 Coal Mines Trail

RATING/DIFFICULTY: **/1
ROUNDTRIP: 6.2 miles
ELEV GAIN/HIGH POINT: 460 feet/2370 feet
SEASON: Year-round

Maps: Green Trails Maps Cle Elum No. 241 and Easton No. 240; **Contact:** This trail runs through multiple jurisdictions, depending on your location: City of Cle Elum, City of Roslyn, or Kittitas County; **Notes:** No permit required. Pit toilets and picnic area at trailhead. Trail description from the Cle Elum trailhead, but you could start in Roslyn and hike either direction. Roslyn Historical Museum en route (see Resources). "Coal Mines Trail" pamphlet available at Cle Elum City Hall (see Resources). Open to leashed dogs, mountain bikes, stock, snowshoeing, cross-country skiing, dogsledding, snowmobiling; **GPS:** N 47 11.824, W 120 56.659

Three decades ago, a trail emerged along the path once traversed by the Northern Pacific Railway. Its creation was a nod to history, an educational journey that whispered tales of coal mining from the past. The remnants of that era linger nearby—a handful of cement foundations, weathered interpretive signs—but it

Little legs and big grins turn this historic path into a playground of joy.

is the trail itself that stands as the true protagonist. The hero of this tale is not the coal mines but the very earth beneath our feet, the nearby trees that guard its secrets, and the creek that murmurs its own history. This lovely rails-to-trails walk cruises along a crushed-gravel surface as it wanders through healthy pines and deciduous forests. The full distance goes from Cle Elum to the tiny hamlet of Ronald, but you can go as far as you like before turning back. What's more, it crosses right through the town of Roslyn, so you could even add shopping, dining, and sightseeing mid-hike. It's your day to play—do what makes you happy.

GETTING THERE

Cle Elum trailhead: From I-90 eastbound near Cle Elum, take exit 84 and bear left onto

W. 1st Street. Continue through town for 1 mile, then turn left onto Stafford Street, passing Flag Pole Park. Cross W. 2nd Street and find the trailhead immediately to the left. If parking is full, you could return to Flag Pole Park and leave your vehicle in the obvious pullouts along the roadside.

Roslyn trailhead: From I-90 near Cle Elum, take exit 80 toward Roslyn and Suncadia. Head north on Bullfrog Road. In 2 miles, at the roundabout, continue straight to remain on Bullfrog Road. In another 0.7 mile, reach a second roundabout, and this time, take the second exit, signed toward Roslyn. You are now on State Route 903, which is also called Salmon La Sac Road. Continue for 1.1 miles and go right on E. Pennsylvania Avenue. Follow this for 0.1 mile, and then turn right at an unsigned road (S. A Street). Find a large visitors parking area immediately to the left. The trail is directly in front of the parking area to the northeast.

ON THE TRAIL

Starting out in Cle Elum, you might want to wander back toward Flag Pole Park (see driving directions) and take a picture of the interpretive sign if you are interested in trying to figure out the former mining locations along the route. Even with the picture, you'll likely struggle a little to interpret what facility was where, since Mother Nature has mostly taken over. If you are here more for the exercise—carry on!

Back at the trailhead, a rather large sign points out the Rat Pack Trails, a network of trails for mountain bike uses. Another sign states that the Coal Mines Trail is closed to motorized vehicles, but just below it, on yet another sign, it contradicts itself by saying snowmobiles are allowed in winter. Still scratching your head at that one, continue down the path.

Homes are visible through the trees and shrubs on either side of the trail, reminding you that you are still in a town, but it feels like the outskirts, especially as you get farther along the path. Small boot paths come in from several of the homes and communities, and a purring seasonal brook jumps from one side of the trail to the other through culverts.

The occasional aspen grove pops up between ponderosa and white pines, while nuthatches and crows sing and clack in the trees. Several benches along the route provide places to stop and take a load off, should you need a break.

In 1.1 miles, the trail crosses under some powerlines and across a primitive road. Just after it, to the right, is a concrete foundation from the coal washing plant. Sadly, the foundation has been tagged with spray paint, and what appears to be an abandoned camp is in the area, making this otherwise historic area look run-down. Keep walking; it gets better.

At 1.5 miles, cross the paved Alliance Road and continue to the other side through the pines on the same pleasant grade. The path you are following was once a branch line of the Northern Pacific Railway, created as a link between Cle Elum, Roslyn, and Ronald to transport coal. Coal was discovered in Roslyn in 1884, and a few years later, the railroad arrived. Coal mining thrived in Kittitas County and peaked in the early 1900s. However, by the 1930s, the Great Depression had an impact, resulting in reduced demand and declining prices. Consequently, coal mining slowly began to decline. The last mine closed in 1963. Shortly afterward, in 1964, with the completion of I-90, Cle Elum transformed itself into a freeway town, dependent on travel and tourism. In 1987, the railroad tracks and ties were removed, and in 1994,

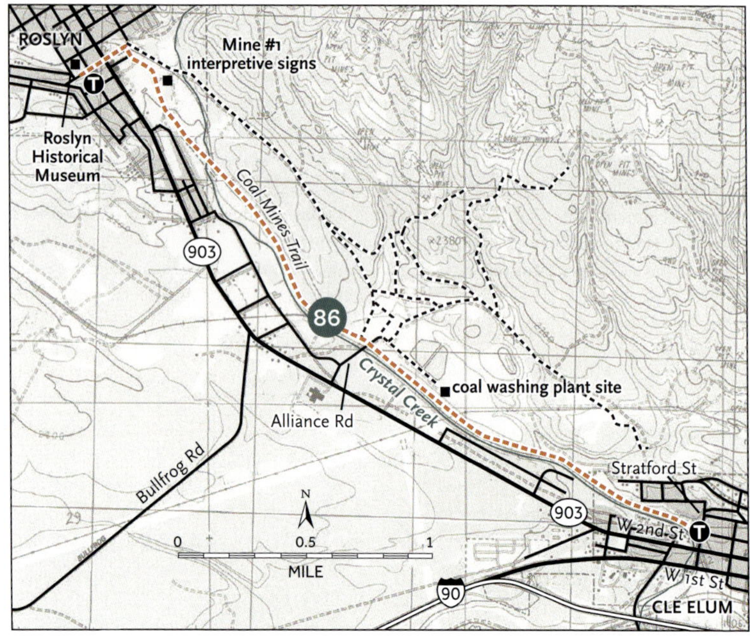

the mutual governments of Roslyn, Cle Elum, and Kittitas County created the Coal Mines Trail as a means of recreation and an underground utilities corridor.

While history whirls in your head, pass a dirt road at 2.9 miles. A couple of interpretive signs are notable here, including one pointing out where an explosion took place on Sunday, October 3, 1909. The mining business was difficult, both in terms of labor and hazards. When the explosion happened that day without any warning, flames shot up as high as 400 feet from deep within the mine. Some bodies were badly burned and thrown hundreds of feet, while others were never found and presumed dead. The deceased men, ranging in age from twenty to sixty, left behind nine widows and twenty-one children. Many more might have died were it not for the fact that it was a Sunday, and fewer workers were on duty. Such darkness for such a light, beautiful trail! But those were tough times, and life was hard.

Onward we go, reaching the town of Roslyn at 3.1 miles. You have options! You could call this your destination and grab lunch, do a little shopping, or visit the Roslyn Historical Museum (see Resources). Or keep going and hike the entire trail, or . . . do it all!

EXTENDING YOUR HIKE

Once you arrive in Roslyn, the Coal Mines Trail delivers you to E. Washington Avenue. Follow this street through town for 0.3 mile until arriving at Roslyn Pioneer Park, with a large field and playground, on your right. To the left, bathrooms are available, and straight ahead is the continuation of the Coal Mines Trail. To complete your journey, follow the well-marked railroad grade for another 1.3 miles, crossing SR 903 along the way. The trail ends rather uneventfully at a Coal Mines Trail sign in Ronald, a tiny community with a general store and fire station. Turn back at this point and follow the chronical of history back to your waiting vehicle, or do a thru hike by using two cars.

87 North Fork Taneum Creek

RATING/DIFFICULTY: **/2
ROUNDTRIP: 10 miles
ELEV GAIN/HIGH POINT: 1520 feet/3570 feet
SEASON: mid- to late May–Oct

Maps: Green Trails Maps Cle Elum No. 241 and Easton No. 240; **Contact:** Okanogan-Wenatchee National Forest, Cle Elum Ranger District; **Notes:** No facilities at trailhead. Open to leashed dogs, motorcycles, mountain bikes, stock; **GPS:** N 47 06.754, W 120 56.072

While this trail is open to motorcycles, it's one of the few that isn't too tough. What's more, it's not open to motorized traffic until June 15, so you might be able to sneak up here on a low-snow year and enjoy the quietness before the machines. This isn't the kind of trail where there are big landmarks—in fact, the destination is wherever you'd like it to be along the way. If the kids are with you, turn back when little feet have had enough. You may want to touch a bridge or two over the North Fork Taneum Creek, or just stroll along quietly and look for wildlife such as black-tailed deer or woodpeckers until you are ready to call it a day.

GETTING THERE

From I-90 east of Cle Elum: Take exit 93, signed for Elk Heights Road. Turn north, and in 0.3 mile, turn right onto Thorp Prairie Road. At 3.8 miles, turn right onto E. Taneum Road and cross back over the interstate. At 4 miles, turn right onto W. Taneum Road. Continue driving as the county road becomes Forest Road 33. At 10 miles, pass Taneum Campground, followed by Icewater Creek Campground at 12.5 miles. At 12.8 miles, stay straight and avoid turning onto FR 3330 to the left. At 14.1 miles, stay straight again, avoiding the left turn with another branch of FR 3330, which crosses North Fork Taneum Creek. You're now on FR 33-133. At 15.3 miles, when the road turns to the right, locate an unsigned but obvious trail to the road's left. Parking is roadside wherever it is safe and clear to do so.

ON THE TRAIL

The trail starts off gentle and continues that grade for most of the way. If you come here in autumn, you might be surprised to see the golden needles of larch trees, which are green during summer months. Shrubs such as huckleberry, elderberry, snowberry, kinnikinnick, and grouseberry shape the trail's edges, springing life and color to the otherwise muted soil.

You can hear the North Fork Taneum Creek for most of the walk, then in 0.8 mile, you can see it through the trees, tucked into the valley to the left. The vegetation is thick, so visiting is only for those up for a bushwhack.

The pathway skips through similar landscape, with the creek playing the ever-present natural music of white noise, giving you even more glimpses of the water. A couple of cascades gurgle during high water, while quiet

Amid vibrant fall colors, a wooden bridge crosses the gentle flow of North Fork Taneum Creek.

pocket water purrs. This is a fantastic place to look for songbirds, both common and uncommon, as they travel through the vicinity. Keep your eyes out for song sparrows, spotted towhees, belted kingfishers, American dippers, and American goldfinches as they flit and chatter from sturdy tree limbs in the riparian zones. And watch for black-tailed and mule deer, as they love this creek too. On my last visit, I was enjoying watching one munch vegetation when a motorcycle came by. I waved a hello to the rider; he waved back. The deer and I both watched the rider pass, then continued doing what we were doing, neither of us deterred by the noise.

At 3.8 miles, after roughly 690 feet of cumulative climbing, reach the first bridge. This is one of six bridges the trail crosses as it jumps back and forth in this stunning drainage. You can stop at whichever one you fancy or keep walking until, at 5.2 miles, it reaches a signed intersection with Fishhook Flat Trail No. 1378, which goes toward Taneum Ridge. All are good milestones, so pick your spot and call it a day before turning around and repeating the path back to your vehicle.

EXTENDING YOUR HIKE

Those who want to make a big loop may consider following Fishhook Flat Trail to Taneum Ridge Trail No. 1363 as it climbs high and showcases gorgeous, forested mountain layers. In autumn, this is a great larch march—with golden eye candy for days. Eventually, this trail will lead you back to the road where you parked your vehicle, and there are options. Turn left and walk the road back, or cross it and follow the North Fork Taneum Trail northwest back to your ride. Following trails the whole way, with the exception of road crossings, is 15 miles with 3150 feet of elevation gain. Having a good map is important, as the trail crosses a couple of forest roads and there are a few confusing intersections. You got this, boss!

88 Taneum Ridge

RATING/DIFFICULTY: **/4
ROUNDTRIP: 9.4 miles
ELEV GAIN/HIGH POINT: 2580 feet/4290 feet
SEASON: June–Oct

Maps: Green Trails Maps Cle Elum No. 241 and Easton No. 240; **Contact:** Okanogan-Wenatchee National Forest, Cle Elum Ranger District; **Notes:** No facilities at trailhead. Open to leashed dogs, motorcycles, mountain bikes, stock; **GPS:** N 47 06.693, W 120 56.112

This is a multiuse trail, which means it's popular with the wheeled ones. Before you turn the page and move on to the next hike, know that you might be pleasantly surprised by how much you enjoy this workout and views, especially in the fall when the gilded larch trees speckle adjacent ridgelines. Spring is a good time to visit too, as the trail is rarely open to motorized traffic before June 15. But if you find yourself here sharing the trail, remember that two-stroke exhaust clears out quickly, along with the riders themselves.

GETTING THERE

From I-90 east of Cle Elum: Take exit 93, signed for Elk Heights Road. Turn north, and in 0.3 mile, turn right onto Thorp Prairie Road. At 3.8 miles, turn right onto E. Taneum Road, and cross back over the interstate. At 4 miles, turn right onto W. Taneum Road. Continue driving as the county road

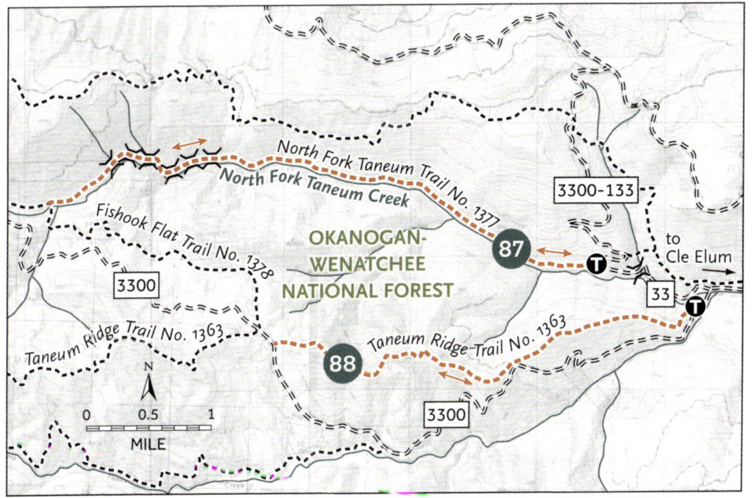

Gilded larches mingle with evergreens, casting a golden glow across the hillside in autumn.

becomes Forest Road 33. At 10 miles, pass Taneum Campground, followed by Icewater Creek Campground at 12.5 miles. At 12.8 miles, stay straight and avoid turning onto FR 3330 to the left. At 14.1 miles, take the left turn when you see another branch of FR 3330, which crosses North Fork Taneum Creek. Just after the creek crossing, locate the trail signed for Taneum Ridge Trail No. 1363 to road's right. Park roadside where safe to do so.

ON THE TRAIL

From the trailhead, climb steeply at times to gain the spine of the ridge. Dwarf huckleberries, mountain junipers, and various grasses gather near your feet while firs, pines, and larches provide a canopy overhead. In places, the trail is narrow, loose, and somewhat rounded, thanks to wheeled traffic, but most years, it's in decent shape compared to many multiuse options.

The trail ducks and dodges in and out of Pacific silver fir, western larch, Englemann spruce, and Douglas-fir mixed with small grassy patches, getting you higher and higher as it scales the ridge. Views through the trees open, but the bigger picture isn't visible until you hit the high point along the ridge.

At 2 miles, the trail drops toward FR 3300 and skirts the edges by crossing through a pullout before continuing on the other side. Ups and downs guide you along the ridge, until at around 3.8 miles, it levels off a bit and showcases northward views of the southern Cle Elum peaks and the unnamed mountain layers in the foreground. In the fall, you'll be walking through golden larches up here, a magical experience. If you wanted to pick a spot along the trail to call the destination—go for it! Otherwise, you could keep walking until the trail drops again to cross FR 3300, 4.7 miles from where you started. Pick your goal for your views and high-fives before heading back home.

EXTENDING YOUR HIKE

After the Tanuem Ridge Trail meets up with FR 3300, you have so many options. This is a giant network of intersecting trails (some signed, some not), and you could spend the whole day, if not week, exploring. You could go straight ahead and continue following the Taneum Ridge Trail as it wanders more of the ridgeline. Or you may want to make a big loop by walking FR 3300 to the right for 0.2 mile, and locating another trail signed Fishhook Flat Trail No. 1378. Follow Fishhook Flat as it descends to North Fork Taneum Creek (Hike 87) and eventually winds you around to where you parked—a big day of 15 miles with 3150 feet of elevation gain. No matter what you choose, have a good map for navigation.

89 Palouse to Cascades: South Cle Elum

RATING/DIFFICULTY: ****/2
ROUNDTRIP: 4.9 miles
ELEV GAIN/HIGH POINT: Negligible/1980 feet
SEASON: Year-round

Maps: Green Trails Maps Cle Elum No. 241 and Easton No. 240, Washington State Parks Map (see Resources); **Contact:** Washington State Parks; **Notes:** Discover Pass required. Pit toilets at trailhead, picnic areas nearby. Open to leashed dogs, bicycles, stock; **GPS:** N 47 11.008, W 120 57.265

Besides the many tunnels along the Palouse to Cascades Trail (see Hikes 73 and 125), this area might be one of the best places to experience the railroad's

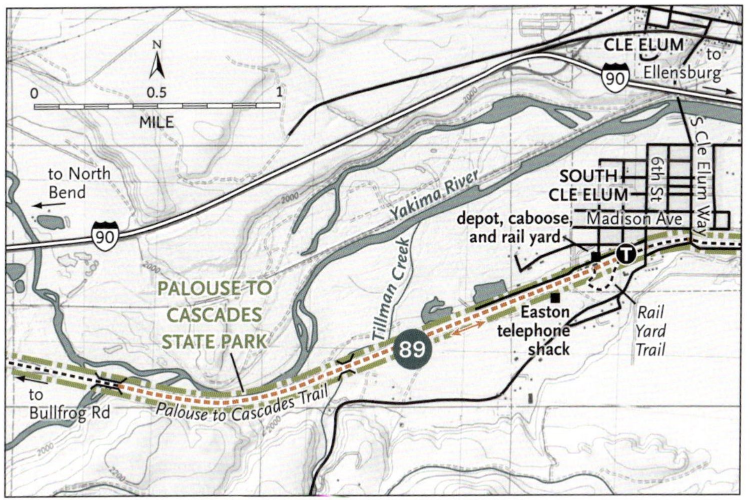

history. Though you can go either direction on this 287-mile trail that spans the state, the best history and closest river views are found by going west. Whether you are interested in the exhibits of yesteryear or simply want to walk along a primarily flat rail-turned-trail and view the Yakima River from a few vantage points, you can't go wrong here.

GETTING THERE

From I-90 eastbound near Cle Elum: Take exit 84 and curve left, passing businesses. In 0.9 mile, turn right on S. Cle Elum Way/Hartwig Boulevard and continue, crossing the bridge over the Yakima River. At 1.8 miles, turn right onto Madison Avenue, then turn left at 1.9 miles on 6th Street. In a couple hundred feet, turn right onto Milwaukee Avenue. Find the well-signed trailhead ahead on your left in roughly 450 feet.

From I-90 westbound near Cle Elum: Take exit 84. Turn right onto Oakes Avenue and follow it for 0.3 mile, then turn left onto W. Railroad Avenue. At 0.5 mile, turn left onto S. Cle Elum Way/Hartwig Boulevard. At 1.3 miles, turn right onto Madison Avenue. At 1.4 miles, turn left onto 6th Street. In a couple hundred feet, turn right onto Milwaukee Avenue and find the well-signed trailhead to your left in roughly 450 feet.

ON THE TRAIL

From the trailhead, go right, and in 240 feet, arrive at a Chicago, Milwaukee, St. Paul, and Pacific Railway caboose exhibit on the right. From 1908 to 1974, Cle Elum was a thriving railroad town that provided jobs and economic stability for the railroad crews that lived and worked in the area. With the arrival of the postwar train the *Olympian Hiawatha*, even more staff was needed for the substation and maintenance it took to run the steel, passenger-centric, electric speed liner. This area, known as the rail yard, was used as a facility for adding or changing railroad cars from the trains.

Next door to the caboose is the depot, which was built in 1909 and was the beating heart of the facilities for the crew. Included inside were a kitchen and lunchroom, a ticket agency, a telegraph office, and a freight and baggage area. Next door to it is the former substation, where you can check out the electrification system of the former train.

Across from all the buildings is the well-signed Rail Yard Trail, a railroad graveyard of sorts, which makes an additional 0.3-mile loop (bicycles are not permitted on this trail). You can take it, save it for later, or skip it. Start in either direction to read the interpretative signs and see the remains of things like the water tank for the steam trains, the turntable that was used to pivot and rotate the locomotives, the roundhouse or repair facilities, and many more artifacts. Nature has tried to take over what was abandoned nearly fifty years ago, but it's fun to see the pictures on the signs and use your imagination about what this area used to look like.

The Palouse to Cascades Trail continues to the west. In 0.5 mile from the trailhead, pass the Easton telephone shack to the left, along with an interpretive sign explaining the communication needs of the railroad and the importance of small buildings like this. Across from the telephone shack is another sign, this one sharing the various train cars along with their horsepower and their purpose.

With most of the exhibits behind us, the former railroad grade passes around the sides of a closed car gate, and the wide, crushed-gravel surface continues westbound.

This trestle over the Yakima River is a perfect stopping point to enjoy the rippling water.

At 1.3 miles, reach a series of picturesque ponds to the right, which attract a variety of migratory songbirds during springtime and often come alive with the sounds of happy frogs in early summer. In fall, the neighboring shrubs take on a tapestry of earth tones, making this a great spot to indulge your senses in autumn splendor.

At 1.4 miles, cross a bridge with metal chain link railings over Tillman Creek. Peek into the quiet trickle and find a little zen in the way the reeds gently dance in the water's current.

The first clear views of the Yakima River show up at 1.8 miles and then continue periodically until the trail reaches a trestle over the waterway at 2.4 miles, where the Cle Elum River joins the Yakima in a picture-perfect setting. Pine trees mix with cottonwoods along the river's edges, while the white noise of a few excited ripples provide ambiance for the moment. A few large sit rocks are scattered around the river's edges for taking it in. Enjoy before retracing your steps.

EXTENDING YOUR HIKE

After the trestle, you could continue onward along the trail to reach Bullfrog Road at 3.8 miles from the trailhead, or head back and make it 5.2 miles total for your day by enjoying the Rail Yard Trail.

90 Cathedral Rock

RATING/DIFFICULTY: *****/3
ROUNDTRIP: 9.2 miles
ELEV GAIN/HIGH POINT: 2280 feet/5525 feet
SEASON: July–Oct

Map: Green Trails Maps Stevens Pass No. 176; **Contact:** Okanogan-Wenatchee National Forest, Cle Elum Ranger District; **Notes:** Northwest Forest Pass or Interagency Pass required. Free wilderness-use permit required—attained

The trail beckons, leading you straight to the towering spire of Cathedral Rock.

at the trailhead. Vehicle ford of Scatter Creek required—high-clearance vehicles recommended. Pit toilets and picnic tables found in the area. Open to leashed dogs, stock; see map, page 278; **GPS:** N 47 32.618, W 121 05.810

This is a fantastic hike for anyone looking for big payback without huge efforts. The trail has a few stops along the way to catch your breath, so the climb doesn't feel like a huge push. You'll pass the sparkling Nosh Nosh Wahtum Lake before cruising past some tranquil tarns to finally arrive at the meadows below the impressive Cathedral Rock, where views await!

GETTING THERE

From I -90 near Cle Elum: Take exit 80 toward Roslyn and Suncadia. Head north on Bullfrog Road. In 2 miles, at the roundabout, continue straight to remain on Bullfrog Road. At 2.7 miles, reach a second roundabout, and this time, take the second exit, signed toward Roslyn. You are now on State Route 903, which is also called Salmon La Sac Road. Follow this road through Roslyn and continue, turning left onto W. Nevada Avenue at 4.3 miles. Pass the town of Ronald and continue along the east shore of Cle Elum Lake.

In 16.9 miles from I-90, the road narrows, and at 17.1 miles, it splits, with one branch going straight ahead toward the Salmon La Sac Campground and the other turning to gravel and going right and uphill. Turn right here, signed for Tucquala Lake (Forest Road 4330). Stay on this road for 12.7 miles. You'll pass private cabins, other trailheads, and a vehicle ford of Scatter Creek, which is dry by late summer. You'll also pass the Fish Lake Guard Station and the Tucquala trailhead. The Cathedral trailhead is to the road's left. If this area is full, get creative with parking options where signed permissible; however, avoid parking in the designated areas for horses and horse trailers.

ON THE TRAIL

From the trailhead, pass the large sign announcing Cathedral Trail No. 1345 (also called Cathedral Pass Trail on other signs), and in 100 feet, cross over a creek by rock- or log-hopping. In another couple hundred feet, arrive at a wooden pedestrian bridge over the Cle Elum River. Stop to admire the ripples, then continue with the trail, which beings its climb. At 0.3 mile, reach the Alpine Lakes Wilderness boundary, announced with a tree sign to the right. From here, the shaded forest climb is pleasant, and the understory of twinflower, foam flower, vanilla leaf, devil's club, and huckleberry is luxuriant.

At 2 miles, after nearly 1220 feet of climbing, reach the signed Trail Creek Trail junction heading off to the left. Our trail continues straight, and at 2.6 miles, it levels out before arriving at Nosh Nosh Wahtum Lake. This lake was recently renamed from the derogatory term Squaw Lake, which may still appear on some maps. Nosh Nosh Wahtum Lake translates to "Salamander Lake," so keep your eyes open for the little amphibians, which have been known to use this perfect body of water to hatch their young. The larvae (juveniles) and neotenes (gilled adults) are often spotted with dragonlike gills (called balancers) on the sides of their heads.

A primitive toilet is found here, along with a couple of pleasant tent sites on the southeastern shore of the lake. You'll most likely be pulling out your camera to snap a few pictures before you make your way around the lake to the northeastern lakeshore, where a large equestrian camp is located.

From here, the way ascends through evergreens on an intermittently rocky trail before it reaches a series of meadows filled with lupine, dwarf huckleberry, Sitka valerian, paintbrush, aster, and other native wildflowers and shrubs. At 4 miles, a couple of tarns to the right attract frogs and aquatic life and make for a tranquil scene. Towering above the meadows, Cathedral Rock overlooks the landscape with its lofty pillars and proud prominences.

Beyond the meadows, at 4.4 miles, the trail touches a signed intersection with the Pacific Crest Trail (PCT). You've arrived! This area is called Cathedral Pass, and should you want to explore more, go either direction in the quest for your perfect snack break nook. Left takes you to a rocky ridge in 0.2 mile, while right drops you down a tiny bit of elevation to explore the trail in the northbound direction. Please use care in the meadows and avoid traveling or picnicking on foliage, which struggle with the short growing season and a lot of curious feet.

EXTENDING YOUR HIKE

If you are a hiking superstar, you can make a big loop by following the PCT to the right (northbound) at Cathedral Pass until you reach Deception Pass, a forested intersection, 5.1 miles from Cathedral Pass. At this point, you'll turn right and follow the signs toward Deception Pass Trail No. 1376, which goes toward Hyas Lake. The trail wanders south, passing the lake and delivering you to a trailhead on the final leg of your loop. From there, follow FR 4330 for 0.1 mile to the southeast to find the Cathedral trailhead and your waiting vehicle, on the road's right.

This whole loop, including the portion to Cathedral Pass, is 14.2 miles, with 3130 feet of total elevation gain. You'll need to cross a somewhat hazardous, swift-water ford 3.3 miles from Cathedral Pass on an unnamed creek along the PCT; be mentally and physically prepared.

91 Hyas Lake

RATING/DIFFICULTY: ***/2
ROUNDTRIP: 5.4 miles
ELEV GAIN/HIGH POINT: 400 feet/3550 feet
SEASON: June–Oct

Map: Green Trails Maps Stevens Pass, WA No. 176; **Contact:** Okanogan-Wenatchee National Forest, Cle Elum Ranger District; **Notes:** Northwest Forest Pass or Interagency Pass required. Pit toilet and picnic areas near trailhead. Free wilderness-use permit available at trailhead. Open to leashed dogs, stock; **GPS:** N 47 32.698, W 121 05.867

This is the perfect hike for a family with younger kids or those who want something mellow that doesn't feel like a big haul or an exhausting day. The trail rolls gently as it cruises through the evergreens and meadows, then arrives near the lake with several spots to access the lake's shoreline.

GETTING THERE

From I-90 near Cle Elum: Take exit 80 toward Roslyn and Suncadia. Head north on Bullfrog Road. In 2 miles, at the roundabout, continue straight to remain on Bullfrog Road. In another 0.7 mile, reach a second roundabout, and this time, take the second exit, signed toward Roslyn. You are now on State Route 903, which is also called Salmon La Sac Road. Follow this road through Roslyn and continue, turning left onto W. Nevada Avenue at 4.3 miles. Pass the town of Ronald and continue along the east shore of Cle Elum Lake.

At 16.9 miles, the road narrows, and at 17.1 miles, it splits, with one branch going straight ahead toward the Salmon La Sac Campground and the other turning to gravel and going right and uphill. Turn right here, signed for Tucquala Lake (Forest Road 4330). Stay on this road until 21.8 miles. You'll go by private cabins, pass other trailheads, and maneuver a vehicle ford of Scatter Creek, which is dry by late summer. You'll also pass the Fish Lake Guard Station and the Tucquala trailhead, before the road dead-ends at our trailhead. If it's full, get creative with parking options where signed permissible; however, avoid crushing vegetation and parking in the designated areas for horse trailers.

ON THE TRAIL

I can't help but snicker at the sign simply saying "trail" right next to a wide, obvious pathway. Good thing it's there or you might just start walking down the forest road back to civilization. Much less obvious and perhaps less duh-invoking is the sign for Deception Pass Trail No. 1376, which we will be following as we make our way to the lake. This trail is also an access trail to several other Alpine Lakes Wilderness overnight destinations, so don't be surprised to see folks with backpacks or equestrians all saddled up for longer trips.

In 0.3 mile, pass the Alpine Lakes Wilderness sign firmly attached to a tree. Huckleberries, Indian plum, vanilla leaf, dwarf dogwood, rosy spirea, and other PNW players are abundant in this area. The trail tucks safely under the boughs of a forest of western

Hyas Lake sparkles in a peaceful setting under jagged Cascade peaks.

hemlock and Douglas-fir as you make your way northwest.

At 0.8 mile, views open into a large, swampy meadow that serves as an important wetland during the rainy season. Aquatic waterfowl, such as ducks, teals, goldeneyes, and even the occasional migratory sandhill crane, have been seen in this area.

Over the next mile, dribbling waterways cross the trail, each time requiring a log-wobble or a rock-hop as you make your way closer and closer to the lake's southeastern shore.

At 1.9 miles, arrive at the first of many tent sites that—over the next 0.5 mile—will show up to the left. A primitive toilet and the spur trail to it is also found in this area, this time to the main trail's right. The tent sites are your access points to the lake's shoreline and lake views, so if they are all occupied, you might want to kindly ask the occupants if they wouldn't mind having you tiptoe through. Usually, you can find at least one that isn't occupied, especially on a weekday, if you just keep walking.

Once at the shoreline, views of Cathedral Rock, Mount Daniel, and others are reflected in the waters on windless days. The bottom is muddy, but some people pay good money for that at a spa, so stick your feet in if the mood strikes.

Onward from the tent site access points, the trail eventually brings a decent view of the lake at 2.7 miles, but it's narrow and not a place for lunch—just a photo opportunity. Eventually, the trail leaves the lake's shoreline and climbs toward junctions with Tuck and Robin Lakes (Hike 93) and the Pacific Crest Trail (Hike 90). Explore away!

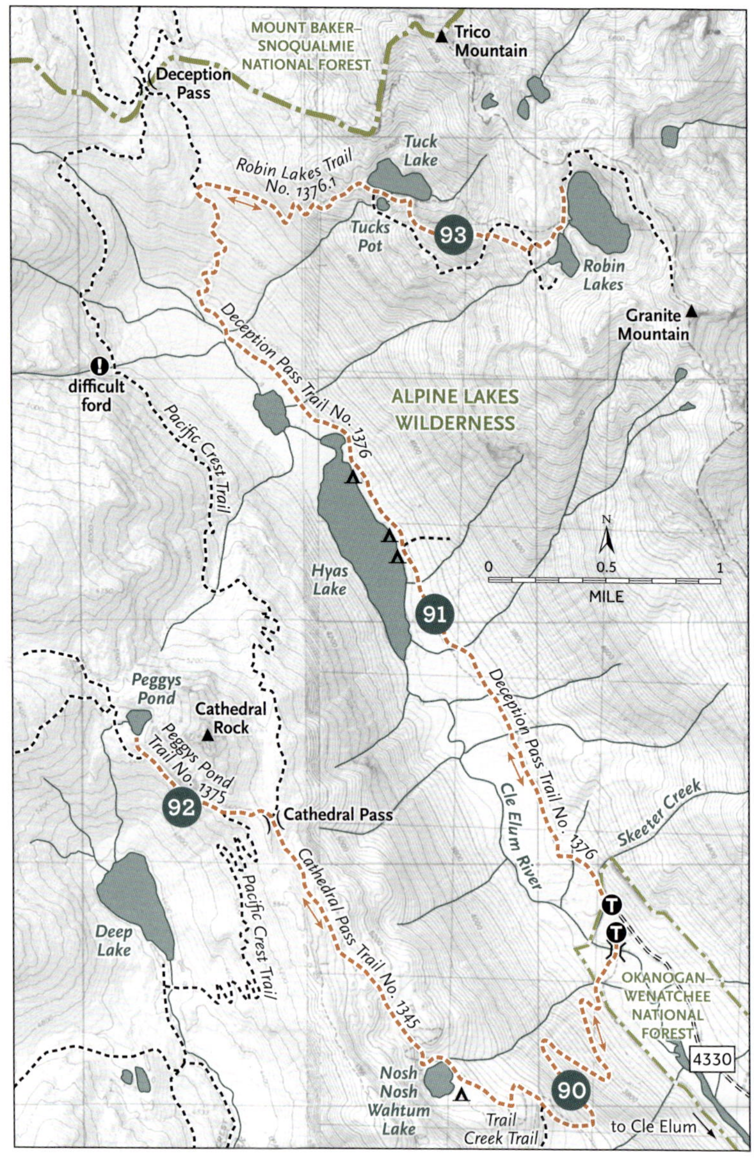
MOUNT BAKER–SNOQUALMIE NATIONAL FOREST
Trico Mountain
Deception Pass
Tuck Lake
Robin Lakes Trail No. 1376.1
Tucks Pot
93
Robin Lakes
Granite Mountain
Deception Pass Trail No. 1376
difficult ford
Pacific Crest Trail
ALPINE LAKES WILDERNESS
Hyas Lake
0
0.5
1
MILE
91
Deception Pass Trail No. 1376
Peggys Pond
Cathedral Rock
Peggys Pond Trail No. 1375
92
Cathedral Pass
Cle Elum River
Skeeter Creek
Cathedral Pass Trail No. 1345
Pacific Crest Trail
Deep Lake
OKANOGAN–WENATCHEE NATIONAL FOREST
4330
Nosh Nosh Wahtum Lake
90
Trail Creek Trail
to Cle Elum

92 Peggys Pond

RATING/DIFFICULTY: *****/5
ROUNDTRIP: 11 miles
ELEV GAIN/HIGH POINT: 2490 feet/5580 feet
SEASON: July–Oct

Map: Green Trails Maps Stevens Pass No. 176; **Contact:** Okanogan-Wenatchee National Forest, Cle Elum Ranger District; **Notes:** Northwest Forest Pass or Interagency Pass required. Free wilderness-use permit required—attained at the trailhead. Vehicle ford of Scatter Creek required; high-clearance vehicles recommended. Pit toilets and picnic tables found in the area. Open to leashed dogs, stock (on all but Peggys Pond Trail No. 1375); **GPS:** N 47 32.618, W 121 05.810

There are some landscapes so beautiful that they stick to your soul like a tattoo, and Peggys Pond is just that. Set in an alpine basin with views of Mount Daniel, the pond is more like a crystal-blue lake, teeming with small fish and wildflower-filled shorelines. The challenge of this place is getting here. This hike follows a primitive pathway across exposed rock bands with narrow footing and fall hazards. Those with a sincere fear of heights, navigational challenges, or limited scrambling experience might want to consider this one to be off the table. But folks with good balance, strong routefinding skills, and confident feet will sail up it without issues.

GETTING THERE

From I-90 near Cle Elum: Take exit 80 toward Roslyn and Suncadia. Head north on Bullfrog Road. In 2 miles, at the roundabout, continue straight to remain on Bullfrog Road. At 2.7 miles, reach a second roundabout, and this time, take the second exit, signed toward Roslyn. You are now on State Route 903, which is also called Salmon La Sac Road. Follow this road through Roslyn and continue, turning left onto W. Nevada Avenue at 4.3 miles. Pass the town of Ronald and continue along the east shore of Cle Elum Lake.

At 16.9 miles, the road narrows, and at 17.1 miles, it splits, with one branch going straight ahead toward the Salmon La Sac Campground and the other turning to gravel and going right and uphill. Turn right here, signed for Tucquala Lake (Forest Road 4330). Stay on this road until 29.8 miles. You'll go by private cabins, pass other trailheads, and maneuver a vehicle ford of Scatter Creek, which is dry by late summer. You'll also pass the Fish Lake Guard Station and the Tucquala trailhead before arriving at the Cathedral trailhead to the left. If this area is full, get creative with parking options where signed permissible; however, avoid parking in the designated areas for horse trailers.

ON THE TRAIL

Locate the large Cathedral Trail No. 1345 sign and, in just 100 feet, cross a creek by log- or rock-hops. In another couple hundred feet, cross the Cle Elum River on a wooden pedestrian bridge and enjoy the purr of the water below the sturdy structure.

The trail dips into the evergreens and begins a moderate climb, reaching the Alpine Lakes Wilderness boundary in 0.3 mile.

Become one with your breathing, your footwork, and the tall green canopy above you, and at just 2 miles, meet up with a signed junction for Trail Creek Trail heading off to the left. Continue straight, climbing up and away until, at 2.6 miles, you reach Nosh Nosh Wahtum Lake (formerly Squaw Lake,

Cathedral Rock rises behind Peggy's Pond, which is so clear and turquoise it feels like a secret kept by the mountains.

which may still be labeled as such on some maps). The translation means "Salamander Lake," so look for little amphibians, their eggs, larvae, and neotenes (gilled adults) in and around the lake.

A primitive toilet is found here, along with a couple of pleasant campsites on the southeastern shore. You'll most likely be pulling out your camera to snap a few pictures before you make your way around the lake to the northeastern lakeshore, where a large equestrian camp is located.

The trail continues climbing before passing a series of trailside tarns sporting seasonal wildflowers near the moist, mossy edges. Ahead on the trail, Cathedral Rock dominates the skyline with its jagged pillars and rocky spires.

At 4.4 miles, the trail dead-ends at an intersection with the Pacific Crest Trail (PCT).

This is the Cathedral Pass area, and the PCT goes both right and left near a large meadow at the Cathedral Rock base. To get to Peggys Pond, turn left and follow the PCT as it ascends to the top of a rocky slope and drops down the other side. At 4.7 miles, on a switchback to the left, find a signed junction saying, "Hiker Trail. Trail Closed to Pack and Saddle Stock," located straight ahead. This is us—onward!

From here the trail narrows and becomes loose dirt with exposed rock, but at first, it's obvious. The views of Deep Lake in the valley below make you stop for pictures, so be sure to come to a full stop instead of trying to multitask. The trail becomes slightly less apparent at 4.9 miles and might cause you to question direction. In one spot near here, the trail seems to end, and the natural tendency is to want to go downhill where others have fearfully, steeply gone. However, look closely. A better path goes straight ahead and slightly uphill at this point but is hidden by shrubs. At 5 miles, find yourself at a junction sometimes noted with a rock pile or cairn. One branch traverses the slope straight ahead and leads to more off-trail navigation, but our path goes uphill. Wiggle through the dirt, moon-walking with one foot sliding back as the other tries to gain traction.

After the struggle of the steeps, find yourself popping over the ridge and standing on the shores of Peggys Pond at 5.5 miles. The pond serves as the basecamp for climbers summiting Mount Daniel, so don't be surprised to have company. A few forested camps are found to the west of the lake, and a primitive box-style privy is located to the north. This is a fragile subalpine environment, so please park your weary bones on one of many durable surfaces and do your best to avoid using or creating social trails. It's easier said than done, as this area has so many.

The pond is magical under the shoulders of Cathedral Rock, and when it catches the light just right, it's a brilliant deep-teal color. Mountain heather, aster, lupine, Sitka valerian, mountain bistort, and others are found in the many sunlit meadows that thrive here. Soak in every bit of this perfect scene before heading back the way you arrived.

93 Tuck and Robin Lakes

RATING/DIFFICULTY: *****/5
ROUNDTRIP: 15 miles
ELEV GAIN/HIGH POINT: 3610 feet/6320 feet
SEASON: July–Oct

Map: Green Trails Maps Stevens Pass, WA No. 176; **Contact:** Okanogan-Wenatchee National Forest, Cle Elum Ranger District; **Notes:** Northwest Forest Pass or Interagency Pass required. Free wilderness-use permit required—attained at the trailhead. Pit toilet and picnic areas near trailhead. Open to leashed dogs, stock; see map, page 278; **GPS:** N 47 32.698, W 121 05.867

This is a very full day and one that requires some fancy footwork. If you aren't up for the full 15-mile day, you could cut it short and do 11 miles and about 2030 feet of elevation gain to reach the first lake, Tuck. Robin is subalpine and grand, but you'll work for it in your climbing, scrambling, and navigating efforts.

GETTING THERE

From I-90 near Cle Elum: Take exit 80 toward Roslyn and Suncadia. Head north on Bullfrog Road. In 2 miles, at the roundabout, continue straight to remain on Bullfrog Road. At

2.7 miles, reach a second roundabout, and this time, take the second exit, signed toward Roslyn. You are now on State Route 903, which is also called Salmon La Sac Road. Follow this road through Roslyn and continue, turning left onto W. Nevada Avenue at 4.3 miles. Pass the town of Ronald and continue along the east shore of Cle Elum Lake.

At 16.9 miles, the road narrows, and at 17.1 miles, it splits, with one branch going straight ahead toward the Salmon La Sac Campground and the other turning to gravel and going right and uphill. Turn right here, signed for Tucquala Lake (Forest Road 4330). Stay on this road until 29.8 miles. You'll go by private cabins, pass other trailheads, and maneuver a vehicle ford of Scatter Creek, which is dry by late summer. You'll also pass the Fish Lake Guard Station and the Tucquala trailhead before the road dead-ends at our trailhead. If it's full, get creative with parking options where signed permissible; however, avoid crushing vegetation and parking in the designated areas for horse trailers.

ON THE TRAIL

From the parking area, find the obvious signed trail located to the northwest and start your walk toward Hyas Lake.

At 0.3 mile, enter the Alpine Lakes Wilderness, announced by a tree sign to the left as you make your way through the hemlocks and firs. Playful creeks and dribbles accompany you all the way to the turnoff for Tuck and Robin Lakes, but they all are easily crossed with dry shoes by log-teetering or rock-hopping.

The first of many camps comes up to the left at 1.9 miles, with more over the next 0.5 mile. A toilet trail is also found in this area, to the main trail's right. These camps also serve as the access trails to the lake's shoreline, so you'll want to find one, preferably unoccupied, and check out the views of Cathedral Rock and other peaks reflected in the water on a calm day. If they are all occupied, you may want to respectfully ask to peek at the lake via their thoroughfare.

You'll pass a good view of the lake at approximately 2.7 miles, so if you skip the camps, you'll still get to see it. Onward you go, eventually leaving the easy cruising grade along the lake and climbing to the north. A few switchbacks help you gain elevation until, at 4.4 miles, you reach a signed junction with Robin Lakes Trail No. 1376.1. This is us! Head right and soon find yourself up close and personal with the earth. The primitive trail with loose rock and dirt sometimes requires hand pulls on roots or stabilization on neighboring trees to get you up and around the steepest parts. Trekking poles are helpful in giving you both balance and cadence as you haul your heinie into the hinterlands.

The sweeping views of Mount Daniel and neighboring peaks as you get higher take your mind off the labored crawl, and at 5.3 miles, arrive at a pass with several rocky outcroppings to the right. Perch yourself if you need a break or want to suck in every drop of that incredible view. When you've taken it in, keep walking to find yourself at the shores of Tuck Lake at 5.5 miles. A few sitting logs are sprinkled around the shoreline, providing places to sit and watch the rising fish. Many folks are content to hang out here, eat some lunch, and maybe buzz around the granite knolls nearby before heading back; however, others won't be happy with loitering and will want to keep going to Robin Lakes.

March forth, hardy souls; this is the hard part. The route scrambles over bulbous, rocky terrain, going up and down rocky shelves and through dwarf huckleberries,

A meandering pathway leads to subalpine bliss near Robin Lake.

mountain heather, and juniper bushes, with routefinding sometimes questionable. Rock cairns are found along the route, which are often helpful, and the trail is obvious in places where vegetation is worn away. This is where having a good map is key! If it feels like you are off-trail, you probably are. At times, hands are helpful in pulling yourself up rocky slopes. This puppy is steep!

The higher you get, the more eye-popping the area becomes, with Tuck Lake far below you and Mount Daniel and Mount Hinman in the distance, with their deep glaciers begging you to stop and gawk. If you hear a clickity-clack, look for mountain goats, who are often found in this area as well as the upper Robin Lakes basin.

At 7 miles, find yourself at the top of the ridge, where you can finally see Robin Lakes and the gorgeous granite basin below you. This place is a gem, and you'll want to drop down and explore it all—the clear, twinkling blues of the ice-cold lake water, the nooks and crannies to hide from the elements, and even the peaks on the lake's shoulders where more panoramas are found. This is paradise—pure and simple—and tearing yourself away to head back will be hard when that time comes. Use care and caution on tired quads, taking plenty of breaks on your way back down the hazardous slopes.

94 Cooper River

RATING/DIFFICULTY: **/2
ROUNDTRIP: 6.6 miles
ELEV GAIN/HIGH POINT: 960 feet/2930 feet
SEASON: July–Oct

Map: Green Trails Maps Kachess Lake No. 208; **Contact:** Okanogan-Wenatchee National Forest, Cle Elum Ranger District; **Notes:** Northwest Forest Pass or Interagency Pass required. Free wilderness-use permit required—attained at the trailhead. Pit toilet and picnic areas at trailhead. Stick to designated parking for hikers, and avoid horse trailer parking areas. This trailhead gets full

A hiker and his loyal dog wind through the deep forest along the Cooper River Trail.

quickly in summer months; arrive early for best opportunities; **GPS:** N 47 24.569, W 121 06.415

This one is a great option for kids or those who want a mellower hike in the often-steep Cascades. It's not without a few short hills here and there to get the heart pumping, but for the most part, it's an easy place to wander, complete with the occasional river access to cool off.

GETTING THERE

From I-90 near Cle Elum: Take exit 80 toward Roslyn and Suncadia. Head north on Bullfrog Road. In 2 miles, at the roundabout, continue straight to remain on Bullfrog Road. At 2.7 miles, reach a second roundabout, and this time, take the second exit, signed toward Roslyn. You are now on State Route 903, which is also called Salmon La Sac Road. Follow this road through Roslyn and continue, turning left onto W. Nevada Avenue at 4.3 miles. Pass the town of Ronald and continue along the east shore of Cle Elum Lake.

At 16.9 miles, the road narrows, and in 17.1 miles, it splits, with one branch going straight ahead toward the Salmon La Sac Campground and the other turning to gravel and going right and uphill to Forest Road 4330, signed for Tucquala Lake. Go straight here (FR 4216-111) and cross the Cle Elum River. Pass the entrance to the Salmon La Sac Campground to the left and proceed straight ahead until the road dead-ends in a parking loop, 0.5 mile past the campground.

ON THE TRAIL

The trail starts at the obvious signed trailhead, located to the parking area's northwest. Several trails kick off from this point, so don't be surprised to see backpackers or equestrians loaded up for several days heading off in different directions.

In roughly 400 feet, reach a signed junction with the Cooper River Trail heading off to the left and the Polallie Ridge Trail (Hike 95) to the slight right. Bear left and soon the trail arrives at an overlook with a well-worn game trail dropping steeply to the Cooper River. In the summer, folks enjoy the deep, slow pool, complete with a rope swing and a small beach. Don't be surprised to see coolers, lawn chairs, and plastic blow-up flamingos making their way down this slope to the river below. Even though this trail goes along a river, it stays high almost until the end, when it drops down to it, so if you need water, this is your only access for a couple of miles.

From here, begin a gentle climb through sunlit forest high above the river. The trail ebbs and flows with ups and downs as it makes its way northwest, following the river but staying high above it, as if to make your anticipation to see it grow.

In 2.3 miles, reach a reliable unnamed creek crossing the trail, the first water since the overlook. If you brought the pup in the warm summer, she will likely be happy to see it—and you might want a handful to splash on your face. The trail is almost all shaded, but this area still gets warm during summer months, and the creek is cool and pleasant.

Rock-hop your way across, then descend, and at 2.5 miles, arrive on the banks of the Cooper River. Stop here to visit the water and snap your pictures, or keep going as the trail flirts with the river in more spots. Pick your picnic location and either turn back after your snack or keep going to reach the end at FR 4616 at 3.3 miles. The road here goes to Cooper Lake, the Owhi Campground, and eventually the Pete Lake trail (Hike 101). If you have

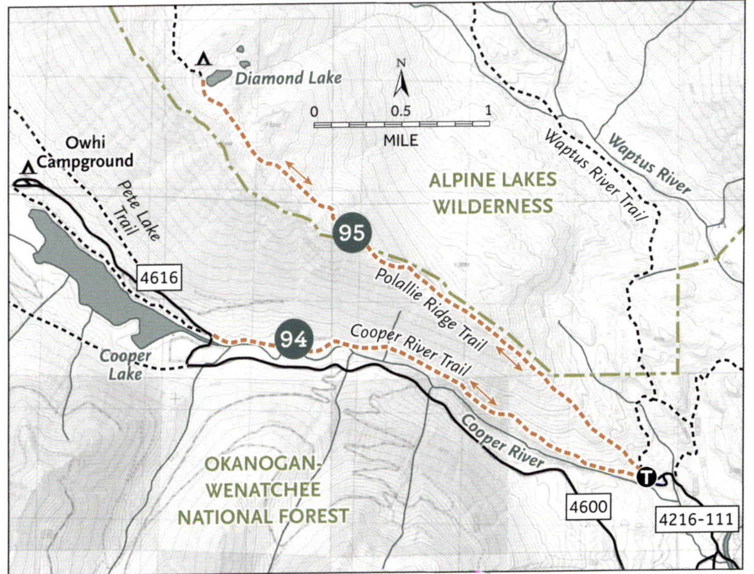

more energy, you could check out Cooper Lake before turning back, or just stop at the road and consider your work here done.

95 Polallie Ridge to Diamond Lake

RATING/DIFFICULTY: ***/4
ROUNDTRIP: 8.5 miles
ELEV GAIN/HIGH POINT: 3150 feet/5150 feet
SEASON: July–Oct

Map: Green Trails Maps Kachess Lake No. 208; **Contact:** Okanogan-Wenatchee National Forest, Cle Elum Ranger District; **Notes:** Northwest Forest Pass or Interagency Pass required. Free wilderness-use permit required—attained at the trailhead. Pit toilet and picnic areas at trailhead. Stick to designated parking for hikers, and avoid horse trailer parking. This trailhead gets full quickly in summer months; arrive early for best opportunities. Open to leashed dogs, stock; see map, page 285; **GPS:** N 47 24.569, W 121 06.415

Polallie Ridge is not a swoon-worthy hike with crazy views and plentiful break locations. In fact, it's a challenging grind through the mixed forest with only a few spots to see the surrounding mountains. But what it lacks in viewpoints it gives back in the form of peacefulness, as it's one of our less crowded PNW options. What's more, this trail description ends at the tranquil lapping shores of Diamond Lake—a true gem after walking through the thick forest. The lake makes a perfect destination for the day.

GETTING THERE

From I-90 near Cle Elum: Take exit 80 toward Roslyn and Suncadia. Head north on Bullfrog Road. In 2 miles, at the roundabout, continue straight to remain on Bullfrog Road. At 2.7 miles, reach a second roundabout, and this time, take the second exit, signed toward Roslyn. You are now on State Route 903, which is also called Salmon La Sac Road. Follow this road through Roslyn and continue, turning left onto W. Nevada Avenue at 4.3 miles. Pass the town of Ronald and continue along the east shore of Cle Elum Lake.

At 16.9 miles, the road narrows and at 17.1 miles, it splits, with one branch going straight ahead toward the Salmon La Sac Campground, and the other going right on Forest Road 4330, signed for Tucquala Lake. Go straight here (FR 4216-111) and cross the Cle Elum River. Pass the entrance to the Salmon La Sac Campground to the left and proceed straight ahead until the road dead-ends in a parking loop, 0.5 mile past the campground.

ON THE TRAIL

Locate the signed trailhead to the parking area's northwest and head on up. In around 400 feet, at the signed junction with the Cooper River Trail, we bear right on the Polallie Ridge Trail. In 0.1 mile, arrive at a second signed trail junction, this time with the Waptus River Trail. Continue following the Polallie Ridge Trail, which bears slightly left at this point and wastes no time getting down and dirty with the climbing.

The trail cruises up the spine of the ridge, though you are enjoying the firs and pines and you probably don't even realize it. There aren't many switchbacks, which helps it feel like you are getting somewhere fast, without many bonus miles. After 1.7 miles, the trail gives you a bit of a reprieve with a couple of flattish areas where a handful of downed

Though not as dramatic as some, Diamond Lake's beauty is a pleasant surprise amid forested Pollallie Ridge.

trailside trees give you options to sit for a break if one is needed.

Continue ascending the ridge, until at around 2.8 miles, the trail changes topographically with a more consistent series of ups and downs. Just after that, the Alpine Lakes Wilderness boundary shows up on a tree to the left, followed by a view to the north, just when you need a break from evergreen views. Across the valley, Mount Daniel, Mount Jerry Garcia, the Citadel, and others shine tall above the surrounding ridges. At this point, you are probably thinking, *Where in the world is Diamond Lake?* The topography doesn't seem like it would hold a lake as you look farther ahead. Keep going—I promise it's there!

At 4.2 miles, the lake shows up to the right. Your instinct is to follow the first social path you see leading to the lake, but if you stay on the trail for another 250 feet, you'll find a tent site and a much less impactful approach to the lake's western shoreline. There aren't many places to sit, save for a small log or two, so pick the best spot to plop down for a rest and a handful of trail mix. You likely won't want to swim, as the bottom is muddy and silty, but if it's not too buggy, it's a good place to saturate yourself in backcountry bliss. Listen—no cars, just perhaps a passing plane and the hum of happy pollinators. You have earned this solitude! Soak it up before retracing your steps.

96 Davis Peak

RATING/DIFFICULTY: *****/5
ROUNDTRIP: 10.4 miles
ELEV GAIN/HIGH POINT: 4160 feet/6430 feet
SEASON: July–Oct

Map: Green Trails Maps Kachess Lake No. 208; **Contact:** Okanogan-Wenatchee National Forest, Cle Elum Ranger District; **Notes:** Northwest Forest Pass or Interagency Pass required. Free wilderness-use permit required—attained at the trailhead. No facilities at trailhead. Open to leashed dogs; **GPS:** N 47 25.167, W 121 05.116

If you go into this knowing that this hike is hard and has umpteen switchbacks to the top, you might find it easier than you think. And there is ample reward to be found in solitude, outstanding views, and even occasionally an adorable hoary marmot. What's more, the workout is commendable, and you walk away a hero in your own mind: #truth.

GETTING THERE

From I-90 near Cle Elum: Take exit 80 toward Roslyn and Suncadia. Head north on Bullfrog Road. In 2 miles, at the roundabout, continue straight to remain on Bullfrog Road. At 2.7 miles, reach a second roundabout, and this time, take the second exit, signed toward Roslyn. You are now on State Route 903, which is also called Salmon La Sac Road. Follow this road through Roslyn and continue, turning left onto W. Nevada Avenue at 4.3 miles. Pass the town of Ronald and continue along the east shore of Cle Elum Lake.

At 16.9 miles, the road narrows, and at 17.1 miles, it splits, with one branch going straight ahead toward the Salmon La Sac Campground and the other turning to gravel and going right and uphill. Turn right here, signed for Tucquala Lake (Forest Road 4330). Stay on this road until 18.5 miles, and turn left on FR 134, signed for Davis Peak. In 0.5 mile from your last turn, find a large parking area to the road's right. If you are not in a high-clearance vehicle, you should park here

A stone wind block marks the spot where a fire lookout once stood on Davis Peak.

and walk 0.2 mile down the road to find the trailhead (add 0.4 mile to this hike description), or continue on to the trailhead and find parking in adjacent pullouts.

ON THE TRAIL

From the signed Davis Peak Trail No. 1324 trailhead, descend on a gentle slope to cross the Cle Elum River on a high wooden footbridge. The bridge has shown some wear, and is currently closed to stock, but is safe and suitable for hikers. Enjoy the river view from the lofty bridge deck, then once across, drop down to let the dog swim or to filter for a water bottle top off if need be. The hike is usually bone dry after this point, and you'll want to stay well-hydrated as you make your sweaty climb to the summit.

Up you go, with firs and smatterings of huckleberry shrubs keeping you company as you zig and zag your way up the peak's shoulders. As you get higher, views of Cle Elum Lake are visible behind you to the south. After 2 miles, arrive at the start of a silver forest, or leftover dead-standing trees from a hot fire in late summer and early fall of 2006. There's no place to plunk down for a break yet, but you can get creative and park your sit pad on a sooty log if desperate times call for desperate measures. The silver lining of the silver forest is that it opens up some views to the west of Thomas Mountain, Mount Clifty, Mount Baldy, and others. Soak it in, then continue your uphill grunt.

Pass a few steep meadows as your switchbacks continue. Don't let the adrenaline-provoking kerfuffle of the sooty grouse flaps give you a jump scare. They are often found here and wait until the very last minute to take flight, only to land a few feet away from where they were. While they aren't the sharpest birds in the animal kingdom,

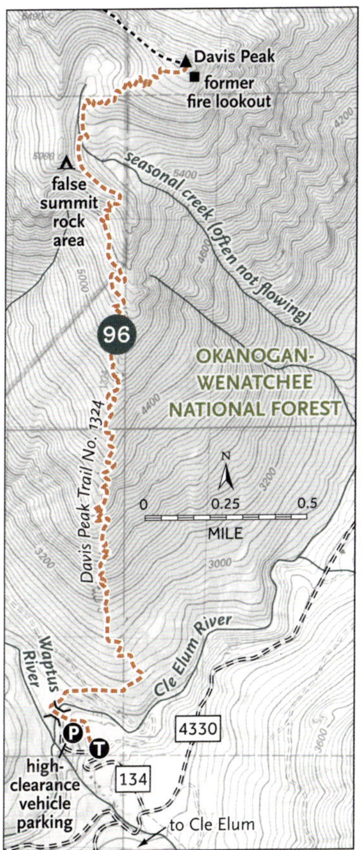

they are fun to see, especially when they have fledglings with them.

At 3.5 miles, reach a rocky boulder field that has a much more alpine feel. Whew, it feels like you are finally getting somewhere! The top of this boulder-laden, fire-burned ridge is the false summit and a good place to take it all in. Across the valley to the northwest, Chikamin Peak, Polallie Ridge, Lemah Mountain, and others are visible and swoon worthy, and this time there are a few places to sit and rest your weary carcass. Looking across the valley to the northeast, you can see the real summit, which seems discouraging, since it feels so far away. Rest assured this next part goes quickly and you'll be there before you know it. If life can't wait . . . you may even have a pop of cell service here.

Carry on from the false summit and wind your way across a talus field, reaching a forested area with a campsite at 4.4 miles. Continue up with a song in your heart and a smile on your face until, at 5.2 miles, you arrive at a rock pile and base of the former fire lookout. The tower that used to stand here was a classic L-4 cabin style with a deck that went around all the sides and a tall chimney for the stove. It stood here proudly for thirty-four years, from 1934 until its destruction in 1968. Look for marmots near Davis Peak on the rocky outcroppings to the north.

You can call this your destination for the day and find a place to land with your lunch, or if you want to extend your trip, keep following the ridgeline to the northwest for views, until it's too sketchy to continue. Davis has both a central and a southwest peak, but they require scrambling and mountaineering skills, so know your limits. Be smart, be safe, and enjoy the heck out of the soul food up here before retracing your steps.

97 French Cabin Creek

RATING/DIFFICULTY: **/3
ROUNDTRIP: 4.6 miles
ELEV GAIN/HIGH POINT: 1130 feet/4850 feet
SEASON: late June–Oct

Map: Green Trails Maps Kachess Lake No. 208; **Contact:** Okanogan-Wenatchee National Forest, Cle Elum Ranger District; **Notes:** No facilities at trailhead. Open to leashed dogs, mountain bikes, stock; see map, page 292; **GPS:** N 47 19.980, W 121 11.164

This hike is often used as an access trail to Kachess Ridge, which leads in a couple of different directions with options for longer, further exploration. But sometimes the side trail *is* the adventure, and this one can hold its own, with good surrounding views of lofty peaks. What's more, it attracts only a handful of users and can be a quiet option for contemplative hikes or catching up with friends.

GETTING THERE

From I-90 near Cle Elum: Take exit 80 toward Roslyn and Suncadia. Head north on Bullfrog Road. In 2 miles, at the roundabout, continue straight to remain on Bullfrog Road. At 2.7 miles, reach a second roundabout, and this time, take the second exit, signed toward Roslyn. You are now on State Route 903, which is also called Salmon La Sac Road. Follow this road through Roslyn and continue, turning left onto W. Nevada Avenue at 4.3 miles. Pass the town of Ronald and continue along the east shore of Cle Elum Lake.

At 13.7 miles, slow down so you don't miss the left turn onto the unsigned Forest Road 4308, which immediately crosses a sturdy car bridge over the Cle Elum River and turns to gravel. Stay on FR 4308, avoiding all smaller side roads, until you reach a significant intersection at 16.9 miles. Go straight here, avoiding the right-hand turn, to stay on FR 4308. At 20.3 miles, near the road's end, locate a spur road, FR 4308-132, to the right. The road is overgrown and has received little maintenance over the years—in fact, the sign pointing to the trailhead is barely legible, but you are a navigational genius, so no worries.

If you have a high-clearance, narrow vehicle and don't value your paint job, you *might* make it, but it's best to leave the gambling to Vegas. Park roadside near this spur road and walk the spur to the official trailhead, which is just a weathered sign 0.6 mile from where you parked.

ON THE TRAIL

You'll feel like the apocalypse hit and you are the only one left when you are standing at this trailhead, 0.6 mile up the spur road. A battered sign, now hiding in the cradled arms of an evergreen, calls out the trail next to a small car turnaround that is overgrown and void of vehicles. It looks like no one has been here in decades. Rest assured, at least I have. See what I mean about solitude?

Up you go, with the hum of West Fork French Cabin Creek keeping you company. The trail switches back through the evergreens and reaches a couple of open grassy knolls to the right 0.5 mile from the official trailhead. This is a great sneak preview of coming attractions, with some pretty views of the French Cabin Mountains, including French Chin and French Tongue to the southwest. If you are wanting a short hike or just a pretty place for a picnic without much work, these sloped grassy knolls are your plop-n-drop spots.

At 1 mile from the trailhead, arrive at a former clear-cut, which mercifully has now begun to grow in. Huckleberries, fireweed, elderberry, and other shrubs and wildflowers fringe the ground, but your eyes are directed up into the stony walls and peaks of the Frenchies (cool kid slang). The views are simply gorgeous of these big walls.

At 1.2 miles, arrive at a signed junction with Kachess Ridge Trail No. 1315. You could go either direction to continue your

The craggy spines of the French Cabin Mountains rise above the French Cabin Creek Trail.

exploration: Thorp Mountain is to the right in 3 miles (6 roundtrip from this spot), but it's great to see the French Cabin Mountains closer, and this is your chance. Turn left and follow the trail as it gently climbs and descends, until, at last, it pushes to reach a pass between French Chin and French Tongue at 1.7 miles. French Tongue to your right is the hero of this pass—with its massive stone walls now in your face. What a place! You could keep going, dropping into Silver Creek basin with gorgeous meadows and pretty quiet places, or turn back here. Explore to your heart's content!

98 French Cabin Mountain

RATING/DIFFICULTY: **/4

ROUNDTRIP: 11.4 miles

ELEV GAIN/HIGH POINT: 3210 feet/5520 feet

SEASON: July–Oct

Map: Green Trails Maps Kachess Lake No. 208; **Contact:** Okanogan-Wenatchee National Forest, Cle Elum Ranger District; **Notes:** No facilities at trailhead. A ford of French Cabin Creek is required, either by foot or vehicle—this may be hazardous in early season. Open to leashed dogs, mountain bikes, dirt bikes (on the Domerie Peak Trail), stock; **GPS:** N 47 21.048, W 121 08.205

This is a long, crazy mountain with all kinds of summits, knobs, and peaks, some directionally named, and others named amorously. The path of least resistance to see most of them is utilizing the Domerie Peak Trail, then connecting with the Silver Creek Tie Trail to get the best views. This requires a road walk and a steep slog up a trail that is open to dirt bikes, but it's

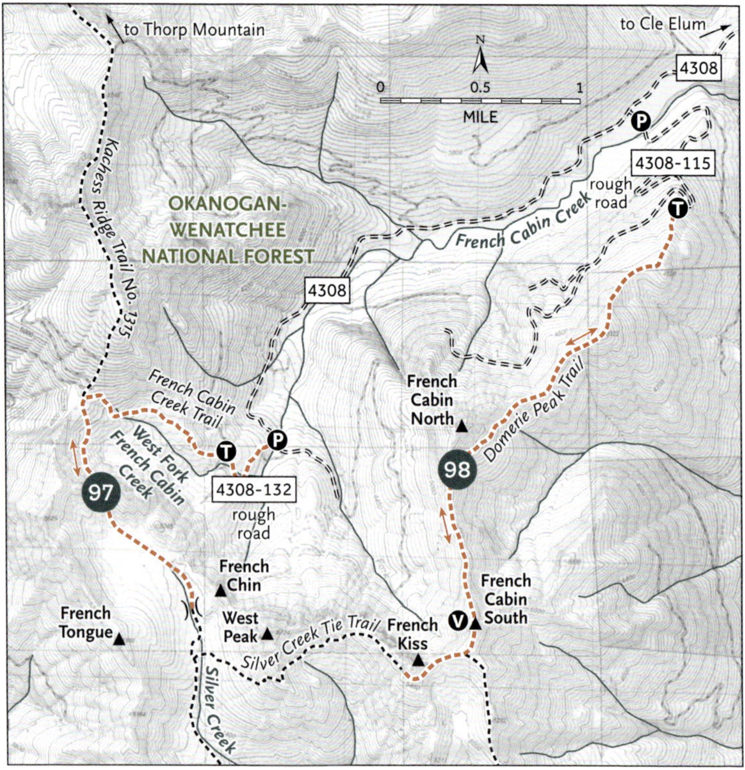

Serrated summits reaching for the clouds is one of many good views in the French Cabin Mountains.

worth the grunt and occasional sputtering exhaust to get to the ultimate view-smackeroo: the French Kiss! It's a big day and the terrain is not for everyone, but like so many places near here, its solitude is worthy, and it's a good place to clean out the mind-cobwebs and maybe even a few actual ones.

GETTING THERE

From I-90 near Cle Elum: Take exit 80 toward Roslyn and Suncadia. Head north on Bullfrog Road. In 2 miles, at the roundabout, continue straight to remain on Bullfrog Road. In another 0.7 mile, reach a second roundabout, and this time, take the second exit, signed toward Roslyn. You are now on State Route 903, which is also called Salmon La Sac Road. Follow this road through Roslyn and continue, turning left onto W. Nevada Avenue at 4.3 miles. Pass the town of Ronald and continue along the east shore of Cle Elum Lake.

At 13.7 miles, slow down so you don't miss the left turn onto the unsigned Forest Road 4308, which immediately crosses a sturdy car bridge over the Cle Elum River and turns to gravel. Stay on FR 4308, avoiding all smaller side roads, until you reach a significant intersection at 16.9 miles. Go straight here, avoiding the right-hand turn, to stay on FR 4308. At 17.3 miles, locate spur road FR 4308-115 to the left. It is signed "115," but the sign is weathered and hard to read. Take the turn and drive 0.1 mile to find a crossing of French Cabin Creek. You can either park before the creek at a pullout to ford it with feet, or bomb through it with a high-clearance vehicle and park on the other side. The road was gated before the gate fell apart, so technically you could drive past this point, but the road gets rough and hard to turn around, so it's best to park here.

ON THE TRAIL

Could this trail be more of a party pooper at the start? First, walk through a very cold creek, next . . . drag your bones up a gated road, then on to a humorously steep, loose trail. I can almost hear you cursing my name for sending you here. Bear with it; it's tough trails like these that earn you grit and character. It gets better.

In 1.5 miles, after around 640 feet of climbing, arrive at the road's end, signified by a large rock pile. Find the trailhead to the left, without much fanfare until a tree sign announces you are on the Domerie Peak Trail. The next 1.3 miles are like a treadmill prank where someone has cranked it to full incline. Thankfully they haven't monkeyed with the pace, so stop often to beg your lungs to forgive you. You'll marvel that dirt bikes can get up this crazy vertical slope, but some folks just have mad skills; I prefer my feet even though they fail me now and again. Peekaboo views help take your mind off the burn, but there's no easy way up this. Let it out—scream, cry, grunt, toot . . . it's all fair game.

After climbing nearly 1240 feet in just 1.3 miles from the trailhead (2.8 miles total), arrive at a well-earned ridgeline where views of Mount Stuart and the Stuart Range are seen, as well as vistas down into the Cle Elum Lake basin.

The trail bobs up and down, much more gently than the initial push, and guides you through a lovely evergreen forest replete with huckleberries and viewpoints. At 2.5 miles from the trailhead (4 miles total), the trail unassumingly ducks under French Cabin North, which has no trail to the summit. In fact, you won't even know you are below it unless you are looking at a map and finding your position. Peak baggers with sound navigational talent may enjoy some off-trail exploration to its summit, but the rest of us will keep walking and enjoying the ridgeline none the wiser.

At 3.5 miles from the trailhead (5 miles total), a pleasant viewpoint arrives to the left, near French Cabin South. If you're spent from the schlep, you could stake it, claim it, and call it lunch, then head back.

Otherwise, in 0.2 mile farther, arrive at a signed junction with the Silver Creek Tie Trail, which heads right and makes its way more primitively toward the French Kiss, which really is just a rocky knob. This trail has a peaceful ambiance with a few open sloping meadows, some open views, and a vibe of being a long way from civilization. At 4 miles from the trailhead (5.5 total), the trail crosses under the French Kiss. There is no trail, but it's open country with sustainable rock for travel, so head up to the line-of-sight summit. Bust out your lunch and swoon in the quiet of this hidden gem.

But wait, there's more! In just another 0.2 mile, there is yet another knob to check out. Find it by cutting upslope, where rocky outcroppings magically pull you toward the peak. It's still part of French Kiss, but I might suggest we call it First Kiss, as it's not quite as impressive as its passionate companion. At this point, head back—or see below for an option to stretch out your adventure.

EXTENDING YOUR HIKE

You could make a big loop by using Kachess Ridge Trail No. 1315, French Cabin Creek Trail No. 1305 (see Hike 97), and FR 4308-132, FR 4308, and FR 4308-115 for a total of 14 miles and close to 4000 feet of total elevation gain. A map will be your friend if you decide to go for it.

99 Jolly Mountain

RATING/DIFFICULTY: ****/5
ROUNDTRIP: 14 miles
ELEV GAIN/HIGH POINT: 4040 feet/6447 feet
SEASON: July–Oct

Map: Green Trails Maps Kachess Lake No. 208; **Contact:** Okanogan-Wenatchee National Forest, Cle Elum Ranger District; **Notes:** No facilities at trailhead. There are two trailheads. Open to leashed dogs, mountain bikes, motorcycles, stock; **GPS:** N 47 23.619, W 121 05.445

This trail is multiuse and popular with the motorized crowd. Despite that, the ridge at the top is outstanding, and the location of the former fire lookout is a vision, with valleys and peaks in all directions. Though you'll work hard to get there, the summit is well worth it. There are two trailheads—the alternative trailhead starts from the Cayuse Horse Camp. However, it's frequently muddy, with huge puddles and plenty of horse droppings from constant use. I've listed both, but my trail description is from the sno-park trailhead, as it's a bit more hiker-friendly.

GETTING THERE

From I-90 near Cle Elum: Take exit 80 toward Roslyn and Suncadia. Head north on Bullfrog Road. In 2 miles, at the roundabout, continue straight to remain on Bullfrog Road. At 2.7 miles, reach a second roundabout, and this time, take the second exit, signed toward Roslyn. You are now on State Route 903, also called Salmon La Sac Road. Follow this road through Roslyn and continue, turning left

Don't let the multiuse trail system on Jolly Mountain scare you away; the vistas are well worth the dusty soil!

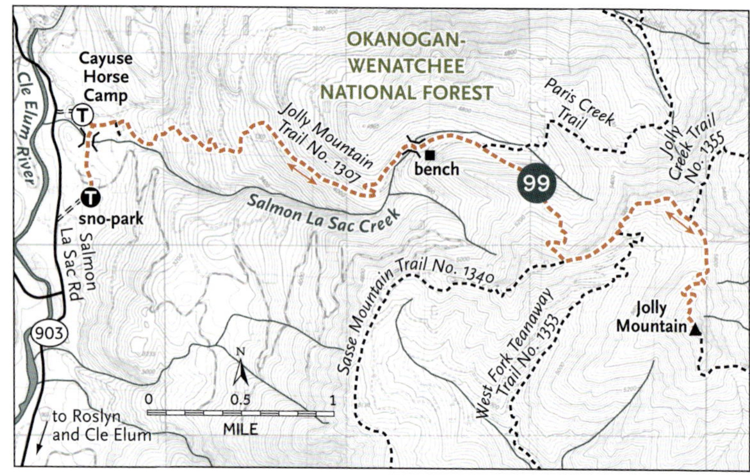

onto W. Nevada Avenue at 4.3 miles. Pass the town of Ronald and continue along the east shore of Cle Elum Lake. From here, follow the specific directions below for the trailhead you plan to start at.

Salmon La Sac Sno-Park: At 16.4 miles from leaving I-90, turn right on Forest Road 4315, following the signs for the Salmon La Sac Sno-Park. At 16.5 miles, the pavement ends and the gravel road begins, passing the sno-park spur road on the right. Proceed to 16.6 miles to find the trailhead on a former road to the left. Parking is to the right in one of several pullouts and campsites. If this parking is occupied, you could park at the sno-park and walk to the trailhead, adding 0.4 mile roundtrip to your day.

Cayuse Horse Camp (alternative trailhead): At 16.9 miles from leaving I-90, follow the signed entrance to the Cayuse Horse Camp on the right. At 17 miles, park across from the corral, ensuring you aren't in the way of campsites or passing trailers. Locate the trailhead on a former road to the south with a sign saying, "Closed to all motorized vehicles."

ON THE TRAIL

From the parking area, locate the road-turned-trail with a pictorial sign with a line through an ATV. A second sign below it notes that motorcycles, mountain bikes, stock, and hikers are permitted.

In 300 feet, bear right (signed with an arrow). Continue along the road-turned-trail, now signed with the trail number 1307 (Jolly Mountain Trail). In 0.3 mile, cross a wooden bridge over a frequently dry creek, then immediately arrive at a Y, where you'll bear right.

At 0.4 mile, the trail meets up with the wide road-turned-trail that comes in from the horse camp and is signed with a Jolly Mountain Trail Detour sign, though technically, this is the main thoroughfare to Jolly, so the detour part is puzzling. Turn right and follow this path. What a befuddling start, right?

At 0.5 mile, arrive at another junction, where the left branch is signed Jolly Mountain Trail No. 1307, and breathe deeply. You're in the right place!

The Jolly Mountain Trail is exactly what you'd expect from a multiuse trail with loose pebbles and dirt that covers your shoes in dust. Pearly everlasting, huckleberries, and salmonberries grow near the evergreens as you cruise uphill. A couple of defunct forest roads are crossed, though the main trail is obvious and if you are busy visiting, you probably won't even notice them.

At 3.5 miles, after just shy of 2000 feet of climbing, the trail crosses Salmon La Sac Creek on a wooden bridge. Near the creek on the far side of the bridge is a wooden bench and the perfect place to stop for a break and to filter water or let the pup drink. There aren't too many quality break spots, so make this one a goal.

Arrive at a signed intersection with the Paris Creek Trail heading off to the left at 3.9 miles. Our trail bears right and continues going into the sky. After 4.5 miles, it reaches a level area where it crosses a seasonal dribble. This area is peaceful, with the occasional colorful wildflower and tweeting songbird.

At 5.2 miles, the ridgeline is finally attained at a junction with Sasse Mountain Trail No. 1340. This feels like victory, as the climbing at this point is much less difficult and more like a gentle stroll as you turn left. What's more, it has a fantastic ambiance, with open views of neighboring peaks as well as grassy meadows containing other shrubs such as fireweed and elderberry. Sadly, in 2017, lightning started a fire that ripped through this area, consuming most of the timber and understory.

At 5.5 miles, bear left at a junction with a badly burned sign heading off toward West Fork Teanaway Trail No. 1353. Stay with the ridge as it guides you along the heights, reaching views of the Stuart Range and beautiful deep valleys in surrounding basins. You'll also pass Jolly Creek Trail No. 1355, though the fire has destroyed much evidence of it.

After 7 miles and over 4030 feet of elevation gain, reach a rocky knob and the large rock pile built as a wind block at the top of Jolly Mountain. This rock pile has a reputation of being the home to an infestation of lady bugs that thrives here for unknown reasons. Despite being called bugs, they are technically beetles and are known for being docile and chill. If you set your pack down or sit near this wind block, you may have a couple of hitchhikers when you leave.

The twisted metal remnants of the old fire lookout are still stuck in the ground, honoring days past, when a classic L-4 style cabin stood here. Built in 1936 to replace an aging cupola cabin, the new lookout stood here for thirty-two years before its removal. The wind whips up here, so stay as long as your cold bones and sticky skin will allow before heading back the way you came.

100 Paddy-Go-Easy Pass to Sprite Lake

RATING/DIFFICULTY: *****/4
ROUNDTRIP: 7.7 miles
ELEV GAIN/HIGH POINT: 2990 feet/6090 feet
SEASON: July–Oct

Map: Green Trails Maps Alpine Lakes West Stevens Pass No. 176S; **Contact:** Okanogan-Wenatchee National Forest, Cle Elum Ranger District; **Notes:** Northwest Forest Pass or Interagency Pass required. Free wilderness-use permit required—attained at the trailhead. Pit toilet and picnic areas near trailhead. Open to leashed dogs, stock; **GPS:** N 47 31.994, W 121 04.951

This is one of my favorite hikes in the Cascades, primarily because the lake's setting in a wide-open basin has such a great vibe. In the fall, a few larches pop with golden tones as you hike toward the lake, a vision of earthy colors when framed against the burgundy carpets of dwarf huckleberries. Mountain goats and mule deer frequent the area too. Overall, it's a hard hike, but the rewards are worth the grunt.

GETTING THERE

From I-90 near Cle Elum: Take exit 80 toward Roslyn and Suncadia. Head north on Bullfrog Road. In 2 miles, at the roundabout, continue straight to remain on Bullfrog Road. At 2.7 miles, reach a second roundabout, and this time, take the second exit, signed toward Roslyn. You are now on State Route 903, which is also called Salmon La Sac Road. Follow this road through Roslyn and continue, turning left onto W. Nevada Avenue at 4.3 miles. Pass the town of Ronald and continue along the east shore of Cle Elum Lake.

At 16.9 miles, the road narrows and at 17.1 miles, it splits, with one branch going straight ahead toward the Salmon La Sac Campground and the other turning to gravel and going right and uphill. Turn right here, signed for Tucquala Lake (Forest Road 4330). You'll go by private cabins, pass other trailheads, and maneuver a vehicle ford of Scatter Creek, which is dry by late summer. Stay on this road until 28.2 miles, when you reach the signed Paddy-Go-Easy Pass trailhead to the road's right. If it's full, get creative with parking options where signed permissible; however, avoid crushing vegetation or parking in the designated areas for horse trailers.

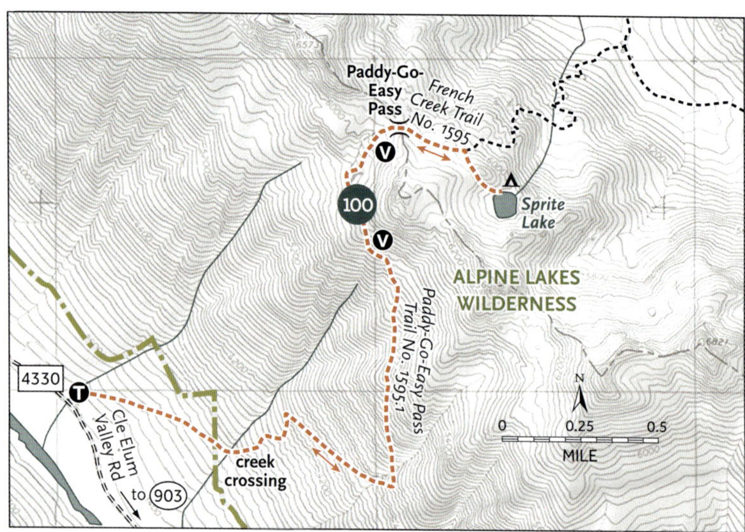

Thanks to the rocky scrambles and huge views, Paddy-Go-Easy Pass is a veritable playground of exploration opportunities.

ON THE TRAIL

After just 90 feet, the trail crosses a drippy creek on a wobbly log. Storms have taken their toll on this hike, and the Forest Service and trail volunteer groups such as Washington Trails Association have done a fantastic job cutting blowdowns. It's an annual effort to keep this trail open, so be sure to admire their work as you hike through the obstacle-free zones.

In 0.6 mile, the Alpine Lakes Wilderness boundary is crossed, with a trail sign on a tree to the right. The climbing is stout at times, but as you get higher, you are treated to views of Cathedral Rock and the glaciers of Mount Daniel sticking up behind you. The switchbacks guide you from forest to more open slopes with sun-loving shrubs, a welcome sign of progress. Deer frequent these slopes, as do sooty grouse, so keep your eyes and ears open.

After almost 2.8 miles, near the top, a few rocky viewpoints pop up to the right. Some of the rocks in this area take on mineral colorations of yellows and pinks, making the ground and surrounding knolls quite colorful. At 3 miles, find yourself cresting Paddy-Go-Easy Pass, where there are plenty of rocks to sit and take it in. The neighboring crags attract mountain goats, so be sure to quietly scan. This is Paddy's pass, and Sprite Lake isn't far off, so you might also give a look around for leprechauns.

The firs and pines are rather short, a testament to harsh weather and a short growing season, and the shrubs are colorful, with mountain heather in the summer and dwarf huckleberry in the fall. You'll be tempted to explore to the left and right, but for now, save your energy and see if it's still there after a visit to Sprite Lake.

Continue onward, descending the back side of the pass. Here's where things get interesting, as the lake is not visible and it's a fun puzzle to find it. Two unsigned boot paths are located off this main trail to the right (southeast), and they eventually rejoin, delivering you to Sprite Lake. The first is almost 0.2 mile downhill from the top of the pass, the second is farther down the main trail by 0.1 mile. Use the second one if you can, since the Forest Service has attempted to decommission the first one, but its continued use is making this a tough task. Having an app or map in this area is helpful. Both paths hide well in rocks and shrubs, but if you are looking diligently to the right as you descend, you'll notice them.

Take the boot path, and in 0.2 mile from the main trail (3.4 miles from the trailhead), arrive at a tree sign stating that no pack and saddle stock is permitted within 200 feet of the lake. You're almost there, and the tree sign is reassuring. A small rise gives way to views down to the lake basin, which is right below you—you've found it! Pikas squeak like dog toys in the rocks as you make your way down to the water's edge. A trail to the lake's left leads to tent sites where you can sit for lunch or just enjoy the moment. A sprite is a fairy or supernatural creature primarily found in or near water in Irish folklore. This lake, with its deep-blue water and tranquil shoreline, is just magical enough to have a sprite or two. Small trout sip hatching insects off the surface as you marinate in this backcountry perfection and soak up the day.

Pull your full, happy heart away and head back to where you started when time is up.

101 Pete Lake

RATING/DIFFICULTY: *****/3

ROUNDTRIP: 9.1 miles

ELEV GAIN/HIGH POINT: 800 feet/3050 feet

SEASON: late May–Oct

Map: Green Trails Maps Kachess Lake No. 208; **Contact:** Okanogan-Wenatchee National Forest, Cle Elum Ranger District; **Notes:** Northwest Forest Pass or Interagency Pass required. Pit toilet and picnic area at trailhead. Open to leashed dogs, stock, mountain bikes until the wilderness boundary (2.1 miles in); **GPS:** N 47 26.046, W 121 11.210

The gentle trail to Pete Lake is a gem for new or young hikers or for those who aren't ready for the tough stuff. Wandering through pines and firs, the path leads to the shoreline of the quiet Pete Lake framed by the rugged ridges of Lemah Mountain, a true reward for a fairly mild approach.

GETTING THERE

From I-90 near Cle Elum: Take exit 80 toward Roslyn and Suncadia. Head north on Bullfrog Road. In 2 miles, at the roundabout, continue straight to remain on Bullfrog Road. At 2.7 miles, reach a second roundabout, and this time, take the second exit, signed toward Roslyn. You are now on State

With minimal elevation gain, the hike to Pete Lake makes for a perfect full-day adventure.

Route 903, which is also called Salmon La Sac Road.

Follow this road through Roslyn and continue, turning left onto W. Nevada Avenue at 4.3 miles. Pass the town of Ronald and continue along the east shore of Cle Elum Lake.

At 18.4 miles, turn left onto Forest Road 46, also signed for the Pete Lake Trail. Cross the Cle Elum River on a wide bridge, then continue on the paved road until 23.1 miles at FR 4616, where you turn right, signed for the Pete Lake Trail. The road turns to gravel, crosses the river again, and passes the Cooper River Trail to the right. At 23.7 miles, bear left at a Y; the right branch is gated. At 24 miles, after passing the Owhi Campground, arrive at another Y. A large sign for the Pete Lake trailhead, a self-pay station, is straight ahead here. Equestrians go to the right branch, while other users continue to the left and follow the one-way loop around until reaching the large parking area, pit toilets, and the start of the trail.

ON THE TRAIL

The well-signed Pete Lake Trail No. 1323 begins with the first of several rock-hops across seasonal streams, just 450 feet from where you started. Sunny days will provide the scents of warm sunshine on firs and make the area smell naturally glorious. In 0.1 mile, catch the first glimpse of the teal-colored Cooper River winding through back eddies and clumps of willows to the left.

Another seasonal creek with a rock-hop arrives at 0.5 mile. Serenading you are the haunting, hollow calls of nuthatches and the scolding chatter of Douglas squirrels. In the late spring and early summer, colorful western tanagers frequent these areas and sing out a series of short, clear calls. These birds, just a little smaller than a robin, have a bright-yellow body, black wings, and red head (male) and hiding isn't easy! If you haven't seen one before, you might think someone's exotic parrot got lost in these parts.

A series of dark swamps, left behind by rains and flooding, arrive to the left, along with horrible mosquitos if you are here in early summer—jog to shake them, as they seem to get better after this stretch.

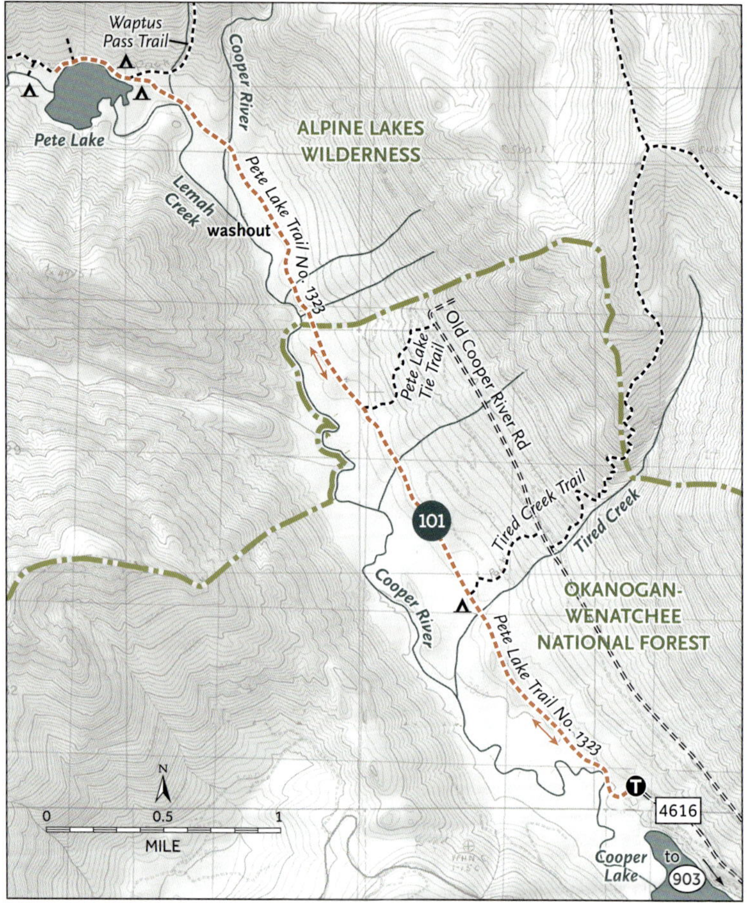

At 1.1 miles, a lovely campsite arrives to the left, followed by a makeshift log bridge (or rock-hop in low season) allowing you to cross Tired Creek with dry feet. At 1.2 miles, the signed Tired Creek Trail comes in from the right, while our trail continues through the forest straight ahead.

Over the next 0.9 mile, the trail provides more of the same scenery and crosses a couple of seasonal creeks by rock-hopping. A brief talus field breaks the monotony in the middle, the only true change along the path.

At 2.1 miles, the signed Pete Lake Tie Trail arrives from the right, and a sign reminds those on wheels that this is their turnaround, as bikes are no longer permitted past this point. Shortly after, the trail enters the Alpine Lakes Wilderness.

The trail is picturesque as it gently guides you through evergreens, some ancient giants, and passes over four seasonal creeks and dribbles, until it arrives at the Cooper River, a much larger water crossing than any so far. A behemoth log has fallen across the river to the right, and you practice parkour as you climb up and over, ultimately making it across with dry shoes. In most summers, a rock-hop is also possible. Trekking poles are helpful as you navigate the tippy tops of the rocks, which stick out with dry tops.

At 3.7 miles, a funky junction makes you scratch your head. Several years ago, the path used to go straight ahead here, but Mother Nature took her water chisel, also known as Lemah Creek, to the banks and made a mess. Instead, the trail now goes sharply to the right, making a bend as it winds around the washout for 0.1 mile. If you aren't paying attention, you might end up in a bushwhack, so keep on your toes.

The signed Waptus Pass Trail comes in from the right, while a large, flat camping area suitable for a group arrives to the left at 4 miles. Shortly after that, views of the lake are visible to the left, along with a couple of camps on a rocky hillside; you've made it! The best views of Lemah Mountain are found by dropping down to the lake's eastern shoreline where a few dirt perches make for a decent snack break.

To get the full experience, or to use the backcountry box-style privy, continue around the lake's northern shoreline for another 0.3 mile to arrive at the signed junction with the toilet trail headed uphill at 4.4 miles. Another camping area is found 0.2 mile from the toilet trail, near Lemah Creek on the lake's western edge, and might be a good turnaround goal for the day.

EXTENDING YOUR HIKE

For those who wish to keep going, the Pete Lake Trail continues westbound by bearing left at the toilet trail and eventually ends up fording the swift Lemah Creek and finally connecting with the Pacific Crest Trail in 1.7 miles and 250 feet of elevation gain. Trail runners or those with a fast gait, endless energy, and plenty of daylight may even consider a trip to Spectacle Lake, south on the PCT. This adds an extra 5.8 miles roundtrip and 1500 feet more of elevation gain to your day once you arrive at the PCT. Consult your map, as a few old trails exist and it's possible to take a wrong turn—stay safe!

102 Thorp Lake and Thorp Mountain Lookout

RATING/DIFFICULTY: ****/4

ROUNDTRIP: 8 miles

ELEV GAIN/HIGH POINT: 2350 feet/5850 feet

SEASON: July–Oct

Built in 1930 and restored in 2007, the Thorp Mountain Lookout offers a scenic stop with a side of history.

Maps: Green Trails Maps Kachess Lake No. 208 and Alpine Lakes East No. 208SX; **Contact:** Okanogan-Wenatchee National Forest, Cle Elum Ranger District; **Notes:** Parking is roadside. No facilities at trailhead. Open to leashed dogs, stock; **GPS:** N 47 22.363, W 121 09.444

Who doesn't love fire lookouts? The one at Thorp Mountain is one of the finest in the Cascades, especially since its facelift in recent years. Like most lookouts, it's a workout to get there, but when you do, the views of surrounding peaks are sublime. While there are other approaches, I prefer the Thorp Creek Trail approach. It doesn't beat up your vehicle too much (passenger cars will make it), finding the trailhead is not too difficult, and you have the option of visiting Thorp Lake, which is a happy bonus. But be prepared to huff and puff to the top.

GETTING THERE

From I-90 near Cle Elum: Take exit 80 toward Roslyn and Suncadia. Head north on Bullfrog Road. In 2 miles, at the roundabout, continue straight to remain on Bullfrog Road. At 2.7 miles, reach a second roundabout, and this time, take the second exit, signed toward Roslyn. You are now on State Route 903, which is also called Salmon La Sac Road. Follow this road through Roslyn and continue, turning left onto W. Nevada Avenue at 4.3 miles. Pass the town of Ronald and continue along the east shore of Cle Elum Lake.

In 13.7 miles from leaving I-90, slow down so you don't miss the left turn onto the unsigned Forest Road 4308, which immediately crosses a sturdy car bridge over the Cle Elum River and turns to gravel. Stay on FR 4308, avoiding all smaller side roads, until you reach a significant intersection at 16.9 miles. Turn right onto FR 4312 (signed shortly after turning) and continue until 18.4 miles, finding roadside parking near a defunct road (FR 4312-121) with a yellow gate to the road's right.

ON THE TRAIL

Locate the trail by walking around the yellow gate of the former road, placed here during the logging efforts of 1988. It hasn't seen vehicle traffic in eons, so it will soon feel more like a trail and less like a road. At 0.1 mile, cross Thorp Creek, which is usually a rock-hop, though after heavy rains or in early season, it may require a ford.

The trail continues on the former road, which is more of a single track at this point. In 0.2 mile, reach a tree sign pointing out options, including our trail, Thorp Creek Trail No. 1316, which goes left. You'll probably feel like this trail is easy breezy at this point, but around 1.5 miles, the thing shoots skyward at a harsh pitch, so make sure your mind and body are prepared. Right about here, a trailside "chair" carved from a stump gives you a place to stop, rest, and adjust your gear.

Wheeze your way up the heights, stopping to catch your breath and look around in a couple of rocky areas that offer views to neighboring ridgelines. At 2.2 miles, arrive at a signed trail junction with Thorp Lake Trail No. 1316.1 to the left. Follow it for 0.5-mile roundtrip and only 105 feet of total elevation gain to this restful nook. Forested tent sites surround the lake which, at just over 9 acres, is home to a small population of rainbow trout and a swarm of dragonflies that live as larvae in the reed-filled plants on shore before they hatch. They are mosquito eaters,

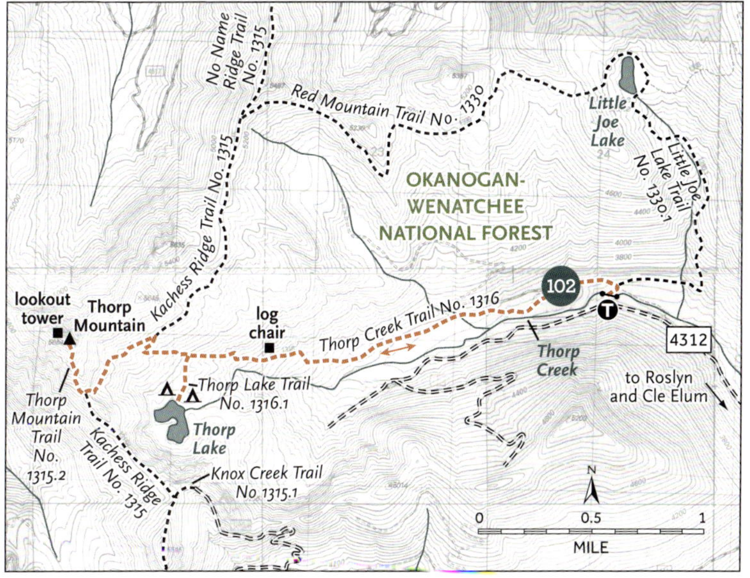

so they aren't only graceful and delicate, but they are also beneficial!

Back on the Thorp Creek Trail, continue pushing uphill to reach the signed junction with Kachess Ridge Trail No. 1315 and head left, now 3.1 miles from the trailhead. Up you go to reach a signed junction pointing toward the Knox Creek Trail and Cooper Pass to the left at 3.6 miles. Go right here for Thorp Mountain, though the sign isn't visible until about 50 feet past this intersection.

At exactly 4 miles, reach the fire lookout tower. This classic L-4 cabin was placed here in 1930 and given renovations in 2007. At that point, the aging structure received a new foundation, roof, windows, partial catwalk, and shutter hangers as well as modernization of the structural architecture. The Forest Service still uses the tower periodically, though most fire-spotting these days is done from the air with the help of planes, drones, and satellites. The views from the tower and its base are outstanding, with the peaks of Mount Daniel, Lemah Mountain, and Chikamin Peak to the north, and Mount Rainier dominating the southern skyline. There are plenty of places around this area to flop down, so find a spot and own it before heading back or further exploring this awesome area.

OPPOSITE: *Peaceful Gallagher Head Lake lies tucked into the Teanaway backcountry, with a backdrop of rugged mountains.*

TEANAWAY AREA AND BLEWETT PASS

WIDE OPEN VIEWS, WARM SUNSHINE, wildflowers, remoteness, and wonderful opportunities to see wildlife are what this area is all about. Elk, mountain goats, and deer are frequent visitors, as are wide varieties of residential and migratory birds. It's a place to lose yourself on trails that lead to postcard-worthy views and give your heart and soul a reprieve from the daily grind.

103 Standup Creek Trail

RATING/DIFFICULTY: ***/3
ROUNDTRIP: 9.3 miles
ELEV GAIN/HIGH POINT: 2890 feet/6200 feet
SEASON: July–Oct

Maps: Green Trails Maps Mount Stuart No. 209 and Alpine Lakes East No. 208SX; **Contact:** Okanogan-Wenatchee National Forest, Cle Elum Ranger District; **Notes:** No facilities at trailhead. High-clearance vehicle necessary on Forest Road 9703-112—or walk from FR 9703. FR 9703-112 may be tight and brushy. Open to leashed dogs, mountain bikes, stock; see map, page 311; **GPS:** N 47 22.140, W 120 50.321

Not many people use the Standup Creek Trail, which sits in the valley to the west of the more popular Stafford Creek Trail (Hike 104). Because of this, the path is brushy and primitive in places, but it still offers outstanding value. There is solitude to be found in the quiet creek basin and on the strong mountain ridges. Good views of Navaho Peak with the rugged McClellan Peak in the distance are found from the final overlook. What's more, there are plenty of connecting options for those who want a longer day.

GETTING THERE

From I-90 near Cle Elum: Take exit 85 and head north. In 0.3 mile, turn right at a T intersection and merge onto State Route 970. At 6.9 miles, turn left onto Teanaway Road, which eventually turns to North Fork Teanaway Road. At 20 miles, the road meets a Y and turns to gravel. Bear right onto the signed FR 9737. At 21.4 miles, turn right onto the signed FR 9703, which is also signed for Trail No. 1351. At 22.2 miles, find the smaller and more primitive FR 9703-112 to the left. If you have a high-clearance vehicle and don't mind a few branches hitting your paint, turn left and follow this road for 0.9 mile to its end, with room for about five parked cars.

Alternatively, you can park in a large pullout at the intersection of FR 9703 and FR 9703-112 and walk the spur road (FR 9703-112) to the trailhead. Doing this adds a roundtrip distance of 1.8 miles and 320 feet of cumulative elevation gain to your trip.

ON THE TRAIL

From the well-signed trailhead, cross the sturdy wooden bridge over Standup Creek and begin your gradual ascent up the valley. For the first couple of miles, the trail stays near the creek, where brushy riparian foliage such as thimbleberry, salmonberry, and slide alder try to crowd you out. The trail is still visible, but you occasionally need to whack a plant or two, and in early season, you may need to do some parkour over blowdowns.

As you climb, you'll be hopping back and forth across the creek at least five more times, doing your best to keep your feet dry. This can be a challenge when the water is flowing heavily in early summer, but usually by mid- to late July, you can rock- or log-jump through each crossing.

After a couple of miles, the trail gets less brushy and begins switching back up a steep slope to put you on a ridgeline. The ridge isn't flat and level but does give you a change of scenery with more rocky outcroppings, scattered pine and fir trees, and some light and open views into neighboring ravines.

After 3.1 miles, a rocky outcropping to the right provides a pleasant place to stop and catch your breath while soaking in views of the distant Teanaway Community Forest. You really haven't gone that far in terms of miles, but it feels like a long way from anywhere up here.

The trail breaks out into pocket meadows where spirited feeder creeks skip down the path of least resistance. Wildflowers such as columbine, paintbrush, lupine, lewisia, and aster make a seasonal appearance as the trail reaches a signed junction for Bean Basin Trail No. 1391.1 to the left at 3.7 miles. Our path turns right at this point and pushes up some short switchbacks to reach a flat saddle with a camp spot and rocky protrusions. This is the top! Walk a few steps farther along the trail for even better views of Earl Peak and the Stuart Range before heading back or exploring more turf.

EXTENDING YOUR HIKE

If you have extra dance in your prance, you could make a big loop by continuing on the Standup Creek Trail, which drops into the valley and meets up with the Stafford Creek Trail (Hike 104). From there, turn left and visit Navaho Pass (a must-do) before returning to this trail junction. Then hike south 3.8 miles to the Stafford Creek trailhead and walk FR 9703 west and 9703-112 north back to your vehicle. The whole loop will be approximately 15.5 miles with 4500 feet of elevation gain.

Yellow posies scattered across a rugged hillside along the Standup Creek Trail, where solitude blooms as freely as the wildflowers

If you brought your superhero cape, you could do the hike to Navaho Pass (see above), then head east and climb Navaho Peak. Doing it all and making a full loop back will be 17.5 miles with 5660 feet of elevation gain on the day.

You also have options from the Bean Basin Trail junction. At that junction, you could head west and follow the trail up a slope to reach a ridge below Earl Peak. From there, it's a steep, loose climb to Earl Peak's sweeping panoramic views (Hike 107). From the Bean Basin Trail junction, this roundtrip distance and cumulative elevation gain is approximately 2.1 miles and 1360 feet more than the trail description.

Even more connecting trails are sprinkled around this area, so consult your map and make it full, great day!

104 Navaho Pass via Stafford Creek

RATING/DIFFICULTY: ****/4

ROUNDTRIP: 10.8 miles

ELEV GAIN/HIGH POINT: 3080 feet/6030 feet

SEASON: July–Oct

Maps: Green Trails Maps Mount Stuart No. 209 and Alpine Lakes East No. 208SX; **Contact:** Okanogan-Wenatchee National Forest, Cle Elum Ranger District; **Notes:** Northwest Forest Pass or Interagency Pass required. Pit toilet at trailhead. Open to leashed dogs, mountain bikes, stock; **GPS:** N 47 21.978, W 120 48.157

The popularity of this hike has greatly increased over the last ten years, and for good reason. Sweeping panoramic views into the Stuart Range as spectacular as this are what dreams are made of. The trail is a moderate climb, with a few steep sections to get you to the pass, but it's worth every grunt, grind, and bead of sweat.

GETTING THERE

From I-90 near Cle Elum: Take exit 85 and head north. In 0.3 mile, turn right at a T intersection and merge onto State Route 970. At 6.9 miles, turn left onto Teanaway Road, which eventually turns to North Fork Teanaway Road. At 20 miles, the road meets a Y and turns to gravel. Bear right onto the signed FR 9737. At 21.4 miles, turn right onto the signed FR 9703, which is also signed for Trail No. 1351. At 23.9 miles, find the parking area for the Stafford Creek trailhead (the one we take to Navaho Peak) on the right. The actual trail is found to the left, across from the parking area.

ON THE TRAIL

Stafford Creek Trail No. 1359 is the path we take to Navaho Pass, though it's not marked for our destination. From the start, the trail cruises gently next to Stafford Creek in brushy riparian foliage with an easy grade. At 0.4 mile, you reach a couple of steep switchbacks that take you over a washout and back down the other side. Though we get back closer to Stafford Creek, the path has more elevation gain now as it heads up the valley.

At 0.8 mile, reach a rock-hop across a burbling tributary brook. This is the first of at least seven or eight water crossings you'll encounter, depending on the snowpack and time of year. Usually, all are manageable with either a jump or a toddle to keep your shoes dry.

The trail takes on a more open feel as you get higher up the valley, displaying a variety of pines (ponderosa, western white, lodgepole, and whitebark) and the classic semiarid feeling of the eastern side of the Cascade Crest. A few meadows and a smattering of hillsides spring to life with wildflowers such as yarrow, pearly everlasting, aster, paintbrush, tiger lily, groundsel, lousewort, skyrocket, columbine, and a plethora of others. Notice how specific arrays favor the wetter areas near the creek, such as Jeffrey's shooting star, elephant's head, and streambank springbeauty, while others thrive in the well-drained sandy soils of the subalpine and alpine landscapes, where they cling to the ground to stabilize their roots in the high winds. In those areas look for moss campion, subalpine daisy, saxifrage, spreading phlox, Columbia lewisia, and others.

The trail stays to the east of Stafford Creek, but dropping down to the water is perfect for a backcountry overnight. Find tent sites to the left at 2.3 miles and again at 3.3 miles,

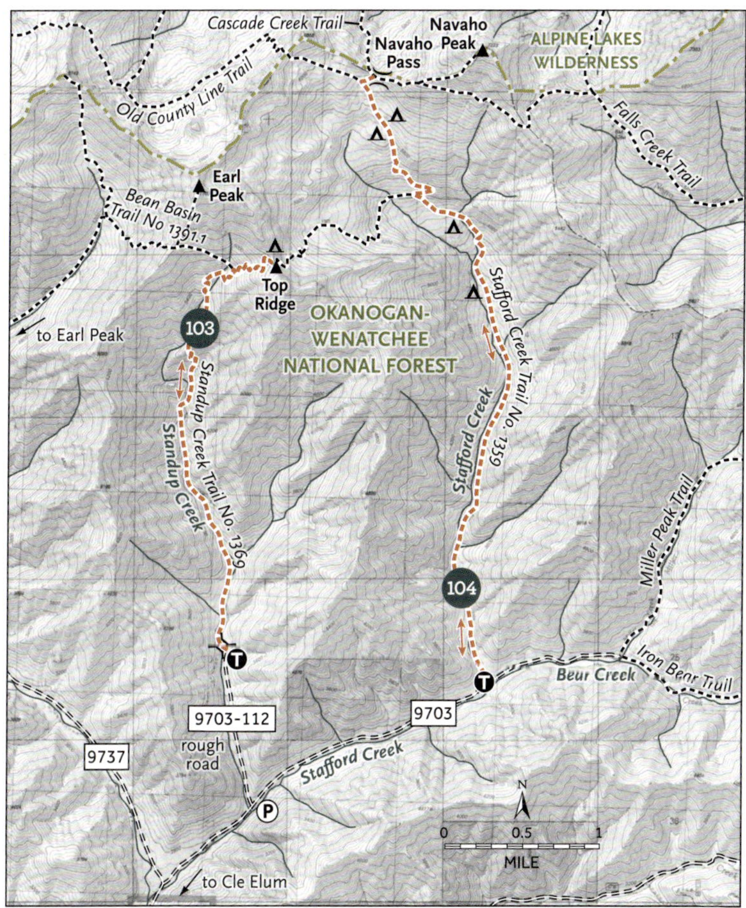

just after a tributary of Stafford Creek comes down a high ravine across the trail.

At 3.8 miles, you might walk right by the signed junction with Standup Creek Trail No. 1369, which comes in from the left, if you are deep in conversation or focused on your feet. If you want a break, duck over to the creek in this spot—there are a few rocks around for sitting. On a hot day, it feels blissful.

After the junction, the trail makes quick work of climbing, taking you up a couple of swooping switchbacks through rocky, loose tread. The area is getting more subalpine as you keep ascending, and the excitement builds to what's ahead.

At 5 miles, reach a meadowy plateau with a handful of tent sites. This is a grand place for a break with plenty of places to sit, so long as you use care to avoid any fragile plants. The remarkable grasses and flowers have a tough survival situation in this exposed, short-growing season.

Beyond the meadow, the way feels more alpine, with sandy, tundra-like soils difficult for vegetation growth and a lighter-colored soil where the trail cuts through it. The last slope before the pass has grasses and wildflowers, as if to welcome you warmly to your destination. Reach the pass with a little huff and puff in your lungs and a little thumping in your heart. Signed junctions with connecting trails are in almost all directions. The Old County Line Trail goes both left and right (east and west), though neither way is well-traveled beyond a few miles from this spot. Straight ahead is the Cascade Creek Trail, which drops you toward Ingalls Creek. You can go up the slopes for views; I prefer to turn left at the pass (west) and wander up the hill, where a few perches provide opportunities to smack down the sit pad and immerse your soul in the crazy beauty stretched out to the north. The jagged spires of the Enchantments—Little Annapurna, Enchantment Peak, Crystal Lake Tower, Fantasia Tower, McClellan Peak, and others—are so incredibly picturesque from this spot, it almost feels like a green screen with imaging. Is it even real? Keep exploring if you've got it in you!

EXTENDING YOUR HIKE

Why not climb Navaho Peak while you are at it? It's only 0.8 mile to the top (one way) from here . . . but it's 1150 feet higher—you've been

Navaho Peak and the Enchantments are a feast for the eyes near Navaho Pass.

warned. Yes, it's absurdly steep, but one foot in front of the other, and plenty of sucking wind, get you there. To climb it, turn right (east) at the pass and walk the Old County Line Trail for 0.3 mile, then bear left when the trail splits on a primitive boot path that leads up the mountain. In the fall, a smattering of larch trees exhibit their golden needles as you scale the stony slope. Find a rugged rock pile when you reach the summit, but the summit isn't why you come. Your eyes nearly pop out of your head with the ridgeline of the Stuart Range staring you back. Mount Stuart's pointing summit shoots toward the stars, while the others follow suit. The world would be a better place if everyone had a chance to stand here.

Another option for a hike extension or a trail run is to make a loop with the Standup Creek Trail (Hike 103). On your way back down, turn right for Standup Creek and follow it back to its trailhead off FR 9703-112. Walk the road south, back to FR 9703 and make a left (east). Find your vehicle again at the Stafford Creek Trail parking area. Doing this loop—including a trip to Navaho Pass and back—is approximately 15.5 miles with 4500 feet of elevation gain.

105 Bean Basin

RATING/DIFFICULTY: ***/4
ROUNDTRIP: 8.2 miles
ELEV GAIN/HIGH POINT: 3260 feet/7040 feet
SEASON: late May–Oct

Map: Green Trails Maps Alpine Lakes East Stuart Range No. 208SX; **Contact:** Okanogan-Wenatchee National Forest, Cle Elum Ranger District; **Notes:** Northwest Forest Pass or Interagency Pass required. Port-a-potties are occasionally at trailhead. Dirt road to trailhead; AWD or higher clearance suggested but not required. Creek fords in early season may get feet wet. While this trail may be open to mountain bikes and equestrians, very few people will attempt biking or riding up to this point. Open to leashed dogs, mountain bikes, stock; see map, page 317; **GPS:** N 47 23.355, W 120 52.328

Day hikers will be captivated by the vibrant wildflowers and sweeping slopes beneath Bean Peak's rugged summit. A tranquil campsite tucked among evergreens offers the perfect retreat where you can savor your lunch and reflect on life's finest moments under the watchful gaze of towering peaks.

GETTING THERE

From I-90 near Cle Elum: Take exit 85 and head north. In 0.3 mile, turn right at a T intersection and merge onto State Route 970. At 6.9 miles, turn left onto Teanaway Road, which eventually turns to North Fork Teanaway Road. At 20 miles, the road meets a Y and turns to gravel. Bear right onto the signed FR 9737. Stay on this road, avoiding all other turns, until 23.8 miles and the signed junction for Beverly-Bean trailhead, then turn right. The road is bumpy with water berms and large rocks until it dead-ends at the trailhead at 25 miles.

ON THE TRAIL

From the parking area, the trail is obvious as the large wooden informational kiosk stands proudly. Free wilderness-use permits are available here if you intend to go to the ridgeline above Bean Creek basin or farther north beyond the wilderness boundary. The trailhead serves both the Beverly Turnpike Trail and Bean Creek Trail and is signed for both.

Shooting star flowers burst into bloom across Bean Basin, adding vibrant color to the alpine meadows.

Right from the parking area, cross Beverly Creek on a sturdy wooden bridge. The creek often attracts migratory songbirds, so keep your birding ears and eyes open.

Next, the trail follows a former road-turned-trail on a gentle grade until it reaches a signed junction with Bean Creek Trail No. 1391.1 in 0.5 mile, where we go right. The trail now narrows and climbs through a ravine to the soundtrack of Bean Creek babbling to the left. If you brought the pup, there are a couple of spots for him to dip down to the water for a drink.

At 0.8 mile, the trail crosses Bean Creek on makeshift logs or non-submerged rock tops, before continuing the climb on the other side. In early season or when flows are high after rains, this crossing might result in wet shoes. The ravine curves slightly to the left, passing groves of firs and pines as it climbs higher into the Bean basin. Chipmunks scurry around intermittent deadfall, and in springtime, the occasional balsamroot plant shows off yellow daisy-like faces. When water is high, the creek rips and roars through the canyon to the right.

At just shy of 2 miles, the trail crosses Bean Creek again with a log wobble and, immediately afterward, reaches a signed junction with a trail coming in from the right. The right-hand trail is the continuation of Bean Creek Trail 1391.1, though that direction isn't signed. It traipses off to Earl Peak and other connecting options, but a new signed trail, now called Bean Basin Trail No. 1391.2, continues straight. Keep 'er rollin'!

A rocky trail tread guides us higher into the hinterlands to 2.5 miles, where Bean basin welcomes us with a level grade and a large patch of packed soil known as the Bean Basin Backcountry Camp. This is a good turnaround spot for most, but some will decide to go farther.

EXTENDING YOUR HIKE

To hit the ridge, turn back the way you came, and in a few steps, locate an unmaintained, unsigned, but obvious trail that goes north through the meadow. It starts innocently enough but then begins a somewhat vertical grade, with loose rocks and soil up the basin's barren shoulders. You slip, you slide, you glide, and you ride as one foot attempts to make it in front of the other. In 0.6 mile and over 780 feet of climbing in that short distance (#sweaty-torso), you arrive at a ridgeline with big rewards. Argonaut, Sherpa, Colchuck, and other peaks shoot skyward in the distance, while the evergreens in the basin to the north dot the vast landscapes. Look for mountain goats—they love this area! Lots of rocky perches are available for sitting, eating, dreaming, and enjoying this piece of Cascade heaven. When you head back down . . . show that loose dirt who's boss, or at least entertain your friends with your unexpected dance moves.

106 Beverly Turnpike and Iron Peak

RATING/DIFFICULTY: ****/4
ROUNDTRIP: 10.2 miles
ELEV GAIN/HIGH POINT: 2860 feet/6490 feet
SEASON: June–Oct

Maps: Green Trails Maps Mount Stuart No. 209 and Alpine Lakes East Stuart Range No. 208SX; **Contact:** Okanogan-Wenatchee National Forest, Cle Elum Ranger District; **Notes:** Northwest Forest Pass or Interagency Pass required. Port-a-potties at trailhead occasionally. Dirt road to trailhead; AWD or higher clearance suggested but not required. Creek fords in early season may get feet wet. Open to leashed dogs, mountain bikes, stock; **GPS:** N 47 23.355, W 120 52.328

Beverly Turnpike Trail No. 1391 takes you to a pretty drainage with views of jagged cliffs where you feel quite small at the base of the lofty peaks. While this trail does eventually head up to the forested Turnpike Pass, I recommend summiting Iron Peak to the valley's south, where you'll experience views of the Stuart Range that will knock your socks off . . . shoes, laces, and all.

GETTING THERE

From I-90 near Cle Elum: Take exit 85 and head north. In 0.3 mile, turn right at a T intersection and merge onto State Route 970. At 6.9 miles, turn left onto Teanaway Road, which eventually turns to North Fork Teanaway Road. At 20 miles, the road meets a Y and turns to gravel. Bear right onto the signed Forest Road 9737. Stay on this road, avoiding all other turns, until 23.8 miles and the signed junction for Beverly-Bean trailhead, then turn right. The road is bumpy with water berms and large rocks until it dead-ends at the trailhead at 25 miles.

ON THE TRAIL

Wander across the parking area to find an informational kiosk and free wilderness-use permit station. You'll want to fill out the wilderness-use permit if you plan to follow the Beverly Turnpike Trail past Turnpike Pass down toward Ingalls Creek.

On the trail, cross a sturdy wooden pedestrian bridge over Beverly Creek, which is signed for both the Beverly Turnpike Trail and Bean Creek Trail, as both leave from this trailhead. The trail continues following a former road-turned-trail until at 0.5 mile,

Leaving Beverly Turnipike Trail and heading toward Iron Peak, the rugged splendor of the trail unfolds with every step.

it narrows, and Bean Creek Trail No. 1391.1 comes in from the right. Stay left here and rock- or log-hop your way across Bean Creek, just after the intersection.

The climbing gets steeper as you wander through the rather sparse forest of grand fir, Engelmann spruce, whitebark pine, western hemlock, and Douglas-fir. In summer, shrubs such as elderberry and mountain huckleberry grow happily in the sunlight as Beverly Creek babbles in the valley to the left.

At 1.5 miles, the trail takes on a more open feeling and offers glimpses of the walls of Judis and Marys Peaks. The orangeish pink gives the valley a warm feeling as the earth tones surround you and the ascent continues.

At nearly 3 miles, reach a flat area with a couple of lightly used tent spots. A keen eye will catch the signed junction for the Fourth Creek Trail coming in from the right. Because the sign is buried in the trees and the trail isn't one that's frequently used, you might walk right by it. Beverly Creek's headwaters dribble in this area, with usually enough flow to catch in a filter in early season.

After 3.7 miles, arrive at a signed intersection for Iron Peak Trail No. 1399 and the continuation of the Beverly Turnpike Trail. Turn left on Iron Peak Trail; the views and openness of the hillsides here are what we live for! There are several awe-inspiring spots where you can turn around—one just 0.3 mile past the junction, and another in 0.6 mile, where a saddle called Eldorado Pass has you standing between Iron Peak and Teanaway Peak. Those with a spring in their step will want to make a hard left at Eldorado Pass on the unsigned but wide-open and easy-to-find boot path leading to the top of Iron Peak 1.4 miles from the junction (5.1 miles from the trailhead). Peak baggers will want to look for the old mountaineer canister at the top that holds the summit register to add your name and the date. To see all this natural eye candy in one hike makes for a perfect mountain romp. Follow the path you took back, or roam if you want to.

EXTENDING YOUR HIKE

After visiting Iron Peak, you could return to the signed junction with the Beverly Turnpike Trail and follow it as it dashes upward to reach the forested Turnpike Pass in another 0.4 mile. From there, it drops down toward Ingalls Creek and even more opportunities to explore if you are a backpacker or runner.

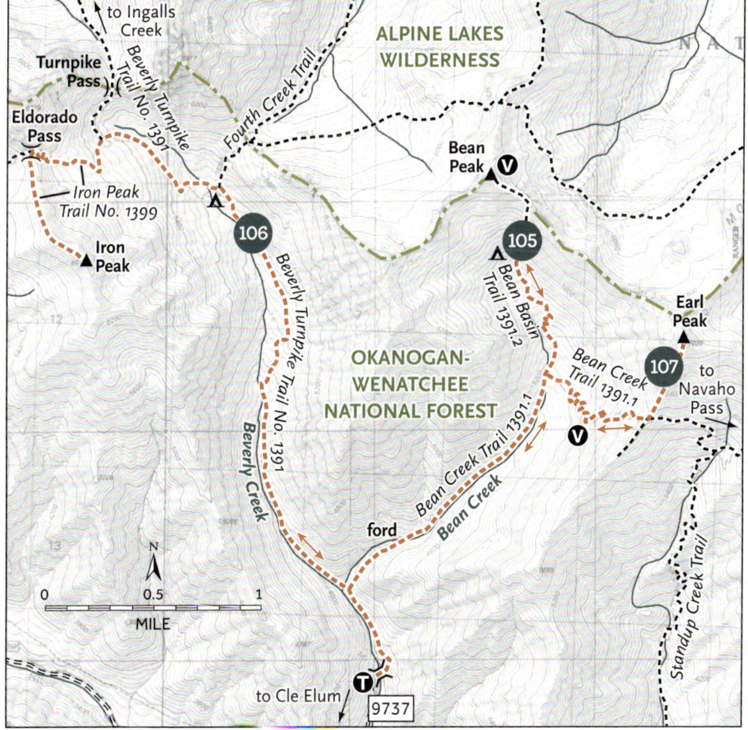

107 Earl Peak via Bean Creek Trail

RATING/DIFFICULTY: *****/5
ROUNDTRIP: 8 miles
ELEV GAIN/HIGH POINT: 3260 feet/7040 feet
SEASON: June–Oct

Map: Green Trails Maps Alpine Lakes East Stuart Range No. 208SX; **Contact:** Okanogan-Wenatchee National Forest, Cle Elum Ranger District; **Notes:** Northwest Forest Pass or Interagency Pass required. Port-a-potties at trailhead occasionally. Dirt road to trailhead; AWD or higher clearance suggested but not required. Creek fords in early season may get feet wet. While this trail may be open to equestrians, very few people will attempt riding to the summit, as it's steep and loose even on two feet. Open to leashed dogs, stock; see map, page 317; **GPS:** N 47 23.355, W 120 52.328

The trail to Earl Peak is a long, tough climb, with the final 0.6 mile throwing down a loose, rocky, steep tread, where at times you may even want to use your hands. This climb isn't for everyone, and the final push doesn't show up on all maps. Yet, it's an obvious path and the word has gotten out about the incredible panorama from the top. Your soul might get misty when you stand at the summit and see the mountain showcase of the Stuart Range sprawling out in front of you; it's one of Washington's best views.

GETTING THERE

From I-90 near Cle Elum: Take exit 85 and head north. In 0.3 mile, turn right at a T intersection and merge onto State Route 970. At 6.9 miles, turn left onto Teanaway Road, which eventually turns to North Fork Teanaway Road. At 20 miles, the road meets a Y and turns to gravel. Bear right onto the signed Forest Road 9737. Stay on this road, avoiding all other turns, until 23.8 miles and the signed junction for Beverly-Bean trailhead, then turn right. The road is bumpy with water berms and large rocks until it dead-ends at the trailhead at 25 miles.

ON THE TRAIL

Locate the trail across the parking area near a large, wooden informational kiosk. If you intend to venture farther north, beyond Earl Peak, you'll want to fill out a free wilderness-use permit located here. This route serves both the Beverly Turnpike and Bean Creek Trails and is signed for both.

Cross the wooden pedestrian bridge over Beverly Creek, and then head up the road-turned-trail for a gentle grade. In 0.5 mile, keep your eyes open to the right for a signed junction with Bean Creek Trail No. 1391.1 and follow it.

The trail narrows and enters a ravine, where the smaller Bean Creek trips and falls to the left. Some cutovers provide access if the pup is thirsty or if you need to load up on water. There isn't any for the last 1.6 miles of this climb, and it's exposed, so make sure you are well hydrated.

At 0.8 mile, the trail log-hops across Bean Creek and delivers you to the other side. As you continue your climb through sparse evergreens, the melodic white noise of the creek is heard to your right now. Keep your ears open for the haunting, hollow call of the red-breasted nuthatch, and watch for songbirds such as the song sparrow and Bewick's wren as they flit from tree to tree.

At nearly 2 miles, cross the narrow Bean Creek again with the help of a skinny log

After marinating in alpine delight, hikers depart the summit of Earl Peak.

and arrive at a signed junction on the other side. To the right is an unsigned trail, which is just a continuation of the trail we've been following (Bean Creek Trail No. 1391.1). A wooden sign points toward Bean Basin Trail No. 1391.2. You may want to visit Bean basin (Hike 105) if you have time and energy after summiting Earl, but for now you still have a big climb ahead, so maybe make that decision on the way back. Follow the unsigned trail to the right.

A seasonal dribble comes down from the top in springtime at 2.2 miles. In average seasons, this is the last chance to get water if you need it before the summit.

At 2.9 miles, as you huff and puff up switchbacks, take a couple of steps south off the switchback to a rocky overlook with a view of Mount Rainier on the horizon. It's a good place to catch your breath for a second if you need to.

Up you go as the trail switches back and forth to get you higher and higher, showcasing a few more peaks and giving you even better views as it climbs. Earl Peak is in view now, looking large and ominous each time you take your eyes off your feet. It goes quicker than you think, so don't feel intimidated; soon you'll be on top!

The way levels off as it reaches a ridge and arrives at an unsigned four-way junction at 3.2 miles. Straight ahead, a trail leads toward the Standup Creek Trail (Hike 103) and the Stafford Creek Trail (Hike 104), while the right branch is a primitive, boot-beaten path heading off to the other knolls. Our trail, to the top of Earl Peak, is an obvious-looking, loose-soiled game trail to the left. Follow it and soon find yourself doing some huffs and puffs mixed with the rest-step to catch your breath as you gain elevation. The views get better and better, making the anticipation build.

Pick your way up and over (and sometimes around) boulders and rocky stretches until the rocky ridge finally guides you to the summit, nearly 4 miles from where you started. Find a good butt rock and take a load off—you earned it. You'll have a hard time leaving this magical place with in-your-face views of Mount Stuart, Fortune Peak, Mount Daniels, Ingalls Peak, Solomon Mountain, Harding Mountain, and so many others. Linger to your heart's content, soaking in the peace of this place like a salve on your skin. When you turn back, be sure to do the nose-over-toes moves to prevent the toes-over-nose moves, which are never executed with grace.

108 Elbow Peak via Yellow Hill

RATING/DIFFICULTY: **/4
ROUNDTRIP: 11.5 miles
ELEV GAIN/HIGH POINT: 3410 feet/5710 feet
SEASON: July–Oct

Maps: Green Trails Maps Kachess Lake No. 208 and Mount Stuart No. 209; **Contact:** Okanogan-Wenatchee National Forest, Cle Elum Ranger District; **Notes:** No facilities at trailhead. Seasonal closure to motorized use prior to June 15, snow dependent. Water is scarce and trail is exposed—bring plenty. Open to leashed dogs, mountain bikes, motorcycles, stock; **GPS:** N 47 17.725, W 120 57.931

If you are looking for a hike without many people, spectacular mountain scenery, and a killer workout, this is the place. You might think, *THIS is the trailhead?* when you arrive at a big dirt patch with very little signage in the middle of the boonies, but stay with me. Eventually you'll get to a proper trail along a ridge, and it will offer you gorgeous views of the Stuart Range. The trail is shared with motorized traffic, but it's generally not much of an issue, as it's a technical pursuit, reserved for the most skilled riders. In my experience, there aren't many bikes, and those that I have met have been courteous.

GETTING THERE

From I-90 in Cle Elum: Take exit 85 and head north. In 0.3 mile, turn right at a T intersection and merge onto State Route 970. At 6.9 miles, turn left onto Teanaway Road, which eventually turns to North Fork Teanaway Road. At 14.2 miles, turn left on W. Fork Teanaway Road. Then turn right on Middle Fork Teanaway Road at 14.8 miles. Drive until 19.7 miles, passing an equestrian campground (the Indian Campground), crossing a bridge over the Middle Fork Teanaway River, and following the road as it turns sharply to the left. Turn right onto an unsigned side road at 20 miles (0.3 mile beyond the bridge). At 20.1 miles (0.1 from turning off onto the side road), find a large turnaround and area to park in a large dirt patch. Please be mindful of horse trailers or other users, and park with them in mind.

ON THE TRAIL

From the parking area, head north and follow the wide road-turned-trail with a sign on a tree showing the trail number 1222. This isn't a fancy trailhead with a kiosk and the like—more of what looks like a barrow pit. You'll get to what looks more like a conventional trail soon enough. For now, walk over large dirt berms intended to keep jeeps and other vehicles out, and in 0.1 mile, stay left when an old forest road heads right. Over the next 1.5 miles, you'll discover steep, loose side trails made by motorized traffic. Most of the shortcuts reconnect you to the former double-track road, so explore them if you wish, but the less steep option is to stick to the road. As you traipse higher along the road, the top half of Mount Rainier comes into view in the southern sky. Like so many of these warm, dry areas, a recent fire swept through here but surprisingly didn't kill every tree. You'll still see pops of pine here and there, along with Cascade mountain ash, fireweed, and multiple varieties of sedge.

At 2.2 miles, reach a ridgeline where you get a small reprieve from stout climbing, and the double track unofficially gives way to the single track. Due to the motorized and hoofed traffic, the trail is dusty and has loose rock, especially as it climbs up rather steep pitches. Pin your boot-throttle and motor your muscles forward—you got this!

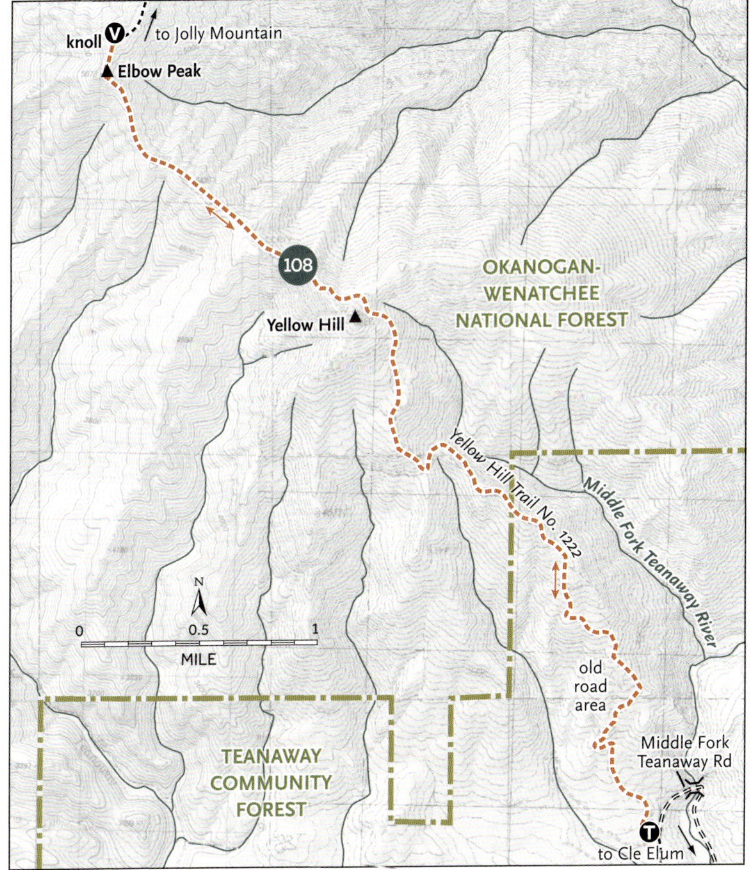

From Yellow Hill, visitors are treated to expansive views of Mount Stuart and the Stuart Range.

After 4 miles, the trail skirts around the base of Yellow Hill with its rocky summit pointing skyward. A primitive game trail hits the top, but if you stick with the trail, you'll get the same views. Mount Stuart, Teanaway Peak, Argonaut Peak, Colchuck Peak, and many others are now visible on the horizon to the northeast, and it only gets better when you get closer to Elbow Peak!

From here the ridge bobs and weaves up and down, most of the time rather barren, so views abound in all directions. Lake Cle Elum even comes to the pretty party. The trail can be a bit dicey as it climbs through scree, loose dirt, and talus, so watch your footing and marvel at the fact that some people do this on wheels!

At 5.7 miles, reach the shoulders of Elbow Peak. A treeless knoll just above the trail, with no official path, marks the actual summit. Wander up to it and marvel at the sweeping vista. From here, the Stuart Range is in-your-face spectacular, as are so many other distant peaks. The foreground holds the charred tree skeletons from the Jolly Mountain Fire, started by lightning in August 2017. The wind can whip up on this knoll and the insects can be obnoxious, but if your timing is right, the wind will gently blow them away and you can sit here and dream until it's time to return to the real world.

EXTENDING YOUR HIKE

You can continue along this ridge northbound for as long your feet hold the beat. Trail runners or those with fast toes may want to make their goal Jolly Mountain, which is another 8.2 miles, with 3240 extra feet of elevation gain roundtrip from this location.

109 Esmerelda Basin and Fortune Creek Pass

RATING/DIFFICULTY: ****/3
ROUNDTRIP: 7 miles
ELEV GAIN/HIGH POINT: 1750 feet/5970 feet
SEASON: June–Oct

Maps: Green Trails Maps Mount Stuart No. 209 and Alpine Lakes East Stuart Range No. 208SX; **Contact:** Okanogan-Wenatchee National Forest, Cle Elum Ranger District; **Notes:** Northwest Forest Pass or Interagency Pass required. Free wilderness-use permit available at the trailhead. Pit toilet at trailhead. Rough road to trailhead, but passenger cars will make it by going slowly. Parking is often full by 9 AM; get there early or later in the day, or hike on a weekday if possible. Obey all roadside parking signage, avoid blocking traffic, and have a plan B. Water can be scarce, so carry extra. Open to leashed dogs, mountain bikes, stock; see map, page 326; **GPS:** N 47 25.105, W 120 56.265

Compared to the more popular Lake Ingalls side, which is also accessed from this trailhead, Esmerelda basin is a less-traveled option. While it's not as scenic as its trailhead-mate, it offers the tranquility of a quiet basin, ascending to the wide-open, welcoming Fortune Creek Pass. From here, a side jaunt takes you to even better views and, with any luck, a bit of solitude from the crowds.

GETTING THERE

From I-90 in Cle Elum: Take exit 85 and head north. In 0.3 mile, turn right at a T intersection and merge onto State Route 970. At 6.9 miles, turn left onto Teanaway Road, which eventually turns to North Fork Teanaway Road. At 20 miles, the road meets a Y and turns to gravel. Bear right onto the signed Forest Road 9737. At 21.3 miles, stay left at a signed fork for the Beverly Campground. At 27.9 miles, bear right at another fork, this time signed Trail No. 1394. At 29.6 miles, find a large parking area and trailhead at the end of the road.

ON THE TRAIL

From the trailhead, follow Esmerelda Basin Trail No. 1394 along a defunct forest road, climbing beside the soundtrack of the North Fork Teanaway River. At 0.4 mile, pass a signed junction for Ingalls Way Trail No. 1390, and continue straight ahead, gaining elevation steadily.

The trail tapers to a smaller path as you continue climbing through the basin. Sturdy limbs of the pines: western white, lodgepole, and whitebark; along with the firs: Douglas, Pacific silver, and subalpine; and a smattering of other evergreens protect you from hot sun with their gracious shade. Marshy meadows in early summer give way to wildflowers like elephant's head, which holds a stock of multiple hot-pink flowers that each look just like a pachyderm with its ears flopped down and its long trunk reaching out to touch the air.

In 2 miles, the trail meets up with an unsigned game path to the left that can be a bit confusing if you aren't paying attention. This little spur trail peters out in 0.2 mile and doesn't offer much more than you'll already see as you climb higher. Instead, continue on the obvious main trail, switching back now to ascend a hill, where the trees become less dense and views open up to the unnamed ridgelines to the west. A couple of creeklets dribble across the trail and provide a good place for the pup to stop for a drink as you climb. Bright-red scarlet gilia—or skyrocket—thrives in the well-drained soil. Its

The welcoming Fortune Creek Pass area offers commanding vistas in a dramatic setting.

stalks hold multiple long, star-shaped flowers that attract hummingbirds.

After the switchbacks, at 3.1 miles, a signed junction with Lake Ann Trail No. 1226.2 turns to the right. Our trail continues traversing the more open-feeling, rockier hillside toward Fortune Creek Pass at 3.4 miles. The exposed pass takes on broad views of the basin and the craggy peaks in all directions, including Hawkins Mountain and Esmerelda Peaks and well as many other jagged spires. As a bonus, you may want to hang a left (south) on a well-used spur trail leading 0.2 mile more up to the top of a knoll where even better views abound and perhaps a little less wind. Enjoy your day, go back the way you arrived, or explore more!

EXTENDING YOUR HIKE

If you really want to test your fitness prowess, a big loop can be made by continuing west and dropping steeply down to reach the Fortune Creek Jeep Trail. Turn left (south) and follow the dusty, steep, rocky Jeep trail past Gallagher Head Lake to reach Boulder–De Roux Trail No. 1392 (Hike 115). From there, wind back left (southeast) until you reach the De Roux trailhead. At this point you can either follow FR 9737 north or take the extremely horsey and wet North Fork Teanaway Trail back to the Esmerelda trailhead. This loop, known unofficially as the Esmerelda Peaks Loop, will be a total of 12.5 miles with close to 3000 feet of elevation gain.

Another option for extending your hike is to visit the shallow but scenic Lake Ann. From Fortune Creek Pass, return 0.3 mile east to the junction with the signed Lake Ann Trail No. 1226.2 and head north. Climb up a rocky subalpine pass, then drop into the lake basin on the other side. The roundtrip distance from the trail junction is a bit under 2.3 miles with an extra 1030 feet of elevation gain. Mountain goats frequent this area, so keep dogs tightly on leash.

110 Lake Ingalls

RATING/DIFFICULTY: *****/3
ROUNDTRIP: 9 miles
ELEV GAIN/HIGH POINT: 2580 feet/6500 feet
SEASON: June–Oct

Maps: Green Trails Maps Mount Stuart No. 209 and Alpine Lakes East Stuart Range No. 208SX; **Contact:** Okanogan-Wenatchee National Forest, Cle Elum Ranger District; **Notes:** Northwest Forest Pass or Interagency Pass required. Free wilderness-use permit available at the trailhead. Pit toilet at trailhead. Rough road to trailhead, but passenger cars will make it by going slowly. Habituated mountain goats in area can be aggressive; give them space. Minor rock scrambling is necessary to get to the lake area, and navigation can be tricky—have a good map. Parking is often full by 9 AM; get there early or later in the day, or hike on a weekday if possible. Obey all roadside parking signage, avoid blocking traffic, and have a plan B. Water can be scarce, so carry extra. Open to hikers only. Dogs are not permitted past the Alpine Lakes Wilderness Boundary at Ingalls Pass; **GPS:** N 47 25.105, W 120 56.265

Lake Ingalls is one of the more popular destinations in the state, and once you visit, you'll know why. Between the incredible close-up views of Mount Stuart, the trickling waterways through green meadows, a peaceful azure lake, and the herds of mountain goats, you'll think you dropped into a Disney movie. You'll work for those moments, but the reward is well worth the grind.

GETTING THERE

From I-90 in Cle Elum: Take exit 85 and head north. In 0.3 mile, turn right at a T intersection

Near Ingalls Pass, Mount Stuart hides behind late season larch trees while mountain goats graze in the meadows.

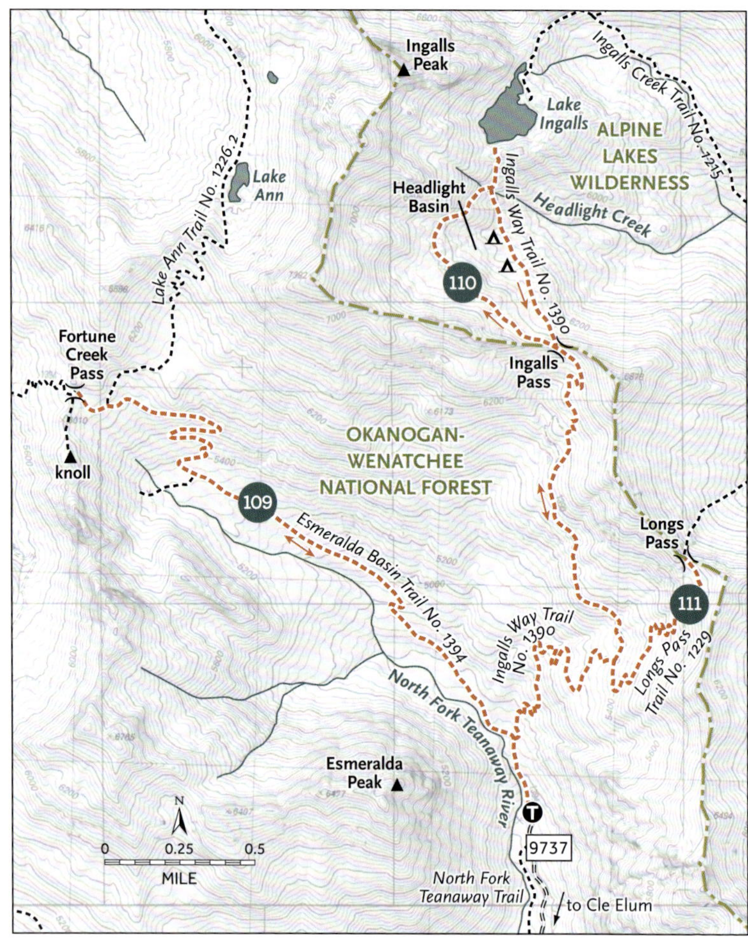

and merge onto State Route 970. At 6.9 miles, turn left onto Teanaway Road, which eventually turns to North Fork Teanaway Road. At 20 miles, the road meets a Y and turns to gravel. Bear right onto the signed Forest Road 9737. At 21.3 miles, stay left at a signed fork for the Beverly Campground. At 27.9 miles, bear right at another fork, this time signed Trail No. 1394. At 29.6 miles, find a large parking area and trailhead at the end of the road.

ON THE TRAIL

The path gets rolling on Esmerelda Basin Trail No. 1394, which cruises up a road-turned-trail alongside the churning North Fork Teanaway River. At 0.4 mile, look to the right for a signed junction for Ingalls Way Trail No. 1390 and follow it as it heads up pleasantly graded switchbacks under pines, firs, and hemlocks. Because you are officially on the drier eastern side of the Cascade Crest, the area lacks the dense understory of the wet western side, and as you climb higher, the trees become sparser and views open up to Esmerelda Peaks to the west and Fortune Peak to the north.

At 1.7 miles, arrive at a signed junction for Longs Pass (Hike 111) heading off to the right and going up to spectacular views. Check it out if time allows, or hit it on the way back when you can better gauge your energy. Bear left and continue climbing on the trail built into the side of shale and sandy mountain, lightly sprinkled with earth-grabbing, erosion-preventing ground cover. As you continue onward and upward, the path leads through rocky outcroppings, groves of evergreens, and seasonal runoff until you crest the top of the climb, known as Ingalls Pass at 3.4 miles. If you are visiting in fall, you are now looking at a sea of subalpine larch trees below you in Headlight Basin. Mount Stuart is front and center, and you probably won't get too far without digging out your camera for some pictures—it's drop-dead gorgeous. This is why we hike!

There are two trails to the lake, an upper and a lower. I suggest following the upper trail, then returning on the lower trail, making a loop so you can see different scenery. Turn left (west) on the other side of the pass and weave your way through small talus fields, tarns, and dribbling creeks under picturesque larch trees. With so much use, you'd think these trails would be straightforward, but you'll need to be paying attention in some places, as the path through the rocks blends well and isn't always obvious. Often cairns mark the way, so look around and retrace your steps if you get off track.

At 4.3 miles (0.9 from the pass), reach a signed junction with the lower trail trotting off to the right, which will be our return path. At this point, both trails join into one and head north/northeast, picking their way through a series of boulders to arrive at the southern shoreline of Lake Ingalls at 4.5 miles from the trailhead.

Ingalls Peak, popular with rock climbers, shows off its stony face to the lake's west. Technically, you can walk through the large boulders all the way around the lake, but it takes fancy footwork, so most folks will be content busting out snacks on a suitable rock on the western side, where Mount Stuart takes over the skyline and Lake Ingalls dances on the horizon.

Retrace your steps to return the way you arrived, only this time, follow the lower trail through Headlight Basin, which is tucked deeper into the valley. Scenery and camping options abound!

111 Longs Pass

RATING/DIFFICULTY: ****/4
ROUNDTRIP: 5.8 miles
ELEV GAIN/HIGH POINT: 1970 feet/6230 feet
SEASON: June–Oct

Maps: Green Trails Maps Mount Stuart No. 209 and Alpine Lakes East Stuart Range No. 208SX; **Contact:** Okanogan-Wenatchee National Forest, Cle Elum Ranger District; **Notes:** Northwest Forest Pass or Interagency Pass required. Free wilderness-use permit available at the trailhead. Pit toilet at trailhead. Rough road to trailhead, but passenger

Longs Pass trades crowds for quiet and a front-row seat to Mount Stuart's granite face.

cars will make it by going slowly. Habituated mountain goats in area can be aggressive; give them space. Parking is often full by 9 AM; get there early or later in the day, or hike on a weekday if possible. Obey all roadside parking signage, avoid blocking traffic, and have a plan B. Water can be scarce, so carry extra. Open to hikers only. Dogs are not permitted past the Alpine Lakes Wilderness boundary at Longs Pass; **GPS:** N 47 25.105, W 120 56.265

There are only a handful of places where you can observe a sweeping panorama of Mount Stuart, the second highest nonvolcanic peak in the state—this is one of them. From the top of Longs Pass, pull up your sit pad and marinate in the euphoria that seizes you when awe-inspiring scenery and endorphins hold hands.

GETTING THERE

From I-90 in Cle Elum: Take exit 85 and head north. In 0.3 mile, turn right at a T intersection and merge onto State Route 970. At 6.9 miles, turn left onto Teanaway Road, which eventually turns to North Fork Teanaway Road. At 20 miles, the road meets a Y and turns to gravel. Bear right onto the signed Forest Road 9737. At 21.3 miles, stay left at a signed fork for the Beverly Campground.

At 27.9 miles, bear right at another fork, this time signed Trail No. 1394. At 29.6 miles, find a large parking area and trailhead at the end of the road.

ON THE TRAIL

From the trailhead, follow Esmerelda Basin Trail No. 1394 for 0.4 mile to a signed junction with Ingalls Way Trail No. 1390, which eventually leads to Lake Ingalls (Hike 110). Turn right here and proceed up the pleasantly graded switchbacks under the canopy of pines, firs, and hemlocks. As you get higher, views open to Esmeralda Peaks to the west and Fortune Peak to the north. The understory in this dry, sandy soil can have some colorful wildflowers tucked into the grasses, such as lupine, skyrocket, phlox, larkspur, and yarrow, to name a few.

The pines give way to more exposed hillside, and at 1.7 miles, arrive at a signed junction for Longs Pass. Because of the openness of the area, the trail is visible as it switchbacks up the hillside and might cause you to groan—that puppy looks steep! Turn right and follow Longs Pass Trail No. 1229 as it climbs back and forth aggressively through the sandy, rocky soil. You might notice what used to be an old mining road built back in the 1930s as you head up the path. The road has long since been taken over by nature, but is still slightly visible in places.

Reach the top of the climb, Longs Pass, at 2.9 miles. This view was worth it! Mount Stuart's southern exposure with its many columns and couloirs takes up the skyline like it owns the place, because, well, it does. Rising 5000 feet and stretching out over 2 horizontal miles, the mountain is a fortress of strength and power—and you worked hard for these views! Pickle yourself in the expansive perspective before heading back.

EXTENDING YOUR HIKE

From Longs Pass, you can keep going, but the trail is somewhat hard to locate and slightly sketchy. From the top, head left for about 100 feet, until the trail drops down the loose, crumbling, exposed slope toward the basin below. In just over 1 mile, it meets up with Ingalls Creek Trail No. 1215, and you can follow that in either direction. Folks who can find their way out of a paper bag and don't mind some unmarked intersections, routefinding, and straightforward scrambling can even make a loop leading back up to Lake Ingalls: At the Ingalls Creek Trail, turn left and continue your challenging voyage to the northwest, then back south toward the lake. From there, connect with Ingalls Way Trail south and back to your car. If you are successful and don't end up with bonus miles, the full loop, including Longs Pass, costs you approximately 11.5 miles with 3650 feet elevation gain. Be sure you have a good map, and be prepared to turn back if you start feeling like you've stepped out of your comfort zone.

112 Miller Peak

RATING/DIFFICULTY: ****/5
ROUNDTRIP: 8.9 miles
ELEV GAIN/HIGH POINT: 3110 feet/6370 feet
SEASON: June–Oct

Map: Green Trails Maps Alpine Lakes East Stuart Range No. 208SX; **Contact:** Okanogan-Wenatchee National Forest, Cle Elum Ranger District; **Notes:** Northwest Forest Pass or Interagency Pass required. Pit toilet at trailhead. Blowdowns common in early season; exposed, warm trail in summer months. Dirt road to trailhead is rough; AWD or high clearance suggested but not required. Creek fords in early season may get feet wet;

bring water shoes or prepare to wade. Seasonal closure to motorized use Oct. 15–June 15, snow dependent. Watch for ticks. Open to leashed dogs, motorcycles, mountain bikes, stock; **GPS:** N 47 22.123, W 120 47.078

Don't let the shared-use aspect of this trail discourage you from hiking it. We often have the dirt bike folks to thank for clearing the blowdowns and fixing washouts along this trail. That said, expect a few bikes here and there. Also expect some crazy-good, front-and-center views of Mount Stuart, Navaho Peak, Earl Peak, and so many others. What's more, mountain goats love this area and are often seen wandering around near the summit.

GETTING THERE

From I-90 in Cle Elum: Take exit 85 and head north. In 0.3 mile, turn right at a T intersection and merge onto State Route 970. At 6.9 miles, turn left onto Teanaway Road, which eventually turns to North Fork Teanaway Road. At 20 miles, the road meets a Y and turns to gravel. Bear right onto the signed Forest Road 9737. At 21.4 miles, turn right onto signed FR 9703, which is also signed for Trail No. 1351. Pass the Stafford Creek Trail (see Hike 104) and continue to the road's end at 24.9 miles. Find the Miller Peak and Iron Bear trailhead, along with a pit toilet and picnic area in the dead end's roundabout. Park along the sides of the road, using care not to block access.

ON THE TRAIL

There are two trails at this trailhead—Miller Peak Trail No. 1379 and Iron Bear Trail No. 1351. If you are a strong hiker with ample time, or a trail runner, you could make a big loop of about 17 miles and utilize them both, with County Line Trail No. 1226 and Teanaway Ridge Trail No. 1364 as hand-holders. Otherwise, the out-and-back to Miller Peak

Clouds drift low, but Miller Peak still delivers jagged skylines and alpine summit serenity.

provides a fantastic workout with plenty of eye candy and soul food.

Start off by heading out on the well-signed Miller Peak Trail, listening to the white noise of nearby Miller Creek. In late spring and early summer, the mosquitos here will have you trotting through this section doing the hand jive as you attempt to get a reprieve. A few pockets of dark standing water in the area are mostly to blame, along with the slower-moving sections of Miller Creek. Walk faster or hose those little jokers down with some insect goo. Rest assured, they get less and less prolific as you get higher. In the first 0.7 mile, the trail crosses the shallow creek two times, both resulting in wet shoes during most springs and early summers.

Three more shallow and easy water crossings arrive as you carry on, some rock-hops or teeter-totters on logs, and some soaking sloshes. Springtime trillium displays here are some of the most beautiful in the area and, if you are like me, you'll want to pull out the camera again and again. How many pictures of trillium does one need? Huckleberries are scattered around the area too, making this a good place for bears to nibble in the late summer.

At 1.6 miles, the trail kicks into high gear, and the climbing—at times steep—makes you grateful for this gorgeous outdoor gym. Up you go, puffing and sweating, crossing the final waterway at nearly 1.8 miles.

The views expand as you get higher and higher, and during autumn, the larch trees showcase their golden needles and the area is quite a vision! Distant rugged peaks start to show up, as do adjacent hillsides dotted with pines and firs until at 3.1 miles, you reach a ridge, where the trail bears left. A social trail leads to an overlook straight ahead, and it's a good place to catch your breath before carrying on.

The path keeps you below the spine of the ridge but does a fine job of showcasing gorgeous peaks and valleys, all views you'll see from the top of Miller Peak. This is your appetizer for the main course! If you hit the timing right—in most years early to mid-June—the balsamroot and lupine explode around these parts, and the flower show is an eye-popping extravaganza.

At nearly 3.8 miles, the trail comes to an unsigned three-way junction, with the trail you came in on being one branch. The descending trail straight ahead is County Line Trail, while the Miller Peak Trail, leading us to our destination, bears left here and continues climbing.

Continue on the Miller Peak Trail as it switchbacks uphill until it reaches a gruelingly steep rise that places you closer to the rocky summit. Bob and weave through the rocky areas at the top until you find yourself standing on the uppermost reaches. The trail continues past the high point on the ridge to a sparsely treed prominence at the far northeastern side, perfect for a meal break. Views of Ingalls Peak, Fortune Peak, Navaho Peak, Mount Stuart, Argonaut Peak, Earl Peak, and others make you want to plant a flag and call this home.

If the dirt bikers come up while you are here, you might get an unexpected treat. The mountain goats that hang out near Miller Peak are drawn to the *brap, brap, brap* of the engine and often show up because they crave the salts found in urine. Gross, right? Bikes mean people, people mean urine, urine means salt, salt mean goats.

When you have enjoyed all there is to see, head back the way you came, your life sufficiently enriched from your adventure.

EXTENDING YOUR HIKE

If you are interested in doing the big loop, return to the junction with County Line Trail

No. 1226 when you come back down from Miller Peak and there, turn east to follow the County Line Trail. Then, in 4 miles, follow the Teanaway Ridge Trail for another 1.7 miles until it reaches the Iron Bear Trail, which guides you back to the trailhead. From the Miller Peak trailhead, this loop is just shy of 14 miles and 4000 feet of elevation gain. A good map is definitely your friend here!

113 Iron Bear and Teanaway Ridge

RATING/DIFFICULTY: ****/3
ROUNDTRIP: 6.5 miles
ELEV GAIN/HIGH POINT: 1930 feet/5520 feet
SEASON: mid June–Oct

Maps: Green Trails Maps Alpine Lakes East No. 208SX, Mount Stuart No. 209, and Liberty No. 210; **Contact:** Okanogan-Wenatchee National Forest, Cle Elum Ranger District; **Notes:** No facilities at trailhead. Rough road to trailhead; high clearance vehicles recommended. Seasonal closure to motorized use Oct. 15–June 15, snow dependent. There are two approaches to this hike's destination, one as described with driving directions on Hike 112, and the shorter, more direct approach as described here. Watch for ticks. Open to leashed dogs, mountain bikes, motorcycles, stock; **GPS:** N 47 21.349, W 120 43.053

This hike on the drier side of the Cascade Crest embraces open slopes with sweeping views of Miller and Navaho Peaks as well

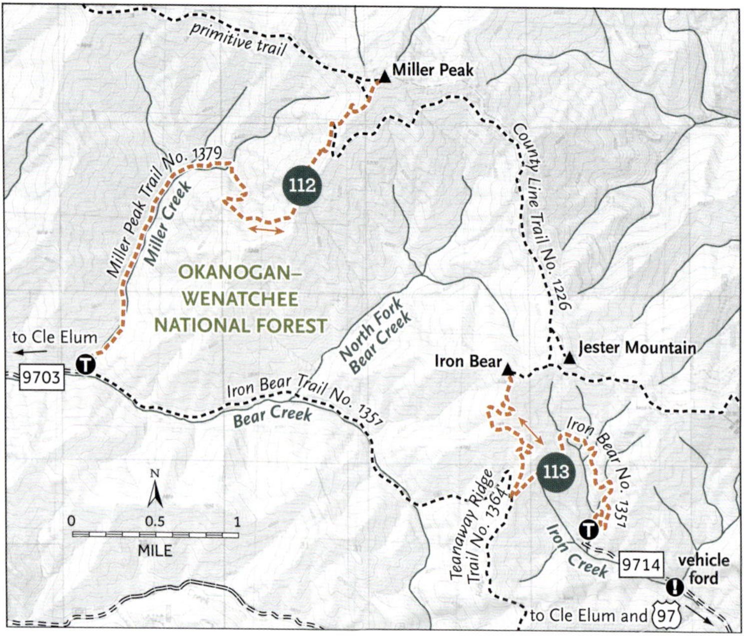

as the tippy top of Mount Stuart. Visit in the summer to see balsamroot and other sun-loving wildflowers or in the fall for an abundant sprinkling of western larch trees.

GETTING THERE

From I-90 in Cle Elum: Take exit 85 and head north. In 0.3 mile, turn right at a T intersection and merge onto State Route 970. Eventually SR 970 becomes US Highway 97. Keep your eyes open for mile marker 158, and shortly after it—18.7 miles from merging onto SR 970—turn left (north) onto Forest Road 9714, signed for Iron Bear Trail No. 1351. Follow the dirt road, which has a few ruts and bumps, until 21.7 miles to find several makeshift parking areas and one designated parking lot near the trailhead. A car ford of Iron Creek is necessary just prior to the trailhead, so if you are worried about your passenger car scraping the creek bed, park just before it, then rock-hop and walk a short distance up the roadway. A tree sign here points cars (or feet if you didn't drive the ford) to the signed trailhead.

ON THE TRAIL

Just after starting the trail, jump across a branch of Iron Creek, then begin a climb through firs and pines that wakes up the quads and gets the heart pumping. After 1 mile, hop across another branch of Iron Creek as the trail traverses its way into more open, airy hillsides. This creek is often dry by summer, so bring extra water for the pup if you plan to hike in the warmer months.

The trail wanders west up a rock-filled slope with views of neighboring hillsides, some lit up with autumn larches. At 1.6 miles, reach the top of the ridge and a signed four-way intersection. The Iron Bear Trail

A row of gilded larches creates a natural border under the open slopes near Iron Bear's summit.

continues straight ahead, and to the right and left is Teanaway Ridge Trail No. 1364. Turn right (north) and begin your climb up the ridge.

The Teanaway ridgeline gets you higher, and Mount Adams and Mount Rainier begin to show off their summits to the southwest. Arrowleaf balsamroots, with their huge yellow daisy-like flowers, display their happy faces in the sunny aspects. The views are so picturesque in a few spots, you'll have a hard time keeping your camera in your pocket. Concrete erosion-prevention blocks give the trail a durable surface in places like switchbacks or step-ups where the trail risks eroding with motorized traffic.

In just over 3 miles, the trail breaks out into rocky outcroppings with peekaboo views of Miller and Navaho Peaks as well as the summit of Mount Stuart, the second highest nonvolcanic peak in the state. At 3.2 miles, reach an unsigned trail junction to the left. This well-traveled short spur leads you to the rocky summit of Iron Bear, our destination. The top is swoon-worthy with sweeping views and plenty of places to stop, plop, and nosh. For most, this makes a perfect day, with mountain vistas in your eyes and endorphins flowing from your brain.

EXTENDING YOUR HIKE

If you haven't had enough hiking, you could follow the Teanaway Ridge Trail past Iron Bear to County Line Trail No. 1226 and take an off-trail romp to the top of the wide-open, trailless Jester Mountain. Doing this will add 1.3 roundtrip miles and 520 feet of elevation gain to your day.

You could even make a big old loop using County Line Trail, Miller Peak Trail, and Iron Bear Trail, which, from the trailhead described here, totals 16.7 miles and 5000 feet of elevation gain, including a side trip to Miller Peak. From the Miller Peak trailhead (see Hike 112), it is just shy of 14 miles and slightly over 4000 feet.

114 Red Top Lookout

RATING/DIFFICULTY: ****/2
ROUNDTRIP: 1.3 miles
ELEV GAIN/HIGH POINT: 350 feet/5360 feet
SEASON: mid-June–Oct

Maps: Green Trails Maps Liberty No. 210 and Mount Stuart No. 209; **Contact:** Okanogan-Wenatchee National Forest, Cle Elum Ranger District; **Notes:** Pit toilets at trailhead. Rough road to trailhead in places; high-clearance vehicles recommended. Open to leashed dogs; **GPS:** N 47 17.960, W 120 45.672

While short, this trail is a steep little bugger. Once you get to the top, you are treated to a fire lookout that is still in use, as well as outstanding views of Mount Stuart, Earl Peak, Marys Peak, Ingalls, and others.

A quick climb with huge rewards leads to panoramic views from Red Mountain's historic lookout tower.

GETTING THERE

From I-90 in Cle Elum: Take exit 85 and head north. In 0.3 mile, turn right at a T intersection and merge onto State Route 970. Follow SR 970 for 16.7 miles (it becomes US Highway 97), and once you pass the Mineral Spring Campground, keep your eyes to the left for Forest Road 9738. Turn left and follow until 18.9 miles, then turn left onto FR 9702, signed with a pair of binoculars and an arrow toward Red Top Mountain. This road is much rougher than the previous road, so watch for those water berms and rocks. At 23.1 miles, turn right at an intersection signed for Red Top Lookout parking area, and at 23.5 miles, find the pit toilet to the road's left and parking to the right. The trailhead is located at the end of the road, and more spots are located farther along the road, so take your pick.

ON THE TRAIL

Follow the road to its turnaround and continue walking north until the wide path turns narrow and reaches a large trail sign, the official trailhead. Here, a Y junction with Teanaway Ridge Trail No. 1364 goes right, and our trail, Red Top Trail No. 1364.1, goes left. For a change of scenery, we'll take the Teanaway Ridge Trail back down and end up here again, making a loop.

For now, start your grind left up the steep slope. One foot in front of the other has the lookout tower in view until it's right in your face, along with an A-frame outhouse. A few more grueling, sweat-soaked steps gets you to the classic L-4 tower, which is still used for fire spotting, just 0.3 mile from the trailhead. Unless a volunteer is there, generally on weekends, the cabin is usually locked and access from the stairs isn't permitted onto the balcony. Even from the base, views are outstanding, and you'll be happy with gazing

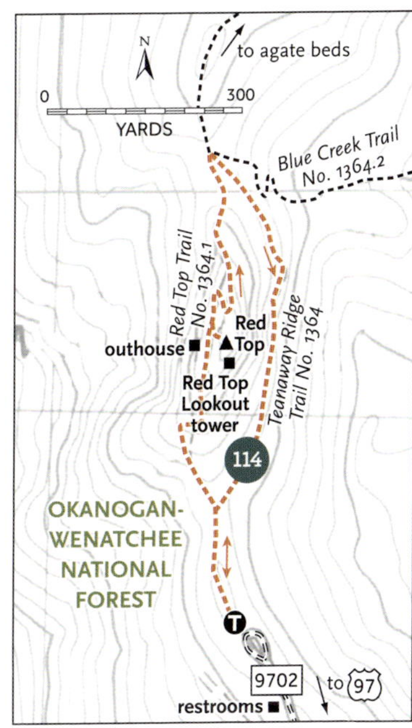

off into the Stuart Range to the many peaks spread out in front of you. Built in 1957, the current lookout replaced the cupola cabin that had been here since 1928.

A rocky prominence to the tower's north is a good place to perch for your snack or to grab a few more pictures. When it's time to head back down, locate the trail to the lookout's north, near the rocky prominence, heading downhill on a narrow tread. This looks fairly sketchy from the top, and it does have exposure, but it's slightly wider than it looks when you get on it. The trail switches back and keeps you on the ridgeline before dropping down to reach a signed trail junction at 0.7 mile. To the left and right is Teanaway Ridge Trail No. 1364, while straight ahead is Blue Creek Trail No. 1364.2. Our trail goes right on the Teanaway Ridge Trail to complete the loop.

When you've reached the large sign again, near where you started, you've completed your mission. Follow the path back toward your waiting vehicle, and buckle up for the rough forest road on the way back down.

EXTENDING YOUR HIKE

If you are curious about the agate beds, where rockhounders dig for volcanic and metamorphic stones, you can turn left on the Teanaway Ridge Trail at the junction 0.7 mile north of the lookout. In roughly 0.5 to 1 mile, you'll find the obvious dig spots. Rock hunters use the tumbled and polished stones for a variety of arts and crafts including rings, earrings, pendants, and tabletop decorations. From here, retrace your steps to the junction with the Red Top Trail and the Blue Creek Trail, but this time stay on Teanaway Ridge Trail No. 1364 to return to your car.

115 Boulder–De Roux Trail

RATING/DIFFICULTY: **/3
ROUNDTRIP: 9 miles
ELEV GAIN/HIGH POINT: 1920 feet/5600 feet
SEASON: July–Oct

Maps: Green Trails Maps Mount Stuart No. 209 and Alpine Lakes East Stuart Range No. 208SX; **Contact:** Okanogan-Wenatchee National Forest, Cle Elum Ranger District; **Notes:** Northwest Forest Pass or Interagency Pass required. Pit toilet and picnic areas at trailhead. Rough road to trailhead, but passenger cars will make it by going slowly. Open to leashed dogs, mountain bikes, motorcycles, stock; **GPS:** N 47 25.151, W 120 56.349

If you crossed this hike off your list simply because it was open to motorized traffic, you'd be missing out on something special. The first part of the trail is dusty, loose, and exactly what you'd expect from pedals, hooves, and wheels, but as you get farther along, the upper De Roux Creek basin and Gallagher Head Lake itself are quite nice and often bursting with wildflowers.

GETTING THERE

From I-90 in Cle Elum: Take exit 85 and head north. In 0.3 mile, turn right at a T intersection and merge onto State Route 970. At 6.9 miles, turn left onto Teanaway Road, which eventually turns to North Fork Teanaway Road. At 20 miles, the road meets a Y and turns to gravel. Bear right onto the signed Forest Road 9737. Stay on this road, avoiding all side roads and at 28.1 miles, after passing Camp Wahoo Outfitter, turn left on a spur road, FR 120, signed for Trail No. 1392. Arrive at the De Roux Campground (horse camp) and find parking roadside at 28.4 miles. The trailhead for Boulder–De Roux Trail No. 1392 is well-signed to the campground's northwest.

ON THE TRAIL

From the trailhead, follow the pathway for 0.2 mile to a sturdy wooden bridge crossing the North Fork Teanaway River, a tranquil, narrow waterway not far from its headwaters. From here, the trail ascends on loose, rocky soil past thick foliage of thimbleberry, huckleberry, grasses, and bracken fern until at 1 mile, it crosses De Roux Creek on a wooden pedestrian bridge. A horse ford is signed near the crossing. This area is not well shaded and can be downright hot on a sunny summer day, so if you brought the pup, this is a good place for him to get a drink and for you to splash your face.

Just after the creek crossing, at 1.2 miles, reach a signed junction with De Roux Spur Trail No. 1392.1 to the left. This trail cruises up toward Koppen Mountain (Hike 116) and is a great place to visit on a different day, or all in one big day if you are tough as a two-day old pizza crust. Our signed trail goes straight ahead.

The birding in this area can be incredible, especially in early summer when migratory birds and their resident friends are hanging out near the creek. Where there is water, there is life! Look for western tanagers, yellow-rumped warblers, evening grosbeaks, mountain chickadees, pine siskins, and many others. Sometimes you must follow their songs to find their perch.

The trail is braided in a couple of spots where the narrowness of the main trail's drop-off edge makes it hazardous for motorcycles. The braids offer a different option for wheels, and thus for feet, so choose your adventure—they reconnect on the same path.

At 2.7 miles, cascading water descending from De Roux Creek is visible through the trees down the slope to the right. Shortly after that, the trail crosses through a gorgeous sedge and wildflower meadow at the base of some barren, rocky ridgelines. Aster, paintbrush, columbine, lupine, bistort, Sitka valerian, elephant's head, and other wildflowers grow happily here while pollinators, such as bumblebees and fritillary butterflies, flicker through the blossoms. You are now in the upper De Roux Creek basin, and it just gets better from here. More meadows and a couple of campsites pop up, as do a smattering of talus fields where pikas—members of the rabbit family—squeak like rubber duckies.

Gallagher Head Lake is a rewarding destination along the multiuse Boulder–De Roux Trail.

Just shy of 4.3 miles, a signed trail junction for Gallagher Head Lake shows up to the right. Turn right and, in a short distance, find yourself in a jeep turnaround with picnic tables and metal fire pits at the southern shore of the shallow Gallagher Head Lake. If you have this place to yourself, you must have done something good in your life recently and the cosmos is paying you back. Often, there are Jeeps or motorcycles sharing the fun. The lake's northwestern shore goes along the Fortune Creek Jeep Trail, and this area is quite popular with folks who test their 4x4s on this exceedingly steep, rutted road, though you wouldn't know it up here. This section of road looks tame, right? You can always make friends and see what might be in their coolers. If the insects aren't too thick, sit for a minute and take it in. Esmeralda Peak stands proudly to the east, with forested slopes below stony outcroppings near its summit. The water laps gently against grassy banks, some containing shooting star or mountain heather. Nature carries on in this peaceful valley, unaware of its frequent visitors. Head back when peace and endorphins merge, or extend your hike.

EXTENDING YOUR HIKE

If you still have energy, vigor, and motivation, you can make a loop, though you'll need to use the Jeep road to complete the task. This sucker was not made for feet! Use care not to twist an ankle or go heinie over teakettle on

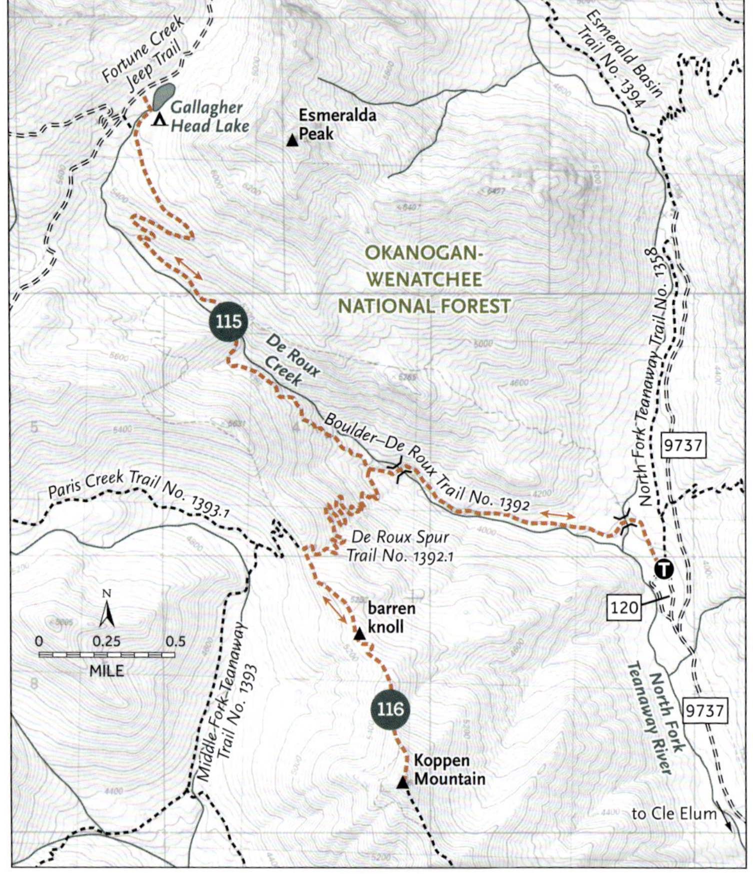

the loose boulders or, just as bad, get sprayed by rocky shrapnel from Jeep tires. To make the loop, follow the Fortune Creek Jeep Trail to the north (on the lake's western side) as it descends for 1.2 crazy, vertical miles to reach a signed junction with Esmeralda Basin Trail No. 1394 to the right. Take this up and over Fortune Creek Pass and back down to where it meets FR 9737. From the trail's terminus with the road, you can either follow FR 9737 to the spur road or take the extremely horsey and wet North Fork Teanaway Trail back to the Boulder–De Roux trailhead. The complete loop will be about 12.5 miles and 3000 feet of elevation gain. This might also be a good time to point out that this whole loop is open to mountain bikes too, should you feel the need for speed and a workout that might blow out your vascular system.

116 Koppen Mountain

RATING/DIFFICULTY: ***/4
ROUNDTRIP: 7.7 miles
ELEV GAIN/HIGH POINT: 2290 feet/6031 feet
SEASON: July–Oct

Maps: Green Trails Maps Mount Stuart No. 209 and Alpine Lakes East Stuart Range No. 208SX; **Contact:** Okanogan-Wenatchee National Forest, Cle Elum Ranger District; **Notes:** Northwest Forest Pass or Interagency Pass required. Pit toilet and picnic areas at trailhead. Rough road to trailhead, but passenger cars will make it by going slowly. Open to leashed dogs, mountain bikes, motorcycles, stock; **GPS:** N 47 25.151, W 120 56.349

You might look at the elevation gain and think it's not too bad, but the end of this hike shoots skyward like a rocket. If you are mentally prepared for the grind, you'll be open to the soaked shirt that earns you the vista at the top, where Mount Stuart and all his friends are bold and showy. What's more, you'll probably have the whole mountain—and its grand view—to yourself.

GETTING THERE

From I-90 in Cle Elum: Take exit 85 and head north. In 0.3 mile, turn right at a T intersection and merge onto State Route 970. At 6.9 miles, turn left onto Teanaway Road, which eventually turns into North Fork Teanaway Road. At 20 miles, the road meets a Y and turns to gravel. Bear right onto the signed Forest Road 9737. Stay on this road, avoiding all side roads, and at 28.1 miles, after passing Camp Wahoo Outfitter, turn left on a side road, FR 120, signed for Trail No. 1392. Arrive at the De Roux Campground (horse camp) and find parking roadside at 28.4 miles. The trailhead for Boulder–De Roux Trail No. 1392 is well-signed to the campground's northwest.

ON THE TRAIL

Boulder–De Roux Trail No. 1392 kicks off with a relatively flat walk for 0.2 mile, where it crosses the North Fork Teanaway River on a sturdy wooden bridge. After that, it slowly starts to gain elevation on loose, rocky soil tossed around by hooves and wheels. Huckleberries provide delicious trailside snacks when they get enough light and heat, usually during mid- to late summer.

At 1 mile, cross De Roux Creek on another wooden pedestrian bridge. This area is somewhat exposed, and this is the last water you'll pass on this hike, so filter up or splash off if you need a moment of refreshment.

Shortly after the creek crossing, at 1.2 miles, reach a signed junction with De Roux

Once home to a 1933 fire spotting camp, Koppen Mountain offers top-of-the-world views—and you may even have it all to yourself.

Spur Trail No. 1392.1 (also signed "M. Fk. Teanaway") to the left. This is us! Turn left and begin a series of seventeen thank-goodness-for-these switchbacks to the top of the ridge. Enjoy the back and forth on a grade that make this climb feel not so grueling, because the top of the ridge has other plans. Mount Stuart shows up to the northeast as you climb, taking your brain off the pain and piquing your curiosity for what's ahead. At 2.5 miles, reach the ridge and stop for a breather if you need one. Otherwise, look to the left (southeast) and notice a curious, unsigned game trail. This is the path to Koppen's summit!

In 1933, Koppen Mountain was the site of a fire-spotting camp but was used only that one summer before it was torn down. In addition to the fire-spotting crews, the Civilian Conservation Corps came to this summit to produce photos requested by the forest service. These images, known as Osborne panoramas, were used to help pinpoint summits for future fire towers and to create useful fire-spotting locator maps. It's a marvel a fire tower was never located here, but they must have had their reasons.

This trail was made and worn in by eighteen- to twenty-year-old young men whose boots were in a hurry to get to the top and couldn't be bothered by the extra distance of switchbacks. Straight up you go! At least it's shaded for now. The climbing ebbs and flows in difficulty, occasionally reaching parts of the trail where your lungs feel a little happier about it all.

After 2.9 miles, the trail reaches a barren knoll before the final summit push. If you are whooped and want to call this your goal for the day, it's a good place to do so. The sweeping vistas are outstanding from this perch—almost as good as the top.

Those with summit fever will keep on pushing, up, up, and up, until reaching the rocky top of Koppen—what a place! South Ingalls Peak, Ingalls Peak, Colchuck Peak, Dragontail Peak, and of course, Mount Stuart are all boasting their burly summits. In the valley far below is the road you came in on (FR 9737). If the wind is still, stay vigilant for pesky horseflies—they like this summit, and sadly, many innocent hikers have donated flesh to their painful bites over the years. But if the bitty biters aren't out and you have luck on your side, savor this delightful landscape for a long time before going back.

117 Johnson Creek to Medra Pass

RATING/DIFFICULTY: ***/4
ROUNDTRIP: 8.2 miles
ELEV GAIN/HIGH POINT: 2230 feet/5420 feet
SEASON: July–Oct

Maps: Green Trails Maps Mount Stuart No. 209 and Alpine Lakes East Stuart Range No. 208SX; **Contact:** Okanogan-Wenatchee National Forest, Cle Elum Ranger District; **Notes:** Northwest Forest Pass or Interagency Pass required. A port-a-potty is often at parking area in summer months; otherwise, the Beverly Campground is close by with pit toilets. Open to leashed dogs, mountain bikes, motorcycles, stock; **GPS:** N 47 22.823, W 120 53.146

Even though this trail is shared with wheels, it's still a beautiful place to visit. The first part of the trail wanders through a riparian zone with a lot of huckleberries for nibbling in season. From there, it climbs to the rocky top of Medra Pass, where you'll have box seats to the top of Mount Stuart, along with other adjacent summits.

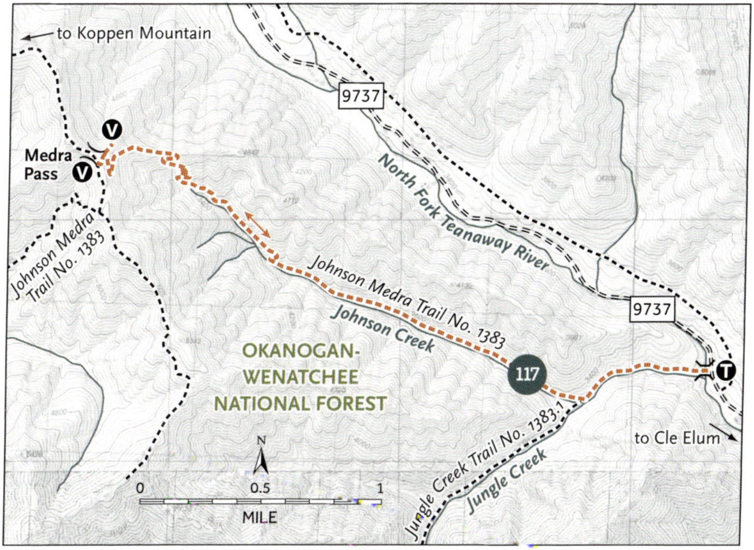

to Koppen Mountain
9737
Medra Pass
Johnson Medra Trail No. 1383
North Fork Teanaway River
Johnson Medra Trail No. 1383
Johnson Creek
9737
117
OKANOGAN-WENATCHEE NATIONAL FOREST
Jungle Creek Trail No. 1383.1
Jungle Creek
to Cle Elum
N
0 0.5 1
MILE

Where wind sculpts silence, Mount Stuart rises as a distant sentinel beyond Medra Pass.

GETTING THERE

From I-90 in Cle Elum: Take exit 85 and head north. In 0.3 mile, turn right at a T intersection and merge onto State Route 970. At 6.9 miles, turn left onto Teanaway Road, which eventually turns into North Fork Teanaway Road. At 20 miles, the road meets a Y and turns to gravel. Bear right onto the signed Forest Road 9737. At 21.3 miles, stay left at a signed fork for the Beverly Campground. Finally, at 25.6 miles, reach the trailhead on the left and the parking area in a wide dirt roundabout to the right.

ON THE TRAIL

Note: In 2024, the trail bridge was closed due to a failed stringer, and access to this hike was cut off. Check its status before you go.

From the parking area, cross the forest road and locate the well-signed Johnson Medra Trail No. 1383 to the west. In just 90 feet from the trailhead, cross a wooden bridge over the North Fork Teanaway River. Continuing west, the trail parallels Johnson Creek, which chatters and coos as it flows to the left. The thick brush makes water access tough, but a primitive cutover at 0.5 mile allows the dog to grab a drink. The trail's grade is gentle and provides a good place for kids to learn about flora and fauna in wet areas.

At 0.6 mile, the trail meets up with Jungle Creek Trail No. 1383.1, which heads left, at a signed junction. Bear right at the intersection and continue up the valley with a tributary to Johnson Creek, following the topographical depression. If you are here in summertime and trail maintenance hasn't been recently tackled, you might find yourself with a brushy bushwhack. Use your trekking poles to whack salmonberries, bracken fern, thimbleberries, and slide alders back to see your feet. The healthy wet climate of this valley makes a perfect place for these shrubs to grow, and they do so with lack of restraint, save for the trail users. If the kiddos are with you, this might be a good place to turn back, since the first part of the trail is much more enjoyable. Otherwise, give them a stick and let them join in the game of walloping the thickets. You might feel a little like a rabbit in a burrow ducking under the overgrown brush.

At just shy of 2 miles, a couple of easy creek crossings are necessary to get you to the end of the valley. A couple of switchbacks after the creek crossings take you higher and start to pull you out of the bushes. The climbing gets steeper, but you are grateful to get out of the dense foliage, so oddly, it's welcomed. Thanks to the various users, the soil and pebbles are loose and dusty, so take your time on what sometimes feels like one step forward equals one step back. When the scenery turns to rocky open slopes, you are officially getting into those high, dry Teanaway landscapes and making good progress.

At 3.5 miles, reach a ridgeline. Glimpses of Mount Stuart are showing up to the north, and you can see all the way out to the windfarms in the far distance to the east. Keeping your heart rate elevated, the trail gives you one last little grunt before delivering you to Medra Pass. Signed junctions point to the Koppen Mountain Trail to the right, as well as the continuation of the Johnson Medra Trail straight ahead and down the other side. You can wander to your heart's delight, but I prefer to follow a faint trail to the right to a series of plentiful rocky outcroppings perfect for parking. Hold little hands and be sure the dogs are leashed in this area, as some of the sit areas are drop-offs.

Feast your eyes on the summits! Fortune Peak, South Ingalls Peak, Ingalls Peak, Teanaway Peak, the tippy top of Dragontail Peak, Navaho and Earl Peaks, and, of course, Mount Stuart are all flaunting their beauty.

EXTENDING YOUR HIKE

If you have more energy to burn, you could follow the faint trail toward Koppen Mountain (Hike 116) by turning right at the signed intersection for Koppen Mountain at Medra Pass. Before doing so, keep in mind that this trail doesn't get much traffic and the pathway is faint and sketchy at times. Have a good map and be prepared for some fancy footwork in rocky areas when you get higher. Going up the ridge all the way to Koppen Mountain and returning to this spot will be just over 3 miles with over 1000 feet more climbing.

118 Tronson Ridge

RATING/DIFFICULTY: ***/3
ROUNDTRIP: 9.4 miles
ELEV GAIN/HIGH POINT: 2180 feet/5810 feet
SEASON: late June–Oct

Map: Green Trails Maps Wenatchee No. 211S; **Contact:** Okanogan-Wenatchee National Forest, Cle Elum Ranger District; **Notes:** Northwest Forest Pass or Interagency Pass required. No facilities at trailhead. Seasonal closure to motorized use Oct. 15–June 15. This area is popular with hunters—wear orange during open season. There are two trailheads for this hike. The one described here starts from the southern end and goes downhill off the jump, whereas the northern trailhead kicks off uphill. High clearance suggested for both approaches, especially the more northerly trailhead; road may be tight, brushy, and rough. The ridge is exposed, and water is unavailable, so bring what you need. Open to

When you want to feel that warm sunshine on the eastern crest of the Cascades, head over to Tronson Ridge to soak in the views.

leashed dogs, mountain bikes, motorcycles, stock; **GPS:** N 47 19.360, W 120 31.618

The dry side of the Cascade Mountains provides the perfect place to enjoy a bounty of wildflowers that thrive in the well-drained soils high upon this ridge. Save for the occasional dirt biker, the trail is free from much traffic, and it's a good place to get a workout as you follow topographical lines up and down the hills and dips. There really isn't a true destination on this journey—the ridge *is* the primary feature, so you can make it as long as you want. The views of the Stuart Range and the copious distant ridgelines make for frame-worthy photos and an opportunity to enjoy some cozy PNW sunshine if luck is on your side.

GETTING THERE

Main trailhead: From I-90 in Cle Elum, take exit 85 and head north. In 0.3 mile, turn right at a T intersection and merge onto State Route 970. Stay on SR 970 as it becomes US Highway 97 and reaches the summit of Blewett Pass in 24 miles. From the summit, turn right (south) onto Forest Road 9716. At 24.4 miles, pass Swauk Forest Discovery Trail. At 27.7 miles, arrive at a T intersection signed for FR 9712 and turn left. At 29.4 miles, continue straight to remain on FR 9712. At 32.5 miles, pass the Ken Wilcox Horse Camp to the left. If you aren't in a high-clearance vehicle, find parking here in a couple of pullouts. Parking here adds an extra roundtrip 2.6 miles and approximately 500 feet of elevation gain to this trail description. Join up with the trail by walking the campground road about 300 feet farther into the campground from the pit toilets. After the campground road bears left, look to the right for Mount Lillian Trail No. 1601. Follow the Mount Lillian Trail for 1.3 miles until it delivers you to an off-road vehicle (ORV) road (4W312). From here, turn left and follow the trail description below.

If you have a high-clearance vehicle, continue past the horse camp, and in 1 more mile, look for the signed spur trail that connects to the Mount Lillian Trail to the left, just prior to a hairpin turn. There isn't parking immediately next to the trail, so continue another 50 feet and look to the left for an unsigned ORV trail (4W312) with scattered spots.

Alternative trailhead: From Blewett Pass, continue north on US 97 for 5 miles, then turn right on Five Mile Road (FR 7224). It comes up quickly and is a little hard to see, so be sure to keep your eyes open. Stay on Five Mile Road for 3.1 miles to an undeveloped trailhead along with a campsite and turnaround.

ON THE TRAIL

If you parked at the horse camp, to reach the trailhead follow the double-track ORV Road (4W312) northbound, passing the Mount Lillian Trail in 0.4 mile. The rough road crosses a burn zone that was part of the lightning-ignited Table Mountain Fire in September of 2012. The meadows underneath the silver forest are stunning when in bloom with wildflowers, usually in the June–July timeframe, making the area fragrant and colorful despite the frozen trees. Thankfully the fire didn't affect most of the ridge—healthy trees for the win!

In 0.8 mile, the road turns left, but our trail to Tronson Ridge No. 1204 is straight ahead angling northwest. The trail is obvious once you see it; look for an outdated sign kiosk, which is visible a few paces downslope of the road on the left. It's showing its age, but underneath, a newer sign shows the classic forest service pictorials announcing permitted user groups. By the time you get out there, the kiosk may have fallen over, so you may just need to follow the mileage. The trail transitions from the double-track road to a narrow single track at this point and begins to descend on the loose, dusty soil.

The trail is often right below the ridge, so social trails to see the high points are frequent; visit if you wish, or just keep walking. Moving forward, you'll have spots where you are close to the top or a few steps away, and the views come easily. Wildflowers in early to midsummer come in all heights, colors, and scents. Look for varieties of pussytoes, balsamroot, paintbrush, lupine, arnica, yarrow, groundsel, aster, phlox, buckwheat, gilia, columbine, larkspur, bitterroot, lewisia, and clover to name a few.

At 2.4 miles from where you parked, the trail reaches a section where the ridge busts you out into open views. Ahead are lightly forested peaks and rocky ledges stretching out to the north with our trail running through them. Views into the Alpine Lakes Wilderness, the Teanaway region, and the Stuart Range are spectacular on a clear day. The tippy tops of Mount Stuart, Argonaut Peak, Pennant Peak, McClellan Peak,

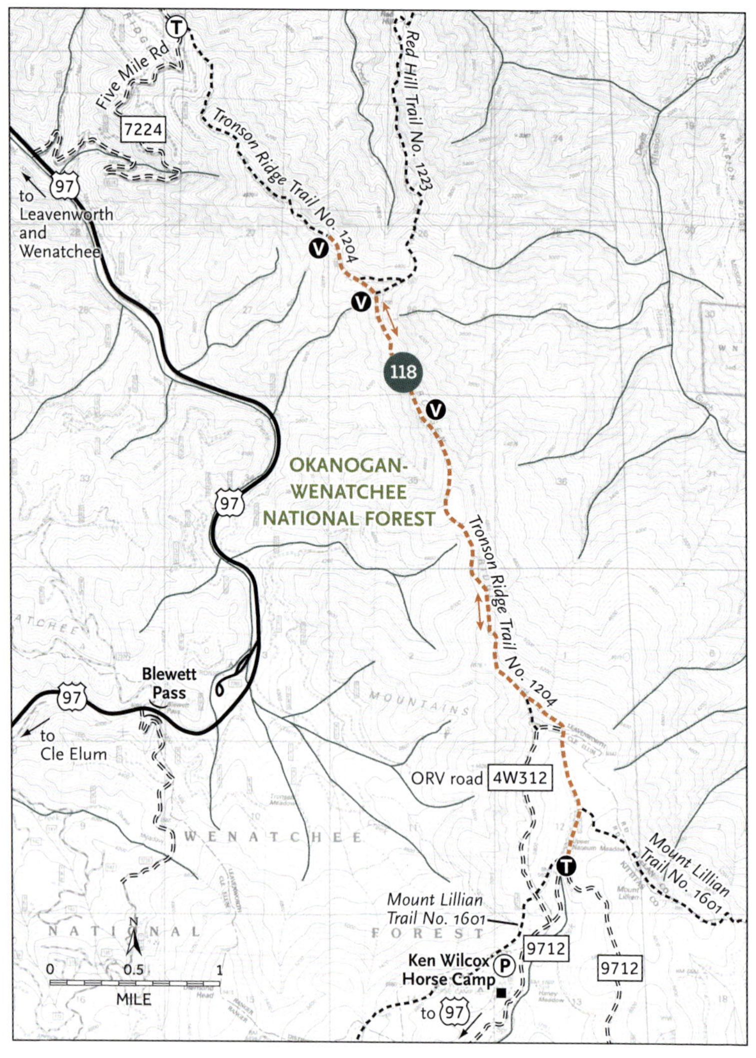

Enchantment Peak, and many others in their foreground make you want to stop and stare. Vehicles zip along the highway far beneath you. This could be a good stopping place if your time is limited or you aren't up for much more.

Otherwise, keep going for more of the same, rolling gently up and down mounds and drops. More spectacular stone bands, more tough evergreens, more eye-popping views, more dazzling wildflowers. If you continue to be drawn forward with mountain magic—keep it rolling!

At 4.1 miles, reach a junction with Red Hill Trail No. 1223 to the right. The sign is on a lovely ponderosa pine; how nice of it to offer this navigational support. A few steps prior to the junction, a spur trail leads up to the top of a knoll opposite the sign (southeast). Climbing up it provides yet another great view if you haven't had your fill.

Stay straight at the junction to 4.7 miles to reach another rocky outcropping to the left, which makes a fine place to pull out the sit pad and drench yourself in a few moments of nature's flawlessness before turning back.

EXTENDING YOUR HIKE

If you keep going, you'll eventually start going downhill on steep, tight switchbacks to reach the northern trailhead. Visiting the northern trailhead and then coming back adds another 3.7 miles of hiking and 1000 feet of elevation gain to this trail description. But wait, there's more! After it reaches the northern trailhead, the Tronson Ridge Trail continues northwest for another 2 miles and connects with several forest roads as well as the Magnet Creek Trail.

Or, on your way back, explore the Mount Lillian Trail, which heads southeast from the Mount Lillian trailhead, leaving the ORV trail to the east. The trail ducks into the forest and pops out at vistas to reach some incredible sheer sandstone walls and freestanding spires. You can go as far as you please on this trail and make several loops, but to see the sandstone features, it's 2.5 miles roundtrip with 615 feet of elevation gain from the intersection with the ORV road.

119 Swauk Forest Discovery Trail

RATING/DIFFICULTY: ****/2
ROUNDTRIP: 2.9 miles
ELEV GAIN/HIGH POINT: 490 feet/4530 feet
SEASON: late May–Oct

Map: Green Trails Maps Wenatchee No. 211S; **Contact:** Okanogan-Wenatchee National Forest, Cle Elum Ranger District; **Notes:** Northwest Forest Pass or Interagency Pass required. Pit toilet at trailhead. This area is prone to blowdowns—contact rangers or check trail reports for latest trail maintenance. See Resources for a brochure for a self-guided tour. Open to leashed dogs; **GPS:** N 47 19.924, W 120 34.728

Loop trails are the best, since you don't have to backtrack and you get new scenery with every turn. This is one of my favorites for an appealing romp with undemanding distance and elevation gain and gorgeous displays of early wildflowers. Audubon Washington has declared this one of the best places to bird-watch in Washington State as part of the Sun and Sage Loop, so bring your binoculars. Hike here in fall and you'll be treated to western larch trees and their gilded needles. Benches and interpretive signage throughout make this a place to come for quiet meditation or an educational opportunity.

GETTING THERE

From I-90 in Cle Elum: Take exit 85 and head north. In 0.3 mile, turn right at a T intersection and merge onto State Route 970. Stay on State Route 970 as it becomes US Highway 97 and reaches the summit of Blewett Pass in 24 miles. From the summit, turn right (south) onto Forest Road 9716. In 0.4 mile, turn right to arrive at the well-signed parking area for Swauk Forest Discovery Trail.

ON THE TRAIL

Locate the trail to the right of the large kiosk, signed Swauk Forest Discovery Trail No. 1334. During your walk, you'll see signposts with numbers that translate to informative details on a self-guided brochure. The brochures are occasionally available in a holder on the sign kiosk, but if they are out, you can download the brochure with the link in Resources. You can go either direction on the trail, but it's easier to find the official path by starting to the right.

The first trailside bench is located off the get-go to the left, a good place to drop a pack and organize gear if need be. In 0.1 mile, another sign to the left discusses forest management and the science behind the craft. The gentle walk continues through the evergreens, passing signs for the various tree and bush varieties, the first with a grand fir. While the sign is still informative, it's a bit outdated. The grand fir behind it isn't quite as grand as it once was, as it appears to be dead. There are healthier specimens around, though, so read the characteristics and see if you can find them.

In the fall, western larch trees are prevalent in this area, and interpretive signage

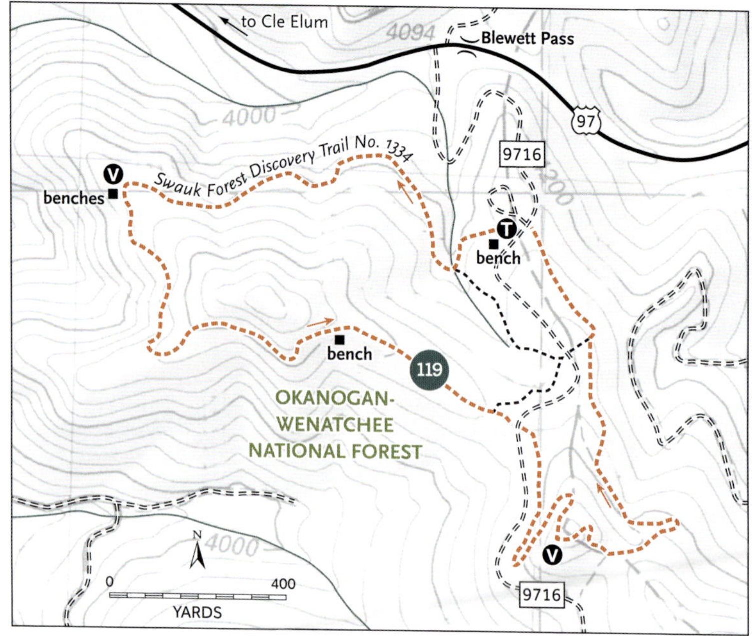

Layers of mountain ridges are visible from the Swauk Forest Discovery Trail.

explains their unique ability to recover after fires and shed their golden needles in the fall. Unlike subalpine larch trees found in places such as Lake Ingalls (Hike 110), the western larch is much taller and more conical in shape.

The traffic from Blewett Pass is noisy at this point, but as you keep trekking along, the hum of the big rigs diminishes. At 0.7 mile, reach an interpretive sign for a ponderosa pine to the left. The trail takes a hard left after this sign, but you may want to check out a boot-beaten viewpoint located on a spur trail a few steps ahead to peek into the forested landscapes to the west. In the fall, the larches can no longer hide tucked in between their fir and pine neighbors. Two benches near the trail's edge offer a spot to sit and relax.

While the wildflowers aren't thick, in the late spring and early summer, they delicately dot the slopes and come in many varieties. Look for flowers such as lupine, paintbrush, penstemon, balsamroot, arnica, sweet cicely, and thistle, which thrive in the sunlight this area receives.

As the trail winds around the mountain, the engine noise from the highway is almost nonexistent, and in its place is the quietness of birds flitting and leaves wiggling on the wind. There is a tranquility in the open airy feeling of this climate, and you can't help but feel that peace through your pores.

Birders, look and listen near the limbs for white-crowned sparrows, yellow-rumped warblers, western tanagers, rock pigeons, western meadowlarks, and red crossbills to name a few. Keep your eyes to the ground, too, for California quail and wild turkeys. Mammals, like deer, elk, porcupines, northern flying squirrels, wood rats, and red foxes also use this area to find sustenance.

At 1.6 miles, find yourself at an unsigned trail Y. If you want to shorten your day, you can go left and get back to your car in 0.3 mile by following the paths—just look for the most used one. If you have small kids whose little legs are spent or others in your group aren't up for anything longer, this might be a good option, since continuing requires a little more elevation gain. For everyone else, there's more to see and you won't want to miss the vistas.

In 180 feet from the Y, cross Forest Road 9716 and climb a few switchbacks through a short stretch of burn zone. In the far distance, Mount Stuart, Navaho Peak, Miller Peak, Earle Peak, and even Mount Rainier are visible, as are carpets of healthy trees on multitudes of ridges. To the south, Diamond Head's summit is sprinkled with evergreens looking a little like hairs on a balding head. Near the No. 20 signpost, an unofficial social trail ascends a small knoll to the northeast, where even more views are found. Check it out if you feel motivated; otherwise, off you go.

From here, the trail promenades north, then descends through larches, pines, and more fantastic foliage to cross FR 9716 again. Directly across the road and clearly visible are the trailhead and your vehicle.

OPPOSITE: *A moody sky looms over a sunlit pathway along the Vista Trail (Hike 126).*

ELLENSBURG AREA

WHERE THE EASTERN EDGE OF THE Cascade Mountains collides with the scrublands of central Washington are a smattering of hikes that are worthy of your footprints. These are the play areas that are often dry when the western slopes are heavy with moisture-rich clouds. They are the hikes where you need to watch for the heat-loving flora and fauna, such as the occasional cactus or rattlesnake. Wildflowers flourish in spring, and sunshine is plentiful, as is wind that can whip with reckless abandon on the barren summits. But there is magic and peace in these areas too, as you can see for miles on most of their pathways.

120 Rattlesnake Dance Ridge

RATING/DIFFICULTY: ****/3
ROUNDTRIP: 2 miles
ELEV GAIN/HIGH POINT: 1220 feet/2646 feet
SEASON: Apr–Oct

Maps: USGS Ellensburg South, USGS Kittitas; **Contact:** Bureau of Land Management Oregon/Washington; **Notes:** No facilities at trailhead. Watch for rattlesnakes and ticks. This hike is almost completely exposed and waterless; avoid hiking in summer or on hot days, as heat exhaustion may occur. Open to leashed dogs; **GPS:** N 46 53.875, W 120 30.253

This trail is wicked steep, and you should probably avoid it on hot days or you might actually do the samba with one of those namesake sassy pit vipers. But it does have some redeeming qualities! First off, it's a great workout and you'll likely hit your daily fitness goals in a short, heart-pounding timeframe. Second, the views from the top of the Stuart Range and the Yakima River canyon are spectacular and worthy of the brief drudgery to the summit. If you only have a little time on your hands to see the high country of the desert, this is the trail!

GETTING THERE

From I-90 near Ellensburg: Take exit 109 and head south on Canyon Road, which

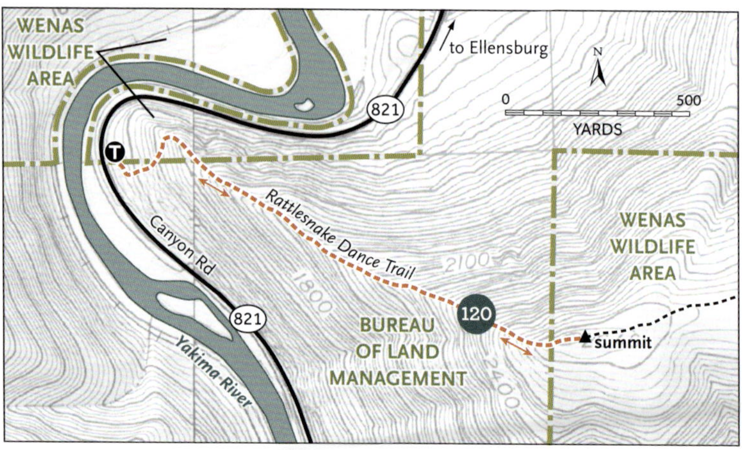

Near the summit of Rattlesnake Dance Trail, balsamroot bursts forth in golden waves.

becomes State Route 821. In 6.3 miles, find a large unsigned parking area to the left on a hairpin turn.

ON THE TRAIL

The trail starts off on an obvious pathway leading you away from the parking area and quickly up into the hinterlands. A sign shortly after starting confirms you are on the Rattlesnake Dance Trail, just in case you thought you might be wandering aimlessly.

The packed soil becomes rockier and gains elevation without wasting any time. In the springtime, the showing of Carey's and Hooker's balsamroots, desert parsley, long-leaf phlox, and other drought-loving flowers bloom with their gorgeous faces to the sun.

In just 0.3 mile, the Stuart Range appears, with main feature Mount Stuart itself rising high above the others. Farmlands sprawl out below you to the north, and the rolling green (or brown in the dry season) hills of the scrublands provide strong bumpers for the Yakima River.

Keep up the steady, tough climbing until you arrive in a ball of sweat and pride at the wooden post held high by a rock pile, typical of desert peaks. An ammo tin holds a journal that awaits your autograph and profound reflections, which perhaps you are too breathless to write. Snap your selfies, pat yourself on your dank backside, and glow with your accomplishment all the way back to the car.

121 Umtanum Creek Falls

RATING/DIFFICULTY: ****/1

ROUNDTRIP: 2 miles

ELEV GAIN/HIGH POINT: 240 feet/2530 feet

SEASON: Mar–Oct

Map: Washington Department of Fish and Wildlife Trail Maps, Wenas Wildlife Area; **Contact:** Washington Department of Fish and Wildlife, Wenas Wildlife Area; **Notes:** Discover Pass required. Creek crossings may get feet wet, depending on height. Watch for rattlesnakes and ticks. No toilets or picnic areas at trailhead. Open to leashed dogs; **GPS:** N 46 53.959, W 120 38.576

Seeing a true waterfall in the desert is a treat, and especially in spring, this one doesn't disappoint. The 25-foot cascade of water over a thin column of basalt can be viewed from several angles. But the journey is also the destination. The great birding en route provides an opportunity to see the usual suspects, such as northern flickers, canyon wrens, and black-capped chickadees, but also a few others like Audubon's warblers, American goldfinches, and spotted towhees.

GETTING THERE

From I-90 near Ellensburg: Take exit 109 and head north on Canyon Road. In 0.8 mile, turn left on Umptanum Road. Follow it into the hills until it turns to gravel at 6.1 miles. Keep going for to 11.1 miles (watch for bluebirds along this road) and arrive at the well-signed parking area and trailhead to the left.

ON THE TRAIL

Umptanum Road (spelled differently than your destination) was part of a historical stagecoach road across the mountains. Can you image the joy of the pioneers finding water in such a dry spot? The trail starts off to the left of the informational kiosk, passing through a couple of large boulders. Most of the birding is around this area, though birds

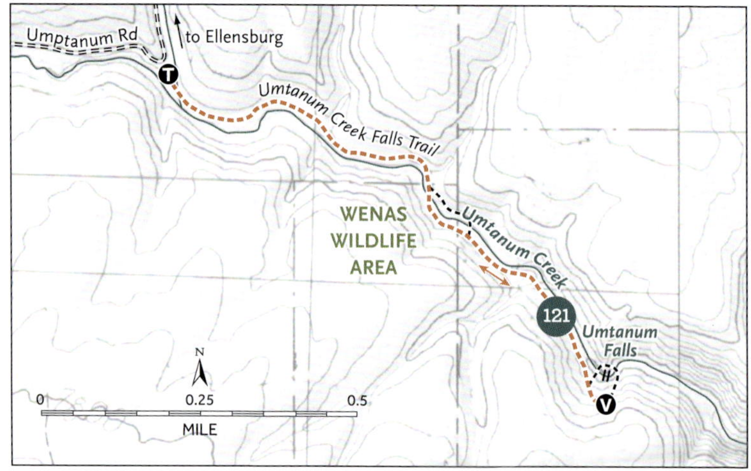

Tucked into the arid landscape, the 25-foot Umtanum Creek Falls spills gracefully through basalt walls.

follow water, so you can sometimes find exotics, such as lazuli buntings in springtime in other spots throughout the hike.

In 0.2 mile, the trail reaches a planked bridge over a swampy area. Almost immediately after that, it's easy to get confused. A well-worn trail goes right toward the water, but the actual trail stays left and climbs up over a rocky outcropping, which may not be obvious. A wetland with a dribble comes up after that, which puts on a show of purple camas in the marsh during springtime. This often attracts pollinators such as monarch or blue copper butterflies, which flirt with the flowers and mud (to derive rotting plant matter) intermittently.

Keep left at 0.5 mile where a boot path drops down to the right to visit the stream. Shortly afterward, arrive at a Y junction in the trail. Both sides of the Y have been created by those who think their way is best for crossing the creek and will meet up at the same place farther along the trail. Pick whichever crossing looks less shoe-wetting. Continue toward the falls through the occasional riparian brush, which can be overgrown at times, until at nearly 1 mile, you reach the top of the falls.

As with most hikes, you have options! Those who trip over air molecules will want to stay above the falls, walking to the right to view them at a safe angle from the side. This vista makes for a beautiful photo, and you can leave content with seeing what you came for.

Those in the more surefooted category may want to also see them from the bottom. There are two paths that lead down into the basin, both on loose dirt requiring somewhat risky maneuvers. One path goes left, crosses the creek above the falls, then drops down a steep slope on loose, rocky soil. The other path goes right and continues following a well-worn trail above the cliffs and eventually down some rocky outcroppings to the bottom. You can make a full loop by going down one trail and coming up the other. Whichever path you choose, please be careful. The rocks are worn and polished from people scrambling on them, and one slip could put an end to a great day. When you are done, head back the way you came, a better person for having enjoyed life to the fullest.

122 Westberg and Boy Scout Trail Loop

RATING/DIFFICULTY: ***/3
ROUNDTRIP: 4.3 miles
ELEV GAIN/HIGH POINT: 1620 feet/3550 feet
SEASON: Mar–Oct

Map: USGS Manastash Creek Quadrangle (7.5-Minute Series); **Contact:** Washington Department of Fish and Wildlife, Wenas Wildlife Area; **Notes:** Please don't hike these trails when muddy, as it erodes the trail (have a plan B). One section of this trail is exposed—avoid it during hot summer months. Watch for rattlesnakes and ticks. While technically these trails are multiuse, hikers are the primary users and others are discouraged. No restrooms or picnic areas at trailhead. Do not drink or filter irrigation water—carry what you need. Open to leashed dogs, stock (on small section), mountain bikes; **GPS:** N 46 58.059, W 120 38.733

Sweeping panoramas await those who work for it! The viewpoint at the top provides a grand vista into Kittitas County, as well as peaks of the Cascade Mountains, such as Mount Stuart, the second highest nonvolcanic peak in the state.

GETTING THERE

From eastbound I-90 near Thorp: Take exit 101 and turn south onto S. Thorp Highway. In 2 miles, turn right onto Cove Road. Continue on Cove Road until 6.4 miles, passing

Enjoy a great workout and a pleasant ramble through wildflowers and desert foliage on the Westberg and Boy Scout Trail Loop.

Robinson Canyon and Manastash Road. An obvious roadside parking area is found to the right prior to Cove Road's dead end at 6.6 miles. It's signed Ridge Trail Parking.

From westbound I-90 near Ellensburg: Take exit 109, Canyon Road. Turn right onto Canyon Road and in 0.5 mile, turn left onto Umptanum Road. At 2.3 miles, turn right onto Manastash Road. At 5.9 miles, turn left onto Cove Road and proceed to 6.1 miles, reaching an obvious spot for roadside parking to the right prior to Cove Road's dead end. It is signed Ridge Trail Parking.

ON THE TRAIL

Walk south from the parking area toward the trailhead and find a large informational kiosk to the right. While this area is multiuse, the land managers have done a fine job of trying to keep each user group to their own trails and making it safe and pleasant for everyone.

Continue walking to the road's end and around a yellow car gate. In about 350 feet, arrive at an irrigation canal with a few concrete pillars on side service roads, and an obvious large sign ahead, announcing you are in the Wenas Wildlife Area and Manastash Ridge Trails. The service road to the right of the irrigation canal is a tiny portion of the return path we will take to get back to this spot, once we've taken the Boy Scout Trail back down. You can go either direction for the loop, but since the Westberg Trail is the most obvious at this point, we will start there.

Continue walking toward the sign, then start your climb, gentle at first, up toward the top. You are now on the Westberg Trail, though it's only signed for the wildlife area, so good directions and a map are helpful. In 0.3 mile, trails come in from both the right and left, but ignore all side trails and continue on the wider, more obvious one you've been following. In many places, the trail splits into a couple of social trails that lead back to the same place—take whichever side suits your fancy; just make sure you continue to climb.

In the springtime, wildflowers such as balsamroot, yarrow, desert parsley, small bluebell, shooting star, stonecrop, paintbrush, lupine, phlox, grass widow, sagebrush violet, larkspur, and many others display their petals and leaves in carpets of grand color, making this somewhat monotone desert pop to life.

Ponderosa pines start arriving as you climb higher, giving this exposed trail a little shade and a different ambiance. Bluebirds use this area, and nesting boxes have been installed to assist them in their quest to survive.

At 1 mile, arrive at a quirky little resting bench clearly built for someone with long legs. This area is known locally as Halfway Pine and provides a place to stop in the shade for a break. You'll want to take a few moments to recharge, as the next push seems to climb straight up to the contrails in the stratosphere. You got this though . . . push through!

You are following an old road-turned-trail, but until now, it hasn't been too obvious. The double track quickly turns back to single track, and before you know it, you are standing at a well-used trail junction at 1.4 miles. Though not signed, the right-hand branch is the Boy Scout Trail and will be the return portion of our loop. First, though, we need to tag the summit—or "The Ridge," as locals calls it—and then return to this point.

Continue onward with the views getting better and better behind you of the central Cascade peaks of the Stuart Range and the pastoral farmlands of Kittitas County.

The Westberg Trail we've been following was named for Ellensburg High School wrestling coach and English teacher Ray

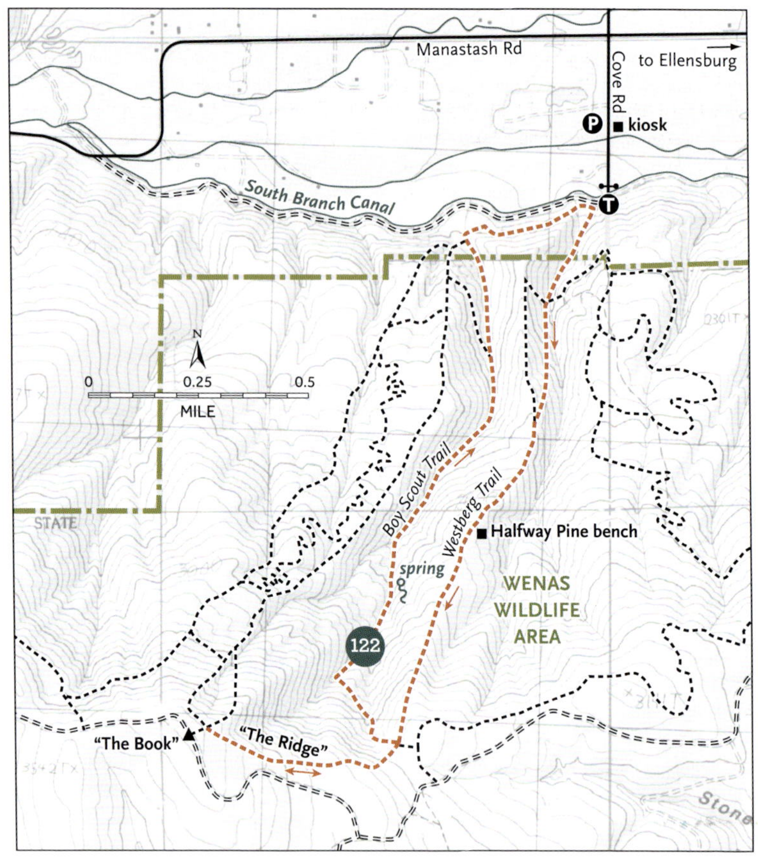

Westberg who passed away suddenly in 1997 at age forty-seven after collapsing in his classroom. He was loved, respected, and amazing at his job, receiving teacher of the year for four years prior to his death and leading his team to consecutive, undefeated seasons of wrestling. A memorial for him is located near the top.

The climbing continues, but the views take your breath away, until, at nearly 2 miles, you reach the summit, marked by a stone pile and a post. This area is called "The Book," thanks to the ammo tin that sits here with pens and a journal for hikers to document thoughts and sign their name. Many other trails connect in this area, so enjoy the top, then take the same one on which you arrived back down to the Boy Scout Trail junction.

Once you get back to the unsigned junction, 0.6 mile from the top (2.6 miles total), take a left and begin your promenade with the pine trees. Almost the whole thing is under the canopy of shade, and the occasional fresh breeze provides a little natural air-conditioning on warm days. At 3.1 miles, a small spring (with an attached pipe) is visible to the right—such a generous gift from Mother Nature in the dry climate.

As you continue downhill, the main trail is larger and obvious as side trails meet up with it. At 4 miles, the trail brings you to a gravel road-turned-trail along an irrigation ditch. Follow it to the right, along the water, until at 4.3 miles you arrive back at the junction where you started, near the Wenas Wildlife Area and Manastash Ridge Trails sign. Turn left toward the yellow gate and your waiting vehicle.

123 Baldy Mountain

RATING/DIFFICULTY: ****/4
ROUNDTRIP: 4.3 miles
ELEV GAIN/HIGH POINT: 1980 feet/3212 feet
SEASON: Apr–Oct

Map: Bureau of Land Management, Big Pines; **Contact:** Washington Department of Fish and Wildlife, Wenas Wildlife Area; **Notes:** Pit toilets, picnic areas, and additional parking at the Big Pines Campground across the street. Bureau of Land Management parking fee required year-round at the Big Pines Campground, payable at self-serve kiosk, or Interagency Pass accepted. Watch for rattlesnakes and ticks. This hike is almost completely exposed and waterless—avoid hiking in summer or on hot days, as heat exhaustion may occur. Open to leashed dogs; **GPS:** N 46 47.712, W 120 27.499

Wonderful views of the Cascades, along with a carpet of springtime wildflowers, await along this highly steep, difficult trail. Get out the turmeric or ibuprofen if you haven't hiked in a while, as your body will no doubt be talking to you post-hike. Yet, the accomplishment is boast-worthy, and you can pat yourself on your sweaty back for tackling this grueling beast and overcoming the challenge. Radio towers on the summit don't make the sweeping views any less desirable, so pretend they aren't there and enjoy the bounty of your hard work.

GETTING THERE

From I-90 near Ellensburg: Take exit 109 and head south on Canyon Road, which becomes State Route 821. Enjoy the drive through the canyon, and at 18.8 miles, find roadside parking to the right, adjacent to the Big Pines Campground. If parking is full, additional parking can be found at the Big Pines Campground.

ON THE TRAIL

The bottom of this hike is like an upside-down lollipop, with two trail options that join into one 0.7 mile farther up the mountain. For the spice of life, I recommend taking one up and the other down. Since this trail can be a slip and slide with loose pebbles and dirt on the way down, I'd recommend taking the steeper of the two trails up and the more forgiving trail on the way back down, but you do you.

To get to the steeper of the two trails, cross the road from the parking area and head toward the rusty propped-open gate. This baby looks like it hasn't moved in years and hangs there defeated in its mission. If you choose to take the other trail, it starts to the left, prior to the gate. The trail is faint, but you'll find it if you look hard enough.

The trail after the gate is named on some maps and navigational systems as TP Jim Trail, and the parking area the TP Jim trailhead. TP Jim was a big help in the community to troubled youth and gangs, so this area was named in honor of him.

For now, follow the trail past the gate as it kicks off with a gentler pitch, followed by a narrow coulee with a what-the-actual-heck steepness. Strange noises wheeze and rasp from your mouth and nose as you cha-cha with the trail, one foot sliding back as the other attempts to find purchase. This is the toughest part of the trail, so hang in there and stop to suck air.

In 0.6 mile, the trail mercifully levels out a bit and reaches a viewpoint overlooking the Yakima River and the scrublands beyond it. If you are ready to throw in the towel, or maybe you set out to do a shorter day, this is a suitable, even noble, goal. Curl up on the rocks for a break before heading back down, or . . . keep going! In 0.1 mile, a junction is reached with the return portion of the lollipop loop and the less hazardous descent. If you are looking to reach the top, keep going at this point.

A cairn shows up to the left as you continue onward and the trail reaches a ridgeline between two peaks. Because you can see the

Baldy Mountain's expansive views into desert scrublands are worth every leg-burning step.

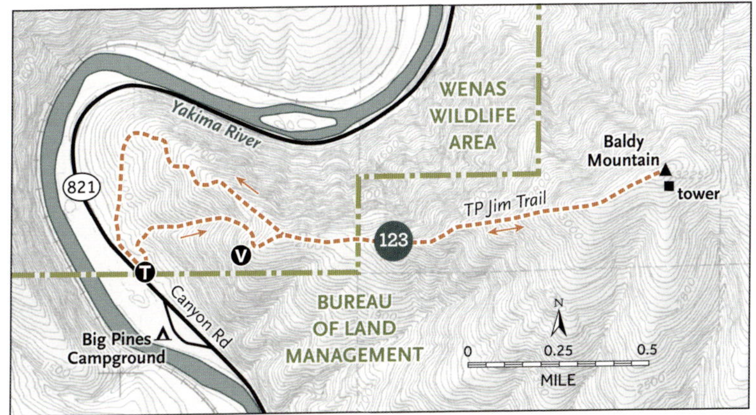

summit clearly now, it begins to wear on you mentally; it looks so far away! But you get there faster than you think, so carry on and maybe pay attention to your feet instead of the goal.

In 0.9 mile, cross between two fence lines, the left one following along with you almost all the way to the summit. Up, up, up you go, higher and higher on the steeps, until you at last arrive at a forgiving trail grade and the final little walk to the towers. On the last push, keep your eyes open for bitterroot, a gorgeous pink-flowered succulent that has an edible root. The plant was harvested by Native people and pioneers in springtime, but by summer, it took on a bitter taste and earned its name. Also, look for hedgehog cactus near the top, which produces an intricate hot-pink flower with a yellow center during late spring.

Most folks stop for lunch or a break away from the tower's eyesore, but if you've come this far, you'll probably want to make the trek up there, to at least stand on the top and maybe even take a victory lap. When you've tagged the top, head back down, and consider taking the right branch of the lollipop trail at the bottom to show your quads and your feet some love.

124 Umtanum Creek Canyon

RATING/DIFFICULTY: **/1
ROUNDTRIP: 5.5 miles
ELEV GAIN/HIGH POINT: 260 feet/1550 feet
SEASON: Mar–Oct

Map: Washington Department of Fish and Wildlife Trail Maps, Wenas Wildlife Area; **Contact:** Washington Department of Fish and Wildlife, Wenas Wildlife Area; **Notes:** Bureau of Land Management parking fee required year-round, payable at kiosk, or Interagency Pass accepted. Pit toilets and picnic areas at trailhead. Trail closed 3.2 miles from the parking area early Feb. through mid-July to protect wildlife. Creek crossings may be hazardous until mid-April or May. Watch for rattlesnakes and ticks. Open to leashed dogs, mountain bikes; **GPS:** N 46 51.337, W 120 29.004

In 2020, this area succumbed to the Evans Creek Fire, and the landscape

Aspens shimmy in the wind along the riparian zones of Umtanum Creek Canyon.

was changed dramatically. Thankfully, many trees were spared, and volunteers have worked to help bring the vegetation back with replanting projects. A few years later, the landscape is flourishing, and songbirds—such as the lazuli bunting, canyon wren, and American goldfinch—are here enjoying the springtime sustenance. The trail, however, is not pristine and has suffered from the creek's mischievous water reroutes throughout the years; dead ends of former trails aren't uncommon. I've done my best to help you navigate with a solid trail description and map.

GETTING THERE

From I-90 near Ellensburg: Take exit 109 and head south on Canyon Road, which becomes State Route 821. Enjoy the drive through the canyon, and at 12.2 miles, find the Umtanum Recreation Site to the right near mile marker 16.

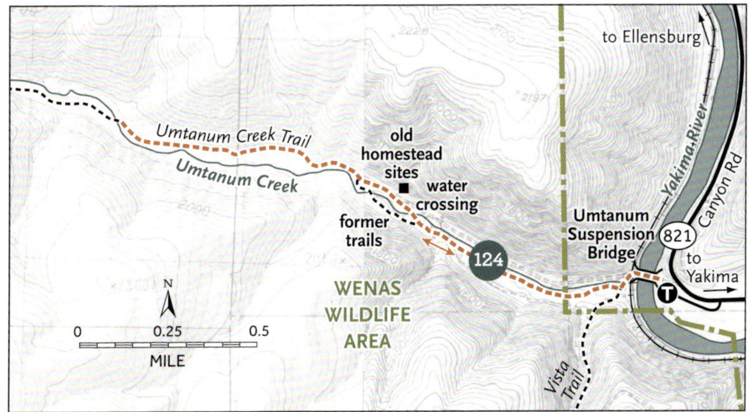

ON THE TRAIL

The trail is overgrown with a few blowdowns here and there, thanks to the fire. The creek crossings don't have bridges, and at times, you wonder if you are the only one who has been here in a while. But rest assured, you are not. This trail sees a fair amount of traffic, despite the lack of maintenance. Maybe because of the natural state, and of course because it follows a creek, it's a hot spot for birding.

Start off by crossing the large engineering marvel of the Umtanum Suspension Bridge. It sways a bit side to side but is sturdy and secure. What's more, you'll be standing in the middle of the Yakima River at some point, able to look down at the water passing underneath you, a fun sensation for all ages.

Just after the suspension bridge, duck your head under the railroad tracks and wind around to the left to find a large informational kiosk along with a map and a few signs, 0.1 mile from the parking area. Two trails diverge here including ours, which goes behind the sign. The other branch goes up to Umtanum Ridge and Vista Trail (Hike 126), a breathtaking hike both in beauty and the lungs!

For now, follow the path as it guides you along the purring Umtanum Creek to the right. A few boot paths scoot off to the creek, but the main trail is obvious. Quaking aspen groves wiggle hello, along with the classic semiarid riparian foliage such as Scouler's willow and box elder. Several social trails split to braid the trail into sections, most coming back to the main trail—take either path, but pay attention because the most important junction is coming up.

At 0.8 mile, reach a junction near a small meadow. Going right here is the correct trail, but the left-hand branch looks better traveled and it's been known to fool many. If you accidentally take the left branch, you'll soon know it, as all the former trails are overgrown and eventually dead-end either at the deep bubbling creek or at talus fields.

The right-hand branch leads down to the creek and crosses it, usually on a makeshift bridge of skinny logs. Having trekking poles helps a bunch with balance on these spindles! Just after the bridge used to be the remnants of an old homestead, with only the foundations and the root cellar still in place. After the fire, the vegetation grew up, making it a scavenger hunt to find them, but the apple trees and walnut trees still give hints of their location.

Continue up the valley, seeing a little more evidence of the fire on the aspen trees and popping in and out of views of the creek. The trail hugs the right bank of the creek for a little while before guiding you up toward the shoulders of the canyon. Eventually, the trail gets harder to follow and crosses a brushy, often shoe-wetting ford of Umtanum Creek. Turn back at this location or whenever you are ready to retrace your steps.

125 Palouse to Cascades: Thorp Tunnels

RATING/DIFFICULTY: ***/1
ROUNDTRIP: 11.8 miles
ELEV GAIN/HIGH POINT: 100 feet/1830 feet
SEASON: Year-round

Map: Washington State Parks Palouse to Cascades State Park Trail Map; **Contact:** Washington State Parks; **Notes:** Discover Pass required. Pit toilets and picnic areas available near the trailhead. Bring a headlamp for the tunnels—the second one is almost pitch black in the middle. Open to leashed dogs, bicycles, stock; **GPS:** N 47 03.552, W 120 40.401

Two engaging former railroad tunnels await those who are willing to walk the distance to see them. Of course, you could ride a bike, but it's doable on foot if you don't mind the monotony of the grade and the relaxing cadence of your footsteps as you make your way along the former tracks. Along the way, verdant farmlands and the peaceful Yakima River keep you company.

GETTING THERE

From I-90 near Thorp: Take exit 101 and head north on Thorp Highway. In 0.3 mile, turn left on the dirt Thorp Depot Road—signed for the trailhead—and follow it until 0.5 mile. Turn right on the trail easement and find the well-signed parking lot/trailhead to the left at 0.6 mile.

ON THE TRAIL

From the trailhead, turn left and wander along the former line of the Chicago, Milwaukee, St. Paul, and Pacific Railway, which followed this route from 1909 to 1980. The railroad delivered freight and passengers from Chicago to Tacoma, chugging along over 2300 miles to various stops and ultimate destinations. Today, the peaceful trail is all that's left to show for the bygone days as it quietly runs through farm county.

In 0.4 mile, cross the lightly traveled Goodwin Road before continuing onward. Cattle in nearby fields look up to see what strange creatures are walking by, as you stare back. An irrigation ditch appears to the right, along with a few migratory birds, drawn to the water in the heat. The fields and farms of this wide-open landscape provide great places to get lost in thought as crunch, crunch, crunch, crunch go your feet on the gravel.

Taneum Road is crossed through two small pedestrian gates at 1.7 miles. Latch them closed behind you as a courtesy to the nearby landowners.

At 2.8 miles, things get a little more interesting as you cross a trestle over the rip-roaring Taneum Creek. In springtime, this puppy churns! Shortly after that, the Yakima River shows up to the right, along with a

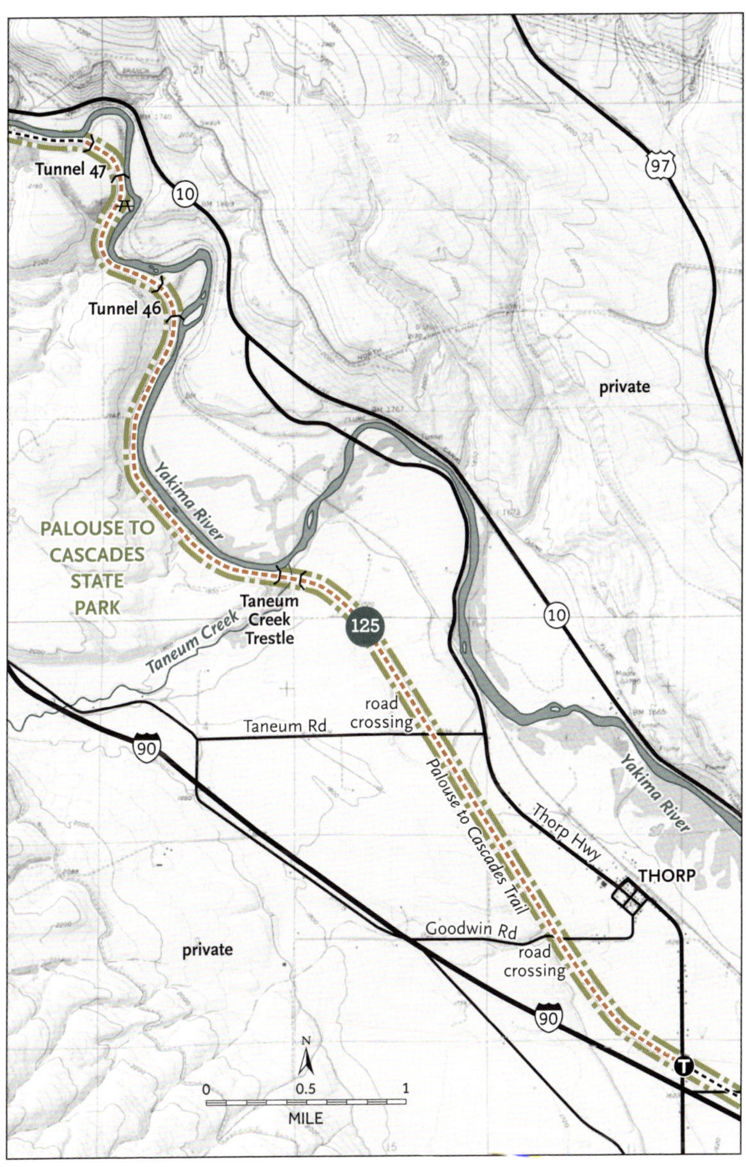
Tunnel 47
10
97
Tunnel 46
private
Yakima River
PALOUSE TO
CASCADES
STATE
PARK
Taneum
Creek
Trestle
Taneum Creek
125
10
road
crossing
Taneum Rd
90
Palouse to Cascades Trail
Yakima River
Thorp Hwy
THORP
Goodwin Rd
road
crossing
private
90
N
0
0.5
1
MILE
T

Once a railway route, the Palouse to Cascades Trail offers a gentle grade, perfect for a walk that blends light exercise with good conversation.

smattering of ponderosa pines and in early season, a pretty spread of colorful wildflowers, such as lupine and balsamroot. Birds such as red-tailed hawks, turkey vultures, and violet-green swallows swirl and dip as they catch a free ride on the wind.

At 4.7 miles, arrive at the first tunnel—number 46. This one is shorter than the next, and you can see the far end almost the whole time. Both tunnels have recently undergone renovations to secure aging concrete, so rest assured you are safe within their nooks. If darkness is a bit unsettling, grab the headlamp and carry on—the tunnel is exactly 0.1 mile long.

With daylight once again showing you the way, continue your adventure, noting the mud nests of the cliff swallow colony on the stone walls to the left. Some nests get occupied in the spring and early summer; their pretty little faces stick out to watch you walk by.

At 5.6 miles, a picnic area to the right provides a much-needed place to rest the feet and bust out the trail mix and your headlamp. An informational sign nearby talks about the *Olympian Hiawatha*, a futuristic passenger train that was introduced in June 1947 for passengers along these tracks.

Just after the picnic area, the trail enters Tunnel 47, which has a slight bend and therefore is dark in the middle. It's also longer, over double the distance of its neighbor, Tunnel 46. Horses use this tunnel too, so don't be like me on my visit and step in a fresh pile; watch your feet! When you've emerged at the far end, turn back satisfied with your accomplishment, or keep going as far as you want—you're the boss! Mysteriously, the way feels a little shorter on the return trip.

126 Vista Trail to Umtanum Ridge

RATING/DIFFICULTY: ***/3
ROUNDTRIP: 5.3 miles
ELEV GAIN/HIGH POINT: 2120 feet/3480 feet
SEASON: Mar–Oct

Map: Washington Department of Fish and Wildlife Trail Maps, Wenas Wildlife Area; **Contact:** Washington Department of Fish and Wildlife, Wenas Wildlife Area; **Notes:** Bureau of Land Management parking fee required year-round, payable at kiosk, or Interagency Pass accepted. Pit toilets and picnic areas at trailhead. Watch for rattlesnakes and ticks. This trail is exposed and may not be suitable for summer travel due to heat. Open to leashed dogs, mountain bikes; **GPS:** N 46 51.337, W 120 29.004

If you have the day to burn and want to enjoy some desert hiking as well as indulge in some distant Cascade views, I can't recommend this trail highly enough. It winds around coulees, springs, and steep hills enough to keep the hike interesting, and gives you a solid, breathtaking goal. The workout is just a bonus.

GETTING THERE

From I-90 near Ellensburg: Take exit 109 and head south on Canyon Road, which becomes

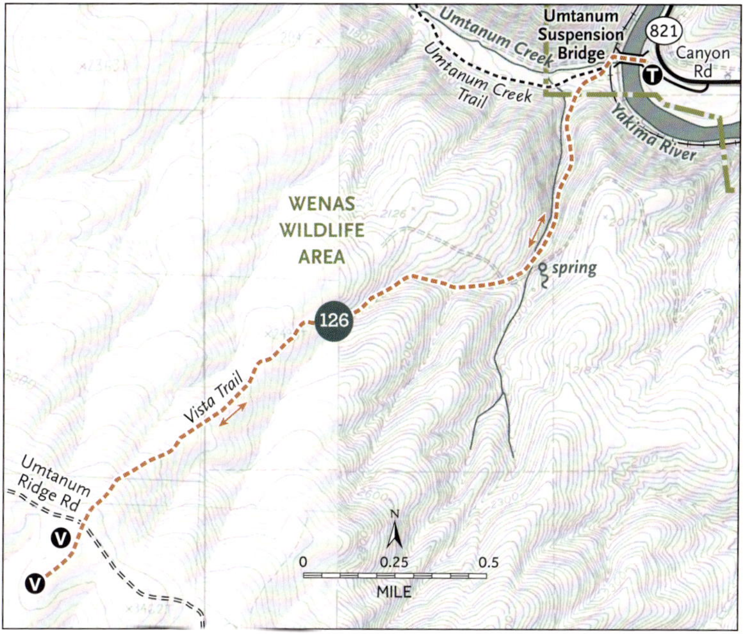

When you need to get away from it all, the Vista Trail offers rolling hills, solitude, and seasonal wildflowers.

State Route 821. Enjoy the drive through the canyon, and in 12.2 miles, find the Umtanum Recreation Site to the right near mile marker 16.

ON THE TRAIL

To find the trail, cross the long, spectacular Umtanum Suspension Bridge as it sways with your weight. From there, duck under the railroad tracks and bear left to find an informational sign with a map, 0.1 mile from the parking area. At the sign, there are two trails—one going behind it (Umtanum Creek Canyon, Hike 124) and our trail, which goes to the left here. Follow it left and before long, find yourself climbing, steeply at times. At 0.4 mile, the grade flattens out a bit and traverses along the canyon, giving you a break from the climb.

A grove of quaking aspens shows up in a topographical depression, along with a piped spring to the left at 0.8 mile. Water in the desert is Mother Nature's olive branch in the harsh climate and offers life to so many plants and animals.

The climbing gets steeper after the watering hole, and in springtime, the flowers show up in great numbers, scenting the air like the perfume from stars at a Hollywood premiere. Prairie lupine, desert parsley, Carey's balsamroot, sagebrush buttercup, lomatium, and many others are near your feet as you get higher onto the hills. Behind you now, the Stuart Range is visible, along with the feature attraction—Mount Stuart himself!

The trail reaches a couple of steep headwalls on the hill climbs, going straight up instead of switchbacking, until at 2.4 miles and just shy of 2050 feet of elevation gain, it arrives at a forest road known as Umtanum Ridge Road. Cross the road and on the other side, follow the trail to reach a couple of high points with amazing views down into the Naches and Tieton valleys. Turn back to the trailhead with endorphins buzzing—or wander either direction on Umtanum Ridge Road to reach a couple of other summits and high points.

Acknowledgments

When one sets out to write a guidebook, the challenge affects many people. First and foremost, thank you to my husband, Vilnis. He stood by as my worn-out feet hiked every one of these trails, syncing up to join me whenever his busy schedule allowed. He pretended to be impressed by my relentless recaps and photos of every giant boulder sighting, marmot encounter, and strange tree that resembled body parts. Thanks to him, I didn't lose my sanity and managed to live my wildest guidebook-writing dreams.

A massive thanks to Dan Nelson and Alan Bauer, who created the first couple of editions of this book and then handed me the torch. You told me that my vision paralleled that of the great Harvey Manning and Ira Spring, and that together we could continue this particular guide in the style and advocacy that was set before us. This book was your baby for years, and I know that the decision to pass it along to me was a difficult one that wasn't without sleepless nights and plenty of conversation. You believed in me, and I thank you immensely! I hope you'll find that I did it justice.

Special thanks to my big furball, rough collie, Scout, who wanted more than anything to come with me every time I left home. I took him on the easier hikes, but his aging bones and muscles wouldn't allow him to join me on longer pursuits. With me on the trail or snuggling at home, he will always have my heart.

To my immediate family and my closest friends—you've been there for victory, celebration, and moments of joy, and I thank you for your support and love. Some of you have

A western tiger swallowtail sips nectar from a blooming Pacific rhododendron.

even put up with being my models for this book. I pointed my camera in your face like an obnoxious paparazzi, and you tolerated it like a boss.

The beautiful humans at Mountaineers Books deserve a hearty thank-you too. Kate, Darryl, Tom, and Mary (who has now set sail for retirement), and all the people who have encouraged my writing and coached my visions, you've made me better through your knowledge and faith in my writing.

A big thank-you to Green Trails Maps staff, especially Chuck Kitterman who was there for me with questions, thoughts, and really great playlist recommendations.

To the land managers and patient folks in the know who endured my constant emails with questions and requests, including Ben Mayberry (DNR), Alex Anderson (City of Issaquah Parks), Nicholas Lichtenstadter (Forest Service), Darian Davis (Watershed Protection, Seattle), Laura Osiadacz (Kittitas County commissioner), Monty Vanderbilt (Middle Fork historian), and so many others: thank you, thank you!

To Mama Nature—we take delight in your peaks and valleys that, through their beauty, sustain our souls. Thank you for showing us that change can be exquisite and that there is no need to hurry; everything is accomplished in perfect timing. Your daylight is only appreciated because of the darkness, and your wind shows us that not all things that exist can be seen or heard—some things are meant to be felt.

Lastly, thank you to my readers and those eager to hike these trails—through these pages, may you find a place to rest the spirit and enjoy a few moments of stillness. You are why I write—we are kindred spirits who can't help falling in love with mountains. I'll see you out there, soon.

Resources

LAND MANAGEMENT AGENCIES

Bureau of Land Management
Oregon/Washington State Office
503-808-6001
www.blm.gov/oregon-washington

City of Cle Elum
City Hall
119 W. 1st St., Cle Elum, WA 98922
509-674-2262
https://cityofcleelum.com

City of North Bend
425-888-1211
https://northbendwa.gov

City of Roslyn
509-649-3105
http://ci.roslyn.wa.us

City of Snoqualmie
425-888-1555
https://snoqualmiewa.gov

King County Parks
206-477-4527
https://kingcounty.gov/en/dept/dnrp/nature-recreation/parks-recreation/king-county-parks

Kittitas County
509-962-7508
https://www.co.kittitas.wa.us/

Mount Baker–Snoqualmie National Forest
Snoqualmie Ranger District
425-888-1421
https://fs.usda.gov/mbs

Okanogan-Wenatchee National Forest
Cle Elum Ranger District
509-852-1100
www.fs.usda.gov/recarea/okawen/recarea/?recid=57117

Puget Sound Energy (Snoqualmie Falls Park)
888-225-5773
www.pse.com/en/pages/tours-and-recreation

Seattle Public Utilities (Rattlesnake Lake Recreation Area and Trails)
206-684-3000
www.seattle.gov/utilities/protecting-our-environment/our-water-sources/cedar-river-watershed/recreation-areas-and-trails

Washington Department of Fish and Wildlife
360-902-2200
https://wdfw.wa.gov

Washington State Department of Natural Resources
360-902-1000
www.dnr.wa.gov

Washington State Parks
360-902-8844
https://parks.wa.gov

MAPS

Baldy Mountain
Washington Department of Fish & Wildlife
Green Dot Maps
www.blm.gov/visit/big-pines

Cougar Mountain Regional Wildland Park
King County Parks
https://aqua.kingcounty.gov/gis/web/VMC/recreation/BCT_CougarMtn_brochure.pdf

Dirty Harrys Peak
Washington State Department of Natural Resources
www.dnr.wa.gov/sites/default/files/publications/amp_rec_dirtyharrypeak_trailmap.pdf

Grand Ridge Park
King County Parks
https://aqua.kingcounty.gov/gis/web/VMC/recreation/BCT_GrandRidge_brochure.pdf

Green Trails Maps
https://greentrailsmaps.com

Lake Easton State Park
Washington State Parks
https://parks.wa.gov/sites/default/files/2023-02/Lake%20Easton%20full%20color%20Map%2002-08-21.pdf

Mount Si National Resources Conservation Area
Department of Natural Resources
www.dnr.wa.gov/geo/mountsi.pdf?y7jqr

Olallie State Park
Washington State Parks
https://parks.wa.gov/sites/default/files/2023-05/Olallie%20full%20color%20Map%2005-31-17.pdf

Palouse to Cascades Trail
Washington State Parks
425-649-4275
www.parks.wa.gov/521/Palouse-to-Cascades-Trail

Pinnacle Peak
King County Parks
https://aqua.kingcounty.gov/gis/web/VMC/recreation/BCT_PinnaclePeak_brochure.pdf

Snoqualmie Falls Park
Snoqualmie Recreation
www.snoqualmiewa.gov/DocumentCenter/View/24420/Map-and-Guide-Trails-and-Landmarks-July-2018-PDF

Squak Mountain State Park
Washington State Parks
https://storage.googleapis.com/stateless-wspf-website/2019/05/cfa5656c-squak-mountain.pdf

Taylor Mountain Forest
King County Parks
https://aqua.kingcounty.gov/gis/web/VMC/recreation/BCT_TaylorMtn_brochure.pdf

Umtanum Creek Falls, Umtanum Creek Canyon, Umtanum Ridge and Vista Trail
Washington Department of Fish & Wildlife
www.dnr.wa.gov/geo/wenas.pdf

PASSES

Federal Interagency Pass
www.nps.gov/planyourvisit/pickup-pass-locations.htm

Northwest Forest Pass
www.fs.usda.gov/detail/crgnsa/passes-permits/recreation/?cid=fsbdev2_027010

Washington State Discover Pass
https://discoverpass.wa.gov

TRAIL AND CONSERVATION CLUBS & ORGANIZATIONS

Issaquah Alps Trails Club
www.issaquahalps.org

King County Parks Foundation
www.kingcountyparks.org

The Mountaineers
www.mountaineers.org

Mountains to Sound Greenway
https://mtsgreenway.org/

Nature Conservancy
www.nature.org

Newcastle Trails
www.newcastletrails.org

Washington State Parks Foundation
www.wspf.org

Washington Trails Association
www.wta.org

Washington Wildlife and Recreation Coalition
www.wildliferecreation.org

OTHER LINKS

Cedar River Watershed Education Center
www.seattle.gov/utilities/protecting-our-environment/our-water-sources/cedar-river-watershed/education-center

Roslyn Historical Museum
509-649-2355
www.roslynmuseum.com

Seattle Paragliding
www.seattleparagliding.com

Snoqualmie Tribe Ancestral Lands Movement
https://snoqualmietribe.us/snoqualmie-tribe-ancestral-lands-movement/

Summit at Snoqualmie parking information
summitatsnoqualmie.com/parking-guide

Swauk Forest Discovery Trail self-guided tour
www.beexploring.com/pdf/swauk-discovery-trail-brochure.pdf

Trailhead Direct Bus
https://trailheaddirect.org

Index

OPPOSITE: *A pair of curious, young hoary marmots pop up to say hello, without straying far from the safety of their burrow.*

1% FOR TRAILS

Where would we be without trails? Not very far into the wilderness. That's why Mountaineers Books designates 1 percent of sales of select guidebooks in our Day Hiking series toward trail maintenance. Since launching this program, we've contributed more than $39,000 toward improving trails.

For this book, our 1 percent of sales is going the Mountains to Sound Greenway Trust. The Mountains to Sound Greenway National Heritage Area stretches 1.5 million acres from Seattle's waterfront over the Cascades to central Washington. Since 1991, the Mountains to Sound Greenway Trust has conserved and reconnected the lands that form the backdrop to many beloved hikes in the I-90 Corridor. Working with land managers and volunteers, they restore habitats and maintain trails, balancing access with preservation so future generations can explore, enjoy, and help care for these treasured public lands. Learn more at mtsgreenway.org.

Mountaineers Books donates many books to nonprofit recreation and conservation organizations. Our 1% for Trails campaign is one more way we help fellow nonprofit organizations as we work together to get people outside, to both enjoy and protect our wild public lands. If you'd like to support Mountaineers Books and our nonprofit partnership programs, please visit our website to learn more or contact mbooks@mountaineersbooks.org.

About the Author

Tami Asars grew up in western Washington, playing in the foothills and mountains of the North Cascades, where hiking and backpacking was a way of life for her family. Asars has completed the Pacific Crest Trail, the Continental Divide Trail, and the Appalachian Trail—making her a Triple Crowner. She has tackled many other long-distance trails as well, including the Colorado Trail, the Arizona Trail, the Tahoe Rim Trail, the West Coast Trail, and the Wonderland Trail.

Asars has served as a professional backpacking guide on the Northern Loop Trail in Mount Rainier National Park and in numerous backcountry locations in Washington State. She teaches classes on outdoor pursuits and dedicates her time to outdoor writing and photography in support of the areas she loves so much. Asars is a full-time freelance writer who has authored several books for Mountaineers Books, including *Hiking the Wonderland Trail*; *Day Hiking: Mount Rainier*; *Day Hiking: Mount Adams and Goat Rocks*; *Fall Color Hikes: Washington*; and *Hiking the Pacific Crest Trail: Washington*. She has contributed to countless magazines including *Washington*, *CityDog*, *Mountaineer*, and *Alaska Airlines*.

She lives in the Cascade foothills with her husband, Vilnis, and their dog, Scout. To learn more about her, visit www.tamiasars.com.

recreation • lifestyle • conservation

MOUNTAINEERS BOOKS, including its two imprints, Skipstone and Braided River, is a leading publisher of quality outdoor recreation, sustainability, and conservation titles. As a 501(c)(3) nonprofit, we are committed to supporting the environmental and educational goals of our organization by providing expert information on human-powered adventure, sustainable practices at home and on the trail, and preservation of wilderness.

Our publications are made possible through the generosity of donors, and through sales of 700 titles on outdoor recreation, sustainable lifestyle, and conservation. To donate, purchase books, or learn more, visit us online:

MOUNTAINEERS BOOKS
1001 SW Klickitat Way, Suite 201 • Seattle, WA 98134
800-553-4453 • mbooks@mountaineersbooks.org • www.mountaineersbooks.org

An independent nonprofit publisher since 1960

Mountaineers Books is proud to support the Leave No Trace Center for Outdoor Ethics, whose mission is to use the power of science, education, and stewardship to ensure a sustainable future for the outdoors and the planet. The Leave No Trace program is focused specifically on human-powered (nonmotorized) recreation. For more information, visit www.lnt.org.